M000240456

Yamaha MT-07 (FZ-07), Tracer & XSR700
Service and Repair Manual

by Matthew Coombs

(6385-304)

Models covered

Model	Displacement	Years
MT-07	689cc	2014 to 2017
FZ-07	689cc	2015 to 2017
MT-07TR Tracer	689cc	2016 to 2017
XSR700	689cc	2016 to 2017

Includes Special Edition models

© Haynes Publishing 2017

ABCDE
FGHIJ
KLMNO
PQRST

A book in the Haynes Service and Repair Manual Series

ISBN: **978 1 78521 385 4**

Library of Congress Control Number 2017947947

Printed in Malaysia

Haynes Publishing
Sparkford, Yeovil, Somerset BA22 7JJ, England

Haynes North America, Inc
859 Lawrence Drive, Newbury Park, California 91320, USA

Printed using NORBRITE BOOK 48.8gsm (CODE: 40N6533) from NORPAC; procurement system certified under Sustainable Forestry Initiative standard. Paper produced is certified to the SFI Certified Fiber Sourcing Standard (CERT - 0094271)

Contents

Contents

Yamaha
Musical instruments to motorcycles

**The FS1E –
first bike of many sixteen year olds in the UK**

The Yamaha Motor Company

The Yamaha name can be traced back to 1889, when Torakusu Yamaha founded the Yamaha Organ Manufacturing Company. Such was the success of the company, that in 1897 it became Nippon Gakki Limited and manufactured a wide range of reed organs and pianos.

During World War II, Nippon Gakki's manufacturing base was utilised by the Japanese authorities to produce propellers and fuel tanks for their aviation industry. The end of the war brought about a huge public demand for low cost transport and many firms decided to utilise their obsolete aircraft tooling for the production of motorcycles. Nippon Gakki's first motorcycle went on sale in February 1955 and was named the 125 YA-1 Red Dragonfly. This machine was a copy of the German DKW RT125 motorcycle, featuring a single cylinder two-stroke engine with a four-speed gearbox. Due to the outstanding success of this model the motorcycle operation was separated from Nippon Gakki in July 1955 and the Yamaha Motor Company was formed.

The YA-1 also received acclaim by winning two of Japan's biggest road races, the Mount Fuji Climbing race and the Asama Volcano race. The high level of public demand for the YA-1 led to the development of a whole series of two-stroke singles and twins.

Having made a large impact on their home market, Yamahas were exported to the USA in 1958 and to the UK in 1962. In the UK the signing of an Anglo-Japanese trade agreement during 1962 enabled the sale of Japanese lightweight motorcycles and scooters in Britain. At that time, competition between the many motorcycle producers in Japan had reduced numbers significantly and by the end of the sixties, only the big-four which are familiar with today remained.

Yamaha Europe was founded in 1968 and based in Holland. Although originally set up to market marine products, the Dutch base is now the official European Headquarters and distribution centre. Yamaha motorcycles are built at factories in Holland, Denmark, Norway, Italy, France, Spain and Portugal. Yamahas are imported into the UK by Yamaha Motor UK Ltd, formerly Mitsui Machinery Sales (UK) Ltd. Mitsui and Co. were originally a trading house, handling the shipping, distribution and marketing of Japanese products into western countries. Ultimately Mitsui Machinery Sales was formed to handle Yamaha motorcycles and outboard motors.

Based on the technology derived from its motorcycle operation, Yamaha have produced many other products, such as automobile and lightweight aircraft engines, marine engines and boats, generators, pumps, ATVs, snowmobiles, golf cars, industrial robots, lawnmowers, swimming pools and archery equipment.

Two-strokes first

Part of Yamaha's success was a whole string of innovations in the two-stroke world. Autolube engine lubrication, torque induction, multi-ported engines, reed valves and power valves kept their two-strokes at the forefront of technology. Many advances were achieved with the use of racing as a development laboratory. They went to the USA in the late 1950s with an air-cooled 250cc twin but didn't hit the GPs until the early 1960s when Fumio Ito scored a hat-trick of sixth places in the Isle of Man TT, the Dutch TT and the Belgian GP. This experiment gave rise to the idea of the over-the-counter racer, an idea that became reality in the TD1, the first in an unmatched series of two-stroke racers that were the standard issue for privateers at national and international level for years and helped Yamaha develop their road engines. While privateers raced the twins, Yamaha built the outrageously complicated vee-four 250 for Phil Read and followed it with a vee-four 125 that Bill Ivy lapped the Isle of Man on at over 100mph! When the FIM regulations were changed to limit the smaller GP classes to two cylinders, these exotic bikes died but set the scene for an unparalleled dynasty of mass-produced racers based on the same technology as the road bikes.

In the 1960s and 70s the two-stroke engined YAS3 125, YDS1 to YDS7 250 and YR5 350 formed the core of Yamaha's range. By the mid-70s they had been superseded by the RD (Race-Developed) 125, 250, and 350 range of two-stroke twins, featuring improved 7-port engines with reed valve induction. Braking was improved by the use of an hydraulic brake on the front wheel of DX models, instead of the drum arrangement used previously, and cast alloy wheels were available as an option on later RD models. The RD350 was replaced by the RD400 in 1976.

Running parallel with the RD twins was a range of single-cylinder two-strokes. Used in a variety of chassis types, the engine was used in the popular 50 cc FS1-E moped, the V50 to 90 step-thrus, RS100 and 125, YB100 and the DT trail range.

The TD racers got water-cooling in 1973 to become the TZs, the most successful and numerous over-the-counter racers ever built. That same year, Jarno Saarinen became the first rider to win a 500cc GP on a four-cylinder two-stroke on the new in-line four which was effectively a pair of TZs side-by-side. TZs won everywhere – including the Daytona 200 and 500 races when overbored to 351cc. A 700cc TZ also appeared, one year later taken out to 750cc. Steve Baker won the first Formula 750 world title – one of the precursors of Superbike – on one in 1977. The following year Kenny Roberts won Yamaha's first world 500 title and would be succeeded by Wayne Rainey and Eddie Lawson before Mick Doohan and the NSR500 took over.

The air-cooled single and twin cylinder RD road bikes were eventually replaced by the LC series in 1980, featuring liquid-cooled engines, radical new styling, spiral pattern cast wheels and cantilever rear suspension (Yamaha's Monoshock). Of all the LC models, the RD350LC, or RD350R as it was later known, has made the most impact in the market. Later models had YPVS (Yamaha Power Valve System) engines, another first for Yamaha – this was essentially a valve located in the exhaust ports which was electronically operated to alter port timing to achieve maximum power output. The RD500LC was the largest two-stroke made by Yamaha and differed from the other LCs by the use of its vee-four cylinder engine.

The Four-strokes

Yamaha concentrated solely on two-stroke models until 1970 when the XS1 was produced, their first four-stroke motorcycle. It was perhaps Yamaha's success with two-strokes that postponed an earlier move into the four-stroke motorcycle market, although their work with Toyota during the 1960s had given them a sound base in four-stroke technology.

The XS1 had a 650 cc twin-cylinder SOHC engine and was later to become known as the XS650, appearing also in the popular SE custom form. Yamaha introduced a three cylinder 750 cc engine in 1976, fitted in a

The distinctive paintwork and trim of the RD models

sport-tourer frame and called the XS750, TX750 in the USA. The XS750 established itself well in the sport tourer class and remained in production with very few changes until uprated to 850 cc in 1980.

Other four-strokes followed in 1976, with the introduction of the XS250/360/400 series twins. The XS range was strengthened in 1978 by the four-cylinder XS1100.

The 1980s saw a new family of four-strokes, the XJ550, 650, 750 and 900 Fours. Improvements over the XS range amounted to a slimmer DOHC engine unit due to the relocation of the alternator behind the cylinders, electronic ignition and uprated braking and suspension systems. Models were available mainly in standard trim, although custom-styled Maxims were produced especially for the US market. The XJ650T was the first model from Yamaha to have a turbo-charged engine. Although these early XJ models have now been discontinued, their roots live on in the XJ600S and XJ900S Diversion (Seca II) models.

The FZR prefix encompasses the pure sports Yamaha models. With the exception of the 16-valve FZR400 and FZR600 models, the FZ/FZR750 and FZR1000 used 20-valve engines, two exhaust valves and three inlet valves per cylinder. This concept was called Genesis and gave improved gas flow to the combustion chambers. Other features of the new engine were the use of down-draught carburetors and the engine's inclined angle in the frame, plus the change to liquid-cooling. Lightweight Deltabox design aluminium frames and uprated suspension improved the

The XS650 led the way for Yamaha's four-stroke range

bikes's handling. The Genesis engine lives on in the YZF750 and 1000 models.

The Genesis concept was the basis of Yamaha's foray into four-stroke racing, first with a bike known simply as 'The Genesis', an FZ750 motor in a TT Formula 1 bike with

which the factory attempted to steal the Honda RVF750's thunder at important events like the Suzuka 8 Hours and the Bol d'Or although they never fielded it for a whole World Championship season. That had to wait for the advent of the World Superbike Championship, although there was no full works team until 1995, instead it was left to individual importers to support teams. It was the Australian Dealer Team Yamaha which scored the factory's first World Superbike win in the series debut year of 1988. The rider? Mick Doohan. Slightly, embarrassingly, it was the steel framed FZ750 rather than the FZR homologation special that won races. The OW01 was a race winner, mainly in the hands of Fabrizio Pirovano, the factory's most successful Superbike racer with ten victories, but national success in the UK, Japan, and in the Daytona 200 has not been translated into World Championships for any of Yamaha's 750s.

The vee-twin engine has been the mainstay of the XV Virago range. Since 1981 XVs have been produced in 535, 700, 750, 920, 1000 and 1100 engine sizes, all using the same basic air-cooled sohc vee-twin engine. Other uses of vee engines have been in the XZ550 of the early 1980s, the XVZ12 Venture and the mighty VMX-12 V-Max.

Yamaha has always been a sporting-orientated company whose motto could be 'Racing Improves the Breed', so it's no surprise that the latest generation of lightweight sportsters are at the cutting edge of performance on and off the track. The R6

Yamaha's XS750 was produced from 1976 to 1982 and then uprated to 850 cc

won more races than any other machine in the inaugural year of the World Supersports Championship, the R7 won a race in its debut year in World Superbike in the hands of the mercurial Noriyuki Haga, and the mighty 1000cc R1 ended Honda's domination of the Isle of Man F1 TT when David Jefferies won three races in a week in 1999.

Cheap thrills

How does a major motorcycle manufacturer respond to a global financial crisis? The crash of 2008/09 coupled with super sports bikes falling out of fashion asked some serious questions of the mass-market companies, in other words the Japanese big four. It didn't take Yamaha long to work out their response. The first we knew was a set of crankcases at the big Winter shows with dozens of wires attached to various points. It looked like it should have been in the Tate Modern rather than the National Exhibition Centre, but this was Yamaha's artistic hint at the future: a completely new generation of engines to power the MT range. MT? Masters of Torque although the old FZ designation was rolled out for some markets including North America.

The first MT was the MT-09, a triple, quickly followed by a twin-cylinder 700cc, the MT-07, which turned out to be even more fun than its big brother. Who'd have thought it? A DOHC parallel twin in a tubular steel frame with low-rent suspension and no electronics turns out to be the most fun since, well… Yamaha's RD350LC or FZS600 Fazer if you're four-stroke

A new family of four-strokes was released in 1980 with the introduction of the XJ range

inclined. Yamaha have certainly refrained from throwing money at the MT-07. That's not surprising in a post-recession design, but the 270-degree crank can claim to be inspired by the MotoGP-derived cross-plane bottom end, which has the happy side-effect of making the engine sound and feel a bit like a V-twin. Also, there are no alternative engine maps or other electronic fripperies to confuse the issue on this the perky little motor. The result is a crisp but above-all fun power unit in a steel chassis cleverly using different stiffness tubes in different areas, and it works. Even the non-adjustable forks and rear shock adjustable for pre-load only add to the fun. If this is budget biking, nobody is complaining.

Of course the financial climate demands that you make best use of your resources, so having produced a brand new engine Yamaha couldn't use it in just one bike. Enter the Tracer 700, a sports tourer by any other name. The transformation from revvy, nippy naked to two-up tourer is another minor miracle given the engine hasn't been touched. The rear subframe and suspension are beefed up to cope with luggage and a pillion and there's a twin-headlamp half-fairing, but the character-changing modification is an extra 50mm on the swinging arm which gives the stability you expect from a tourer. The other clever trick is keeping the price low, just like the base model MT-07, low enough in fact to force rival manufacturers into price cuts.

But if there's an MT variant that really catches the zeitgeist of post-recession biking, it's the XSR700. If you wanted proof that Yamaha understand what's going on out there, the sight of various SR400s modified by well-known customisers doing the rounds at the big shows should have done it. The point being that they were on the official Yamaha stand alongside a black-and-yellow Kenny Roberts tribute MT-09 from top California

The MT-07 Moto Cage

The Tracer

The XSR700

trend-setter Roland Sands. Yamaha hit every trend by employing Japan's main man Shinya Kimura to style the XSR. He wanted it to be 'timeless', not retro. Nevertheless, the key retro styling cues are apparent: one-piece bars, round headlight shell, what can only be described as retro paint. That other essential of modern customs, the short single seat, is catered for by an abbreviated rear subframe. There is also encouragement to do a few easy modifications from the front mudguard mount and detachable tank panels. Most of the encouragement comes from Yamaha themselves who have a range of accessories ready to bolt on.

The factory says the bike harks back to their first four-stroke, the XS-1 and the better known XS650 and is the first of a range that will be known as the Faster Sons, tributes to earlier landmark Yamaha models. Very Japanese and very clever that, referencing history while still being right up to date. That's a clever trick and one the MT-07 has pulled off with aplomb

Acknowledgements

Our thanks are due to Bransons Motorcycles of Yeovil, who supplied the machines featured in the illustrations throughout this manual. We would also like to thank NGK Spark Plugs (UK) Ltd for supplying the colour spark plug condition photographs, the Avon Rubber Company for supplying information on tyre fitting and Draper Tools Ltd for some of the workshop tools shown.

Thanks are also due to Yamaha Motor (UK) Ltd who supplied model photographs, and to Julian Ryder who wrote the introduction 'Musical Instruments to Motorcycles'.

About this Manual

The aim of this manual is to help you get the best value from your motorcycle. It can do so in several ways. It can help you decide what work must be done, even if you choose to have it done by a dealer; it provides information and procedures for routine maintenance and servicing; and it offers diagnostic and repair procedures to follow when trouble occurs.

We hope you use the manual to tackle the work yourself. For many simpler jobs, doing it yourself may be quicker than arranging an appointment to get the motorcycle into a dealer and making the trips to leave it and pick it up. More importantly, a lot of money can be saved by avoiding the expense the shop must pass on to you to cover its labour and overhead costs. An added benefit is the sense of satisfaction and accomplishment that you feel after doing the job yourself.

References to the left or right side of the motorcycle assume you are sitting on the seat, facing forward.

We take great pride in the accuracy of information given in this manual, but motorcycle manufacturers make alterations and design changes during the production run of a particular motorcycle of which they do not inform us. No liability can be accepted by the authors or publishers for loss, damage or injury caused by any errors in, or omissions from, the information given.

Illegal copying

Frame and engine numbers

The frame serial number is stamped into the right-hand side of the steering head. The engine number is stamped into the left-hand side of the crankcase. The model code label is under the passenger seat. These numbers should be recorded and kept in a safe place so they can be given to the police in the event of a theft.

The frame serial number, engine serial number, and model code should also be kept in a handy place (such as with your driver's licence) so that they are always available when ordering parts for your machine.

There are three models covered, the MT-07 (known as the FZ-07 in the US and Canada), the MT-07TR Tracer (MTT690), and the XSR700 (MTM690). The procedures in this manual identify the bikes by model name, and if necessary by whether or not it has ABS, and where changes have been made over the model life by model year, as required.

Europe models

Model	Code	Year
MT-07	1WS1/1WS2/1WS6/1WS7/ 1WS8/1WS9/1WSA/1WSG	2014
MT-07	1WSB/1WSC	2015
MT-07	1WSH/1WSJ	2016
MT-07A	1XB1/1XB2/1XB5/ 1XB6/1XB7/1XB8/1XBE	2014
MT-07A	1XBA/1XBB	2015
MT-07A	1XBH/1XBJ	2016
MT-07A	BU21/BU23	2017
MT-07TR	BC61	2016/2017
XSR700	B341/B344	2016
XSR700	B347	2017

US models

Model	Code	Year
FZ-07	F	2015
FZ-07	G	2016
FZ-07	H	2017

Buying spare parts

Once you have found all the identification numbers, record them for reference when buying parts. Since the manufacturers change specifications, parts and vendors (companies that manufacture various components on the machine), providing the ID numbers is the only way to be reasonably sure that you are buying the correct parts.

Whenever possible, take the worn part to the dealer so direct comparison with the new component can be made. Along the trail from the manufacturer to the parts shelf, there are numerous places that the part can end up with the wrong number or be listed incorrectly.

The two places to purchase new parts for your motorcycle – the accessory store and the franchised dealer – differ in the type of parts they carry. While dealers can obtain virtually every part for your motorcycle, the accessory dealer is usually limited to normal high wear items such as spark plugs, chains, sprockets, brake pads, etc.

Used parts can be obtained for roughly half the price of new ones, but you can't always be sure of what you're getting. Once again, take your worn part to the breaker's yard for direct comparison.

Whether buying new, used or rebuilt parts, the best course is to deal directly with someone who specialises in parts for your particular make.

The frame number is stamped into the right-hand side of the steering head

The engine number is stamped into the left-hand side of the crankcase

Label provides the model code and colour code

Professional mechanics are trained in safe working procedures. However enthusiastic you may be about getting on with the job at hand, take the time to ensure that your safety is not put at risk. A moment's lack of attention can result in an accident, as can failure to observe simple precautions.

There will always be new ways of having accidents, and the following is not a comprehensive list of all dangers; it is intended rather to make you aware of the risks and to encourage a safe approach to all work you carry out on your bike.

Asbestos

● Certain friction, insulating, sealing and other products - such as brake pads, clutch linings, gaskets, etc. - contain asbestos. Extreme care must be taken to avoid inhalation of dust from such products since it is hazardous to health. If in doubt, assume that they do contain asbestos.

Fire

● Remember at all times that petrol is highly flammable. Never smoke or have any kind of naked flame around, when working on the vehicle. But the risk does not end there - a spark caused by an electrical short-circuit, by two metal surfaces contacting each other, by careless use of tools, or even by static electricity built up in your body under certain conditions, can ignite petrol vapour, which in a confined space is highly explosive. Never use petrol as a cleaning solvent. Use an approved safety solvent.

● Always disconnect the battery earth terminal before working on any part of the fuel or electrical system, and never risk spilling fuel on to a hot engine or exhaust.

● It is recommended that a fire extinguisher of a type suitable for fuel and electrical fires is kept handy in the garage or workplace at all times. Never try to extinguish a fuel or electrical fire with water.

Fumes

● Certain fumes are highly toxic and can quickly cause unconsciousness and even death if inhaled to any extent. Petrol vapour comes into this category, as do the vapours from certain solvents such as trichloro-ethylene. Any draining or pouring of such volatile fluids should be done in a well ventilated area.

● When using cleaning fluids and solvents, read the instructions carefully. Never use materials from unmarked containers - they may give off poisonous vapours.

● Never run the engine of a motor vehicle in an enclosed space such as a garage. Exhaust fumes contain carbon monoxide which is extremely poisonous; if you need to run the engine, always do so in the open air or at least have the rear of the vehicle outside the workplace.

The battery

● Never cause a spark, or allow a naked light near the vehicle's battery. It will normally be giving off a certain amount of hydrogen gas, which is highly explosive.

● Always disconnect the battery ground (earth) terminal before working on the fuel or electrical systems (except where noted).

● If possible, loosen the filler plugs or cover when charging the battery from an external source. Do not charge at an excessive rate or the battery may burst.

● Take care when topping up, cleaning or carrying the battery. The acid electrolyte, evenwhen diluted, is very corrosive and should not be allowed to contact the eyes or skin. Always wear rubber gloves and goggles or a face shield. If you ever need to prepare electrolyte yourself, always add the acid slowly to the water; never add the water to the acid.

Electricity

● When using an electric power tool, inspection light etc., always ensure that the appliance is correctly connected to its plug and that, where necessary, it is properly grounded (earthed). Do not use such appliances in damp conditions and, again, beware of creating a spark or applying excessive heat in the vicinity of fuel or fuel vapour. Also ensure that the appliances meet national safety standards.

● A severe electric shock can result from touching certain parts of the electrical system, such as the spark plug wires (HT leads), when the engine is running or being cranked, particularly if components are damp or the insulation is defective. Where an electronic ignition system is used, the secondary (HT) voltage is much higher and could prove fatal.

Remember...

✗ **Don't** start the engine without first ascer-taining that the transmission is in neutral.

✗ **Don't** suddenly remove the pressure cap from a hot cooling system - cover it with a cloth and release the pressure gradually first, or you may get scalded by escaping coolant.

✗ **Don't** attempt to drain oil until you are sure it has cooled sufficiently to avoid scalding you.

✗ **Don't** grasp any part of the engine or exhaust system without first ascertaining that it is cool enough not to burn you.

✗ **Don't** allow brake fluid or antifreeze to contact the machine's paintwork or plastic components.

✗ **Don't** siphon toxic liquids such as fuel, hydraulic fluid or antifreeze by mouth, or allow them to remain on your skin.

✗ **Don't** inhale dust - it may be injurious to health (see Asbestos heading).

✗ **Don't** allow any spilled oil or grease to remain on the floor - wipe it up right away, before someone slips on it.

✗ **Don't** use ill-fitting spanners or other tools which may slip and cause injury.

✗ **Don't** lift a heavy component which may be beyond your capability - get assistance.

✗ **Don't** rush to finish a job or take unverified short cuts.

✗ **Don't** allow children or animals in or around an unattended vehicle.

✗ **Don't** inflate a tyre above the recommended pressure. Apart from overstressing the carcass, in extreme cases the tyre may blow off forcibly.

✔ **Do** ensure that the machine is supported securely at all times. This is especially important when the machine is blocked up to aid wheel or fork removal.

✔ **Do** take care when attempting to loosen a stubborn nut or bolt. It is generally better to pull on a spanner, rather than push, so that if you slip, you fall away from the machine rather than onto it.

✔ **Do** wear eye protection when using power tools such as drill, sander, bench grinder etc.

✔ **Do** use a barrier cream on your hands prior to undertaking dirty jobs - it will protect your skin from infection as well as making the dirt easier to remove afterwards; but make sure your hands aren't left slippery. Note that long-term contact with used engine oil can be a health hazard.

✔ **Do** keep loose clothing (cuffs, ties etc. and long hair) well out of the way of moving mechanical parts.

✔ **Do** remove rings, wristwatch etc., before working on the vehicle - especially the electrical system.

✔ **Do** keep your work area tidy - it is only too easy to fall over articles left lying around.

✔ **Do** exercise caution when compressing springs for removal or installation. Ensure that the tension is applied and released in a controlled manner, using suitable tools which preclude the possibility of the spring escaping violently.

✔ **Do** ensure that any lifting tackle used has a safe working load rating adequate for the job.

✔ **Do** get someone to check periodically that all is well, when working alone on the vehicle.

✔ **Do** carry out work in a logical sequence and check that everything is correctly assembled and tightened afterwards.

✔ **Do** remember that your vehicle's safety affects that of yourself and others. If in doubt on any point, get professional advice.

● If in spite of following these precautions, you are unfortunate enough to injure yourself, seek medical attention as soon as possible.

Engine oil level

Before you start:

✔ Support the motorcycle upright on level ground.
✔ Start the engine and let it idle for several minutes until it reaches normal operating temperature, then stop the engine.
Caution: Do not run the engine in an enclosed space such as a garage or workshop.
✔ Leave the motorcycle undisturbed for a few minutes to allow the oil level to stabilise.

Bike care:

● If you have to add oil frequently, check whether you have any oil leaks. If there is no sign of oil leakage from the joints and gaskets the engine could be burning oil (see *Fault Finding*).

The correct oil:

● Modern, high-revving engines place great demands on their oil. It is very important that the correct oil for your bike is used – do not use car engine oils.

● Always top up with a good quality motorcycle oil of the specified type and viscosity and do not overfill the engine.

Oil type	API grade SG or higher, JASO grade MA
Oil viscosity	SAE 10W40

1 The oil level is visible in the inspection window in the left-hand side of the crankcase. If the window is dirty, wipe it clean. The oil level must lie between the level lines (arrowed).

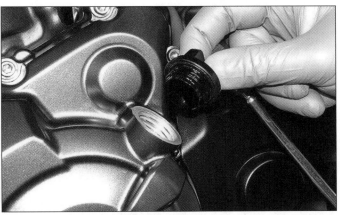

2 If the level is below the lower level line unscrew the filler cap from the alternator cover

3 Add the recommended grade and type of oil to bring the level almost up to the upper level line. Do not overfill.

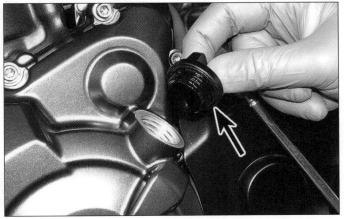

4 Check the filler cap O-ring (arrowed) is in place, then screw the cap in. Run the engine, switch it off and wait a few minutes, then check the level again.

Suspension, steering and drive chain

Suspension and Steering:

● Check that the front and rear suspension operates smoothly without binding.
● Check that the rear suspension pre-load is adjusted as required.
● Check that the steering moves smoothly from lock-to-lock.

Drive chain:

● Check that the drive chain slack isn't excessive, and adjust it if necessary (see Chapter 1).
● If the chain looks dry, lubricate it (see Chapter 1).

Coolant level

Before you start:
✔ Check the coolant level when the engine is cold.
✔ Support the motorcycle upright on level ground.

> ⚠ **Warning: DO NOT remove the radiator pressure cap to add coolant. Topping up is done via the coolant reservoir tank filler. DO NOT leave open containers of coolant about, as it is poisonous.**

Bike care:
● Use only the specified coolant mixture, either a pre-mix coolant for motorcycle engines or a 50/50 mix of distilled water and corrosion inhibited ethylene glycol anti-freeze. It is important that anti-freeze is used in the system all year round, and not just in the winter. Do not top the system up using only water, as the system will become too diluted. If necessary tap water can be used as long as it is soft – do not use hard water.

● Do not overfill the reservoir. If the coolant is significantly above the FULL level line at any time, siphon or drain the surplus to prevent the possibility of it being expelled out of the overflow hose.

● If the coolant level falls steadily, check the system for leaks (see Chapter 1). If no leaks are found and the level continues to fall, fit a new pressure cap. If this does not solve the problem take the bike to a Yamaha dealer for a pressure test.

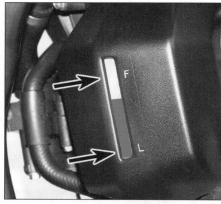

1 The reservoir is mounted at the front of the engine on the left-hand side. The coolant level must be between the F (full) and L (low) level lines (arrowed) marked on the reservoir cover

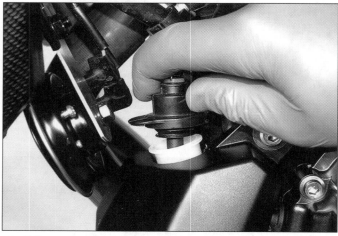

2 If the coolant level does not lie between the F and L level lines, open the reservoir filler cap

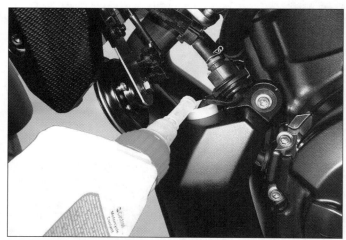

3 Top the coolant level up with the recommended coolant mixture, then fit the cap.

Legal and safety

Lighting and signalling:
● Take a minute to check that the headlight, tail light, brake light, instrument lights and turn signals all work correctly.
● Check that the horn sounds when the switch is operated.
● A working speedometer graduated in mph is a statutory requirement in the UK.

Safety:
● Check that the throttle grip rotates smoothly and snaps shut when released, in all steering positions. Also check for the correct amount of freeplay (see Chapter 1).
● Check that the steering moves freely from lock-to-lock.
● Check that the brake lever and pedal, clutch lever and gearchange lever operate smoothly. Lubricate them at the specified intervals or when necessary (see Chapter 1).
● Check that the engine shuts off when the kill switch is operated.

● Check that the sidestand return springs hold the stand up securely when it is retracted.

Fuel:
● This may seem obvious, but check that you have enough fuel to complete your journey. If you notice signs of fuel leakage rectify the cause immediately.
● Make sure you use the correct grade fuel – see Chapter 4 Specifications.

Tyres

Tyre tread depth:

● At the time of writing UK law requires that the tread depth must be at least 1 mm over the entire tread breadth all the way around the tyre, with no bald patches. Many riders, however, consider 2 mm tread depth minimum to be a safer limit. Yamaha recommend a minimum of 1.6 mm.

● Tyres incorporate wear indicators in the tread. Identify the triangular pointer or TWI mark on the tyre sidewall to locate the indicator bar and fit a new tyre if the tread has worn down to the bar.

The correct pressures:

● The tyre pressures must be checked when cold, not immediately after riding. Note that low tyre pressures will cause abnormal tread wear and unsafe handling, and may cause the tyre to slip on the rim or come off. High tyre pressures will cause abnormal tread wear and unsafe handling.

● Use an accurate pressure gauge. Many garage forecourt gauges are wildly inaccurate. If you buy your own, spend as much as you can justify on a quality gauge.

● Correct air pressure will increase tyre life and provide maximum stability, handling capability and ride comfort. Tyre pressures are printed on a label stuck to the swingarm.

| Front pressure | 33 psi (2.25 Bar) |
| Rear pressure (all loads) | 36 psi (2.5 Bar) |

Tyre care:

● Check the tyres carefully for cuts, tears, embedded nails or other sharp objects and excessive wear. Operation of the motorcycle with excessively worn tyres is extremely hazardous, as traction and handling are directly affected.

● Check the condition of the tyre valve and make sure a dust cap is fitted.

● Pick out any stones or nails which may have become embedded in the tyre tread. If left, they will eventually penetrate through the casing and cause a puncture.

● If tyre damage is apparent, or unexplained loss of pressure is experienced, seek the advice of a tyre fitting specialist without delay.

1 Remove the cap from the valve – if it's missing, fit a new one.

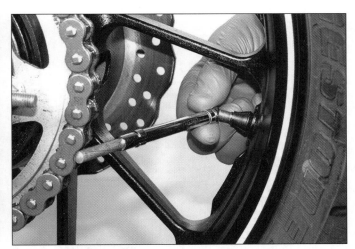

2 Check the tyre pressures when the tyres are cold and keep them properly inflated. Fit the cap on completion.

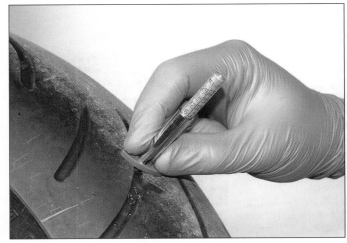

3 Measure tread depth at the centre of the tyre using a tread depth gauge.

4 Tyre tread wear indicator bar (A) and its location marking (B) (usually either an arrow, a triangle or the letters TWI) on the sidewall.

Brake fluid levels

> **Warning:** *Brake hydraulic fluid can harm your eyes and damage painted surfaces, so use extreme caution when handling and pouring it and cover surrounding surfaces with rag. Do not use fluid that has been standing open for some time, as it absorbs moisture from the air which can cause a dangerous loss of braking effectiveness.*

Before you start:

✔ The front brake fluid reservoir is on the right-hand handlebar. The rear brake fluid reservoir is between the seat and the rear footrest bracket on the right-hand side.
✔ Make sure you have a supply of DOT 4 hydraulic fluid.
✔ Wrap a rag around the reservoir being worked on to ensure that any spillage does not come into contact with painted surfaces.
✔ Support the bike upright on level ground.

Bike care:

● The fluid in the front and rear brake master cylinder reservoirs will drop very gradually as the brake pads wear down. When the level is low check the brake pads for wear (see Chapter 1).
● If either fluid reservoir requires repeated topping-up there could be a leak somewhere in the system, which must be investigated immediately.
● Check the operation of both brakes before taking the machine on the road; if there is evidence of air in the system (spongy feel to lever or pedal), it must be bled (see Chapter 6).

FRONT BRAKE

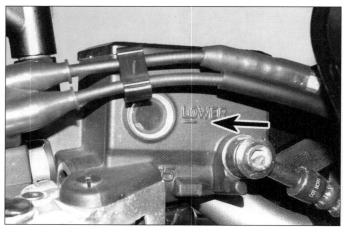

1 The front brake fluid level is visible through the window in the reservoir body – it must be above the LOWER level line (arrowed).

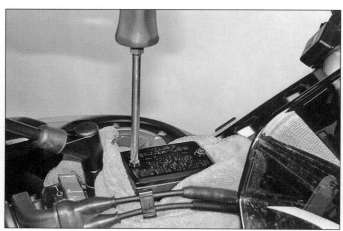

2 If the level is low undo the reservoir cover screws and remove the cover, the diaphragm plate and the diaphragm.

3 Top-up with new DOT 4 hydraulic fluid until the level is just below the UPPER level line (arrowed) cast on the inside of the reservoir. Take care to avoid spills (see Warning) and do not overfill.

4 Wipe any moisture out of the diaphragm using a clean lint-free cloth.

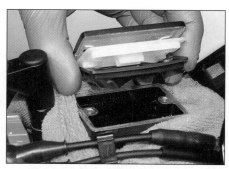

5 Make sure the diaphragm is correctly seated before fitting the plate and cover.

REAR BRAKE

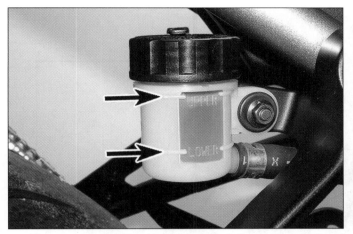

1 The rear brake fluid level is visible through the reservoir body – it must be between the UPPER and LOWER level lines (arrowed).

2 On MT-07 (FZ-07) and MT-07TR models, if the level is on or below the LOWER level line, unscrew the nut and remove the security bracket.

3 On XSR models, if the level is on or below the LOWER level line undo the mounting screw and draw the reservoir out so the cap is clear of the security tab.

4 Hold the reservoir, unscrew the cap and remove the diaphragm plate and diaphragm.

5 Top-up with new DOT 4 hydraulic fluid until the level is just below the UPPER level line. Take care to avoid spills (see **Warning**) and do not overfill.

6 Wipe any moisture out of the diaphragm using a clean lint-free cloth.

7 Make sure the diaphragm is correctly seated before fitting the plate and cap. Fit the reservoir and tighten the nut or screw.

Dimensions and weights

Overall length
MT-07 (FZ-07) .... 2085 mm
MT-07TR .... 2138 mm
XSR700.. 2075 mm

Overall width
MT-07 (FZ-09) .... 745 mm
MT-07TR .... 806 mm
XSR700.. 820 mm

Overall height
MT-07 (FZ-07)... 1090 mm
MT-07TR .... 1270 mm
XSR700.. 1130 mm

Seat height
MT-07 (FZ-07)... 805 mm
MT-07TR .... 835 mm
XSR700.. 815 mm

Wheelbase
MT-07 (FZ-07)... 1400 mm
MT-07TR .... 1450 mm
XSR700.. 1405 mm

Ground clearance..................................... 140 mm

Wet weight (with all fluids and full fuel tank)
MT-07 (FZ-07)... 179 kg (182 kg on models with ABS)
MT-07TR .... 196 kg
XSR700.. 186 kg

Max. load (weight of rider/passenger/luggage)
MT-07 (FZ-07)... 176 kg (173 kg on models with ABS)
MT-07TR .... 180 kg
XSR700.. 172 kg

Engine

Type	Four-stroke 8-valve parallel twin
Capacity	689 cc
Bore	80.0 mm
Stroke	68.6 mm
Compression ratio	11.5 to 1
Cooling system	Liquid cooled
Clutch	Wet multi-plate
Transmission	Six-speed constant mesh
Final drive	Chain and sprockets
Camshafts	DOHC, chain-driven
Throttle body	Mikuni EHDW38
Ignition system	Digital electronic CDI

Chassis

Frame type	Tubular steel, backbone	
Rake and trail		
MT-07 (FZ-07)	24.80°, 90.0 mm	
MT-07TR and XSR700	25°, 90.0 mm	
Fuel tank capacity (including reserve)		
MT-07 (FZ-07) and XSR700	14 litres	
MT-07TR	17 litres	
Reserve capacity (when fuel warning flashes)		
MT-07 (FZ-07) and XSR700	2.7 litres	
MT-07TR	3.5 litres	
Front suspension		
Type	41 mm oil-damped telescopic forks	
Travel	130 mm	
Adjustment	None	
Rear suspension		
Type	Single shock absorber, rising rate linkage, swingarm	
Travel		
MT-07 (FZ-09) and XSR700	55 mm at shock, 130 mm at wheel	
MT-07TR	65 mm at shock, 142 mm at wheel	
Adjustment	Spring pre-load	
Wheels	17 inch 10-spoke alloys	
Tyres	**Front**	**Rear**
MT-07 (FZ-07) and MT-07TR	120/70-ZR17 M/C (58W) tubeless	180/55-ZR17 M/C (73W) tubeless
XSR700	120/70-R17 M/C (58V) tubeless	180/55-R17 M/C (73V) tubeless
Front brake	Twin 282 mm discs with 4 piston opposed calipers	
Rear brake	Single 245 mm disc with single piston sliding caliper	

Model development

The MT-07 (FZ-07)

The MT-07 was launched in Europe in 2014, and became available as the FZ-07 in the US and Canada in 2015.

The engine is a liquid-cooled parallel twin with two chain driven overhead camshafts actuating on four valves per cylinder. Power is routed through a cable-operated wet multi-plate clutch to a six-speed constant mesh gearbox. Drive to the rear wheel is by chain and sprockets.

Yamaha's engine management system controls the amount of fuel supplied and the timing of the ignition.

The exhaust system is an under-slung one-piece unit, incorporating a catalytic converter and oxygen sensor.

The engine is housed in a tubular steel frame that uses the engine as a stressed member. The front suspension has non-adjustable 41 mm oil-damped telescopic forks. The rear suspension has a single shock absorber acting on a steel swingarm via a rising-rate linkage. The shock absorber has adjustable spring pre-load.

Seventeen-inch cast aluminium wheels are fitted front and rear, with twin four opposed-piston disc brakes at the front and one single-piston sliding caliper disc brake at the rear.

MT-07A models have an anti-lock brake system (ABS). An immobiliser is fitted as standard on UK models.

In 2015 the MT-07 Moto Cage version was launched. The Moto Cage is an MT-07 with colour-co-ordinated extras such as engine guards, hand guards, a screen and radiator trim panels, and it has mis-matched wheels, all aimed at creating a stunt-style bike.

There have been no major changes since the model was launched.

The MT-07TR Tracer

The Tracer was launched in 2016, and is a half-faired version of the MT-07. Apart from the fairing and bodywork, the only differences are in the fuel tank, seat, handlebars, headlight, and instruments, a longer aluminium swingarm and revised suspension spring rates and damping to cope with passenger and luggage loading, a stronger rear sub-frame and a different tail section. ABS and an immobiliser are fitted as standard on UK models.

There have been no major changes since the model was launched.

The XSR700

The XSR was launched in 2016, and is a retro version of the MT-07. Differences are in the fuel tank, seat, handlebars, a different rear sub-frame, bodywork and trim, headlight, tail light, and instruments. ABS and an immobiliser are fitted as standard on UK models.

There have been no major changes since the model was launched.

Chapter 1
Routine maintenance and servicing

Contents

Degrees of difficulty

Easy, suitable for novice with little experience		**Fairly easy,** suitable for beginner with some experience		**Fairly difficult,** suitable for competent DIY mechanic		**Difficult,** suitable for experienced DIY mechanic		**Very difficult,** suitable for expert DIY or professional	

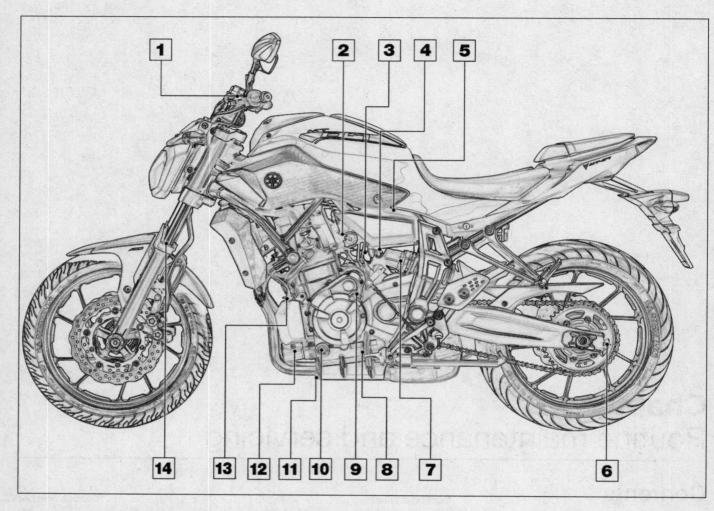

Component locations on the left side – MT-07 (FZ-07)

1 Clutch cable upper adjuster
2 Throttle cable lower adjusters
3 EVAP canister (where fitted)
4 Air filter housing drain
5 Air filter element

6 Drive chain adjuster
7 Rear shock pre-load adjuster
8 Engine number
9 Oil filler cap
10 Oil level window

11 Oil drain plug
12 Oil filter
13 Coolant reservoir filler cap
14 Fork seal

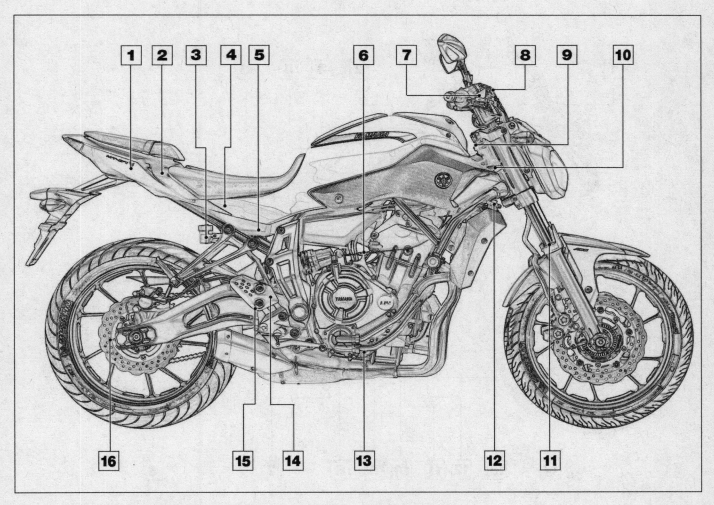

Component locations on the right side – MT-07 (FZ-07)

1 Model/colour code label
2 Diagnostic plug
3 Rear brake fluid reservoir
4 Fuses
5 Battery
6 Clutch cable lower adjuster

7 Front brake fluid reservoir
8 Throttle cable adjuster
9 Steering head bearing adjuster
10 Frame number
11 Fork seal
12 Radiator pressure cap

13 Coolant drain bolt
14 Rear brake light switch
15 Rear brake pedal height
   adjuster
16 Drive chain adjuster

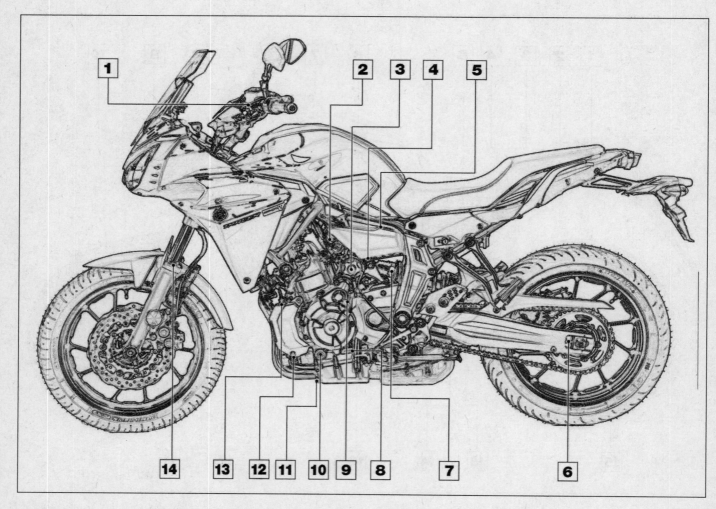

Component locations on the left side – MT-07TR

1 Clutch cable upper adjuster
2 Throttle cable lower adjusters
3 EVAP canister
4 Air filter housing drain
5 Air filter element

6 Drive chain adjuster
7 Rear shock pre-load adjuster
8 Engine number
9 Oil filler cap
10 Oil level window

11 Oil drain plug
12 Oil filter
13 Coolant reservoir filler cap
14 Fork seal

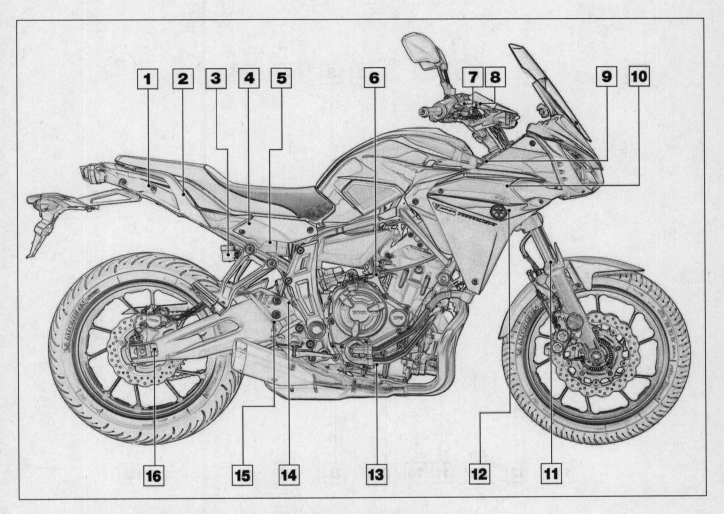

Component locations on the right side – MT-07TR

1 Model/colour code label
2 Diagnostic plug
3 Rear brake fluid reservoir
4 Fuses
5 Battery
6 Clutch cable lower adjuster

7 Front brake fluid reservoir
8 Throttle cable upper adjuster
9 Steering head bearing adjuster
10 Frame number
11 Fork seal
12 Radiator pressure cap

13 Coolant drain bolt
14 Rear brake light switch
15 Rear brake pedal height
   adjuster
16 Drive chain adjuster

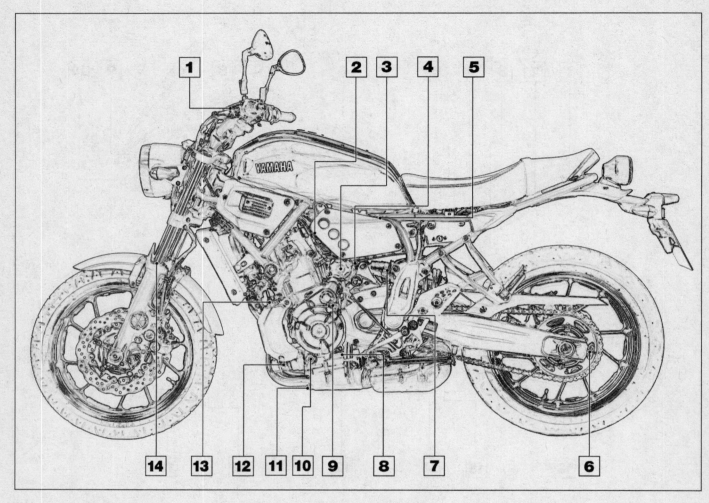

Component locations on the left side – XSR700

1 Clutch cable upper adjuster
2 Throttle cable lower adjusters
3 EVAP canister
4 Air filter housing drain
5 Air filter element

6 Drive chain adjuster
7 Rear shock pre-load adjuster
8 Engine number
9 Oil filler cap
10 Oil level window

11 Oil drain plug
12 Oil filter
13 Coolant reservoir filler cap
14 Fork seal

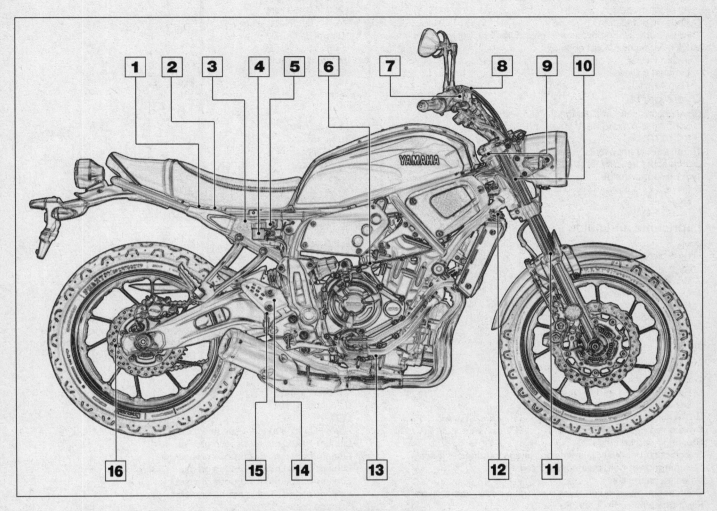

Component locations on the right side – XSR700

1 Model/colour code label
2 Diagnostic plug
3 Fuses
4 Rear brake fluid reservoir
5 Battery
6 Clutch cable lower adjuster

7 Front brake fluid reservoir
8 Throttle cable upper adjuster
9 Steering head bearing adjuster
10 Frame number
11 Fork seal
12 Radiator pressure cap

13 Coolant drain bolt
14 Rear brake light switch
15 Rear brake pedal height
   adjuster
16 Drive chain adjuster

Engine

Spark plugs
    Type . . . . NGK LMAR8A-9
    Electrode gap . . . . 0.8 to 0.9 mm
Engine idle speed
    2014/15 MT-07 (FZ-07) models . . . . 1100 to 1300 rpm
    All other models . . . . 1250 to 1450 rpm
Cylinder identification. . . . . No. 1 – left, No. 2 – right
Throttle body synchronisation – max. difference between bodies. . . . . 10 mmHg
Valve clearances (COLD engine)
    Intake valves. . . . . 0.11 to 0.20 mm
    Exhaust valves . . . . 0.24 to 0.30 mm

Cycle parts

Drive chain slack (on sidestand) – see text
    MT-07 (FZ-07) and XSR . . . . 51 to 56 mm
    MT-07TR. . . . . 30 to 35 mm
Throttle cable freeplay . . . . 3 to 5 mm
Clutch cable freeplay (at lever ball end) . . . . 5 to 10 mm
Tyre pressures (cold)
    Front . . . . 33 psi (2.25 Bar)
    Rear . . . . 36 psi (2.5 Bar)

Lubricants and fluids

Fuel . . . . see Chapter 4
Engine oil type . . . . API grade SG or higher, JASO grade MA, SAE 10W40
Engine oil capacity
    Oil change. . . . . 2.3 litres
    Oil and filter change . . . . 2.6 litres
    Following engine overhaul – dry engine, new filter. . . . . 3.0 litres
Coolant type. . . . . Pre-mixed coolant for motorcycle engines, or a mixture of 50% distilled water and 50% ethylene glycol anti-freeze with corrosion inhibitors for aluminium engines. Note that Yamaha specify that soft tap water can be used, but NOT hard water. If in doubt use only distilled water.
Coolant capacity
    Radiator, hoses and all passages. . . . . 1.6 litres
    Reservoir. . . . . 0.25 litre
Brake fluid . . . . DOT 4
Drive chain . . . . Aerosol chain lubricant suitable for O-ring chains
Steering head bearings . . . . Lithium-based multi-purpose grease
Shock absorber bush, suspension linkage bearings and seals . . . . Lithium-based multi-purpose grease
Swingarm pivot bolt, bearings and seals. . . . . Lithium-based multi-purpose grease
Wheel bearing seals. . . . . Lithium-based multi-purpose grease
Gearchange lever, clutch lever, rear brake pedal, stand pivots . . . . Lithium-based multi-purpose grease
Front brake lever pivot and tip . . . . Silicone grease
Cables . . . . Aerosol cable lubricant
Throttle twistgrip. . . . . Lithium-based multi-purpose grease

Torque wrench settings

Cooling system drain bolt . . . . 7 Nm
Crankshaft end cap . . . . 10 Nm
Fork clamp bolts (top yoke) . . . . 26 Nm
Oil drain plug . . . . 43 Nm
Oil filter . . . . 17 Nm
Rear axle nut
    MT-07 (FZ-07) and XSR models. . . . . 105 Nm
    MT-07TR models . . . . 150 Nm
Spark plugs . . . . 13 Nm
Steering head bearing adjuster nut – using Yamaha tool
    Initial setting . . . . 52 Nm
    Final setting . . . . 18 Nm
Steering head bearing adjuster nut clamp bolt
    MT-07 (FZ-07) and XSR models. . . . . 21 Nm
    MT-07TR models . . . . 35 Nm
Timing inspection bolt . . . . 15 Nm

Pre-ride

☐ See Pre-ride checks at the beginning of this manual.

After the initial 600 miles (1000 km)

Note: *This check is performed by a Yamaha dealer after the first 600 miles (1000 km) from new. Thereafter, maintenance is carried out according to the following intervals of the schedule.*

Every 600 miles (1000 km)

☐ Check, adjust, clean and lubricate the drive chain (Section 4)

Every 6000 miles (10,000 km) or 12 months

☐ Check and adjust the spark plugs (Section 5)
☐ Check the idle speed (Section 6)
☐ Check/adjust throttle body synchronisation (Section 7)
☐ Check the fuel system (Section 8)
☐ Check and adjust the throttle cables (Section 9)
☐ Check and adjust the clutch cable (Section 10)
☐ Lubricate the clutch/gearchange/brake lever/brake pedal/stand pivots and cables (Section 11)
☐ Check the cooling system (Section 12)
☐ Change the engine oil (Section 13)
☐ Check the brake system (Section 14)
☐ Check the condition of the wheels, wheel bearings and tyres (Section 15)
☐ Check the front and rear suspension (Section 16)
☐ Check and adjust the steering head bearings (Section 17)
☐ Check the sidestand and starter safety circuit (Section 18)
☐ Check the tightness of all nuts, bolts and fasteners (Section 19)
☐ Check the battery (Section 20)

Every 12,000 miles (20,000 km)

☐ Fit new spark plugs (see Section 5)
☐ Check the EVAP system (where fitted) (Section 8)
☐ Fit a new engine oil filter (Section 13)
☐ Re-grease the steering head bearings (Chapter 5)
☐ Re-grease the suspension linkage bearings (Chapter 5)

Every 24,000 miles (40,000 km)

☐ Fit a new air filter and clean the filter housing (Section 21)
☐ Check and adjust the valve clearances (Section 22)

Every 30,000 miles (50,000 km)

☐ Re-grease the swingarm bearings (Chapter 5)

Every two years

☐ Change the brake fluid (Chapter 6)

Every three years

☐ Change the coolant (Section 12)

Every four years

☐ Fit new brake hoses (Chapter 6)

Pre-ride
- [ ] See Pre-ride checks at the beginning of this manual.

After the initial 600 miles (1000 km)
Note: *This check is performed by a Yamaha dealer after the first 600 miles (1000 km) from new. Thereafter, maintenance is carried out according to the following intervals of the schedule.*

Every 500 miles (800 km)
- [ ] Check, adjust, clean and lubricate the drive chain (Section 4)

Every 4000 miles (7000 km)
- [ ] Check and adjust the spark plugs (Section 5)
- [ ] Check the idle speed (Section 6)
- [ ] Check/adjust throttle body synchronisation (Section 7)
- [ ] Check the fuel system (Section 8)
- [ ] Check the crankcase breather hose (Section 21)
- [ ] Check the exhaust system for leaks (Section 19)
- [ ] Check and adjust the throttle cables (Section 9)
- [ ] Check and adjust the clutch cable (Section 10)
- [ ] Lubricate the clutch/gearchange/brake lever/brake pedal/sidestand pivots and cables (Section 11)
- [ ] Check the cooling system (Section 12)
- [ ] Change the engine oil (Section 13)
- [ ] Check the brake system (Section 14)
- [ ] Check the condition of the wheels, wheel bearings and tyres (Section 15)
- [ ] Check the front and rear suspension (Section 16)
- [ ] Check and adjust the steering head bearings (Section 17)
- [ ] Check the sidestand and starter safety circuit (Section 18)
- [ ] Check the tightness of all nuts, bolts and fasteners (Section 19)
- [ ] Check the battery (Section 20)

Every 8000 miles (13,000 km)
- [ ] Fit new spark plugs (Section 5)
- [ ] Fit a new engine oil filter (Section 13)

Every 12,000 miles (20,000 km)
- [ ] Check the air induction system (AIS) and the EVAP system (Section 8)
- [ ] Re-grease the steering head bearings (Chapter 5)

Every 24,000 miles (38,000 km)
- [ ] Fit a new air filter and clean the air filter housing (Section 21)

Every 26,000 miles (42,000 km)
- [ ] Check and adjust the valve clearances (Section 22)

Every 30,000 miles (50,000 km)
- [ ] Re-grease the swingarm and suspension linkage bearings (Chapter 5)

Every two years
- [ ] Change the brake fluid (Chapter 6)
- [ ] Change the coolant (Section 12)

Every four years
- [ ] Fit new brake hoses (Chapter 6)

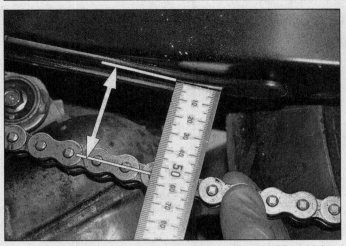

4.4a Measuring chain slack on MT-07 (FZ-07) and XSR models

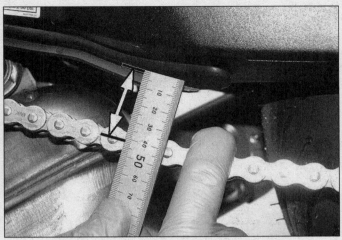

4.4b Measuring chain slack on MT-07TR models

3 General information

1 This Chapter is designed to help the home mechanic maintain his/her motorcycle for safety, economy, long life and peak performance.

2 Deciding where to start or plug into the routine maintenance schedule depends on several factors. If the warranty period on your motorcycle has just expired, and if it has been maintained according to the warranty standards, you may want to pick up routine maintenance as it coincides with the next mileage interval. If you have owned the machine for some time but have never performed any maintenance on it, then you may want to start at the beginning and include all frequent procedures to ensure that nothing important is overlooked. If you have just had a major engine overhaul, then you should start the engine maintenance routines from the beginning. If you have a used machine and have no knowledge of its history or maintenance record, you should combine all the checks into one large initial service and

4.7 Neglect has caused the links in this chain to kink

then settle into the maintenance schedule prescribed.

3 Before beginning any maintenance or repair, the machine should be cleaned thoroughly, especially around the oil filter, drain plugs and valve cover. Cleaning will help ensure that dirt does not contaminate the engine and will allow you to detect wear and damage that could otherwise easily go unnoticed.

4 Certain maintenance information is sometimes printed on decals attached to the motorcycle. If any information on the decals differs from that included here, use the information on the decal.

> ⚠️ *Warning: Read the Safety first! section of this manual carefully before starting work.*

4 Drive chain and sprockets

Check

1 A neglected drive chain won't last long and can quickly damage the sprockets. Routine chain adjustment and lubrication isn't difficult and will ensure maximum chain and sprocket life.

Caution: Riding the bike with excess slack in the chain could lead to damage.

2 Check chain slack with the bike on the sidestand. There should be no weight on the bike.

3 Make sure that the transmission is in neutral.

4 Hold a ruler behind the chain in the centre of the lower run, with the top (zero end) of the ruler against the underside of the rear end of the chain slider on the swingarm – push down lightly on the chain to take out all the slack and measure the distance between the

chain slider and the centre of the chain **(see illustrations)**.

5 Compare the result with the range given in the Specifications.

6 Since the chain will rarely wear evenly, roll the bike forward so that another section of chain can be checked; do this several times to check the entire length of chain, and mark the tightest spot.

7 In some cases where lubrication has been neglected, corrosion and dirt may cause the links to bind and kink, which effectively shortens the chain's length and makes it tight **(see illustration)**. Thoroughly clean and work free any such links, then highlight them with a marker pen or paint. Take the bike for a short ride, then repeat the measurement for slack in the highlighted area.

8 If the chain has kinked again and is still tight, fit a new one (see Chapter 6). A rusty, kinked or worn chain will damage the sprockets and can damage transmission bearings. If in any doubt as to the condition of a chain, it is far better to fit a new one than risk damage to other components and possibly yourself.

9 Check the entire length of the chain for worn or damaged rollers and sideplates, loose links and pins, and missing O-rings and fit a new one if necessary. From time to time, and particularly if the chain is old and most of the adjustment has been taken up, or if the sprockets are wearing, refer to Chapter 6 and check the amount of chain stretch.

Caution: Never fit a new chain onto old sprockets, and never use the old chain if you fit new sprockets – replace the chain and sprockets as a set – see Chapter 6.

Adjustment

10 If the amount of slack at the tightest point exceeds the upper limit of the specified range it must be adjusted. Rotate the rear wheel until the chain is positioned with the tightest spot at the centre of its bottom run.

4.11a Rear axle nut (arrowed) – MT-07 (FZ-07) and XSR models

4.11b Rear axle nut (arrowed) – MT-07TR models

4.12a Slacken the locknut (arrowed) on each side

4.12b Turn the adjuster nuts as required

11 Loosen the rear wheel axle nut **(see illustrations)**.

12 On MT-07 (FZ-07) and XSR models loosen the locknut on the adjuster on each side of the swingarm, then turn the adjuster nuts evenly and a small amount at a time, clockwise to reduce slack and anti-clockwise to increase it, keeping some forward pressure on the wheel to make sure the adjuster plates remain butted against the swingarm, until the amount of slack is within the specified range **(see illustrations)**. Now check that the alignment marks on the swingarm are equally aligned relative to the axle plate on each side of the swingarm – if not, the rear wheel will be out of alignment with the front **(see illustration)**.

13 On MT-07TR models loosen the locknut on the adjuster bolt on each side of the swingarm, then turn the adjuster bolts evenly and a small amount at a time, anti-clockwise to reduce slack and clockwise to increase it, keeping some forward pressure on the wheel to make sure the adjuster plates remain butted against the bolt heads, until the amount of slack is within the specified range **(see illustration)**.

4.12c Make sure the position of the adjuster plate relative to the lines on the swingarm is the same on each side

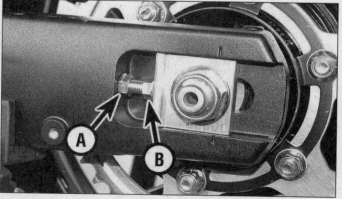

4.13a Slacken the locknut (A) on each side and turn the adjuster bolts (B) as required

4.13b Make sure the position of the adjuster plate relative to the index notches (arrowed) on the swingarm is the same on each side

4.16 Counter-hold the adjuster when tightening the locknut to prevent it turning

Now check that the alignment marks on each adjuster plate are equally aligned relative to the index notches in each side of the swingarm **(see illustration)** – if not, the rear wheel will be out of alignment with the front.

14 If there is a discrepancy in the position of the alignment marks, correct it with the adjusters and then check the chain tension again as described above.

15 Push the wheel forwards to make sure the adjuster plates butt against the swingarm on MT-07 (FZ-07) and XSR models and the adjuster bolt heads on MT-07TR models, then tighten the axle nut to 105 Nm on MT-07 (FZ-07) and XSR models and 150 Nm on MT-07TR models.

16 Counter-hold the adjuster nuts or bolts and tighten the locknuts **(see illustration)**. Recheck the adjustment.

17 If the chain is difficult to adjust satisfactorily, or if it is close to the end of available adjustment, check the chain stretch as described in Chapter 6.

Cleaning and lubrication

Note: *If using a Scottoiler or equivalent automatic chain lubrication system you do not need to manually apply any other lubricant.*

18 The best time to lubricate the chain is after the motorcycle has been ridden. When the chain is warm, the lubricant will penetrate the joints between the sideplates better than when cold.

19 If required, wash the chain using a dedicated aerosol cleaner or paraffin (kerosene), then wipe it off and allow it to dry, using compressed air if available **(see illustration)**.

Caution: Don't use petrol (gasoline), solvent or other cleaning fluids which might damage the internal sealing properties of the chain. Don't use high-pressure water. The entire process shouldn't take longer than five to six minutes – if it does, the O-rings in the chain rollers could be damaged.

20 Use an aerosol chain lube that is specifically for O-ring chains. Engine oil can be used but it will not stick to the chain as well as dedicated chain lube and therefore not provide long lasting lubrication. Apply the lubricant to the area where the sideplates overlap – not the middle of the rollers. Protect the tyre from overspray with a rag or piece of cardboard **(see illustration)**.

⚠️ *Warning: Take care not to get any lubricant on the tyre or brake system components. If any of*

4.19 Specially shaped chain cleaning brushes are available from good suppliers

the lubricant inadvertently contacts them, clean it off thoroughly using a suitable solvent or dedicated brake cleaner before riding the machine.

Sprocket wear check

21 If the drive chain is worn or damaged, it is likely that the sprockets will also be worn.

22 Remove the front sprocket cover (see Chapter 6). Check the teeth on the front and rear sprockets for wear **(see illustration)**. If the sprocket teeth are worn excessively,

4.20 Apply the lubricant to the overlap between the sideplates

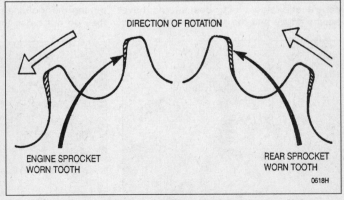

DIRECTION OF ROTATION

ENGINE SPROCKET WORN TOOTH

REAR SPROCKET WORN TOOTH

0618H

4.22 Check the sprockets in the areas indicated to see if they are worn excessively

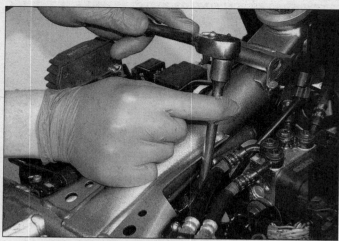

5.4a Unscrew and remove each plug...

5.4b ... use a magnet to lift the plugs out if necessary

follow the procedure in Chapter 6 and replace the chain and both sprockets with a new set.

23 Check the front and rear sprocket nuts are tight (refer to Chapter 6 for torque settings).

24 Inspect the drive chain slider on the front of the swingarm for excessive wear and damage and fit a new one if necessary (see Chapter 5).

5 Spark plugs

1 To remove the spark plugs you need a 14mm spark plug socket.

2 Remove the ignition coils (see Chapter 4).

3 If available, blow compressed air down into each spark plug bore to get rid of any dirt that may otherwise fall into the cylinders when the plugs are removed.

4 Using either the Yamaha plug socket provided in the toolkit or a deep socket type wrench, unscrew the plugs and lift them out of the cylinder head **(see illustrations)**. Lay each plug out in relation to its cylinder so that if either plug shows up a problem it is easy to identify the troublesome cylinder.

5 Inspect the electrodes for wear. Both the centre and side electrodes should have square edges and the side electrode should be of uniform thickness. Look for excessive deposits and evidence of a cracked or chipped insulator around the centre electrode.

6 Compare your spark plugs to the firing end examples on the inside rear cover of this manual. Check the threads, the washer and the ceramic insulator body for cracks and other damage.

7 If the electrodes are not excessively worn, and if the deposits can be easily removed with a wire brush, and there are no cracks or chips visible in the insulator, the plugs can be re-gapped and re-used. If in doubt concerning the condition of the plugs, replace them with new ones, as the expense is minimal. Note that new spark plugs should be fitted at every second service interval.

8 Before installing the plugs, refer to the Specifications and make sure they are the correct type and heat range and check the gap between the side (earth) electrode and the centre electrode **(see illustrations)**. Adjust the gap as necessary by bending the side electrode, but be very careful not to chip or crack the insulator nose **(see illustration)**. Make sure the sealing washer is in place on the plug before installing it.

9 Carefully thread the plugs into the head turning the tool shaft by hand, making sure they do not cross-thread – if they become prematurely tight remove them and start again, do not force them or you will damage the threads in the cylinder head. Once the plugs are finger-tight, the job can be finished with the tool handle or a socket wrench. If a torque wrench is available, tighten the spark plugs to 13 Nm. Otherwise tighten them by 1/4 to 1/2 turn after they have been fully hand tightened and have seated. Do not over-tighten them.

10 Install the ignition coils (see Chapter 4).

6 Idle speed

1 Engine idle speed is controlled electronically and cannot be adjusted manually. If the idle speed is not within the range given in the Specifications when the engine is at normal temperature, check the throttle bodies are synchronised (balanced) (Section 7), the valve clearances are correct (Section 22), the air filter is clean (Section 21), and the spark plugs are clean and their gaps are correct (Section 5). Also, with the engine running turn the handlebars back-and-forth and see if the idle speed changes – if it does, the throttle cables may not be adjusted or routed correctly, or may be worn out. This is a dangerous

5.8a Using a feeler gauge to measure the spark plug electrode gap

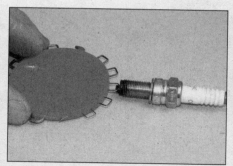

5.8b Using a wire type gauge to measure the spark plug electrode gap

5.8c Adjust the electrode gap by bending the side electrode only

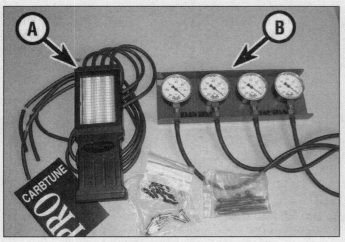

7.3 Manometer (A) and vacuum gauges (B)

7.5a IAP sensor hose (arrowed)

condition that can cause loss of control of the bike. Be sure to correct this problem before proceeding (Section 9). Also check for loose intake duct clamps between the throttle bodies and the cylinder head, and make sure the ducts are in good condition (see Chapter 4) – a loose or split duct will cause an air leak and affect the idle speed. If all is good so far check cylinder compression (see Chapter 2).

2 If no problem can be found take the bike to a Yamaha dealer for assessment of the idle speed control system using the diagnostic tester.

7.5b Intake air flap diaphragm hose (arrowed)

7.6 Blanking cap (arrowed)

7 Throttle body synchronisation

⚠️ **Warning: Petrol (gasoline) is extremely flammable, so take extra precautions when you work on any part of the fuel system. Don't smoke or allow open flames or bare light bulbs near the work area, and don't work in a garage where a natural gas-type appliance is present. If you spill any fuel on your skin, rinse it off immediately with soap and water. When you perform any kind of work on the fuel system, wear safety glasses and have a fire extinguisher suitable for a Class B type fire (flammable liquids) on hand.**

⚠️ **Warning: Do not allow exhaust gases to build up in the work area; either perform the check outside or use an exhaust gas extraction system.**

Special tool: *A set of vacuum gauges or a manometer is necessary for this job.*

1 Throttle body synchronisation ensures each throttle body passes the same amount of fuel/air mixture to each cylinder. This is done by measuring the vacuum produced in each cylinder. Throttle bodies that are out of

synchronisation will result in increased fuel consumption, higher engine temperature, less than ideal throttle response and higher vibration levels.

2 If the service intervals coincide, before synchronising the throttle bodies check the valve clearances (Section 22), fit a new air filter (Section 21), and clean the spark plugs and check their gaps, or fit new ones (Section 5). Also check for loose intake duct clamps between the throttle bodies and the cylinder head, and make sure the ducts are in good condition (Section 8) – a loose or split duct will cause an air leak and affect the idle speed.

3 To synchronise the throttle bodies you will need a set of vacuum gauges or a manometer **(see illustration)**. These instruments measure engine vacuum, and can be obtained from motorcycle dealers or mail order parts suppliers – usually there is an option to buy either a two-gauge or a four-gauge set, and come complete with the necessary adapters and hoses to fit the take-off points. You also need two three-way hose joints and two auxiliary lengths of hose on 2014 to 2016 MT-07 (FZ-07) models, and a single three-way joint and auxiliary hose on 2017-on MT-07 (FZ-07), all MT-07TR and all XSR models. These are available from Yamaha parts stockists.

4 Start the engine and let it run until it reaches normal operating temperature, then shut it off. Support the motorcycle upright on level ground using an auxiliary stand. Remove the fuel tank (see Chapter 4).

5 On 2014 to 2016 MT-07 (FZ-07) models disconnect the intake air pressure sensor hose from the vacuum take-off point on the left-hand throttle body, and the intake air flap diaphragm valve hose from the take-off point on the right-hand throttle body **(see illustrations)**. Connect the auxiliary hoses to the take-off points, then fit the three-way joints into the other end, and connect the IAP sensor and diaphragm valve hoses to one of the unions on the respective joints. Connect the hose from the No. 1 vacuum gauge to the remaining union on the left-hand joint, and the No. 2 gauge hose to the right-hand one.

6 On 2017-on MT-07 (FZ-07), all MT-07TR and all XSR models disconnect the intake air pressure sensor hose from the vacuum take-off point on the left-hand throttle body **(see illustration 7.5a)**, and remove the blanking cap from the take-off point on the right-hand throttle body **(see illustration)**. Connect the auxiliary hose to the take-off point on the left-hand throttle body, then fit the three-way joint into the other end, and

7.8 Checking throttle body synchronisation

7.9a By-pass air screw (arrowed), left-hand throttle body – DO NOT adjust this screw

7.9b By-pass air screw (arrowed), right-hand throttle body – adjust this screw

8.1 Check the tank and hoses as described

connect the IAP sensor hose to one of the unions on the joint. Connect the hose from the No. 1 vacuum gauge to the remaining union on the left-hand joint, and the No. 2 gauge hose to the take-off point on the right-hand throttle body.

7 Position the fuel tank on the frame and connect the wiring and hoses (see Chapter 4) – leave the tank supported in the raised position, and make sure none of the gauge hoses are trapped or kinked.

8 Start the engine and let it idle, making sure the speed is still correct. If the gauges are fitted with damping adjustment, set this so that needle flutter is just eliminated but so that they can still respond to small changes in pressure. The difference in the vacuum reading on each gauge should be within the maximum difference given in the Specifications **(see illustration)**.

9 If the vacuum readings vary by more than the maximum difference specified and adjustment is necessary identify the by-pass air screws on the throttle bodies – the screw on the left-hand throttle body is the base to which the right-hand one is matched, and must not itself be adjusted **(see illustrations)**. The screw on the right-hand throttle body is best turned

using an angled screwdriver – long-handled ones with an internal flexi-shaft turned from the end of the handle, specially built for this purpose, are available, either from Yamaha (part No. 90890-03173), or there are many after-market equivalents.

10 Turn the right-hand by-pass air screw until the gauge readings are the same **(see illustration 7.9b)**. After each adjustment, open and close the throttle quickly to settle the setting and check the reading on the gauges again. If the adjuster screw is inadvertently unscrewed, screw it back in, then set it according to the gauge readings.

11 When the throttle bodies are synchronised, open and close the throttle quickly to settle the settings, and recheck the gauge readings, readjusting if necessary. If the throttle bodies cannot be synchronised, remove the throttle bodies and clean and check them as described in Chapter 4, and if necessary fit new ones.

12 Remove the gauges and fit the IAP sensor hose and the diaphragm valve hose or blanking cap, according to model **(see illustrations 7.5a and b and 7.6)**.

13 Install the fuel tank (see Chapter 4).

8 Fuel system and EVAP system

⚠ *Warning: Petrol (gasoline) is extremely flammable, so take extra precautions when you work on any part of the fuel system. Don't smoke or allow open flames or bare light bulbs near the work area, and don't work in a garage where a natural gas-type appliance is present. If you spill any fuel on your skin, rinse it off immediately with soap and water. When you perform any kind of work on the fuel system, wear safety glasses and have a fire extinguisher suitable for a Class B type fire (flammable liquids) on hand.*

Fuel system

1 Raise the fuel tank (see Chapter 4) and check the underside of the tank, the fuel supply hose and its connectors, and the tank overflow and breather hoses for signs of leaks, cracking, hardening or damage **(see illustration)**. Replace any hose that has deteriorated with a new one (see

8.6 Check all six clamp screws are tight (arrowed)

8.7 Check the drain collector (arrowed)

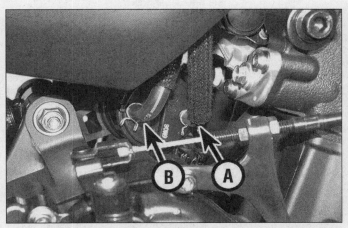

8.9a Fuel tank breather hose at canister end (A), canister to throttle body hose (B)

8.9b Canister to throttle body hoses (arrowed)

Chapter 4). Check the lower end of the overflow and breather hoses for blockages.

2 If the joint between the fuel pump mounting plate and the tank is leaking, check the mounting bolts are tightened to the specified torque setting (see Chapter 4); if the leak persists, remove the pump and fit a new O-ring (see Chapter 4).

3 Remove the tank (see Chapter 4).

4 Inspect the intake air pressure sensor hose, and on 2014 to 2016 MT-07 (FZ-07) models the intake air flap system hoses, for signs of cracking, hardening or damage **(see illustrations 7.5a and b)**. Check that the hoses are fully pushed on to their unions at each end.

5 Inspect the joints between the fuel rail, the injectors and the throttle bodies. If there are any fuel leaks, remove the fuel rail and fit new seals and O-rings to the injectors (see Chapter 4).

6 Make sure the ducts from the air filter housing and between the throttle bodies and the cylinder head are in good condition and correctly seated, and that the clamp screws are tight **(see illustration)**.

7 Check for any deposits in the air filter

housing drain collector, and clean it if required **(see illustration)**. If deposits continue to drain from the air filter housing with the collector removed, remove the air filter and clean the housing (Section 21).

EVAP system (where fitted)

8 The system prevents petrol (gasoline) fumes escaping from the fuel tank into the atmosphere by collecting and storing them in a canister while the bike is not being used, and passes them into the throttle bodies for combustion when the engine is running. The system is fitted in accordance with the legislation of the country in which the bike is registered, and is a requirement of Euro 4 legislation.

9 The system consists of the breather hose from the fuel tank going to a canister via a one-way valve, and the hose from the canister to each throttle body via a three-way joint **(see illustrations)**. The canister is mounted in a rubber sleeve on top of the starter motor.

10 On MT-07 (FZ-07) and XSR models remove the right-hand fuel tank side cover, and on MT-07TR models remove the fuel tank cover (see Chapter 7). Visually inspect all the

hoses between the fuel tank, the one-way valve, the canister and the throttle bodies on the right-hand side **(see illustrations 8.9a and b)**, and the canister breather hose on the left-hand end, for kinks and splits and any other damage or deterioration **(see illustration)**. Make sure that the hoses are securely connected with a clamp on each end. Replace any hoses that are damaged or deteriorated with new ones.

8.10 Canister breather hose (arrowed)

9.3a On MT-07 (FZ-07) and XSR models unscrew the end-weight using a hex key in its end (arrowed)

9.3b On MT-07TR models undo the screw (arrowed) and remove the end-weight

9 Throttle cables

1 Make sure the throttle twistgrip rotates easily from fully closed to fully open with the front wheel turned at various angles. The twistgrip should return automatically from fully open to fully closed when released.

2 If the throttle sticks, this is probably due to a cable fault. Remove the cables (see Chapter 4) and lubricate them (Section 11). If the inner cables still do not run smoothly in the outer cables, replace the cables with new ones.

3 With the cables removed, check that the twistgrip turns smoothly around the handlebar – dirt combined with a lack of lubrication can cause the action to be stiff. If necessary remove the handlebar end-weight and slide the twistgrip off the handlebar (see illustrations). Clean any old grease from the bar and the inside of the tube. Apply a smear of lithium-based multi purpose grease to the bar, then refit the twistgrip and end-weight. While the cables are disconnected also check the action of the throttle linkage and butterflies, turning the cable pulley on the left-hand end of the throttle bodies by hand.

4 Install the lubricated or new cables, making sure they are correctly routed (see Chapter 4).

5 With the throttle operating smoothly, check for a small amount of freeplay in the opening cable, measured in terms of the amount of twistgrip rotation before the throttle opens, and compare the amount to that listed in the Specifications (see illustration). If it is incorrect, adjust the cables as follows:

6 Adjust freeplay using the adjuster near the upper end of the the throttle opening cable – slide the rubber boot off the adjuster, loosen the locknut and turn the adjuster until the specified amount of freeplay is obtained (see illustration). Turn the adjuster towards the nut to increase freeplay and away to reduce it. Tighten the locknut against the adjuster then refit the rubber boot

7 If the adjuster has reached its limit of adjustment, reset it to its start point by turning it most of the way in so freeplay is increased, then adjust the cable at the throttle body end as follows: loosen the locknut holding the opening cable in the bracket and thread it up, then free the adjuster nut from the bracket and thread it down a bit, then re-seat it against the lug on the bracket and tighten the locknut down against the bracket (see illustrations). Further

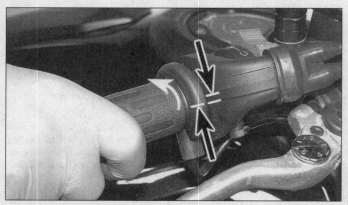

9.5 Check for the specified amount of free rotation in the twistgrip

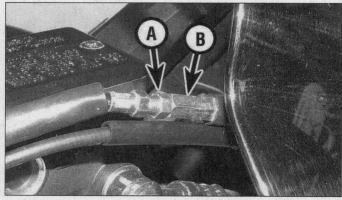

9.6 Pull the boot off, slacken the locknut (A) and turn the adjuster (B)

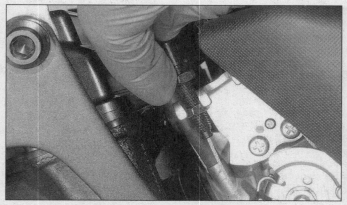

9.7a Slacken the locknut and thread it up...

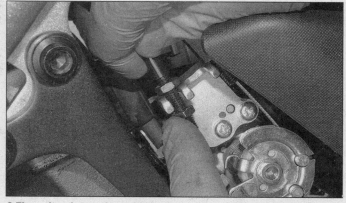

9.7b ... then lower the cable in the bracket to free the adjuster nut so it can be turned

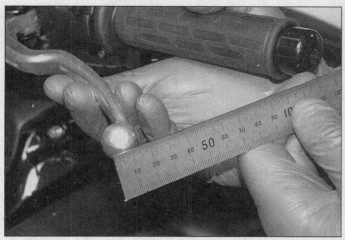

10.5 Clutch cable freeplay is measured at the ball end of the lever

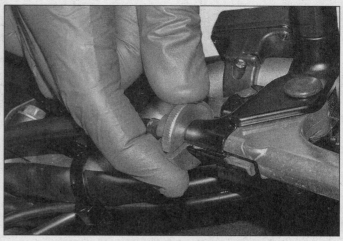

10.6 Turn the adjuster to set the correct freeplay

adjustments can now be made at the twistgrip end as described above. If the freeplay cannot be set within the limits of adjustment at both ends replace the cables with new ones (see Chapter 4).

> ⚠ **Warning: Turn the handlebars all the way through their travel with the engine idling. Idle speed should not change. If it does, the cables may be routed incorrectly. Correct this condition before riding the motorcycle.**

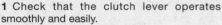

10 Clutch cable

1 Check that the clutch lever operates smoothly and easily.
2 If the lever action is heavy or stiff, disconnect the cable (see Chapter 2) and lubricate it (Section 11). If the inner cable still does not run smoothly in the outer cable, replace the cable with a new one. With the cable disconnected check the action of the lever, and if it is stiff see Step 3. Install the lubricated or new cable (see Chapter 2).
3 If the lever is stiff, remove it (see Chapter 5) and check for damage or distortion, or any other cause, and remedy as necessary. Clean and lubricate the pivot and contact areas (Section 11).
4 If the lever and cable are good, refer to Chapter 2 and check the release mechanism in the clutch cover and the clutch itself.
5 With the clutch operating smoothly, check that the clutch lever is correctly adjusted. Periodic adjustment is necessary to compensate for wear in the clutch plates and stretch of the cable. Check that the amount of freeplay at the clutch lever end is within the range given in the Specifications at the beginning of the Chapter **(see illustration)**.
6 If adjustment is required, thread the

adjuster in or out of the lever bracket on the handlebar until the required amount of freeplay is obtained **(see illustration)**. To increase freeplay, turn the adjuster clockwise (into the lever bracket). To reduce freeplay, turn the adjuster anti-clockwise (out of the lever bracket). Make sure the cable removal slot in the adjuster does not align with the slot in the lever bracket.
7 If all the adjustment has been taken up at the lever end, reset the adjuster to give the maximum amount of freeplay, then set the correct amount of freeplay using the adjuster on the right-hand side of the engine.
8 Slacken the locknut securing the threaded section of the cable in the bracket, then push the cable forwards in the bracket until the adjuster nut is clear of the tab. Now thread the adjuster nut up or down the cable as required to obtain the correct freeplay **(see illustration)** – thread it down the cable to decrease freeplay and up the cable to increase it. When the correct amount of freeplay has been achieved seat the adjuster nut against the tab on the bracket and tighten the locknut against the bracket. Any minor adjustments can now be made at the handlebar end as described above.

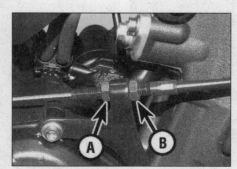

10.8 Clutch cable adjuster locknut (A) and adjuster nut (B)

11 Stand pivot, lever pivots and cable lubrication

Pivot points

1 Since the controls, cables and various other components of a motorcycle are exposed to the elements, they should be checked and lubricated periodically to ensure safe and trouble-free operation.
2 The clutch and brake lever pivots, footrest pivots, brake pedal and gearchange lever pivots and linkage, and stand pivot should be lubricated frequently. In order for the lubricant to be applied where it will do the most good, the component should be removed and cleaned before applying fresh lubricant (see Chapter 5).
3 The lubricant recommended by Yamaha for each application is listed at the beginning of the Chapter. If an aerosol lubricant is being used, it can be applied to the pivot joint gaps and will usually work its way into the areas where friction occurs, so less disassembly of the component is needed (however it is always better to do so and clean off all corrosion, dirt and old lubricant first).
4 If grease is used, apply it sparingly as it may attract dirt (which could cause the controls to bind or wear at an accelerated rate). An alternative lubricant for the control lever pivots is a dry-film lubricant (available from many sources by different names), but it may need to be applied more frequently.

Cables

Special tool: A cable lubricating adapter is necessary for this procedure.
5 To lubricate the cables, disconnect the relevant cable at its upper end, then lubricate it with a pressure adapter and aerosol cable

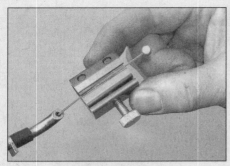

11.5a Fit the cable into the adapter...

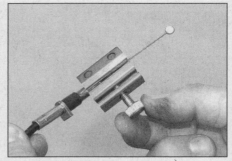

11.5b ...and tighten the screw to seal it in...

11.5c ...then apply the lubricant using the nozzle provided inserted in the hole in the adapter

lubricant **(see illustrations)**. See Chapter 4 for throttle cable removal procedures, and Chapter 2 for the clutch cable.

12 Cooling system

Check

 Warning: The engine must be cool before beginning this procedure.

1 On MT-07TR models remove the right-hand fairing side panel and inner panel (see Chapter 7).

2 Check the coolant level in the reservoir (see *Pre-ride checks*).

3 Check the entire cooling system for evidence of leaks.

4 Examine each coolant hose and pipe along its entire length **(see illustration)**. Look for cracks, splits, abrasions and other signs of damage or deterioration. Squeeze each hose at various points. They should feel firm, yet pliable, and return to their original shape when released. If they are cracked or hard, replace them with new ones. If necessary, tighten the hose clips carefully to prevent future leaks. If there is leakage from the pipe joints to the water pump check the bolt is tight. If necessary remove the pipes and fit new O-rings (see Chapter 3).

5 Examine the oil cooler inlet and outlet hoses on the front of the engine for damage and signs of deterioration. Check that the hose clips are secure and that there are no signs of either coolant or oil leaks at the oil cooler-to-crankcase joint. If there is, refer to Chapter 2 – if coolant is leaking from the body replace the cooler with a new one, and if oil is leaking first remove the oil filter (Section 13) and make sure the cooler bolt is tightened to the specified torque (see Chapter 2 Specifications), and if it is, or if leaks persists, remove the cooler and replace the O-ring with a new one.

6 Check for leaks around the pump on the right-hand side of the engine **(see illustration 12.4)**. If coolant is leaking from between the pump and the clutch cover, check that the pump bolts are tight. If they are, remove the pump and replace the O-ring with a new one (see Chapter 3).

7 To prevent water leaking from the cooling system to the lubrication system and vice versa, two seals are fitted on the water pump shaft. If either seal fails, a drain hole between the seals to the outside of the clutch cover allows the coolant or oil to escape and prevents them mixing. Look for tell-tale signs of leaks from the drain hole **(see illustration)**.

8 The water seal is of the mechanical type and bears on the inner face of the pump impeller. The oil seal is of the normal feathered lip type. If there are signs of coolant leaking, remove the pump and replace the mechanical seal with a new one. If it is oil that is leaking, or if the leaks are white with the texture of emulsion, replace both seals with new ones (the mechanical seal has to be removed in order to remove the oil seal, and it cannot be reused). Refer to Chapter 3 for seal replacement.

9 Check the thermostat cover on the left-hand end of the cylinder head for signs of leakage

12.4 Squeeze the hoses to check for cracks, deterioration and hardening. Make sure all clamps are tight

12.7 Water pump drain hole (arrowed)

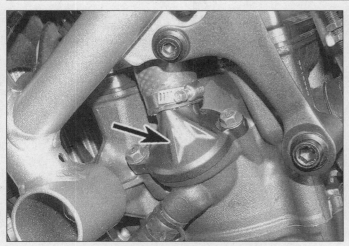

12.9 Thermostat cover (arrowed)

12.11 Check the radiator fins for blockages and carefully straighten any bent ones

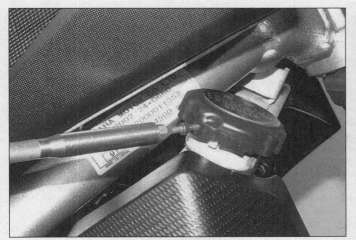

12.12a Undo the lock screw

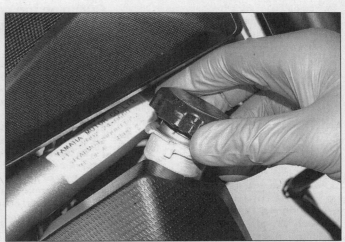

12.12b Remove the pressure cap as described

(see illustration). If coolant is leaking, check that the cover bolts are tight. If they are, fit a new thermostat (see Chapter 3) – it has a seal around its rim which is not available separately. Similarly check the coolant inlet union on the front of the engine – it has an O-ring between it and the engine (see Chapter 3).

10 Check the radiator for leaks and other damage. Leaks in the radiator leave tell-tale scale deposits or coolant stains on the outside of the core below the leak. If leaks are noted, remove the radiator (see Chapter 3) and have it repaired by a specialist.

Caution: Do not use a liquid leak stopping compound to try to repair leaks.

11 Check the radiator fins for mud, dirt and insects, which may impede the flow of air through the radiator. If the fins are dirty, remove the radiator (see Chapter 3) and clean it, using water or low pressure compressed air directed through the fins from the back. If the fins are bent or distorted, straighten them carefully with a screwdriver (see illustration).

Bent or damaged fins will restrict the airflow and impair the efficiency of the radiator causing the engine to overheat. Where there is substantial damage to the radiator's surface area, replace the radiator with a new one.

12 Unscrew the radiator pressure cap locking screw (see illustration). Undo the cap by turning it anti-clockwise until it reaches a stop (see illustration). If you hear a hissing sound (indicating that there is still pressure in the system), wait until it stops. Now press down on the cap and continue turning until it can be removed.

13 Check the condition of the coolant in the system. If it is rust-coloured or if accumulations of scale are visible, drain and flush the system and refill with new coolant (see below). Check the antifreeze content of the coolant with an antifreeze tester if available (see illustration) – a 50% content should give a reading of 1.084 at 5°C to 1.074 at 25°C, varying accordingly in between. The system must have the correct coolant mixture (see Specifications) – if the

coolant is too weak (i.e. too little anti-freeze giving a low reading – anything below 1.07 when cold and 1.06 when hot) there will not be adequate protection against freezing and corrosion, and if it is too strong the ability to cool the engine is reduced. If the hydrometer indicates an incorrect mixture, drain and refill the system (see overleaf).

12.13 Checking the anti-freeze content of the coolant

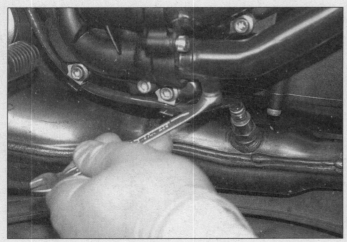

12.21a Unscrew the drain bolt...

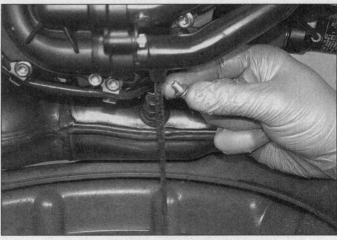

12.21b ...and allow the coolant to drain

14 The function of the pressure cap is crucial to the correct running of the cooling system. Check the cap seal for cracks and other damage. If the coolant level consistently drops and/or the bike overheats, and no evidence of leaks can be found, have the cap pressure checked by a Yamaha dealer, or just fit a new one – they are not expensive.

15 Fit the cap by turning it clockwise until it reaches the first stop then push down on the cap and continue turning until it will turn no further **(see illustration 12.12b)**. Fit the lock screw **(see illustration 12.12a)**.

16 Start the engine and let it reach normal operating temperature, then check for leaks again. As the coolant temperature increases beyond normal, the fan should come on automatically and the temperature should begin to drop. If it does not, refer to Chapter 3 and check the fan circuit.

17 If the coolant level is consistently low, and no evidence of leaks can be found, and you have fitted a new pressure cap to the radiator, have the entire system pressure-checked by a Yamaha dealer.

Changing the coolant

> ⚠️ *Warning: Allow the engine to cool completely before performing this maintenance operation. Also, don't allow antifreeze to come into contact with your skin or the painted surfaces of the motorcycle. Rinse off spills immediately with plenty of water. Antifreeze is highly toxic if ingested. Never leave antifreeze lying around in an open container or in puddles on the floor; children and pets are attracted by its sweet smell and may drink it. Check with local authorities (councils) about disposing of antifreeze. Many communities have collection centres where antifreeze can be disposed of safely. Antifreeze is also combustible, so don't store it near open flames.*

Draining

18 On MT-07TR models remove the right-hand fairing side panel and inner panel (see Chapter 7).

19 Remove the coolant reservoir (see Chapter 3). Empty the contents into a suitable container, rinse the inside with clean water and refit it.

20 Remove the radiator pressure cap (see Step 12).

21 Position a suitable container beneath the drain bolt on the underside of the coolant outlet pipe from the water pump. Unscrew the bolt and allow the coolant to drain **(see illustrations)** – a new sealing washer must be used.

Flushing

22 Flush the system with clean tap water by inserting a garden hose in the radiator filler neck. Allow the water to run through the system until it is clear when it flows out of the drain hole. If there is a lot of rust in the water, remove the radiator (see Chapter 3) and have it professionally cleaned.

Refilling

23 Fit a new sealing washer onto the drain bolt and tighten it to 7 Nm **(see illustration)**.

24 Fill the system via the radiator with the specified coolant mixture (see Specifications) **(see illustration)** – pour the coolant in slowly

12.23 Always use a new sealing washer

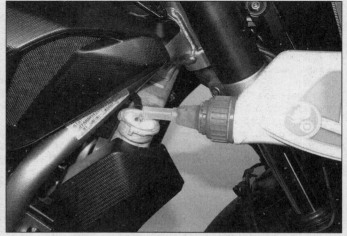

12.24 Fill the system as described

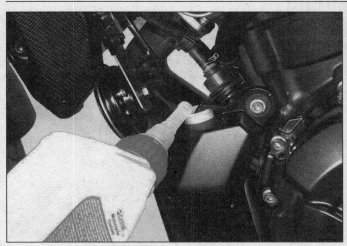

12.25a Fill the reservoir...

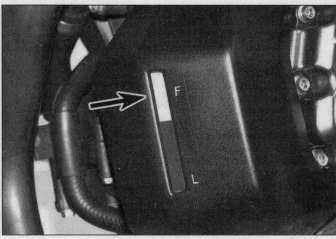

12.25b ...to the F line (arrowed)

to minimise the amount of air entering the system. When the system appears full, move the bike off its stand then squeeze the hoses and shake the bike slightly to dislodge any air bubbles and dissipate the coolant, then place the bike back on the stand and top the system up.

25 When the system is full (all the way up to the top of the radiator filler neck), fit the pressure cap, but do not yet fit the lock screw. Now fill the coolant reservoir to the F mark and fit the cap **(see illustrations)**.

26 Start the engine and allow it to run for several minutes. Flick the throttle open 3 or 4 times, so that the engine speed rises to approximately 4000 – 5000 rpm, then stop the engine. Any air trapped in the system should bleed back to the top of the radiator, and the level will drop.

27 Wait a few minutes for the coolant to settle, then remove the pressure cap as described in Step 12 and check the coolant level in both the radiator and the coolant reservoir. If necessary, top up the radiator to the base of the filler neck, then fit the pressure cap and the lock screw **(see illustrations 12.12b and a)**. Also top up the coolant reservoir to the F mark if necessary.

28 Check the system for leaks.

29 Do not dispose of the old coolant by pouring it down the drain. Instead pour it into a heavy plastic container, cap it tightly and take it into an authorised disposal site or service station.

30 On MT-07TR models fit the fairing inner and side panels.

13 Engine oil and filter

⚠️ **Warning: Be careful when draining the oil, as the exhaust pipes, the engine, and the oil itself can cause severe burns.**

Engine oil

1 Regular oil changes are the single most important maintenance procedure you can perform on a motorcycle. The oil not only lubricates the internal parts of the engine, transmission and clutch, but it also acts as a coolant, a cleaner, a sealant, and a protector. Because of these demands, the oil takes a terrific amount of abuse and must be replaced at the specified intervals with new oil of the recommended grade and type and marked as suitable for motorcycles. Saving a little money on the difference in cost between a good oil and a cheap oil won't pay off if the engine is

damaged. The oil filter should be changed with every second oil change (see Steps 9 to 11).

2 Before changing the oil, warm up the engine so the oil will drain easily.

3 Place a clean drain tray under the oil drain plug. Unscrew the oil filler cap from the alternator cover to vent the engine unit and to act as a reminder that there is no oil in the engine **(see illustration)**.

4 Unscrew the oil drain plug and allow the oil to flow into the drain tray **(see illustrations)**. Remove the sealing washer from the plug **(see illustration)** – a new one must be used. If you are changing the oil filter, do so now (Steps 9 to 11).

13.3 Unscrew the oil filler cap

13.4a Unscrew the oil drain plug...

13.4b ...and allow the oil to drain

13.4c Remove the old washer

13.5 Always use a new sealing washer

13.6a Pour the oil in

13.6b Do not fill beyond the upper level lines (arrowed)

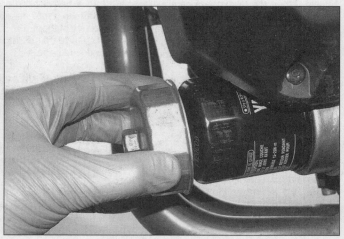

13.10a Fit the tool onto the filter...

5 When the oil has completely drained, clean around the drain plug seat, then fit the plug with its new washer and tighten it to 43 Nm **(see illustration)**. Avoid overtightening, as you will damage the sump.

6 Refill the engine using the type and amount of oil given in the Specifications so the level lies between the upper and lower level lines on the window with the bike upright **(see illustrations)**. Start the engine and let it run for two or three minutes. Stop the engine, wait a few minutes, then check the oil level.

If necessary, add more oil until the level is correct. Check that there are no leaks around the drain plug and filter.

7 The old oil drained from the engine cannot be re-used and must be disposed of properly. Check with your local refuse disposal company, disposal facility or environmental agency to see whether they will accept the used oil for recycling – most will. Don't pour used oil into drains or onto the ground.

Oil filter

Special tool: *A filter removing tool is necessary for this job (see illustration 13.10a).*

8 Drain the engine oil as described in Steps 2 to 4.

9 The oil filter threads onto the oil cooler on the front of the engine. Place the drain tray below it.

10 Unscrew the filter using a filter removal tool **(see illustrations)** – make sure you have the correct size of oil filter tool to fit

13.10b ... then unscrew the filter...

13.10c ...and drain its oil into the tray

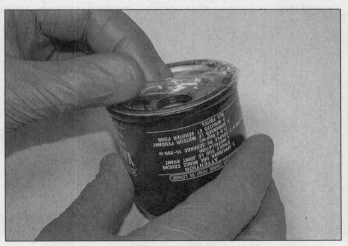

13.11 Remove any packaging

14.5 Check the hoses as described

the Yamaha filter cartridge as many sizes are available (part No. for the Yamaha tool is 90890-01426 or YU-38411). A filter tool that can be used with a socket wrench is the best as it allows the new filter to be tightened to the specified torque. Tip any residual oil into the drain tray.

11 Clean the sealing surface on the oil cooler carefully with a suitable solvent. Remove any protective packaging from the new filter **(see illustration)**. If the filter seal is not pre-greased smear clean engine oil onto it. Screw the filter onto the cooler until the seal just seats. If a suitable oil filter tool is being used, tighten the filter to 17 Nm. Otherwise, tighten the filter as tight as possible by hand, or by the number of turns specified on the filter or its packaging. Do not use a strap or chain wrench to tighten the filter as you will damage it.

12 Fit the drain plug and refill the engine to the specified level (see Steps 5 and 6).

13 Remember to drain all the old oil from the filter into the drain tray. Note that the old filter should be taken to the oil disposal facility rather than disposed of with the household rubbish.

Note: It is illegal and anti-social to dump oil down the drain. To find the location of your local oil recycling bank in the UK, call 03708 506 506 or visit www.oilbankline.org.uk. In the US note that any oil supplier must accept used oil for recycling.

14 Brake system

Brake system check

1 A routine check of the brake system will ensure that any problems are discovered and remedied before the rider's safety is jeopardised.

2 Check the brake lever and pedal for looseness, rough action, excessive play, bends, and other damage. Replace any damaged parts with new ones (see Chapter 5).

Clean and lubricate the lever and pedal pivots if their action is stiff or rough (Section 11).

3 Make sure all brake component fasteners are tight – refer to the torque settings in Chapter 6 Specifications. Check the fluid level in the reservoirs (see *Pre-ride checks*). Inspect the brake pads for wear (see Steps 11 to 13).

4 If the lever or pedal action is spongy, bleed the brakes (see Chapter 7). Change the brake fluid at the specified service interval.

5 Look for leaks at the hose connections and check for cracks in the hoses themselves **(see illustration)**. The hoses should be replaced with new ones at the specified service interval – or sooner if they show signs of damage or deterioration (see Steps 15 and 16).

6 Check the brake master cylinder and caliper seals for signs of leaking fluid (see Steps 17 and 18).

7 Make sure the brake light operates when the front brake lever is pulled in. The front brake light switch, mounted on the underside of the master cylinder, is not adjustable. If it fails to operate properly, check it (see Chapter 8).

8 Make sure the brake light is activated just before the rear brake takes effect. The switch, mounted between the rider's right-hand heel plate and the swingarm, is adjustable. If adjustment is necessary, for best access remove the right-hand frame cover (see Chapter 7). Hold the switch and turn the adjuster nut on the switch body until the brake light is activated when required **(see illustration)**. If the brake light comes on too late, turn the nut clockwise. If the brake light comes on too soon or is permanently on, turn the nut anti-clockwise. If the switch doesn't operate the brake light, check it (see Chapter 8).

9 The front brake lever has a span adjuster that alters the distance of the lever from the handlebar. Each setting is identified by a number on the adjuster, which must align with the triangle mark on the lever **(see illustration)**. Pull the lever away from the

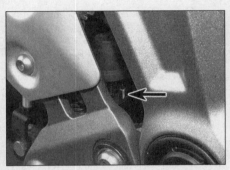

14.8 Rear brake light switch adjuster nut (arrowed)

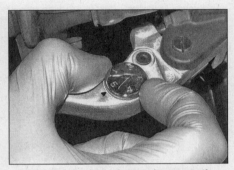

14.9 Hold the lever forwards to turn the adjuster

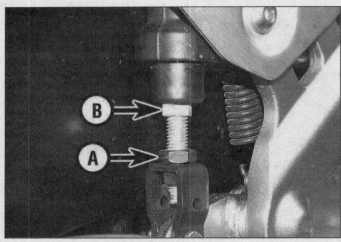

14.10 Adjust pedal height by slackening the locknut (A) and turning the pushrod hex (B)

14.11 Front brake pad wear indicator (arrowed)

handlebar and turn the adjuster until the setting that best suits the rider is obtained. There are five settings – setting 1 gives the largest span, and setting 5 the smallest. Make sure the selected setting number aligns exactly with the mark to ensure correct engagement of the adjuster setting.

10 Sit on the bike and check the position of the brake pedal. If the pedal height is not as required, loosen the locknut on the top of the clevis on the master cylinder pushrod, then turn the pushrod using a spanner on the hex at the top of the rod until the pedal is at the desired height **(see illustration)**. After adjustment check that some of the bottom of the pushrod end is still visible in the hole in the clevis. On completion tighten the locknut. Adjust the rear brake light switch after adjusting the pedal position (see Step 8).

Brake pad wear check

> ⚠️ *Warning: The dust created by the brake system is harmful to your health. Never blow it out with compressed air and don't inhale any of it. An approved filtering mask should be worn when working on the brakes.*

11 The front brake pads can be checked from the front of the caliper **(see illustration)**. The pads fitted as original equipment have turned-in corners, and when these are almost contacting the disc the pads must be replaced with new ones (see Chapter 6). If you are in doubt as to the amount of friction material remaining, or to clean the pads, remove them from the caliper (see Chapter 6).

12 The rear brake pads on all models can be checked from the rear of the caliper **(see illustration)**. The pads fitted as original equipment have a cut-out in the rear edge of the pad, and when the pads have worn down to the beginning of the cut-out they must be

replaced with new ones (see Chapter 6). If you are in doubt as to the amount of friction material remaining, or to clean the pads, remove them from the caliper (see Chapter 6).
Note: *Normal road dirt can be cleaned from the pad friction material, but it is not possible to effectively remove oil or grease – if necessary fit a new set of pads.*

13 Some after-market pads may use different wear indicators. If so a minimum thickness of 0.5 mm is specified for the friction material – if required remove the pads and measure the amount of friction material remaining.

Brake fluid change

14 The brake fluid should be changed at the specified service interval or whenever a master cylinder or caliper overhaul is carried out. Refer to Chapter 6 for details. Make sure that all the old fluid is pumped from the system. Check the levels in the fluid reservoirs and test the brakes before riding the motorcycle.

Brake hoses

15 The hoses will deteriorate with age and even if they appear to be in good condition

14.12 Rear brake pad wear indicator cut-out (arrowed)

they should be replaced with new ones at the specified service interval (see Chapter 6).
16 Always replace the banjo union sealing washers with new ones when fitting new hoses. Refill the system with new brake fluid and bleed the system as described in Chapter 6.

Brake caliper and master cylinder seals

17 Brake system seals will deteriorate over a period of time and lose their effectiveness. Old master cylinder seals will cause sticky operation of the brake lever or pedal or fluid leakage; old caliper seals will cause the pistons to stick or fluid leakage. The seals should be replaced with new ones if defects are evident (see Chapter 6).
18 Replace all the seals in each caliper as a set – a rebuild kit for each caliper is available. Front and rear master cylinder seals are supplied as a kit along with a new piston and spring assembly (see Chapter 6).

15 Wheels, wheel bearings and tyres

Wheels

1 Cast wheels are virtually maintenance free, but they should be kept clean and checked periodically for cracks and other damage. Also check the wheel runout and alignment (see Chapter 6). Never attempt to repair damaged cast wheels; they must be replaced with new ones.
2 Make sure the valve cap is in place and tight **(see illustration)**. Check the tyre valve rubber for signs of damage or deterioration and have it replaced with a new one if necessary. Check that any wheel balance weights are fixed firmly to the wheel rim. If there's sign of any weights having fallen off, have the wheel rebalanced by a motorcycle tyre specialist.

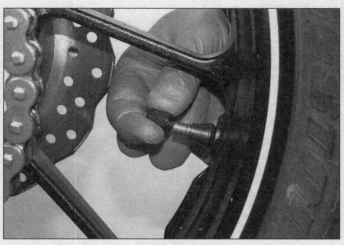

15.2 Make sure a cap is fitted, and check the rubber seal

15.4 Checking for play in the wheel bearings

Wheel bearings

Note: *Avoid using a high pressure cleaner around the wheel hubs. Water may penetrate the wheel bearing seals and wash out the grease, leading to corrosion and premature bearing failure.*

3 Wheel bearings will wear over a period of time and result in handling problems.
4 Support the motorcycle so the wheel being checked is off the ground. Check for any play in the bearings by pushing and pulling each wheel against the hub **(see illustration)**. Also rotate the wheels and check that they spin smoothly and quietly, but do not mistake brake pad-to-disc noise for noisy bearings.
5 If any play is detected in the hub, or if the wheel does not rotate smoothly (and this is not due to brake or chain drag), the wheel must be removed for thorough inspection of the bearings (see Chapter 6).

Tyres

6 Check the tyre condition and tread depth thoroughly (see *Pre-ride checks*).

16 Suspension

1 The suspension components must be maintained in top operating condition to ensure rider safety. Loose, worn or damaged suspension parts decrease the motorcycle's stability and control.
2 Check the tightness of all suspension nuts and bolts to be sure none have worked loose, referring to the torque settings given in Chapter 5 Specifications.

Front suspension check

3 While standing alongside the motorcycle, apply the front brake and push on the handlebars to compress the forks several times **(see illustration)**. Check that they move up and down smoothly without binding. If binding is felt, the forks should be disassembled and inspected (see Chapter 5).
4 Inspect the fork inner tubes for signs of

scratches, corrosion and pitting, and oil leaks **(see illustration)**. Carefully lever the dust seal from the top of each fork outer tube using a flat-bladed screwdriver and inspect the area around the fork seals (see Chapter 5). Any scratches, corrosion and pitting will cause premature seal failure. If the damage is excessive, new tubes should be installed (see Chapter 5).
5 If oil is leaking, new seals must be fitted (see Chapter 5). If there is evidence of corrosion between the seal retaining ring and its groove in the fork outer tube spray the area with a penetrative lubricant, otherwise the ring will be difficult to remove if needed. Press the dust seal back into place on completion.

Rear suspension check

Note: *Avoid using a high pressure cleaner around the swingarm pivots and the suspension linkage and shock absorber pivots. Water may penetrate the bearing seals and wash out the grease, leading to corrosion and premature bearing failure.*

16.3 Pump the forks to check their action

16.4 Check the fork inner tube (arrowed) in the area of travel above the dust seal for leaks, pitting and corrosion

16.7 Pump the rear suspension to check its action

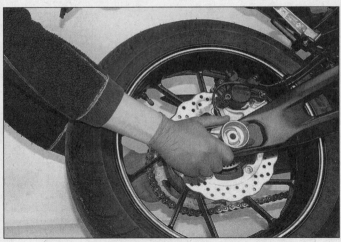

16.8 Checking for play in the swingarm bearings

6 Inspect the rear shock for fluid leaks and loose mountings. If the shock is leaking, a new one should be fitted (see Chapter 5).

7 With the aid of an assistant to support the bike, compress the rear suspension several times **(see illustration)**. It should move up and down freely without binding. If any binding is felt, the worn or faulty component must be identified and checked. The problem could be due to either the shock absorber, the suspension linkage components or the swingarm components (see Chapter 5).

8 Support the motorcycle so that the rear wheel is off the ground. Grasp the swingarm and rock it from side to side – there should be no discernible movement at the ends of the swingarm **(see illustration)**. If there is a little movement or a slight clicking can be heard, inspect the tightness of all the rear suspension mounting bolts and nuts, referring to the torque settings specified at the beginning of Chapter 5, and re-check for movement.

9 Next, grasp the top of the rear wheel and pull it upwards – there should be no discernible freeplay before the shock absorber begins to compress **(see illustration)**. Any freeplay felt in either check indicates worn

bearings in the swingarm or suspenion linkage arm, or worn shock absorber mountings. The worn components must be identified and checked (see Chapter 5).

10 To make an accurate assessment of the swingarm bearings it is necessary to remove the rear wheel (see Chapter 6), and the shock absorber and the linkage arm (see Chapter 5). Grasp the rear of the swingarm with one hand and place your other hand at the junction of the swingarm and the frame. Try to move the rear of the swingarm from side-to-side. Any wear (play) in the bearings should be felt as movement between the swingarm and the frame at the front. If there is any play, the swingarm will be felt to move forward and backward at the front (not from side-to-side).

11 Next, move the swingarm up and down through its full travel – it should move freely, without any binding or rough spots. If any play in the swingarm is noted, or if the swingarm does not move freely, remove the swingarm for inspection of the bearings (see Chapter 5).

12 With the linkage arm removed check its seals and bearings, and check for play between the linkage rod and the frame, and if necessary re-grease the seals and bearings or fit new ones.

Front fork oil change

13 Although there is no set interval for changing the fork oil, note that the oil will degrade over a period of time and lose its damping qualities. Refer to Chapter 5 for details of front fork removal, oil draining and refilling. The forks do not need to be completely disassembled to change the oil.

Rear suspension bearing lubrication

14 Over a period of time the grease in the swingarm and suspension linkage arm bearings will be washed out (especially if pressure washers are used) or will harden allowing the ingress of dirt and water.

15 The suspension linkage and swingarm should be removed at the specified service interval and the bearings cleaned and re-greased, or new ones fitted, as necessary (see Chapter 5).

---

17 Steering head bearings

Freeplay check and adjustment

1 Steering head bearings can become dented, rough or loose during normal use of the machine. In extreme cases, worn or loose steering head bearings can cause steering wobble – a condition that is potentially dangerous.

Check

2 Support the motorcycle in an upright position using an auxiliary stand, and raise the front wheel off the ground by placing a support under the engine.

3 Point the front wheel straight-ahead, and slowly turn the handlebars from side to side. Any notches or roughness in the bearing races will be felt and if the bearings are too tight the bars will not move smoothly and freely. If the bearings are damaged or the action is rough, they should be replaced with new ones (see Chapter 5). If the bearings are too tight they should be adjusted as described below.

4 Again point the wheel straight-ahead, and tap the front of the wheel to one side. The wheel should 'fall' under its own weight to the limit of its lock, indicating that the bearings are not too tight (take into account the restriction that cables and wiring may have). Check for similar movement to the other side.

5 Next, grasp the bottom of each fork and try to pull and push them forwards and

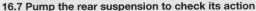

16.9 Checking for play in the suspension bearings and shock mounts

17.5 Checking for play in the steering head bearings

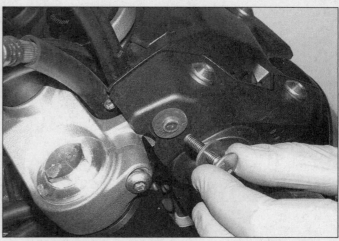

17.7a On MT-07 (FZ-07) models undo the screw on each side...

17.7b ... and move the headlight clear of the yoke

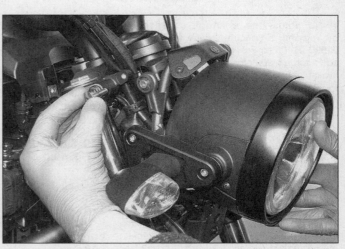

17.7c On XSR models undo the screw on each side and move the headlight clear of the yoke

backwards **(see illustration)**. Any looseness in the steering head bearings will be felt as front-to-rear movement of the forks. If play is felt in the bearings, adjust them as follows.

Adjustment

Special tool: *Either the Yamaha service tool described in Step 10 or a suitably sized*

C-spanner is required for this procedure **(see illustration 17.11).**

6 Remove the fuel tank cover(s) (see Chapter 7), and for best access, particularly if using the Yamaha tool (see Step 10), remove the fuel tank (see Chapter 4).

7 On MT-07 (FZ-07) and XSR models undo the screw securing the headlight assembly

to each side of the top yoke and pivot the headlight forwards **(see illustrations)**.

8 Slacken the fork clamp bolts in the top yoke **(see illustration)**. Slacken the head bearing adjuster nut clamp bolt **(see illustration)**.

9 Ease the top yoke up, but not off, the forks so there is clear access to the head bearing adjuster nut notches **(see illustration)**.

17.8a Slacken the fork clamp bolt on each side of the yoke...

17.8b ... and the adjuster nut clamp bolt in the centre

17.9 Lift the yoke/handlebar assembly up to the tops of the forks

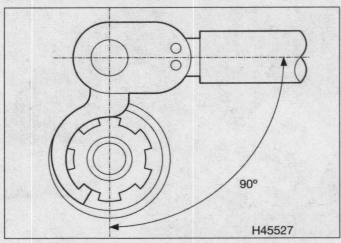

17.10 Make sure the tool and torque wrench are correctly positioned

H45527

90°

17.11 Using a C-spanner to adjust the steering head bearings

10 To adjust the bearings as specified by Yamaha, a special service tool (Pt. No. 90890-01403 for Europe, or YU-A9472 for US) and a torque wrench are required. If the tool is available, first slacken the adjuster nut slightly to take pressure off the bearing, then tighten the nut to 52 Nm – make sure the torque wrench handle is at right-angles (90°) to the centre line between the adjuster nut and the service tool wrench socket **(see illustration)**. Now slacken the nut until loose, then tighten it to 18 Nm.

11 If the Yamaha tool is not available use a C-spanner to slacken the adjuster nut slightly to take pressure off the bearing then tighten the nut until all freeplay is removed **(see illustration)**. Now tighten the nut a little more to pre-load the bearings. Now slacken the nut and retighten it, setting it so that all freeplay is just removed from the bearings, yet the steering is able to move freely from side to side. Tighten the nut only a little at a time, and after each adjustment repeat the checks outlined in Steps 3 to 5, with the bike supported as in Step 2.

12 Turn the steering from lock to lock five times to settle the bearings, then recheck the adjustment or the final torque setting (18 Nm) depending on your method used. The object is to set the adjuster nut so that the bearings are under a very light loading, just enough to remove any freeplay.

Caution: Take great care not to apply excessive pressure because this will cause premature failure of the bearings.

13 Push the top yoke down until it seats **(see illustration 17.9)**. Tighten the adjuster nut clamp bolt to 21 Nm on MT-07 (FZ-07) and XSR models, and to 35 Nm on MT-07TR models, then tighten the fork clamp bolts in the top yoke to 26 Nm **(see illustrations 17.8b and a)**.

14 Recheck the bearing adjustment as described in Steps 3 to 5. Install all remaining components.

Lubrication

15 Over time the grease in the bearings will be dispersed or will harden allowing the ingress of dirt and water.

16 At the specified interval the steering head should be disassembled and the bearings cleaned and re-greased (see Chapter 5, Section 10).

18 Sidestand and starter safety circuit

Sidestand

1 The stand return springs must be capable of retracting the stand fully and holding it retracted when the motorcycle is in use. If a spring has sagged or broken, it must be replaced with a new one (see Chapter 5).

2 Check the stand for cracks and other damage, and check it moves smoothly on its pivot.

Starter safety circuit

3 The sidestand switch prevents the motorcycle being started if the transmission is in gear and the stand is down, and cuts the engine if the stand is put down while the engine is running and in gear.

4 Check the operation of the safety circuit (which incorporates the sidestand, clutch and neutral switches, and the starter circuit cut-off relay) by shifting the transmission into neutral, retracting the stand and starting the engine. Pull in the clutch lever and select a gear. Extend the sidestand. The engine should stop as the sidestand is extended.

5 Also make sure that the engine cannot be started while in gear unless the stand is up and the clutch lever is pulled in. If the circuit does not operate as described, check the individual components of the safety circuit (see Chapter 8).

19 Nuts, bolts and fasteners

1 Since vibration of the machine tends to loosen fasteners, all nuts, bolts, screws, etc. should be periodically checked for tightness.

2 Pay particular attention to the following:
- Brake caliper and master cylinder mounting bolts
- Brake hose banjo bolts and caliper bleed valves
- Brake disc bolts
- Exhaust system bolts/nuts
- Engine oil drain plug
- Engine mounting bolts/nuts
- Lever and pedal bolts
- Handlebar clamp bolts
- Footrest bracket and sidestand pivot and bracket bolts
- Shock absorber and suspension linkage mounting bolts/nuts
- Swingarm pivot bolt nut
- Front fork clamp bolts (top and bottom yoke) and fork top bolts
- Steering head bearing adjuster nut clamp bolt
- Front axle and axle clamp bolt
- Rear axle nut
- Front and rear sprocket nuts
- Chain adjuster locknuts

3 If a torque wrench is available, use it along with the torque settings given in the Specifications at the beginning of this and other Chapters.

20 Battery check

1 A maintenance-free VRLA (valve regulated lead acid) battery is fitted.

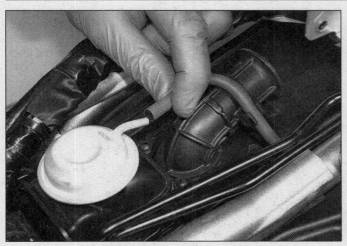

21.2 Hose is a push fit on valve stub

21.4 Undo the four screws

Caution: *Do not attempt to open the battery as resulting damage will mean it will be unfit for further use.*

2 All that should be done is to check that the terminals are clean and tight and that the casing is not damaged or leaking. See Chapter 8 for further details.

3 If the machine is not in regular use, disconnect the battery and give it a refresher charge every month to six weeks (see Chapter 8, Section 4).

21 Air filter

Note: *If the machine is continually ridden in dusty conditions, replace the filter more frequently than specified.*

Note: *All models are fitted with a disposable oil-impregnated paper element that cannot be cleaned. Replace the filter with a new one at the specified service interval.*

1 Raise or remove the fuel tank (see Chapter 4) – you can remove the air filter with the tank in its raised position if you have a stubby screwdriver that fits between the tank and the front air filter cover screws, otherwise it needs to be removed.

2 On 2014 to 2016 MT-07 (FZ-07) models, if you want to remove the air filter cover from the bike rather than leave it displaced to one side, disconnect the vacuum hose from the intake air flap diaphragm valve and release it from the clip on the air duct **(see illustration)**.

3 On MT-07TR models remove the seat bracket.

4 Undo the air filter cover screws and remove the cover **(see illustration)**.

5 Undo the filter screw and lift the filter out of the housing **(see illustrations)**.

6 Clean out any dirt from the filter housing and cover, and check the hole for the crankcase breather hose in the front of the housing is clear.

7 Fit the new filter into the housing, making sure it is the correct way round, and secure it with the screw **(see illustrations 20.5b and a)**.

8 Fit the cover, check that it is seated all the way round, and tighten the screws **(see illustration 21.4)**.

9 On 2014 to 2016 MT-07 (FZ-07) models connect the vacuum hose to the intake air flap diaphragm valve and seat it in the clip **(see illustration 21.2)**.

10 On MT-07TR models fit the seat bracket.

11 Check the crankcase breather hose between the front of the air filter housing and

21.5a Undo the screw down the side

21.5b Lift the filter from the housing

21.11 Crankcase breather hose (arrowed) – engine end

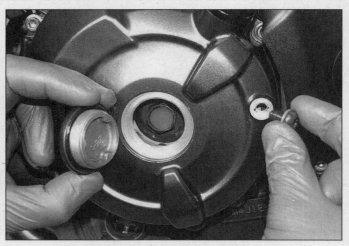

22.4 Remove the inspection bolt and end cap

the top of the engine for loose connections, cracks and deterioration, and fit a new one if necessary **(see illustration)**.

12 Install the fuel tank (see Chapter 4).

22 Valve clearances

1 The engine must be cool for this maintenance procedure.

2 Remove the spark plugs (Section 5).

3 Remove the valve cover (see Chapter 2).

4 Unscrew the timing inspection bolt and the crankshaft end cap from the alternator cover on the left-hand side of the engine **(see illustration)**. You may need a new sealing washer for the bolt and a new O-ring for the cap – check their condition and use new ones if in any doubt.

5 The cylinders are numbered 1 – left, 2 –

right, viewed as normally seated on the bike. Each cylinder has four valves, two on the intake side and two on the exhaust. Make a chart or sketch of all valve positions so that a note of each clearance can be made against the relevant valve.

6 Using a socket on the alternator rotor bolt and rotating in an anti-clockwise direction only, turn the engine until the timing mark on the rotor aligns with the notches in the inspection hole and the camshaft lobes for the No. 1 (left-hand) cylinder face away from each other (i.e. intake camshaft lobes point backwards and exhaust camshaft lobes point forwards) as shown **(see illustrations)**. If the cam lobes are facing towards each other, turn the engine anti-clockwise 360° (one full turn) so that the timing mark again aligns with the notches – the camshaft lobes will now be facing away from each other and the No. 1 cylinder will be at TDC (top dead centre) on the compression stroke.

7 Check the clearances on the No. 1 cylinder intake and exhaust valves. Insert a feeler gauge of the same thickness as the correct valve clearance (see Specifications) between the camshaft lobe and follower of each valve and check that it is a firm sliding fit **(see**

22.6a Turn the engine anti-clockwise...

22.6b ...until the timing line aligns with the notches...

22.6c ...and the No. 1 cylinder cam lobes point away from each other

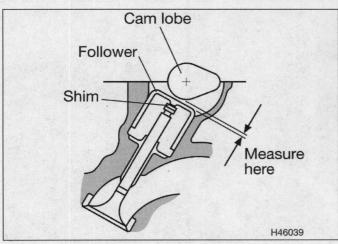

Cam lobe

Follower

Shim

Measure here

H46039

22.7a Measure the valve clearance...

22.7b ...using a feeler gauge

illustrations) – you should feel a slight drag when you pull the gauge out. If not, use the feeler gauges to measure the exact clearance. Record the measured clearance on your chart.
8 Now turn the engine anti-clockwise 270° (3/4 turn) so that the camshaft lobes for the No. 2 cylinder are facing away from each other (i.e. intake camshaft lobes point backwards and exhaust camshaft lobes point forwards) as shown **(see illustration)**. The No. 2 cylinder is now at TDC on the compression stroke. Measure the clearances of the No. 2 cylinder valves using the method described in Step 7.
9 When all clearances have been measured and recorded, identify whether the clearance on any valve falls outside that specified. If it does, the shim between the cam follower and the valve must be replaced with one of a thickness that will restore the correct clearance.
10 Shim replacement requires removal of the camshafts (see Chapter 2). Place rags over the spark plug holes and the cam chain tunnel

to prevent a shim accidentally dropping into the engine on removal.
11 Using a magnet if available, remove the cam follower of the valve in question, then remove the shim from inside the follower **(see illustrations)**. If it is not in the follower, pick it out of the top of the valve using either a magnet, a small screwdriver with a dab of grease on it (the shim will stick to the grease),

22.8 No. 2 cylinder exhaust camshaft lobes (arrowed) showed pointing forwards

or a screwdriver and a pair of pliers **(see illustration 22.14a)**. Do not allow the shim to fall into the engine.
12 Measure the thickness of the shim using a micrometer. A size should be marked on the upper face of the shim (though it could have rubbed off) – a shim marked 175 is 1.75 mm thick, but the shim should measured anyway to allow for wear **(see illustration)**.

22.11a Lift out the cam follower...

22.11b ...and remove the shim (arrowed)

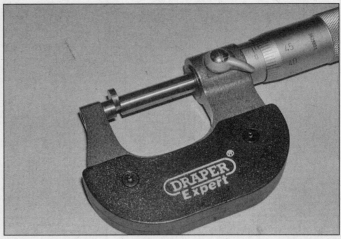

22.12 Measure the shim using a micrometer to confirm its size

22.14a Fit the shim into its recess...

22.14b ...then fit the follower

13 If the measured clearance is greater than the upper limit of the range given, you need a thicker shim, and if it is less than the lower limit of the range you need a thinner shim. Calculate by how much thicker or thinner than the existing shim the replacement shim needs to be to bring the clearance to the middle of the specified range, noting that shims are available in 0.05 mm increments from 1.50 mm to 2.40 mm. For example, if the measured clearance on an intake valve is 0.25 mm, this is 0.1 mm greater than the middle of the range (which is 0.15 mm). So add 0.1 mm to the the size of the current shim to get the size of the required replacement shim. If the required replacement size does not correspond exactly to an available size, round it up or down to the next size that is nearest to bring it closest to the middle of the range.

14 Obtain the replacement shim, then lubricate it with molybdenum disulphide oil (a 50/50 mix of molybdenum disulphide grease and engine oil) and fit it into its recess in the top of the valve, with the size marking facing up **(see illustration)**. Check that the shim is correctly seated, then lubricate the follower with engine oil, and fit it onto the valve **(see illustration)**. Repeat the process for any other valves until the clearances are correct, then install the camshafts (see Chapter 2).

15 Rotate the crankshaft anti-clockwise several turns to seat the new shim(s), then check the clearances again.

16 Install the valve cover (see Chapter 2).

17 Fit the timing inspection bolt using a new sealing washer if necessary and tighten to 15 Nm **(see illustration 22.4)**. Smear the end cap O-ring with grease, using a new one if necessary, then fit the cap and tighten to 10 Nm **(see illustration 22.4)**.

18 Install all remaining components in the reverse order of removal.

Chapter 2
Engine, clutch and transmission

Contents

Degrees of difficulty

| Easy, suitable for novice with little experience | 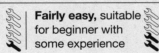 | Fairly easy, suitable for beginner with some experience | | Fairly difficult, suitable for competent DIY mechanic | | Difficult, suitable for experienced DIY mechanic | | Very difficult, suitable for expert DIY or professional | |

Specifications

General

Type	Four-stroke parallel twin
Capacity	689 cc
Bore	80.0 mm
Stroke	68.6 mm
Compression ratio	11.5 to 1
Cylinder numbering	No. 1 – left, No. 2 – right
Cooling system.	Liquid cooled
Clutch	Wet multi-plate
Transmission.	Six-speed constant mesh
Final drive.	Chain

Camshafts

Lobe height	
Intake camshaft	
Standard.	35.610 to 35.710 mm
Service limit	35.510 mm
Exhaust camshaft	
Standard.	35.710 to 35.810 mm
Service limit	35.610 mm
Journal diameter	21.959 to 21.972 mm
Holder diameter	22.000 to 22.021 mm
Journal oil clearance	0.028 to 0.062 mm
Runout (max)	0.03 mm

Cylinder head

Warpage (max) . . . . 0.05 mm

Valves, guides and springs

Valve clearances. . . . . see Chapter 1
Intake valve
  Stem diameter
    Standard . . . . 4.475 to 4.490 mm
    Service limit . . . . 4.445 mm
  Guide bore diameter
    Standard . . . . 4.500 to 4.512 mm
    Service limit . . . . 4.550 mm
  Stem-to-guide clearance
    Standard . . . . 0.010 to 0.037 mm
    Service limit . . . . 0.08 mm
  Stem runout service limit . . . . 0.01 mm
  Seat width. . . . . 0.9 to 1.1 mm
  Valve spring free length
    Standard . . . . 40.30 mm
    Service limit . . . . 38.29 mm
  Valve spring tilt (max) . . . . 1.8 mm
Exhaust valve
  Stem diameter
    Standard . . . . 4.460 to 4.475 mm
    Service limit . . . . 4.430 mm
  Guide bore diameter
    Standard . . . . 4.500 to 4.512 mm
    Service limit . . . . 4.550 mm
  Stem-to-guide clearance
    Standard . . . . 0.025 to 0.052 mm
    Service limit . . . . 0.10 mm
  Stem runout service limit . . . . 0.01 mm
  Seat width. . . . . 0.9 to 1.1 mm
  Valve spring free length
    Standard . . . . 41.39 mm
    Service limit . . . . 39.32 mm
  Valve spring tilt (max) . . . . 1.8 mm

Clutch

Friction plates
  Type 1 plates
    Quantity 2
    Thickness
      Standard . . . . 2.90 to 3.10 mm
      Service limit. . . . . 2.80 mm
  Type 2 plates
    Quantity 5
    Thickness
      Standard . . . . 2.92 to 3.08 mm
      Service limit. . . . . 2.82 mm
Plain plates
  Quantity 6
  Thickness . . . . 1.9 to 2.1 mm
  Warpage (max) . . . . 0.1 mm
Clutch springs
  Free length . . . . 50.0 mm
  Service limit . . . . 47.5 mm

Lubrication system

Engine oil pressure (engine warm) . . . . 40.6 psi (2.8 Bar) @ 5000 rpm
Oil pump
  Inner rotor tip-to-outer rotor clearance
    Standard . . . . less than 0.12 mm
    Service limit . . . . 0.20 mm
  Outer rotor-to-housing clearance
    Standard . . . . 0.09 to 0.15 mm
    Service limit . . . . 0.22 mm

Cylinder bores

Bore . . . . 80.00 to 80.01 mm
Ovality (max). . . . . 0.05 mm
Taper (max) . . . . 0.05 mm
Cylinder compression @ 355 rpm
  No. 1 (left) cylinder
    Standard . . . . 125 psi (8.8 Bar)
    Minimum . . . . 140 psi (10 Bar)
    Maximum . . . . 109 psi (7.7 Bar)
  No. 2 (right) cylinder
    Standard . . . . 112 psi (7.9 Bar)
    Minimum . . . . 98 psi (6.9 Bar)
    Maximum . . . . 125 psi (8.8 Bar)
Piston-to-bore clearance . . . . 0.015 to 0.040 mm

Pistons

Piston diameter (8 mm up from skirt, at 90° to piston pin axis) . . . . 79.970 to 79.985 mm
Piston-to-bore clearance . . . . 0.015 to 0.040 mm
Piston pin diameter
  Standard . . . . 17.990 to 17.995 mm
  Service limit . . . . 17.970 mm
Piston pin bore diameter in piston
  Standard . . . . 18.004 to 18.015 mm
  Service limit . . . . 18.045 mm
Piston pin-to-piston pin bore clearance
  Standard . . . . 0.009 to 0.025 mm
  Service limit . . . . 0.075 mm

Piston rings

Top compression ring
  Type . . . . Barrel
  Ring end gap (installed)
    Standard . . . . 0.15 to 0.25 mm
    Service limit . . . . 0.50 mm
  Piston ring-to-groove clearance
    Standard . . . . 0.030 to 0.065 mm
    Service limit . . . . 0.115 mm
2nd compression ring
  Type . . . . Taper
  Ring end gap (installed)
    Standard . . . . 0.30 to 0.45 mm
    Service limit . . . . 0.8 mm
  Piston ring-to-groove clearance
    Standard . . . . 0.020 to 0.055 mm
    Service limit . . . . 0.115 mm
Oil ring
  Side-rail end gap (installed) . . . . 0.10 to 0.35 mm

Crankshaft and bearings

Main bearing oil clearance . . . . 0.018 to 0.042 mm
Runout (max) . . . . 0.03 mm

Balancer shaft and bearings

Bearing oil clearance . . . . 0.020 to 0.054 mm
Runout (max) . . . . 0.03 mm

Connecting rods

Big-end oil clearance . . . . 0.027 to 0.051 mm

Transmission

Gear ratios (no. of teeth)
  Primary reduction . . . . 1.925 to 1 (77/40)
  Final reduction . . . . 2.688 to 1 (43/16)
  1st gear . . . . 2.846 to 1 (37/13)
  2nd gear . . . . 2.125 to 1 (34/16)
  3rd gear . . . . 1.632 to 1 (31/19)
  4th gear . . . . 1.300 to 1 (26/20)
  5th gear . . . . 1.091 to 1 (24/22)
  6th gear . . . . 0.964 to 1 (27/28)
Shaft runout (max) . . . . 0.08 mm

Gearchange mechanism

Selector fork shaft runout (max)	0.05 mm
Selector fork end thickness	5.76 to 5.89 mm

Torque wrench settings

Balancer shaft end cap bolts	12 Nm
Cam chain holder bolt	10 Nm
Cam chain tensioner blade pivot bolt	10 Nm
Cam chain tensioner cap bolt	7 Nm
Cam chain tensioner mounting bolts	10 Nm
Camshaft holder bolts	10 Nm
Camshaft sprocket bolts	24 Nm
Clutch nut	95 Nm
Clutch cover bolts	12 Nm
Clutch spring bolts	8 Nm
Connecting rod cap bolts	
Initial setting	20 Nm
Final setting (see Section 21)	+ 180°
Coolant inlet and outlet pipe bolts	10 Nm
Crankcase bolts	see Section 19
Crankshaft end cap	10 Nm
Cylinder head bolts	see Section 10
Engine mounting bolts/nuts	see Section 4
Footrest/gearchange lever bracket bolts	30 Nm
Frame inner bracket bolts	45 Nm
Gearchange shaft centralising spring locating pin	22 Nm
Main oil gallery plug	8 Nm
Oil cooler bolt	40 Nm
Oil gallery plug	8 Nm
Oil pump cover screw	4 Nm
Oil pump bracket bolt	10 Nm
Oil pump mounting bolts	12 Nm
Oil strainer bolts	10 Nm
Oil sump bolts	10 Nm
Selector fork shaft retaining plate screws	10 Nm
Shock absorber front mounting bolt nut	44 Nm
Sidestand bracket bolts	63 Nm
Starter clutch bolts	32 Nm
Swingarm pivot bolt nut	110 Nm
Timing inspection bolt	15 Nm
Transmission input shaft bearing housing screws	12 Nm
Valve cover bolts	10 Nm
Water pump cover bolts	10 Nm

1 General Information

1 The engine is a liquid-cooled parallel twin, with four valves per cylinder. The valves are operated by double overhead camshafts that are driven by chain off the right-hand end of the crankshaft. The exhaust camshaft incorporates a decompression mechanism for easier starting. The engine assembly is constructed from aluminium alloy. The crankcase divides horizontally.

2 The crankcase incorporates a wet sump, pressure-fed lubrication system that uses a chain-driven, dual-rotor oil pump, an oil filter, a relief valve and an oil pressure switch. The pump chain runs off the back of the clutch housing. The oil circulates through a cooler located on the front of the crankcases.

3 The alternator is on the left-hand end of the crankshaft, and the starter clutch is on the back of the alternator.

4 Power from the crankshaft is routed to the transmission via the clutch. The clutch is a wet multi-plate type and is gear-driven off the crankshaft. The transmission is a six-speed constant-mesh unit. Final drive to the rear wheel is by chain and sprockets.

5 Read the *Safety First!* section of this manual carefully before starting work.

2 Component access

Operations possible with the engine in the frame

1 The components and assemblies listed below can be removed without having to remove the engine assembly from the frame. If however, a number of areas require attention at the same time, removal of the engine is recommended.
- Valve cover
- Camshafts
- Cam chain and blades
- Cylinder head
- Water pump and thermostat
- Clutch
- Gearchange mechanism
- Alternator stator and crankshaft position (CKP) sensor
- Alternator rotor and starter clutch
- Starter motor
- Oil filter and cooler
- Oil sump and oil strainer
- Oil pump and pressure relief valve

Operations requiring engine removal

2 It is necessary to remove the engine from the frame to gain access to the following components.
- Crankshaft and bearings
- Balancer shaft and bearings
- Connecting rods and bearings
- Cylinder bores, pistons and piston rings
- Transmission shafts
- Selector drum and forks

3 Engine wear assessment

Warning: Be careful when working on the hot engine – the exhaust pipes, the engine and engine components can cause severe burns.

1 Poor engine performance may be caused by leaking valves, incorrect valve clearances, a leaking head gasket, or worn pistons, piston rings or cylinders. A cylinder compression check will highlight these conditions and can also indicate the presence of excessive carbon deposits in the cylinder head, and a leakdown test (for which special equipment is needed – consult a Yamaha dealer) will pinpoint the actual cause(s) of the problem.

Cylinder compression test

Special tools: *A compression gauge with an adapter that matches the spark plug threads (10mm x 1.0mm pitch)is necessary for this procedure.Yamaha can provide a gauge (part no. 90890-03081 in Europe, YU-33223 in the US) and gauge adapter (part no. 90890-04136) for this purpose.*

2 Before carrying out the test, check that the valve clearances are correct (see Chapter 1).

3.5a Select the correct adapter...

3 Run the engine until it reaches normal operating temperature, then turn the ignition OFF.

4 Remove the spark plugs (see Chapter 1). To prevent a fault code being generated reconnect the coil wiring connectors and fit the plugs into the coils, then earth the plugs against the cylinder head, or connect them to a suitable earth point using crocodile clips and an auxiliary wire, or jump leads – keep them away from the plug bores as there could be some fuel/air mix expelled from the cylinder not being tested.

5 Select the correct gauge adapter to match the spark plug thread size and fit it onto the end of the gauge hose **(see illustrations)**. Working on the first cylinder to be tested, thread the gauge adapter into the spark plug hole.

6 Open the throttle fully and crank the engine over on the starter motor until the gauge reading has built up to a maximum figure and then remains stable **(see illustration)**. Make a note of the pressure reading and then repeat the procedure on the other cylinder. Turn the ignition OFF when the test has been completed.

7 Compare the results with the Specifications (see Cylinder bores) – make sure you compare the reading obtained for each cylinder to the correct specification, as each cylinder runs at a different compression. If they are both within the specified range and the maximum difference between the cylinders is less than specified, the engine is in good condition.

8 If there is a marked difference between the readings, or if the readings are lower than specified, it is likely components in the engine top-end are worn. Pour a small quantity of clean engine oil through the spark plug hole of the cylinder being checked, then test for compression again. An increase in pressure indicates worn or broken piston rings. No change in the pressure indicates a problem with the valves or cylinder head gasket.

9 Readings that are higher than specified are unlikely, but if found indicate excessive carbon build-up in the combustion chamber and on the top of the piston. If this is the case, remove the cylinder head and clean the carbon deposits off.

10 When the test is complete, refer to Chapter 1 and install the spark plugs.

Leak-down (cylinder leakage) test

11 A leak down or 'cylinder leakage' test is similar to a compression test in that it tells you how well a cylinder is sealing, but it does so by testing how much pressure is lost through leakage, as opposed to how much pressure is created through compression. Many professionals prefer a leak test to a compression test as it more accurately pin-points the cause of the problem before any disassembly is done, as it is easy to tell where the leakage is occurring. Generally however the required equipment is more expensive than for a compression test and a source of compressed air is essential. If you think a test is needed take the bike to a suitably equipped dealer or workshop. If you decide to purchase your own equipment follow the manufacturer's instructions.

12 A leakage test can also be used in conjunction with a compression test to diagnose other kinds of problems, such as a faulty valve train component, incorrect valve timing, faulty ignition or fuel delivery problems.

Engine oil pressure check

Special tools: *An oil pressure gauge with a 16 mm threaded adapter is necessary for this procedure.Yamaha provide a gauge (part no. 90890-03153 in Europe, YU-03153 in the US) and gauge adapter (part no. 90890-03139) for this purpose.*

13 If there is any doubt about the performance of the engine lubrication system an oil pressure check must be carried out. The check provides useful information about the state of wear of the engine.

14 Check the engine oil level and top up if necessary (see *Pre-ride checks*).

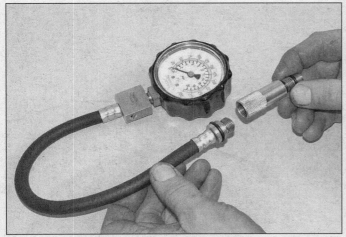

3.5b ... and thread it onto the hose

3.6 Measuring cylinder compression

3.16a Unscrew the oil gallery plug

3.16b Select the correct adapter

3.16c Connect the gauge hose to the adapter – this shows a push-on type, others may thread on

15 Run the engine until it reaches normal operating temperature, then turn the ignition OFF. Support the machine on its sidestand.

16 Place a drain tray under the right-hand side of the engine. Unscrew the main oil gallery plug, then select the matching gauge adapter and thread it into the plug bore **(see illustrations)**. Connect the pressure gauge to the adapter **(see illustration)**.

> ⚠ **Warning: Take great care not to burn your hand on the coolant pipe, engine, exhaust pipe or with engine oil when removing the gallery plug and fitting the gauge – the exhaust will be particularly hot. Do not allow exhaust gases to build up in the work area; either perform the check outside or use an exhaust gas extraction system.**

17 Start the engine and increase the engine speed to 5000 rpm whilst watching the pressure gauge reading **(see illustration)**. Make a note of the reading. The oil pressure should be similar to that given in the Specifications.

18 Stop the engine.

19 Fit a new O-ring smeared with grease onto the oil gallery plug.

20 Remove the gauge and unscrew the adapter from the crankcase, then fit the oil gallery plug and tighten it to 8 Nm. Check the engine oil level (see *Pre-ride checks*).

21 If the pressure is significantly lower than the standard, either the pressure relief valve is stuck open, the oil pump is faulty, the oil strainer or filter is blocked, or there is considerable engine wear. Begin diagnosis by checking the oil filter (see Chapter 1), the strainer and relief valve, then the oil pump (Section 17 and Section 18). If those items check out okay, the engine bearing oil clearances are likely to be excessive and the engine needs to be overhauled.

22 If the pressure is too high, either an oil passage is clogged, the relief valve is stuck closed or the wrong grade of oil is being used.

23 Refer to the appropriate Sections within this Chapter and rectify any problems before running the engine again.

4 Engine removal and installation

Caution: The engine is very heavy. Engine removal and installation should be carried out with the aid of at least one assistant. Personal injury or damage could occur if the engine falls or is dropped. An hydraulic or mechanical floor jack should be used to support and lower or raise the engine, if possible. It is best to remove as many components as possible (particularly the ones with easy access, such as the clutch, oil cooler, alternator and starter motor) to reduce the weight of the engine before removing it.*

Removal

Note: *If you intend to remove the alternator or clutch with the engine removed from the frame, it is best to slacken the rotor bolt and clutch nut while the engine is still in the frame – they are tight and the engine needs to be held securely while they are undone. Refer to Chapter 8 for the alternator, and Section 13 for the clutch.*

1 Support the motorcycle securely in an upright position using an auxiliary stand or stands – the front of the rear shock absorber bolts to the back of the engine, and so you cannot use a rear paddock stand. A good way to support the bike is to pass a sturdy bar through the passenger footrest brackets, using rag to protect them, and support each end of the bar on a tall axle stand, with blocks of wood under the stand if necessary – you can use a paddock stand to initially raise the back of the bike, then take it away after the bar is in place. Alternatively use axle stands positioned as shown once the exhaust system has been removed **(see illustration)** - make

3.17 Checking oil pressure

4.1 Bike supported on axle stands, exhaust removed

4.11 Unscrew the bolt and detach the earth leads

4.12a Release the hoses from the clips

4.12b Release the clip (arrowed)

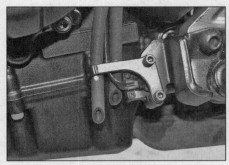

4.12c Draw the hoses out of the guide

4.13a Disconnect the connector(s) …

4.13b … then undo the screw (arrowed) and move the bracket and wiring aside

sure the left-hand stand is under the frame and not the footrest bracket assembly as this needs to be displaced. Place some wood under the rear wheel to prevent it dropping when the shock absorber bolt is removed, but make sure it is not compressing the suspension. Tie the front brake lever on so the bike can't move. Work can be made easier by raising the machine to a suitable working height on an hydraulic ramp or a suitable platform. Make sure the motorcycle is secure and will not topple over. When disconnecting any wiring, cables and hoses, it is advisable to mark or tag them as a reminder of where they connect, and make a note of any ties and guides that secure them and how they are routed.

2 Disconnect the battery (see Chapter 8).
3 If the engine is dirty, particularly around its mountings, wash it thoroughly before starting any major dismantling work. This will make work much easier and rule out the possibility of dirt falling inside.
4 Drain the engine oil and the coolant (see Chapter 1).
5 Remove the fuel tank, the throttle bodies and the air filter housing (see Chapter 4). Plug the intake manifolds with clean rag.
6 Remove the ignition coils (see Chapter 4).
7 Remove the coolant reservoir and the radiator along with their hoses, then remove the inlet and outlet pipes from the water pump (see Chapter 3).

8 Remove the exhaust system if not already done (see Chapter 4).
9 Detach the clutch cable from the release mechanism arm (Section 12).
10 Remove the front sprocket cover (see Chapter 6). Remove the left-hand frame cover (see Chapter 7).
11 Detach the engine earth leads **(see illustration)**.
12 On models without the EVAP canister release the fuel tank drain and breather hoses from the clips **(see illustration)**. Release the clip joining the hose with the blue dot on its end to the sidestand switch wire, then draw the hoses out of the guide on the sidestand bracket and remove them, noting their routing, and that the hose with the blue dot fits to the

rear of the one with the white dot, and the wire sits between them, and remove the hoses **(see illustrations)**.
13 Disconnect the gear position switch wiring connector, and on models without ABS or traction control the speed sensor wiring connector, then undo the screw securing the connector/hose clip bracket and move the wiring out of the way **(see illustrations)**.
14 Peel back the boot on the starter motor terminal, then unscrew the starter motor terminal nut and detach the lead **(see illustration)**. Secure the lead clear of the engine.
15 Pull the rubber boot off the oil pressure switch, undo the screw and detach the wire **(see illustration)**- release the wire from its clips and secure it clear, noting its routing.

4.14 Unscrew the nut (arrowed) and detach the starter lead

4.15 Disconnect the oil pressure switch wiring connector

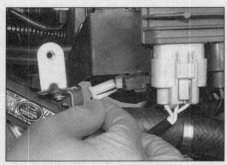

4.16a CKP sensor wiring connector

4.16b Alternator wiring connector

4.18 Undo the screw so the bracket is free to move

4.19a Unscrew the nut and remove the bolt and spacer

4.19b Tie the front of the shock up as shown

4.20a Slacken the tie (arrowed) and slide it rearwards…

4.20b … then disconnect the connector

4.20c Unscrew the bolts and remove the stand assembly

4.21a Slacken the pivot bolt nut (no need to remove it)

4.21b Unscrew the inner bracket bolts

4.21c Swing the bracket back as shown then insert one of the bolts into the front hole

16 Disconnect the CKP sensor and alternator wiring connectors **(see illustrations)**. Feed the wiring down to the alternator cover, releasing it from any clips or ties, and noting its routing.

17 Remove the clutch cable guide from the right-hand side of the frame **(see illustration 6.4)**.
18 Undo the wiring connector/rear brake pipe joint bracket (ABS models) screw on the right-hand side of the frame **(see illustration)**.
19 Unscrew the nut on the shock absorber front mounting bolt and withdraw the bolt with its spacer **(see illustration)**. Lift the shock out of the mount and tie it up using a cable-tie **(see illustration)**.
20 Release the sidestand switch wiring tie then disconnect the wiring connector **(see illustrations)**. Unscrew the sidestand bracket bolts and remove the stand assembly **(see illustration)**.
21 Slacken the swingarm pivot bolt nut **(see illustration)**. Unscrew the frame inner bracket bolts on the left-hand side and pivot the bracket rearwards so access to the lower rear mounting bolt is clear **(see illustration)** - secure the bracket in this position by inserting one of its bolts into the front hole and allowing this to sit against the rear edge of the frame **(see illustration)**.

4.22 Slip the chain off the shaft

4.25a Unscrew the bolts and remove the left-hand bracket...

4.25b ... and the right-hand bracket

4.26a Unscrew the front bolt on the right-hand side...

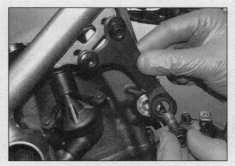

4.26b ... and on the left-hand side, noting the washer with each bolt

4.28a Unscrew the nut and remove the washer

22 Remove the front sprocket (see Chapter 6). Slip the chain off the transmission output shaft **(see illustration)**.

23 At this point, position an hydraulic or mechanical jack under the engine with a block of wood between the jack head and sump. Make sure the jack is centrally positioned so the engine will not topple in any direction when the last mounting bolt is removed and the engine is supported only by the jack. Take the weight of the engine on the jack, but make sure the bike is not being lifted.

24 Check around the engine and frame to make sure that all the necessary wiring, cables and hoses have been disconnected, and that any that remain connected to the engine are not retained by any clips, guides or brackets on the frame, and that any staying behind are not held to the engine.

25 Unscrew and remove the engine mounting bracket bolts and then the upper engine mounting bolt on each side **(see illustrations)**.

26 Unscrew and remove the front mounting bolt and washer on each side **(see illustrations)**.

27 Make sure the engine is properly supported on the jack, and have an assistant support it as well.

28 Unscrew the nut and remove the washer from the left-hand end of the upper rear mounting bolt **(see illustration)**. Withdraw the bolt, on models with ABS holding the brake pipe joint bracket clear **(see illustration)** – do not move the bracket any more than is necessary for the mounting bolt to just clear it as the brake pipes are delicate and could bend and deform or crack if moved too far.

29 Unscrew the nut and remove the washer from the right-hand end of the lower rear mounting bolt **(see illustration)**. Steady the engine, then with the help of an assistant withdraw the bolt, lower the engine and manoeuvre it out of the frame **(see illustration)**.

30 On some models, those with a '1' stamped to the inner side of the frame just to the rear of the front mounting on the right-hand side, there is a spacer plate – remove it if required, or if it is loose and liable to drop off, noting how the projections seat in the slots.

Installation

31 On models with a '1' stamped to the inner side of the frame just to the rear of the front mounting on the right-hand side make sure

4.28b Hold the bracket/pipe assembly aside and withdraw the upper rear bolt

4.29a Unscrew the nut and remove the washer

4.29b Withdraw the lower rear bolt

the spacer plate is fitted with the projections seated in the slots.

32 With the aid of an assistant, place the engine unit onto the jack and block of wood and carefully raise it into position so that the mounting bolt holes align. Make sure no wires, cables or hoses become trapped between the engine and the frame.

33 Fit and tighten the engine mounting bolts in the following order:

● Slide the upper rear mounting bolt in from the right-hand side and the lower rear bolt in from the left **(see illustrations 4.28b and 4.29b)**. Fit the washers and nuts and tighten them finger-tight **(see illustrations 4.28a and 4.29a)**.

● Fit the front mounting bolts with their washers, and tighten them finger-tight **(see illustration 4.26a and b)**.

● Fit the right-hand engine bracket, the bracket-to-frame bolts and the upper mounting bolt and tighten the bolts finger-tight **(see illustration 4.25b)**.

● Tighten the upper rear mounting bolt nut and then the lower rear mounting bolt nut to 55 Nm – counter-hold the bolt heads to prevent them turning.

● Tighten the left-hand front mounting bolt to 75 Nm.

● Fit the left-hand engine bracket, the bracket-to-frame bolts and the upper mounting bolt and tighten the bolts finger-tight **(see illustration 4.25a)**.

● Tighten the left-hand upper mounting bolt to 55 Nm.

● Tighten the right-hand front mounting bolt to 75 Nm.

● Tighten the right-hand upper mounting bolt to 55 Nm.

● Tighten the engine bracket-to-frame bolts on each side to 25 Nm.

34 The remainder of installation is the reverse of removal, noting the following points:

● Reposition the inner bracket on the left-hand side of the frame, clean the threads of the bracket bolts, apply some fresh threadlock and tighten the bolts to 45 Nm **(see illustration 4.21b)**. Tighten the swingarm pivot bolt nut to 110 Nm **(see illustration 4.21a)**.

● Clean the threads of the sidestand bracket bolts, apply some fresh threadlock and tighten the bolts to 63 Nm **(see illustration 4.20c)**.

● Fit the shock absorber bolt with its spacer and tighten the nut to 44 Nm **(see illustration 4.19a)**.

● Make sure all wires, cables and hoses are correctly routed and connected, and secured by any clips or ties.

● Refill the engine with oil and coolant to the correct levels (see Chapter 1).

● Check the throttle and clutch cable freeplay (see Chapter 1).

● Adjust the drive chain tension (see Chapter 1).

● Start the engine and check that there are no oil or coolant leaks.

5 Engine overhaul general information

1 Before beginning the engine overhaul, read through the related procedures to familiarise yourself with the scope and requirements of the job. Overhauling an engine is not all that difficult, but it is time consuming. Check on the availability of parts and make sure that any necessary special tools are obtained in advance.

2 Most work can be done with a decent set of typical workshop hand tools, although a number of precision measuring tools are required for inspecting parts to determine if they are worn.

3 To ensure maximum life and minimum trouble from a rebuilt engine, everything must be assembled with care in a spotlessly clean environment, using the correct lubricant where directed.

Disassembly

4 Before disassembling the engine, thoroughly clean and degrease its external surfaces. This will prevent contamination of the engine internals, and will also make the job a lot easier and cleaner. A high flash-point solvent, such as paraffin (kerosene) can be used, or better still, a proprietary engine degreaser such as Gunk. Use old paintbrushes and toothbrushes to work the solvent into the various recesses of the casings. Take care to exclude solvent or water from the electrical components and intake and exhaust ports.

 Warning: The use of petrol (gasoline) as a cleaning agent should be avoided because of the risk of fire.

5 When clean and dry, position the engine on the workbench, leaving suitable clear area for working. Gather a selection of small containers, plastic bags and some labels so that parts can be grouped together in an easily identifiable manner. Also get some paper and a pen so that notes can be taken. You will also need a supply of clean rag, which should be as absorbent as possible.

6 Before commencing work, read through the appropriate section so that some idea of the necessary procedure can be gained. When removing components note that great force is seldom required, unless specified (checking the specified torque setting of the particular bolt being removed will indicate how tight it is, and therefore how much force should be needed). In many cases, a component's reluctance to be removed is indicative of an incorrect approach or removal method; if in any doubt, re-check with the text.

7 When disassembling the engine, keep 'mated' parts together (including gears, pistons, connecting rods, valves, etc, that

have been in contact with each other during engine operation). These ' mated' parts must be reused or replaced as an assembly.

8 A complete engine disassembly should be done in the following general order with reference to the appropriate Sections (or Chapters, where indicated).

● Remove the clutch cover (if not already done) and the oil sump and strainer – doing this first gives the engine a steady flat base to sit on while removing other components
● Remove the valve cover
● Remove the cam chain tensioner
● Remove the camshafts
● Remove the cylinder head
● Remove the clutch
● Remove the gearchange mechanism
● Remove the oil pump
● Remove the alternator rotor and starter clutch
● Remove the starter motor (see Chapter 8)
● Remove the oil cooler
● Separate the crankcase halves
● Remove the balancer shaft
● Remove the crankshaft
● Remove the connecting rods and pistons
● Remove the transmission output shaft
● Remove the selector drum and forks
● Remove the transmission input shaft

Reassembly

9 Reassembly is accomplished by reversing the general disassembly sequence.

6 Valve cover

Removal

1 Remove the fuel tank and the ignition coils (see Chapter 4). On XSR models remove the air scoops (see Chapter 7).

2 Remove the radiator (see Chapter 3).

3 On 2014 to 2016 MT-07 (FZ-07) models remove the intake air flap solenoid valve and surge tank (see Chapter 4).

4 Remove the clutch cable guide from the right-hand side of the frame **(see illustration)**.

6.4 Undo the screw and remove the guide

6.5 Release the clamp (arrowed) and detach the hose

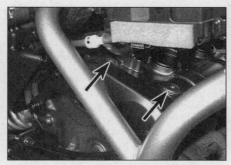

6.6a Unscrew the bolts (arrowed) on each side…

6.6b …and remove the valve cover

5 Disconnect the breather hose from the top of the valve cover **(see illustration)**.

6 Unscrew and remove the valve cover bolts **(see illustration)**. Lift the cover off the cylinder head and remove it **(see illustration)**. If it is stuck, break the gasket seal by tapping gently around the edge with a soft-faced hammer or block of wood. Do not lever the cover off as this will damage the sealing surface.

Installation

7 Examine the valve cover gasket rim and circular spark plug seals for signs of damage or deterioration and fit a new gasket if necessary **(see illustration)**. Similarly check the cover bolt sealing washers for cracks, hardening and deterioration and use new ones if necessary **(see illustration)**.

8 Clean the mating surfaces of the cylinder head and the valve cover with a suitable solvent; Yamaha specify their Yamaha bond 1215.

9 Fit the gasket onto the valve cover, making sure It locates correctly with the projection on the bridging section between the plug hole seals on the front side of the rib on the cover **(see illustration 6.7a)**. If the new gasket has a bridge piece between the cam chain end and the adjacent spark plug seal cut it away using a sharp knife.

10 Position the valve cover on the cylinder head, making sure the gasket stays in place **(see illustration 6.6b)**. Apply a smear of silicone grease to the lips of the sealing washers and fit them if removed **(see**

6.7a Check the gasket…

6.7b …and the sealing washers

illustration 6.7b). Fit the bolts and tighten them to 10 Nm.

11 Install the remaining components in reverse order of removal.

7 Cam chain tensioner

1 The cam chain tensioner is located on the rear of the cylinder head on the right-hand side **(see illustration 7.4b)**.

Removal

2 Remove the valve cover (Section 6). Remove the spark plugs (see Chapter 1).

3 Refer to Section 8, Steps 2 and 3 and align

the camshafts as described. If the camshafts are not being removed as well secure the chain tight on the intake camshaft sprocket using a cable-tie as shown, or the chain could jump teeth which puts the valve timing out **(see illustration)**.

4 Unscrew the tensioner cap bolt, noting its washer **(see illustration)**. Unscrew the two mounting bolts, evenly and a little at a time, and withdraw the tensioner, noting that the plunger will be pushed out under spring pressure **(see illustration)**. Remove the gasket – a new one must be used. You may need a new sealing washer for the cap bolt – check its condition and use a new one if in any doubt.

Inspection

5 Check that the plunger cannot be pushed

7.3 Cable-tie the chain to the sprocket as shown

7.4a Unscrew the cap bolt with its washer…

7.4b … then unscrew the mounting bolts (arrowed) and remove the tensioner

7.5 The plunger must not move in when pushed

into the body (see illustration) – if it can, fit a new tensioner. Draw the plunger into the tensioner using a 3mm hex key and turning it anti-clockwise (see illustration 7.7a) – the plunger should wind in smoothly and easily. Hold the plunger in, then remove the hex key and slowly release the plunger – it should extend smoothly and freely under spring pressure.

Installation

6 Make sure the tensioner and cylinder head mating surfaces are clean and dry.

7 Draw the plunger into the tensioner using a 3mm hex key and turning it anti-clockwise until the plunger is fully retracted **(see illustration)** – do not remove the hex key or the plunger will release, but the key should lock itself in place and so will not need to be held.Fit a new gasket onto the tensioner with the protruding tab to the left of the punch mark on the tensioner, then fit the tensioner with the punch mark and tab facing up, and tighten the bolts to 10 Nm **(see illustration)**. Remove the hex key, and check that the plunger has extended to contact and push on the blade and so tension the chain **(see illustration)**. Fit the tensioner cap bolt, using a new sealing washer if necessary, and tighten it to 7 Nm **(see illustration 7.4a)**.

8 Remove the cable-tie from the camshaft sprocket **(see illustration)**. Turn the engine anti-clockwise through two full turns **(see illustration 8.3a)** – make sure the tensioner

has taken up all slack in the chain, then check again that all the timing marks still align (see Step 3 of Section 8).

9 Install the valve cover (Section 6).

10 Fit the timing inspection bolt using a new sealing washer if necessary and tighten to 15 Nm. Smear the end cap O-ring with grease, using a new one if necessary, then fit the cap and tighten to 10 Nm **(see illustration 8.2)**.

11 Install all remaining components in the reverse order of removal. On completion, check the engine oil level (see *Pre-ride checks*).

8 Camshafts and followers

Removal

1 Remove the valve cover (see Section 6). Remove the spark plugs (see Chapter 1).

2 Unscrew the timing inspection bolt and the crankshaft end cap from the alternator cover on the left-hand side of the engine **(see**

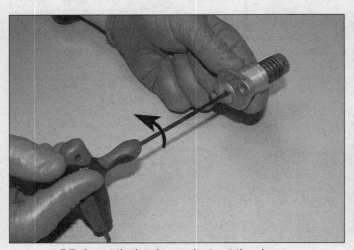

7.7a Insert the hex key and retract the plunger

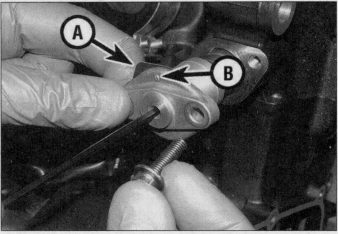

7.7b Gasket tab (A), punch mark (B)

7.7c Remove the key and check the plunger extends

7.8 Cut and remove the cable-tie

8.2 Remove the inspection bolt and the end cap

8.3a Turn the engine anti-clockwise…

8.3b …until the timing mark aligns with the notches…

illustration). You may need a new sealing washer for the bolt and a new O-ring for the cap – check their condition and use new ones if in any doubt.

3 Using a socket on the alternator rotor bolt and rotating in an anti-clockwise direction only, turn the engine until the timing mark on the rotor aligns with the notches in the inspection hole, and the line next to the 'I' on the intake camshaft sprocket faces back and is parallel to the cylinder head top surface, and the lines on the exhaust camshaft sprocket are parallel to the cylinder head top surface and the punch mark is near the top **(see illustrations)**. If the intake camshaft line faces forwards and the punch mark is near the bottom, turn the engine anti-clockwise 360° (one full turn) so that the timing mark on the rotor again aligns with the notches – the line will now face back and the punch mark will be near the top. In this position the No. 1 cylinder is at TDC (top dead centre) on its exhaust stroke, the required position for camshaft removal and installation.

4 Remove the cam chain tensioner (Section 7).
5 Starting with the intake camshaft, unscrew the camshaft holder bolts evenly and a little at a time in a criss-cross pattern, starting from the outside and working towards the centre **(see illustration)**. Remove the bolts, then lift

8.3c …and the sprocket lines are parallel with the head and the punch mark (arrowed) is near the top

off the holder **(see illustration)** – retrieve the dowels from either the holder or the cylinder head if they are loose.
Caution: If the bolts are loosened carelessly and the holders do not come away from the head squarely, a holder is likely to break. If this happens the complete cylinder head

assembly must be replaced with a new one as the holders are matched to the head and cannot be obtained separately. Also, a camshaft could break if the holder bolts are not slackened evenly and the pressure from a depressed valve causes a shaft to bend.

8.5a Camshaft holder bolts (arrowed) – intake camshaft at the rear, exhaust at the front

8.5b Lift the holder off, noting the dowels (arrowed)

8.6 Exhaust camshaft holder dowels (arrowed)

8.8a Lift out the follower using a magnet if available...

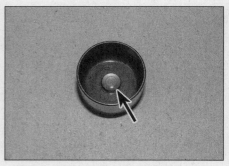

8.8b ...and retrieve the shim (arrowed) from inside it

6 Remove the exhaust camshaft holder in the same way **(see illustration)** – retrieve the dowels from either the holder or the cylinder head if they are loose.

7 Disengage the chain from the intake camshaft sprocket and lift the camshaft out of the head **(see illustration 8.28a)**. Similarly remove the exhaust camshaft **(see illustration 8.27a)**, and rest the cam chain on the bolt in the tunnel – avoid rotating the crankshaft in case the chain jams between the timing sprocket and the case.

8 If the followers and shims are being removed from the cylinder head, obtain a container that is divided into eight compartments, and label each compartment with the location of its corresponding valve in the cylinder head. If a container is not available, use labelled plastic bags (egg cartons also work very well). Remove the cam follower of the valve in question, then retrieve the shim from the inside of the follower **(see illustrations)**. If it is not in the follower, pick it out of the top of the valve using either a magnet, a small screwdriver with a dab of grease on it (the shim will stick to the grease), or a screwdriver and a pair of pliers **(see illustration 8.24a)**. Do not allow the shim to fall into the engine.

Inspection

9 Inspect the bearing surfaces of the cylinder head and camshaft holders and the corresponding journals on the camshaft **(see illustration)**. Look for score marks, deep scratches and evidence of spalling (a pitted appearance) **(see illustration 8.10a)**. If damage

is noted or wear is excessive, the relevant parts must be replaced with new ones. The cylinder head and holders must be replaced as a new matched set – individual parts are not available.

10 Check the camshaft lobes for heat discoloration (blue appearance), score marks, chipped areas, flat spots and spalling **(see illustration)**. Measure the height of each lobe with a micrometer **(see illustration)** and compare the results to the minimum lobe height listed in the Specifications. If damage is noted or wear is excessive, the camshaft must be replaced with a new one. Also check the condition of the cam followers.

11 Check the amount of camshaft runout by supporting each end of the camshaft on V-blocks, and measuring any runout at the journals using a dial gauge. If the runout exceeds the specified limit the camshaft must be replaced with a new one.

12 The camshaft journal oil clearance should now be checked. This is done as follows using a product called Plastigauge.

13 Work on one camshaft at a time and clean the camshaft and the bearing surfaces in the cylinder head and the camshaft holders with a suitable solvent and a clean, lint-free cloth. Lay the camshaft in place in the cylinder head with the lobes clear of the followers.

14 Cut some strips of Plastigauge and lay one piece on each journal, parallel with the camshaft centreline **(see illustration 24.13)**. Make sure the camshaft holder dowels are in place then fit the holders in their correct location (see Step 29). Lubricate the threads of the holder bolts with clean engine oil, then

tighten the bolts evenly and a little at a time in a criss-cross pattern from the centre outwards to 10 Nm. Make sure each holder is being pulled down square and does not bind on the dowels, and don't let the camshaft rotate.

15 Now unscrew the bolts evenly and a little at a time in a criss-cross pattern, starting from the outside and working towards the centre, and carefully lift off the camshaft holders.

16 To determine the oil clearance, compare the crushed Plastigauge (at its widest point) on each journal to the scale printed on the Plastigauge container **(see illustration 24.17)**. Compare the results to the Specifications. Carefully clean away all traces of Plastigauge using a fingernail or other object which will not score the bearing surfaces. If any clearance is greater than specified, it is an indication of wear on the camshaft and/or the cylinder head and holder.

17 First check to see if the camshaft journals are worn below the service limit by measuring them with a micrometer. If they are, a new camshaft must be fitted. If you need a new camshaft calculate whether the specified journal diameter for a new camshaft will restore the oil clearance to within specification.

18 If the camshaft journals are good, or if fitting a new camshaft will not restore the oil clearance to within specification, the holders and cylinder head will have to be replaced – they come as a matched set.

19 Inspect the cam chain guide blade, tensioner blade and cam chain (Section 9).

20 Check the action of the decompression mechanism on the exhaust camshaft – with the weights on the outside of the sprocket at

8.9 Check all related bearing surfaces

8.10a Check the camshaft lobes as described – damage as shown requires immediate attention

8.10b Measure the height of the camshaft lobes with a micrometer

8.20a With the weights at rest the rounded ends of the pins (arrowed) should be extended

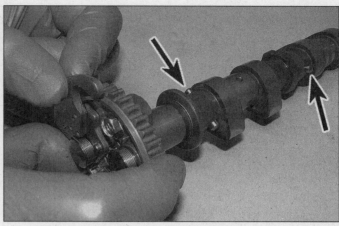

8.20b With the weights pulled out the rounded ends of the pins (arrowed) should be retracted

rest the decompression pins should protrude from the lobes, and when the weights are moved outwards the pins should retract, with everything moving smoothly **(see illustrations)**. To remove the internal shafts and the pins, first remove the sprocket (Step 21). Hold the right-hand pin, withdraw the right-hand shaft and then remove the pin **(see illustrations 8.20h and g)**. Repeat for the left-hand pin and shaft **(see illustrations 8.20e and d)**. Before refitting the components lubricate them with new engine oil. To refit the components, hold the camshaft as shown with the hole in the sprocket flange bottom right, then place and hold the left-hand pin in the hole with its rounded end facing out so it is opposite the lobes and the cut-out facing the sprocket end, then insert the left-hand shaft with the short offset end pin going in first and locating this in the cut-out in the decompression pin **(see illustrations)**. Check that the shaft has engaged with the pin **(see illustration)**. Repeat for the right-hand decompression pin and shaft, making sure the cut-out in its left-hand end aligns with and engages the long thin pin of the left-hand shaft, so that when the right-hand shaft turns it turns the left-hand shaft **(see illustrations)**. Check that all is correctly fitted by turning the right-hand shaft **(see illustration)** – the decompression pins should move in and out smoothly and simultaneously. Fit the sprocket (Step 21).

8.20c Hold the camshaft so the hole (arrowed) is positioned as shown

8.20d Insert the pin with the rounded end (arrowed) opposite to the lobes and the cut-out facing the sprocket end

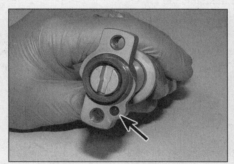

8.20e Insert the shaft...

8.20f ... and check it has engaged with the pin

8.20g Insert the pin with the rounded end (arrowed) opposite to the lobes and the cut-out facing the sprocket end

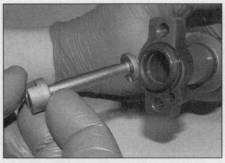

8.20h Insert and engage the shaft as described

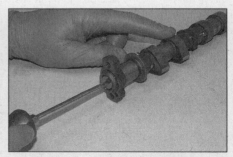

8.20i Turn the right-hand shaft using a screwdriver and check the pins move in and out

8.21a Intake camshaft sprocket bolts (arrowed) – note the positioning of the sprocket marks relative to the camshaft lobes

8.21b Exhaust camshaft sprocket bolts (arrowed)

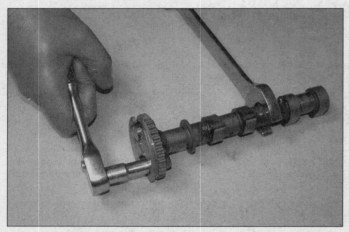

8.21c Hold the exhaust shaft hex using a spanner while unscrewing the bolts

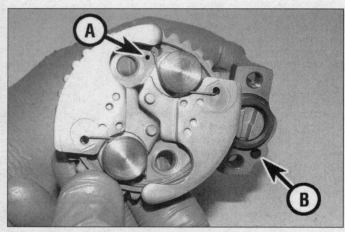

8.21d Align the punch mark (A) on the sprocket and the hole (B) on the flange as shown

21 Inspect the camshaft sprockets; if they show signs of wear, cracks or other damage, replace them and the cam chain with a new set. The camshaft sprockets are retained by two bolts **(see illustrations)**. Unscrew the bolts and remove the sprockets – to hold the intake camshaft use a holding tool with pins located in the holes in the sprocket from the inner side, and to hold the exhaust camshaft use a spanner on the flats cast into the shaft **(see illustration)**. Fit the new sprockets – on

the intake camshaft align the 'I' and "E" marks and the lobes as shown **(see illustration 8.21a)**, and on the exhaust camshaft align the punch mark and the hole in the sprocket flange as shown **(see illustration)**, and make sure the weights engage the outer end of the right-hand decompression shaft so that when the weights move the shaft moves. Tighten the sprocket bolts to 24 Nm, on the exhaust camshaft tightening the bolt adjacent the punch mark first.

22 Inspect the outer surfaces of the cam followers for evidence of wear, scoring or other damage. If the side of a follower is in poor condition, it is probable that the bore in which it works is also damaged. Check for clearance between the followers and their bores. Whilst no specifications are given, if slack is excessive, replace the followers with new ones. If the bores are seriously out-of-round or tapered, then replace the cylinder head and followers with new ones.

Installation

23 If removed, install the cam chain and the tensioner blade (Section 9).
24 Lubricate each shim with molybdenum disulphide oil (a 50/50 mix of molybdenum disulphide grease and engine oil) and fit it into its recess in the top of the valve, with the size marking facing up **(see illustration)**. Check that the shim is correctly seated, then lubricate the top of the follower with molybdenum disulphide oil and the outer wall of the follower with engine oil, and fit it onto the valve **(see illustration)**.

8.24a Fit each shim into its recess...

8.24b ...then fit the follower

8.27a Fit the exhaust camshaft...

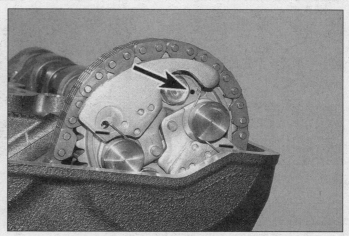

8.27b ... with the lines parallel to the head and the punch mark (arrowed) near the top

8.28a Fit the intake camshaft...

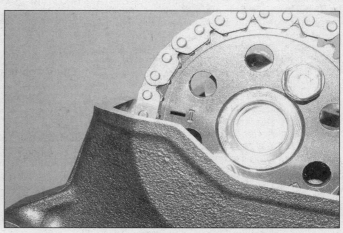

8.28b ... with the line facing back and parallel to the head

Note: *It is important that the shims and followers are returned to their original valves, otherwise the valve clearances will be inaccurate.*

25 Make sure the timing mark aligns with the notches in the timing inspection hole (see Step 3) (see illustration 8.3b).

26 Make sure the camshaft journals and the bearing surfaces in the cylinder head and holders are clean, then apply molybdenum disulphide oil to them and to the camshaft lobes.

27 Fit the exhaust camshaft first with the punch mark on the sprocket at the top and the lines parallel with the cylinder head top surface, fitting the cam chain around the sprocket as you position the camshaft, pulling up on the chain to remove all slack in the front run between the crankshaft and the camshaft (see illustrations).

28 Now fit the intake camshaft with the line next to the 'I' facing back and parallel to the cylinder head top surface, fitting the cam chain around the sprocket and pulling it tight to make sure there is no slack between the two camshaft

sprockets (see illustrations) – any slack in the chain must lie in the rear run, so that it is taken up by the tensioner. With the alignment correct fit a cable-tie through a hole in the sprocket and secure it tightly around the chain to prevent it jumping (see illustration 7.3).

29 Fit the camshaft holder dowels into the holders if removed (see illustrations 8.5b and 8.6). Fit the holders onto the camshafts – the exhaust camshaft holder has a ridged top and the intake camshaft holder has a flatter top (see illustration). Lubricate the threads of the holder bolts with clean engine oil, fit them into the holders and tighten them finger-tight. Starting with the exhaust camshaft tighten the holder bolts evenly and a little at a time in a criss-cross sequence from the centre outwards, until the holder is seated – as you tighten the bolts make sure the holder is drawn down evenly and does not bind on the dowels. Now tighten the holder bolts in the same sequence to 10 Nm. Repeat for the intake camshaft holder bolts.

Caution: The camshaft holder is likely to break if it is not tightened down evenly

and squarely and the camshaft is likely to bend if it is tightened down onto the closed valves before the open ones.

30 Using a piece of wooden dowel, press on the back of the cam chain tensioner blade via the tensioner bore in the crankcase to take up any slack in the cam chain. Check that all the timing marks are still in exact alignment as described in Step 3. If it is necessary to turn

8.29 The exhaust camshaft holder has the ridged top

9.3a Unscrew the bolt...

9.3b ...and remove the chain

9.4 Unscrew the bolt and remove the blade

the engine slightly, keep the wooden dowel pressed onto the tensioner blade. Note that it is easy to be slightly out (by one tooth on a sprocket) without the marks appearing drastically out of alignment.

31 If the timing marks are out, release the tension on the chain and cut the cable-tie around the sprocket and chain **(see illustration 7.8)**. Manually feed the chain around the sprockets as required, then turn the crankshaft and/or camshafts as required so that all timing marks align as specified. Secure the chain tightly on the intake camshaft sprocket with a new cable-tie.
Caution: If the marks are not aligned exactly as described, the valve timing will be incorrect and the valves may strike the pistons, causing extensive damage to the engine.

32 With everything correctly aligned, install the cam chain tensioner (Section 7).

33 Remove the cable-tie **(see illustration 7.8)**. Turn the engine anti-clockwise through two full turns – make sure the tensioner takes up all slack in the chain, then check again that all the timing marks still align (see Step 3).

34 Check the valve clearances and adjust them if necessary (see Chapter 1).

35 Install the valve cover (Section 6).

36 Fit the timing inspection bolt using a new sealing washer if necessary and tighten to 15 Nm. Smear the end cap O-ring with grease, using a new one if necessary, then fit the cap and tighten to 10 Nm **(see illustration 8.2)**.

37 Install all remaining components in the reverse order of removal. On completion,

check the engine oil level (see *Pre-ride checks*).

9 Cam chain, tensioner blade and front guide blade

Removal

Cam chain and tensioner blade

1 Remove the clutch cover (Section 13).

2 Remove the camshafts (Section 8).

3 Unscrew the cam chain holder bolt, then slip the chain off the sprocket and remove it **(see illustrations)**. The sprocket is an integral part of the crankshaft.

4 Unscrew the tensioner blade pivot bolt, then draw the blade out, noting which way round it fits **(see illustration)**.

Front guide blade

5 Remove the cylinder head (Section 10).

6 Lift the front guide blade out, noting how its lugs locate in the cut-outs **(see illustration)**.

Inspection

7 Except in cases of oil starvation, the cam chain wears very little. If the chain is stiff or the links are binding, or if the links are loose, fit a new chain. Check the sprocket teeth for wear and damage – the driven sprockets can be removed from the camshafts and new ones fitted (Section 8), but the drive sprocket is not available separately from the crankshaft.

8 Check the sliding surfaces of the blades for

excessive wear, deep grooves, cracking and other obvious damage, and replace them with new ones if necessary.

Installation

9 Installation is the reverse of removal, noting the following:
● Make sure the front guide blade lugs seat in the cut-outs **(see illustration)**.
● Apply some silicone grease to the cam chain holder bolt rubber, and tighten the bolt to 10 Nm.
● Clean the threads of the tensioner blade pivot bolt and apply some fresh threadlock, and tighten the bolt to 10 Nm.
● Refer to Section 13 for installation of the clutch cover.

10 Cylinder head removal and installation

Note: *On installation new head bolts (10 mm thread diameter) must be used, so it is wise to obtain them before commencing work.*

Removal

1 Remove the fuel tank, the throttle bodies, the ignition coils, and the exhaust system (see Chapter 4).

2 Remove the radiator (see Chapter 3). Disconnect the oil cooler inlet hose from the union on the left-hand end of the cylinder head **(see illustration)**.

9.6 Lift the blade out

9.9 Seat the lugs in the cut-outs

10.2 Release the clamp and detach the hose

10.5a First unscrew the 6 mm bolts on each end

10.5b Cylinder head 10 mm bolts (arrowed)

3 Remove the valve cover (Section 6) and the camshafts (Section 8). Remove the cam chain holder bolt and rest the chain in the tunnel **(see illustration 9.3a)**.

4 Place a support under the engine so the weight is taken without the bike being pushed up. Unscrew and remove the engine mounting bracket bolts and then the upper engine mounting bolt on each side **(see illustrations 4.25a and b)**. Unscrew and remove the front mounting bolt and washer on each side **(see illustrations 4.26a and b)**.

5 The cylinder head is secured by eight bolts. First unscrew and remove the two 6 mm bolts on the right-hand end of the head **(see illustration)**. Now unscrew the six 10 mm bolts **(see illustration)**- unscrew them evenly and no more than a half turn at a time in the reverse of the tightening sequence **(see illustration 10.17b)**. When all the bolts are loose, remove them.

6 Pull the cylinder head up off the cylinder block and remove it **(see illustration)**. If the head is stuck on the block, tap around the joint faces of the head with a soft-faced hammer or block of wood to free it. Do not attempt to free the head by inserting a lever between it and the cylinder block or you might damage the sealing surfaces.

7 Remove the cylinder head gasket, and the dowels if loose **(see illustration 10.15)**. A new gasket must be used.

8 On some models, those with a '1' stamped to the inner side of the frame just to the rear of the front mounting on the right-hand side, there is a spacer plate – remove it if required, or if it is loose and liable to drop off, noting how the projections seat in the slots.

9 Check the cylinder head gasket and the mating surfaces on the cylinder head and block for signs of leaks from the cylinders, or the oil or coolant passages, which could indicate that the head is warped. Refer to Section 11, Step 14, for a warpage check.

10 Lay a clean cloth over the pistons while the head is off to prevent any dirt getting in.

11 If required remove the ECT sensor (see Chapter 3).

Installation

12 Clean all traces of old gasket material from the cylinder head and block. If you need to use a scraper, take care not to scratch or gouge the soft aluminium. Be careful not to let any of the gasket material fall into the crankcase, the cylinder bores or the oil or coolant passages.

13 Fit the ECT sensor if removed (see Chapter 3).

14 On models with a '1' stamped to the inner side of the frame just to the rear of the front mounting on the right-hand side make sure the spacer plate is fitted with the projections seated in the slots.

15 Fit the dowels if removed, then lay the new head gasket over the dowels **(see illustration)**.

16 Carefully position the cylinder head on the cylinder block, making sure it locates onto the dowels **(see illustration 10.6)**.

17 Lubricate the threads, washers and under the heads of the six new 10 mm cylinder head

10.6 Lift and remove the head

10.15 Fit the dowels (arrowed) then lay the new gasket on the block

10.17a Use new bolts and lubricate as described

10.17b Cylinder head 10 mm bolt tightening sequence

bolts with clean engine oil. Fit the bolts and tighten them finger-tight **(see illustration)**. Now tighten the bolts in the sequence shown first to 10 Nm, and then to 40 Nm **(see illustration)**. Working in the same sequence, now loosen all the bolts, then tighten them to 20 Nm, then use a degree disc to tighten the bolts through 90° **(see illustration)**. Mark the top of each bolt with a marker pen once you have completed its angle tightening to ensure none get omitted or done twice.

18 Fit the 6 mm bolts and tighten them to 10 Nm **(see illustration 10.5a)**.

19 Lift the cam chain out of the tunnel using a piece of wire or a magnet and pull it taught, then pass a rod (such as a screwdriver or a socket extension) through it and across the tunnel to keep it up. Apply some silicone grease to the cam chain holder bolt rubber, fit the bolt between the runs of the chain and tighten the bolt to 10 Nm **(see illustration 9.3a)**. Rest the chain on the bolt.

20 Refer to Section 4 and fit and tighten the engine mounting bolts and brackets in the order described, omitting the steps relating to the upper and lower rear mounting bolts.

21 Install the remaining components in the reverse order of removal, referring to the relevant Sections and Chapters as directed.

---

11 Cylinder head and valve overhaul

1 Because of the complex nature of this job and the special tools and equipment required, most owners leave servicing of the valves, valve seats and valve guides to a professional. However, you can make an initial assessment of whether the valves are seating correctly, and therefore sealing, by pouring a small amount of solvent into each of the valve ports. If the solvent leaks past any valve into the combustion chamber area the valve is not seating correctly and sealing.

2 With the correct tools (a valve spring compressor is essential – make sure it is suitable for motorcycle work), you can also remove the valves and associated components from the cylinder head, clean them and check them for wear to assess the extent of the work needed, and, unless seat cutting or guide replacement is required, lap the valves and reassemble them in the head.

3 A dealer service department or engine specialist can replace the guides and re-cut the valve seats.

4 After the valve service has been performed, be sure to clean it very thoroughly before installation on the engine to remove any metal particles or abrasive grit that may still be present from the valve service operations. Use compressed air, if available, to blow out all the holes and passages.

Disassembly

5 Before proceeding, arrange to label and store the valves along with their related components in such a way that they can be returned to their original locations without getting mixed up **(see illustration)**. Either use the same container as the valve shims and followers are stored in (see Section 8), or obtain a separate container which is divided into eight compartments, and label each compartment with the identity of the valve which will be stored in it. Alternatively, labelled plastic bags will do just as well.

6 Compress the valve spring on the first valve with a spring compressor, making sure it is correctly located onto each end of the valve

10.17c Use a degree disc for the final tightening

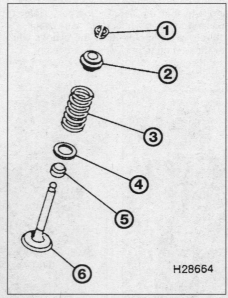

H28664

11.5 Valve components

1 Collets
2 Spring retainer
3 Valve spring
4 Spring seat
5 Valve stem oil seal
6 Valve

11.6a Compressing the valve springs using a valve spring compressor

11.6b Make sure the compressor is a good fit both on the top...

assembly **(see illustration)**. On the top of the valve the adaptor needs to be about the same size as the spring retainer – if it is too big it will contact the follower bore and mark it, and if it is too small it will be difficult to remove and install the collets **(see illustration)**. On the underside of the head make sure the plate (where present) on the compressor only contacts the valve and not the soft aluminium of the head **(see illustration)** – if the plate is too big for the valve, use a spacer between them. Do not compress the spring any more than is absolutely necessary.

7 Remove the collets using needle-nose pliers, tweezers, a magnet or a screwdriver with a dab of grease on it **(see illustration)**. Carefully release the valve spring compressor and remove the spring retainer, noting which way up it fits, the spring and the valve **(see illustrations)**. If the valve binds in the guide (won't pull through), push it back into the head and deburr the area around the collet groove with a very fine file or whetstone **(see illustration)**.

8 Pull the valve stem seal off the top of the valve guide with pliers and discard it (the old seals cannot be reused) **(see illustration)**. Remove the spring seat, noting which way up it fits – using a magnet is the easiest way to lift the seat off the head **(see illustration)**.

9 Repeat the procedure for the remaining

11.6c ...and the bottom of the valve assembly

11.7a Remove the collets with needle-nose pliers, tweezers, a magnet or a screwdriver with a dab of grease on it

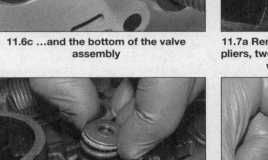

11.7b Remove the spring retainer and the spring...

11.7c ...then push the valve down and draw it out

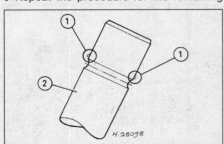

11.7d If the valve stem (2) won't pull through the guide, deburr the area above the collet groove (1)

11.8a Pull the seal off the top of the guide...

11.8b ...then remove the spring seat

11.15 Measure the valve seat width with a ruler (or for greater precision use a Vernier caliper)

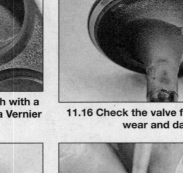

11.16 Check the valve face (arrowed) for wear and damage

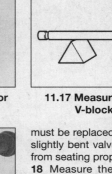

11.17 Measure valve stem runout with V-blocks and a dial gauge

11.18a Measure the valve stem diameter with a micrometer…

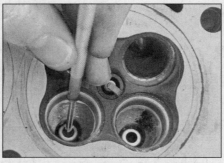

11.18b …and the guide bore width with a bore gauge

valves. Remember to keep the parts for each valve together and labelled so they can be reinstalled in the correct location.

10 Clean the cylinder head with solvent and dry it thoroughly. Compressed air will speed the drying process and ensure that all holes and recessed areas are clean. Do not use a wire brush mounted in a drill motor to clean the combustion chambers as the head material is soft and may be scratched or eroded away by the wire brush.

11 Clean the valve components with solvent and dry them thoroughly – clean the parts from one valve at a time so they don't get mixed up.

12 Scrape off any deposits that may have formed on the valves, using a motorised wire brush if available and necessary. Again, make sure the valves do not get mixed up.

Inspection

13 Inspect the head very carefully for cracks and other damage. If cracks are found, a new head is required. Check the camshaft bearing surfaces for wear and evidence of seizure. Check the camshafts and holders for wear as well (see Section 8).

14 Using a precision straight-edge and a feeler gauge, check the head gasket mating surface for warpage. Refer to *Tools and Workshop Tips* in the Reference section for details of how to use the straight-edge. If the head is warped beyond the limit specified at the beginning of this Chapter, consult your Yamaha dealer or take it to an engineer for correction.

15 Examine the valve seats in the combustion

chamber. If they are pitted, cracked or burned, the head will require work beyond the scope of the home mechanic. Measure the valve seat width and compare it to that given in the Specifications **(see illustration)**. If it is outside of the range, or if it varies around its circumference seek the advice of a Yamaha dealer or engineer.

16 Examine each valve face for cracks, pits and burned spots **(see illustration)**. Slight imperfections between the valve face and seat may be overcome by lapping the valve (see Steps 23 to 26).

17 Rotate the valve and check for any obvious indication that it is bent. Using V-blocks and a dial gauge if available, measure the valve stem runout and compare the results to the specifications at the beginning of this Chapter **(see illustration)**. If the measurement exceeds the service limit specified, the valve

must be replaced with a new one. Note that a slightly bent valve stem will prevent the valve from seating properly in the head.

18 Measure the valve stem diameter **(see illustration)**. Clean the valve guides to remove any carbon build-up, then measure the inside diameters of the guides (at both ends and the centre of the guide) with a small hole gauge and micrometer (see *Tools and Workshop Tips* in the Reference section) **(see illustration)**. Measure the guides at the ends and at the centre to determine if they are worn in a bell-mouth pattern (more wear at the ends). Subtract the stem diameter from the valve guide diameter to obtain the valve stem-to-guide clearance. If the stem-to-guide clearance is greater than given in the Specifications, replace whichever components are worn beyond their specified limits with new ones. If the valve guide is within specifications, but is worn unevenly, fit a new one.

Note: *Note that Yamaha recommend fitting a new valve guide whenever a new valve is fitted.*

19 Inspect the valve stem and collet groove area for scuffing and cracks **(see illustration)**. Check the end of the stem for pitting and wear.

20 Check the ends of each valve spring for wear. Measure the free length of each spring and compare it to that listed in the Specifications **(see illustration)**. If any spring is shorter than specified it has sagged, and it is advisable to replace all springs as a set. Also place the spring upright on a flat surface and check it for tilt by placing a ruler or

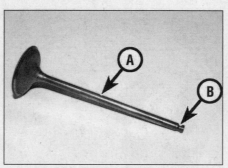

11.19 Check the stem (A) and collet groove (B)

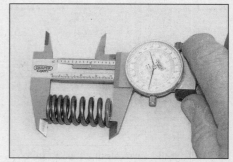

11.20a Measure spring free length with a Vernier caliper…

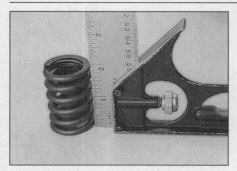

11.20b ...and check the spring is not bent

11.24 Apply small dabs of lapping compound to the valve face only

11.25 Rotate the tool back and forth between the palms of your hands

11.28a Fit the seat over the guide

11.28b Fit the valve stem seal – you can use the shaft of a screwdriver as a guide to locate the seal...

11.28c ... and the handle to push it on

engineer's square against it **(see illustration)**. If the tilt in any spring exceeds the limit given in the Specifications, it must be replaced with a new one.

21 Check the spring retainers and collets for obvious wear and cracks.

22 If the inspection indicates that no overhaul work is required, the valve components can be reinstalled in the head. Any questionable parts should not be reused, as extensive damage will occur in the event of failure during engine operation.

Reassembly

23 Before installing the valves in the head they should be lapped to ensure a positive seal between the valves and seats. If a valve service has been performed by someone else, and if the seats have been re-cut, ask the engineer if they should be lapped – he may have already done it, or might advise against it, depending on the work done. This procedure requires coarse and/or fine lapping compound (depending on the state of the seat) and a valve grinding tool (either hand-held or drill driven). If a grinding tool is not available, a piece of rubber or plastic hose can be slipped over the valve stem (after the valve has been installed in the guide) and used to turn the valve.

24 Apply a small amount of lapping compound to the valve face, starting with coarse paste if necessary, and finishing with fine paste **(see illustration)**. Smear some molybdenum disulphide oil (a 50/50 mixture of molybdenum disulphide grease and engine oil) to the valve stem, then slip the valve into the guide **(see illustration 11.7c)**. Make sure

each valve is installed in its correct guide and be careful not to get any lapping compound on the valve stem.

25 Attach the grinding tool to the valve and rotate the tool between the palms of your hands. Use a back-and-forth motion (as though rubbing your hands together) rather than a circular motion (i.e. so that the valve rotates alternately clockwise and anti-clockwise rather than in one direction only) **(see illustration)**. If a motorised tool is being used, take note of the correct drive speed for it – if your drill runs too fast and is not variable, use a hand tool instead. Lift the valve off the seat and turn it at regular intervals to distribute the lapping compound properly. Continue the procedure until the valve face and seat contact area is of uniform width, and unbroken around the entire circumference.

26 Carefully remove the valve from the guide and wipe off all traces of lapping compound. Use solvent to clean the valve and wipe the seat area thoroughly with a solvent soaked cloth.

27 Repeat the procedure for the remaining valves.

28 Working on one valve at a time, lay the spring seat in place in the cylinder head so that its shouldered side faces upwards **(see illustration)**. Fit a new valve stem seal onto the guide and use your fingers, an appropriate size deep socket or a small screwdriver as shown to press the seal over the end of the valve guide until it is felt to clip into place **(see illustrations)**. Don't twist or cock the seal, or it will not seal properly against the valve stem. Also, don't remove it again or it will be damaged.

29 Coat the valve stem with molybdenum disulphide oil, then slide it into its guide, rotating it slowly to avoid damaging the seal **(see illustration 11.7c)**. Check that the valve moves up and down freely in the guide. Next, fit the spring, with the closer-wound coils facing down into the cylinder head, then fit the spring retainer, with its shouldered side facing down so that it fits into the top of the spring **(see illustrations)**.

11.29a Fit the spring...

11.29b ... then fit the retainer

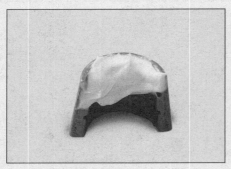

11.30a A small dab of grease will help to keep the collets in place on the valve while the spring is released

11.30b Seat the rib on the inner side of each collet into the groove in the valve stem

12.2 Turn the adjuster fully in then align the slots

30 Apply a small amount of grease to the inside of the collets to help stick them in place when fitting them on the valve stem **(see illustration)**. Compress the spring with the valve spring compressor **(see illustrations 11.6a, b and c)** – when compressing the spring, do so only as far as is necessary to slip the collets into place. Fit the collets with the thick end at the top and seat the ribs in the groove **(see illustration)**. Make certain that the collets are securely located in the groove, then release the spring compressor.
31 Repeat the procedure for the remaining valves. Remember to keep the parts for each valve together and separate from the other valves so they can be reinstalled in their original locations.
32 Support the cylinder head on blocks so the valves can't contact the workbench top,

then very gently tap the top of each valve stem to seat the collets in the groove.
33 After the camshafts have been installed, check the valve clearances (see Chapter 1).

12 Clutch cable

Removal

1 On MT-07TR models remove the fairing side panels and inner panels, and on XSR models remove the right-hand air scoop (see Chapter 7).
2 Turn the adjuster at the handlebar end of the cable fully into the lever bracket, then turn

it out to align the slot in the adjuster with that in the lever bracket **(see illustration)**.
3 Slacken the locknut securing the threaded section of the cable in the bracket on the engine, then push the cable in along the bracket until the adjuster nut is clear of the tab and lower the cable out of the bracket **(see illustrations)**. Bend the tab in the cable retainer on the end of the clutch release mechanism arm up, then release the cable end from the retainer, noting how it fits **(see illustrations)**.
4 At the handlebar end pull the outer cable from the socket in the adjuster and release the inner cable end from the lever **(see illustrations)**.
5 Remove the cable from the machine, releasing it from any ties and guides, and noting its routing.

12.3a Hold the adjuster nut (front) and slacken the locknut (rear)…

12.3b …then release the cable from the bracket

12.3c Bend up the tab in the cable retainer…

12.3d …and release the cable end

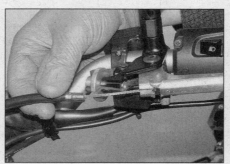

12.4a Release the cable from the adjuster…

12.4b …and the lever

12.6 Bend the retainer tab down

Installation

6 Installation is the reverse of removal. Apply grease to the cable ends and make sure the cable is correctly routed. After connecting the cable end to the release arm pull the cable forwards in the engine bracket to take up most, but not all, of the excess slack, then thread the adjuster nut down and seat it against the

tab and tighten the locknut up against the rear of the bracket **(see illustrations 12.3d, b and a)**. Bend the tab in the retainer on the release mechanism arm down to secure the cable end **(see illustration)**.

7 Adjust the clutch lever freeplay (see Chapter 1).

13 Clutch

Special tool: *A clutch centre holding tool is useful, although not essential – see Step 12.*

Removal

1 If the bike is upright on an auxiliary stand, drain the engine oil (see Chapter 1) – if the bike is on its sidestand there is no need.

2 Drain the cooling system (see Chapter 1).

3 Unscrew the water pump cover bolts and the bolt securing the pipes to the clutch cover, and displace the pump cover, securing it clear

of the clutch cover using a cable-tie around the exhaust **(see illustration)**. Remove the O-ring **(see illustration 13.38)** – a new one must be used. Remove the locating pin if loose **(see illustration)**.

4 Refer to Step 3 in Section 12 and disconnect the clutch cable.

5 Working evenly in a criss-cross pattern, unscrew the clutch cover bolts, noting the positions of the clutch cable bracket and the oxygen sensor wiring clamps **(see illustration)**.

6 Remove the cover, being prepared to catch any residual oil **(see illustration)**. If the cover will not lift away easily, break the gasket seal by tapping gently around the edge with a soft-faced hammer or block of wood.

7 Remove the cover gasket – a new one must be fitted. Note the position of the two dowels and remove them if they are loose – they could be in either the cover or the crankcase **(see illustration 13.35a)**.

8 Working in a criss-cross pattern, gradually slacken the clutch spring bolts until spring

13.3a Unscrew the bolts (arrowed) and displace the pump cover and pipe assembly

13.3b Pump cover locating pin (arrowed)

13.5 Clutch cover bolts (arrowed)

13.6 Remove the cover

13.8 Remove the clutch bolts and springs...

13.9 ...and the pressure plate

13.11 Unstake the rim of the nut...

13.12 ...then unscrew it as described

pressure is released, counter-holding the clutch using a rag (see illustration). Remove the bolts and springs.

9 Remove the pressure plate (see illustration). Remove the pull-rod from the pressure plate bearing.

10 Remove the clutch plates (see Step 32) – unless the plates are being replaced with new ones, keep them in their original order. Note that the outermost (type 1) friction plate perimeter tabs locate in the slots offset from the others in the clutch housing, and that the outer and innermost have different friction pad faces to the other five (type 2) plates.

11 Use a small pointed tool to unstake the rim of the clutch nut from the indent in the end of the shaft (see illustration).

12 To unscrew the clutch nut, the transmission input shaft must be locked. This can be done by selecting top gear and having an assistant hold the brakes on hard with the rear tyre in firm contact with the ground. Alternatively, the Yamaha service tool Pt. No. 90890-04086 (European models) or YM-91042 (US models) or a similar commercially available tool, can be

used to hold the clutch centre while the nut is loosened. With the clutch held, unscrew the nut and remove the washers (see illustration). A new nut should be used on reassembly.

13 Slide the clutch centre and the thrust washer off the input shaft (see illustrations 13.31a and 13.30).

14 Note how the primary driven gear on the clutch housing engages with the primary drive gear on the crankshaft. Note also the run of the oil pump drive chain behind the clutch

housing – the chain loops round a sprocket on the back of the clutch housing.

15 Ease out the bearing centre and needle bearing from between the clutch housing and the input shaft – this can be done using a magnet and/or by sliding the housing on the shaft to help push them along (see illustration).

16 Disengage the chain from the oil pump sprocket and remove the clutch housing (see illustration).

17 Slide the thrust washer off the shaft (see illustrations 13.28).

13.15 Ease the bearing centre and bearing out

13.16 Slip the chain off and remove the housing

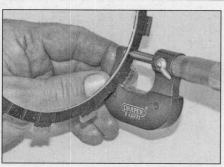

13.18 Measuring clutch friction plate thickness

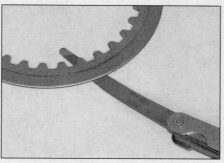

13.19 Checking the plain plates for warpage

13.20 Measure the free length of the clutch springs

13.21a Check for wear of the friction plate tabs and the clutch housing slots...

13.21b ...and of the plain plate tongues and clutch centre slots

13.22 Inspect the needle bearing, the bearing centre and the bearing surface in the housing

Inspection

18 After an extended period of service the clutch friction plates will wear and promote clutch slip. Measure the thickness of each friction plate using a Vernier caliper **(see illustration)**. If any plate has worn to or beyond the service limit given in the Specifications, the friction plates must be replaced with a new set. Also, if any of the plates smell burnt or are glazed, they must be replaced as a set.

19 The plain plates should not show any signs of excess heating (bluing). Check for warpage using a flat surface and feeler gauges **(see illustration)**. If any plate exceeds the maximum amount of warpage given in the Specifications, or shows signs of bluing, all the plain plates must be replaced with a new set.

20 Measure the free length of each clutch spring **(see illustration)**. If any spring is below

the service limit given in the Specifications, replace all the springs with a new set.

21 Inspect the friction plate tabs and the clutch housing slots for burrs and indentations **(see illustration)**. Similarly check for wear between the inner teeth of the plain plates and the slots in the clutch centre **(see illustration)**. Wear of this nature will cause clutch drag and slow disengagement during gear changes as the plates will snag when the pressure plate is lifted. With care a small amount of wear can be corrected by dressing with a fine file, but if this is excessive the worn components should be replaced with new ones.

22 Inspect the needle roller bearing, the internal bearing surface of the clutch housing and the external surface of the bearing centre **(see illustration)**. If there are any signs of wear, pitting or other damage the affected parts must be replaced with new ones.

23 Check the teeth of the primary driven gear on the clutch housing and the corresponding teeth of the primary drive gear on the end of the crankshaft **(see illustration)**. Replace the clutch housing with a new one if any teeth are worn or chipped. The primary drive gear is an integral part of the crankshaft (see Section 24 for removal of the crankshaft).

24 Check the teeth of the oil pump drive sprocket on the back of the clutch housing **(see illustration 13.23)**. If any are worn or chipped, fit a new housing, and check the driven sprocket on the oil pump and the chain (Section 18).

25 Check the pressure plate and its bearing for signs of wear or damage and roughness **(see illustration)**. Check the pull-rod teeth for signs of wear or damage, and check the corresponding teeth on the release shaft in the cover **(see illustration)**. Replace any

13.23 Check the primary driven gear and oil pump drive sprocket

13.25a Check the pressure plate and bearing

13.25b Check the teeth on the pull-rod and shaft

13.26a Remove the E-clip and washer...

13.26b ...then withdraw the shaft

13.26c Lever the seal out...

13.26d ...and check the bearings (arrowed)

13.26e Circlip (arrowed) secures the arm on the shaft

13.26f Push the seal in, setting it flush

13.26g Fit the washer then slide the E-clip into the groove

parts, as necessary, with new ones, referring to the next Step for the shaft. To remove the pressure plate bearing drive it out from the outside using a socket. Drive the new bearing in from the inside using a socket that bears on the outer race until it seats.

26 Check the clutch release mechanism shaft turns smoothly in its housing in the cover. If it is rough, release the E-clip and remove the washer from the bottom of the shaft and draw the shaft out of the cover, noting how the return spring ends locate **(see illustrations)**. Remove the oil seal (a new one will be required), and clean and check the bearings **(see illustrations)**. Replace the bearings with new ones if necessary, referring to *Tools and Workshop Tips*. If the shaft teeth are worn mark the alignment of the release arm on the shaft, then release the circlip from the top and remove the washer, the arm and the spring **(see illustration)**. On reassembly fit the arm onto the shaft with the UP mark facing up, aligning it as marked on removal, fit the washer, and use a new circlip if required. Lubricate the bearings with engine oil. Fit a new oil seal with its marked side facing out, and lubricate its lip with grease **(see illustration)**. Slide the shaft in, fit the washer and the E-clip, and make sure the spring ends locate correctly **(see illustration)**.

Installation

27 Remove all traces of old gasket from the crankcase and clutch cover surfaces.

28 Slide the thrust washer onto the transmission input shaft **(see illustrations)**. Loop the chain around the oil pump drive sprocket on the back of the clutch housing. Slide the clutch housing onto the shaft and loop the oil pump chain around the sprocket on the pump, and make sure each run of the chain seats in the guide **(see illustrations 13.16)**.

29 Lubricate the needle roller bearing and the bearing centre with clean engine oil. Support the clutch housing and engage the primary driven and drive gears, then slide the bearing and the bearing centre onto the shaft and into the housing **(see illustration)**.

30 Lubricate the thrust washer with clean engine oil and slide it onto the shaft **(see illustration)**.

13.28 Fit the thrust washer

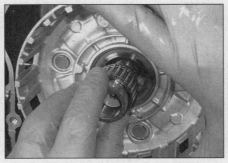

13.29 Centre the housing and insert the bearing and centre

13.30 Fit the thrust washer

13.31a Fit the clutch centre...

13.31b ... the washers ...

13.31c ... and a new clutch nut

13.31d Tighten the nut to the specified torque ...

31 Slide the clutch centre onto the shaft splines **(see illustration)**. Fit the thrust washer, then lubricate the spring washer with oil and fit it with the OUT mark facing out **(see illustration)**. Lubricate the new clutch centre nut threads with oil and fit it with the thin rim facing out, then lock the input shaft as before (see Step 12) and tighten the nut to 95 Nm **(see illustrations)**. Check that the clutch centre rotates freely after tightening the nut. Stake the rim of the nut into the indents in the end of the shaft **(see illustration)**.

32 If new clutch plates are being fitted, or if the order of the old clutch plate pack has been muddled up, first identify the two type 1 friction plates that have different friction pad faces to the five type 2 plates **(see illustration)** – the type 1 plates fit first and last

13.31e ... then stake the rim into the indent

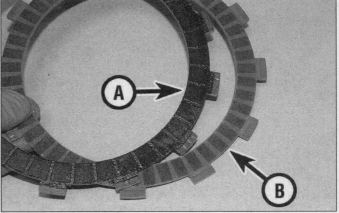

13.32a Type 1 plate (A), type 2 plate (B)

13.32b Fit a type 1 friction plate …

13.32c …then a plain plate…

so they are offset from the other friction plate tabs **(see illustrations)**.

33 Lubricate the bearing in the pressure plate with clean engine oil, then fit the pull-rod. Fit the pressure plate, locating the castellations in its rim into the slots in the clutch centre **(see illustration 13.9)**.

34 Fit the clutch springs and bolts, then hold the clutch housing and tighten the bolts evenly and a little at a time in a criss-cross sequence to 8 Nm **(see illustration 13.8)**.

35 If removed, fit the dowels into the crankcase. Fit the new gasket onto the dowels **(see illustration)**. Align the pull-rod so its teeth point back **(see illustration)**.

36 Align the slot in the water pump impeller shaft with the tab on the oil pump sprocket, and set the release shaft arm so that it points slightly back, then fit the cover, pushing the arm in as you do once the teeth engage

(innermost and outermost). Coat each plate with clean engine oil prior to installation. Build up the plates, starting with a type 1 friction plate and aligning its tabs with the deep

slots, then a plain plate, then alternate type 2 friction plates and plain plates until all are fitted, then lastly fit the second type 1 friction plate, aligning its tabs with the shallow slots

13.32d … then a type 2 friction plate, and so on as described

13.32e Fit the outer type 1 friction plate tabs into the offset shallow slots

13.35a Fit a new gasket onto the dowels (arrowed)

13.35b Point the pull-rod teeth as shown

13.36a Align the slot with the tab …

13.36b … position the release arm as shown and fit the cover as described

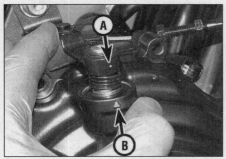

13.36c Push the arm in and check the punch mark (A) and triangular mark (B) align

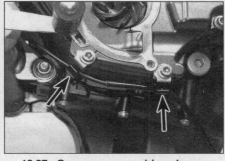
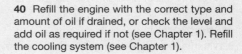

13.37a Oxygen sensor wiring clamps (arrowed)

13.37b Clutch cable bracket

(see illustrations). Check that the cover is located on the dowels and is seated all round, then push the release arm in until it stops and check that the punch mark on the lever aligns with the mark on the shaft casing (see illustration) – if it doesn't, draw the cover off, realign the arm/shaft as required, and refit the cover, checking again that the marks align.

37 Clean the threads of the two clutch cover bolts that secure the cable bracket, and apply some threadlock. Fit the cover bolts, securing the oxygen sensor wiring clamps and the cable bracket, and tighten the bolts evenly in a criss-cross sequence to 12 Nm (see illustrations).

38 Fit the pump cover locating pin if removed (see illustration 13.3b). Fit a new water pump cover O-ring into its groove (see illustration). Clean the threads of the cover bolts and apply some threadlock. Fit the cover and tighten the bolts to 10 Nm (see illustration 13.3a). Fit and tighten the pipe bolt.

39 Connect the clutch cable (Section 12), then adjust it (see Chapter 1).

40 Refill the engine with the correct type and amount of oil if drained, or check the level and add oil as required if not (see Chapter 1). Refill the cooling system (see Chapter 1).

14 Starter clutch and gears

Check

1 The operation of the starter clutch can be checked while it is in place – remove the alternator cover (see Chapter 8). Withdraw the idle/reduction gear shaft and remove the gear (see illustration 14.4), then check that the starter driven gear (on the back of the alternator rotor) is able to rotate freely clockwise as you look at it from the left-hand side of the bike, but locks when rotated anti-clockwise (see illustration). If not, the starter clutch is faulty and should be removed for inspection.

Removal

2 Remove the alternator cover (see Chapter 8).

13.38 Use a new O-ring

14.1 Check the gear rotates clockwise and locks anti-clockwise

14.3 Remove the torque limiter…

14.4 … and the idle/reduction gear

14.6 Check the gear rotates anti-clockwise and locks clockwise, as viewed from above

14.7 Check the sprags in the clutch and the driven gear hub

14.8 Starter clutch bolts (arrowed)

14.9 Check the bush (arrowed) for wear

3 Remove the starter torque limiter **(see illustration)**.
4 Withdraw the idle/reduction gear shaft from the crankcase and remove the gear **(see illustration)**.
5 Remove the alternator rotor (see Chapter 8) – the starter clutch is mounted on the back of it.

Inspection

6 With the alternator rotor face down, check that the starter driven gear rotates smoothly and freely in an anti-clockwise direction and locks solid against the rotor in a clockwise direction **(see illustration)**.
7 Remove the driven gear from the clutch **(see illustration 14.12)**. Inspect the condition of the sprags in the clutch and the outer surface of the driven gear hub **(see illustration)**. If there is wear or damage or it does not operate as described in Step 6 fit a new starter clutch.

8 To remove the starter clutch from the rotor, hold the rotor using a rotor strap and unscrew the clutch bolts **(see illustration)**.
9 Inspect the bush in the driven gear and its bearing surface on the crankshaft for signs of wear and scoring **(see illustration)**. If the bush is worn, evident by the lack of oil retention grooves, replace the gear with a new one.
10 Inspect the teeth on the starter motor shaft, the torque limiter, the idle/reduction gear and the starter driven gear for wear and damage. Check the idle/reduction gear shaft and the bores it runs in, and the torque limiter shaft ends, the needle bearing in the crankcase **(see illustration 14.3)** and the ball bearing in the cover **(see illustration)**. Fit new parts if required.

Installation

11 Clean the starter clutch bolt threads and apply a drop of locking compound. Fit the

clutch onto the back of the alternator rotor with the arrow facing the rotor, then tighten the bolts to 32 Nm, holding the rotor as before **(see illustration 14.8)**.
12 Lubricate the starter driven gear hub with clean engine oil, then fit it into the starter clutch, rotating it anti-clockwise to spread the sprags and allow the hub to enter **(see illustration)**. Check the operation of the starter clutch as described in Step 6.
13 Install the alternator (see Chapter 8).
14 Lubricate the idle/reduction gear shaft with clean engine oil. Position the gear with the smaller pinion facing in, and mesh the teeth with the teeth of the starter driven gear, then insert the shaft **(see illustration 14.4)**.
15 Lubricate the torque limiter bearings in the crankcase and alternator cover with oil then fit the torque limiter, meshing its teeth with the idle/reduction gear and the starter motor shaft **(see illustration 14.3)**.
16 Install the alternator cover (see Chapter 8).

15 Gearchange mechanism

Gearchange shaft oil seal

1 If there is oil leakage from the left-hand end of the gearchage shaft a new seal can be fitted without removing the shaft – refer to Steps 3 and 4 and displace the gearchange linkage arm and remove the E-clip and washer. Lever out the old seal with a small flat-bladed

14.10 Torque limiter ball bearing (arrowed)

14.12 Rotate the gear anti-clockwise as you fit the hub into the clutch

15.1a Lever out the old seal…

15.1b … and push the new one in

15.3 Note the alignment then remove the
pinch bolt and slide the arm off

15.4 Release the clip and remove the
washer

15.6a Unhook the spring…

15.6b …and withdraw the shaft

screwdriver (see illustration). Grease the lips of the new seal, then push it squarely into place, with its marked side facing out, using your fingers or a blunt drift, until it seats, at which point its outer face should be recessed from the end of the housing by 0.6 to 1.1 mm (see illustration).

Removal

2 Remove the clutch (Section 13). If a gear was selected to unscrew the clutch nut, shift the transmission back to neutral.
3 Note the alignment of the line on the gearchange shaft with the punch mark on the gearchange linkage arm, then unscrew the

pinch bolt and slide the arm off the shaft (see illustration).
4 Release the E-clip and remove the washer from the left-hand end of the shaft (see illustration).
5 Note how the gearchange shaft centralising spring ends fit on each side of the locating pin in the crankcase, how the pawls on the selector arm locate onto the pins on the end of the selector drum, how the stopper arm spring locates, and how the roller on the stopper arm locates in the neutral detent on the selector drum (see illustration 15.15b).
6 Unhook the stopper arm spring from its anchor pin, then withdraw the gearchange

shaft assembly (see illustrations). Check whether the washer is on the inner end of the shaft as you remove the assembly – it may stick to the crankcase wall, in which case remove it and slide it onto the shaft.

Inspection

7 Inspect the splines on the end of the gearchange shaft; if they are worn or damaged, or if the shaft is bent, fit a new one.
8 Check the shaft selector arm for cracks, distortion and wear of its pawls, and check for any corresponding wear on the selector pins on the selector drum (see illustrations). Check the stopper arm roller and the detents

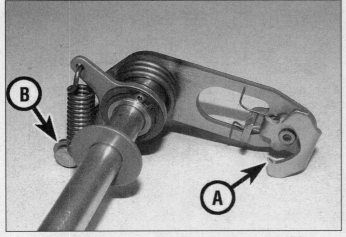

15.8a Selector arm pawls (A), stopper arm roller (B)

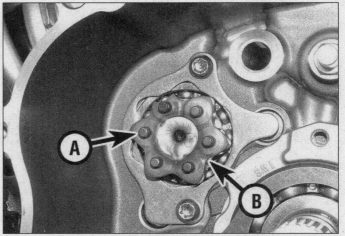

15.8b Selector drum pins (A) and detents (B)

15.9a Centralising spring (A), stopper arm spring (B)

15.9b Check the action of the pawl plate

15.10 Release the circlip (arrowed) to disassemble the shaft

15.11 Check the locating pin (arrowed)

in the selector drum for any wear or damage, and make sure the roller turns freely. Replace any components that are worn or damaged with new ones.

9 Inspect the centralising spring, the stopper arm return spring and the pawl plate spring for fatigue, wear or damage, and make sure the plate turns freely and returns to the centre **(see illustrations)**. If any faults are found, replace the components with new ones. Note

how the ends of the centralising spring locate each side of the tab on the selector arm.

10 To disassemble the shaft, slide the washer off, then remove the circlip, the second washer and the stopper arm **(see illustration)**. Slide the collar off, then the centralising spring. Reassemble in reverse order, making sure the centralising spring ends seat on each side of the tab, and fit the long end of the collar between the spring and the shaft. Make sure

the stopper arm is the correct way round. It is advisable to use a new circlip, and make sure it is seated in the groove.

11 Check that the centralising spring locating pin in the crankcase is tight **(see illustration)**. If it is loose, remove it, clean the threads and apply a non-permanent thread locking compound, then tighten it to 22 Nm.

12 Check the condition of the gearchange shaft oil seal and bearing in the crankcase – it is wise to fit a new seal if the shaft is removed. Lever out the old seal with a flat-bladed screwdriver or seal hook **(see illustration 15.1a)**. If the bearing is damaged or does not run smoothly and freely fit a new one (see *Tools and Workshop Tips* in the Reference section) – make sure the bearing is fully seated in its bore so its outer end does not protrude into the seal housing. Lubricate the bearing with engine oil. Push the new seal squarely into place, with its marked side facing out, using your fingers or a suitable socket, until it seats, at which point its outer face should be recessed from the end of the housing by 0.6 to 1.1 mm **(see illustration 15.1b)**. Grease the lips of the seal.

Installation

13 Lubricate the gearchange shaft with engine oil. If removed, slide the washer onto the shaft, and fit the stopper arm spring onto the stopper arm **(see illustration 15.8a)**.

14 Slide the gearchange shaft assembly into the crankcase, lifting the stopper arm onto the neutral detent on the top of the selector drum, making sure that the centralising spring ends fit on each side of the locating pin and that the selector arm pawls engage the pins on the selector drum **(see illustration 15.6b)**.

15 Hook the stopper arm spring over its anchor pin **(see illustration)**. Check that everything is correctly positioned **(see illustration)**.

16 Fit the washer onto the left-hand end of

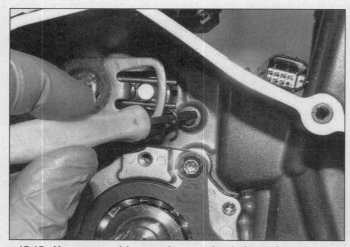

15.15a Use a screwdriver as shown to hook the spring over the pin

15.15b Check that everything is correctly in place

15.16 Slide the washer on and fit the E-clip into the groove

16.2a Release the clamps...

16.2b ...and pull the hoses off

the shaft, then slide the E-clip into its groove **(see illustration)**.

17 Fit the gearchange linkage arm, aligning the punch mark with the line on the shaft, and tighten the pinch bolt **(see illustration 15.3)**.

18 Check the gearchange mechanism by raising the rear wheel off the ground, and spinning it forwards by hand while selecting each gear in turn, then back to neutral.

19 Install the clutch (Section 13).

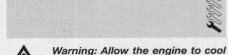

16 Oil cooler

⚠ *Warning: Allow the engine to cool completely before starting work.*

Removal

1 The cooler is located on the front of the engine. Drain the engine oil and remove the filter, and drain the coolant (see Chapter 1) – do not refit the coolant reservoir after draining it. Leave a drain tray under the cooler to catch residual oil and coolant as the cooler is removed.

2 Release the clamps securing the coolant inlet and outlet hoses to the oil cooler and slide them along the hoses, then pull the hoses off **(see illustrations)**.

3 Unscrew the bolt and remove the cooler **(see illustration)**.

4 Remove the O-ring from the cooler body – a new one must be used **(see illustration)**.

5 Check the cooler body for cracks and dents and any evidence of coolant leaking and fit a new one if necessary. Also check the hoses for splits, cracks, hardening and deterioration.

Installation

6 Installation is the reverse of removal, noting the following:

● Clean the mating surfaces of the crankcase and the cooler with a rag and solvent.
● Lubricate the new body O-ring with grease and seat it in the groove in the cooler body **(see illustration 16.4)**.
● Lubricate the bolt with oil. Seat the tab on the rim of the cooler in the cut-out in the crankcase and tighten the bolt to 40 Nm **(see illustration 16.3)**.
● Make sure the coolant hoses are pressed fully onto their unions and secured by the clamps **(see illustrations 16.2b and a)**.
● Install the coolant reservoir (see Chapter 3).
● Fit a new oil filter and refill the engine with oil and the cooling system with coolant, both to the correct levels (see Chapter 1).
● Start the engine and check that there are no leaks before taking the machine on the road.

17 Oil sump and oil strainer

Removal

1 Drain the engine oil (see Chapter 1). Remove the exhaust system (see Chapter 4).

2 Unscrew the sump bolts, slackening them evenly in a criss-cross sequence, and remove

16.3 Unscrew the bolt and remove the cooler, noting how the tab (A) locates in the cut-out (B)

16.4 Remove the O-ring

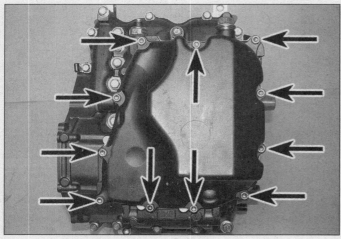

17.2 Sump bolts (arrowed)

17.3 Remove the strainer

the sump (see illustration). If necessary, break the gasket seal by tapping gently around the edge of the sump with a soft-faced hammer or block of wood; do not lever the sump off as this will damage the sealing surface. Remove the gasket – a new one must be used.

3 Unscrew the oil strainer bolts and remove the strainer (see illustration). Remove the O-ring (see illustration 17.6a) – a new one must be used. Note the collar in the rubber grommet (see illustration 17.6b).

Inspection

4 Remove all traces of gasket from the sump and crankcase mating surfaces, and clean the

inside of the sump with a suitable solvent.

5 Clean the strainer in solvent, flushing it through from the inside, and remove any debris caught in the mesh (see illustration). Check the mesh for any signs of wear or damage and fit a new strainer if necessary. Check the condition of the rubber grommet and fit a new one if necessary (see illustration 17.6b).

Installation

6 Lubricate the new O-ring for the oil strainer with grease and fit it into the oil passage (see illustration). Clean the threads of the strainer bolts and apply some fresh threadlock. Make sure the grommet is in place and the collar

is in it (see illustration). Fit the strainer and tighten the bolts to 10 Nm (see illustration 17.3).

7 Lay a new gasket onto the sump (if the engine is in the frame) or onto the crankcase (if the engine has been removed and is upside down on the work surface) (see illustration). Make sure the holes in the gasket align correctly with the bolt holes – if the engine is in the frame insert two bolts into the sump and through the gasket to keep it aligned.

8 Position the sump on the crankcase and finger-tighten all bolts (see illustration). Tighten the bolts evenly and a little at a time in a criss-cross pattern to 10 Nm (see illustration 17.2).

9 Install the exhaust system (see Chapter 4).

10 Fill the engine with the correct type and quantity of oil (see Chapter 1).

11 Start the engine and check that there are no leaks around the sump before taking the bike on the road.

18 Oil pump

Removal

1 Remove the clutch (Section 13).

2 Unscrew the pump bracket bolt and

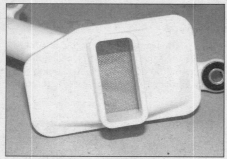

17.5 Clean and check the strainer mesh

17.6a Lubricate the new O-ring and fit it into the groove.

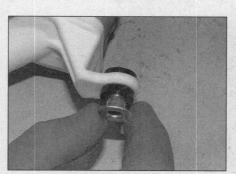

17.6b Make sure the collar is fitted

17.7 Use a new gasket, aligning it with the sump bolt holes

17.8 Keep the gasket aligned when fitting the sump and inserting the bolts

18.2a Unscrew the bolts and remove the bracket...

18.2b ...and the pump

18.3 Undo the screw and remove the cover, noting the locating dowels

mounting bolts and remove the pump and bracket **(see illustrations)**.

Inspection

3 Unscrew the oil pump cover screw and remove the cover from the rotor housing **(see illustration)**. Remove the locating dowels if loose.

4 Remove the inner and outer rotors, noting how they fit **(see illustrations)**.

5 Withdraw the pin from the drive shaft and remove the washer, then withdraw the sprocket and shaft from the pump **(see illustrations)**.

6 Clean all components in solvent. Check that the oilways in the body are clear by blowing them through with compressed air.

7 Inspect the rotors and pump housing for scoring and wear. If any damage, scoring or uneven or excessive wear is evident, replace the pump with a new one – individual components are not available.

18.4a Remove the outer rotor...

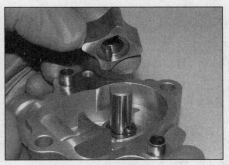

18.4b ... and the inner rotor

8 Reassemble the shaft and rotors in the housing (see Step 11, but do not lubricate the parts), then measure the clearance between the outer rotor and housing with a feeler gauge and compare it to the maximum clearance

listed in the Specifications **(see illustration)**. If the clearance measured exceeds the service limit, fit a new pump.

9 Position the inner rotor as shown and measure the clearance between the inner rotor tip and the outer rotor with a feeler gauge and compare it to the maximum clearance given in the Specifications **(see illustration)**. If the clearance measured exceeds the service limit, fit a new pump.

10 Check the pump driven sprocket and the chain for wear or damage. Also check the condition of the drive sprocket on the back of the clutch housing **(see illustration 13.23)**.

11 If the pump is good, make sure all the components are clean, then lubricate them with clean engine oil. Insert the shaft then fit the washer and slide the drive pin into the hole **(see illustrations 18.5c, b and a)** – keep the pin horizontal and with an equal amount

18.5a Remove the drive pin ...

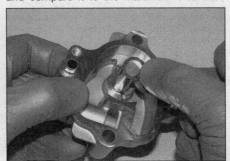

18.5b ... and washer...

18.5c ... and withdraw the sprocket/shaft

18.8 Measure the outer rotor to housing clearance as shown

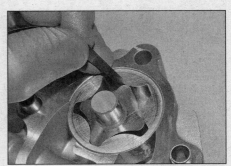

18.9 Measure the inner rotor tip to outer rotor clearance as shown

18.14a Release the circlip…

18.14b … and remove the spring seat…

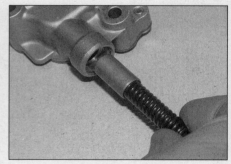

18.14c … and the spring and plunger

protruding from each end of the hole. Fit the inner rotor with its slots facing in and seated over the drive pin ends **(see illustration 18.4b)**. Fit the outer rotor into the pump **(see illustration 18.4a)**.

12 Fit the locating dowels if removed. Fit the cover and tighten the screw to 4 Nm **(see illustration 18.3)**.

13 Rotate the pump by hand and check that the rotors turn freely. If not, strip and reassemble the pump.

14 Release the pressure relief valve circlip, noting that it is under spring pressure, and remove the spring seat, spring and plunger **(see illustrations)**. Clean all the components in solvent and check them for scoring, wear or damage. If any is found, replace the pump with a new one – individual components are not available. Otherwise, coat the inside of the valve body and the plunger with clean engine oil, then insert the plunger and spring, then fit the spring seat with its flat side facing out so the dished inner side seats over the spring, and secure them with a new circlip.

Installation

15 Before fitting the pump, prime it with clean engine oil.

16 Clean the threads of the bracket bolt and apply some threadlock. Fit the pump and the bracket and tighten the pump bolts to 12 Nm and the bracket bolt to 10 Nm **(see illustrations 18.2b and a)**.

17 Install the clutch (Section 13).

18 Fill the engine with the specified quantity and type of engine oil (see Chapter 1).

19 Crankcase separation and reassembly

Note: *On reassembly new crankcase bolts Nos. 1 to 8 must be used. It is wise to obtain them in advance.*

Separation

1 To gain access to the connecting rods, pistons and rings, crankshaft, balancer shaft, transmission shafts, selector drum and forks, and all related bearings, the crankcase must be split into two parts.

2 Remove the engine from the frame (Section 4).

3 Before the separating the crankcases for a full engine strip remove the following components. Note that not all components need be removed for access to the transmission and selector assemblies – see Section 26and Section 28 and.
● Camshafts and cam chain tensioner (Section 7 and Section 8)
● Cylinder head (Section 10)
● Alternator rotor (Chapter 8)

● Starter motor (Chapter 8)
● Cam chain and blades (Section 9)
● Clutch (Section 13)
● Gearchange mechanism (Section 15)
● Oil filter (see Chapter 1) and cooler (Section 16)
● Oil sump and strainer (Section 17)
● Oil pump (Section 18)

4 Remove the balancer shaft end cap **(see illustration 19.21)** – a new gasket must be used.

5 Turn the engine upside down. The crankcases are joined by six M9 (9mm thread diameter) bolts (Nos. 1 to 6), eight M8 (8mm thread diameter) bolts (Nos. 7 to 14), and thirteen M6 (6mm thread diameter) bolts (Nos. 15 to 27) **(see illustration 19.18a)**. The number of each bolt from 1 to 16 is cast into the crankcase near the bolt head **(see illustration)**. First unscrew the M6 bolts (15 to 27) without a cast number a quarter turn at a time in any order. Next unscrew all the remaining bolts a quarter turn at a time in a reverse of the bolt numbering sequence (i.e. from 14 to 1), until they are finger-tight, then remove them – as there are many different types and length of bolt it is best to store them in a cardboard template of the crankcase to ensure correct installation **(see illustration)**. Note the washers fitted to bolts Nos. 1 to 6 – these bolts must be replaced with new ones.

19.5a Numbers are marked on the crankcase for bolts 1 to 16

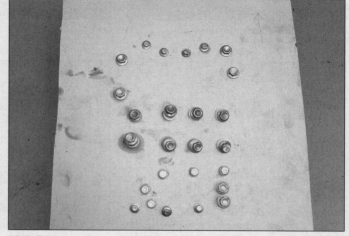

19.5b Example of a cardboard template for storing the crankcase bolts

19.6 Lift the lower half of the crankcase off the upper half

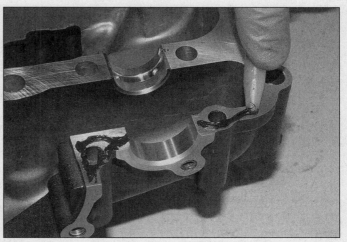

19.12a Apply the sealant…

19.12b …as shown

19.13 Fit the dowels (arrowed) if removed

Note the O-rings fitted with the M8 bolts Nos. 7 to 12.

6 Carefully lift the lower crankcase half off the upper half, using a soft-faced hammer or block of wood to tap around the joint to initially separate the halves, if necessary **(see illustration)**. If the halves do not separate easily, make sure all fasteners have been removed. Do not try and separate the halves by levering between the sealing surfaces as they are easily damaged and will leak oil on reassembly.

7 Remove the three locating dowels from the crankcase (they could be in either half) **(see illustration 19.13)**.

8 Refer to Sections 20 to 28 for the removal and installation of the components housed within the crankcases.

Reassembly

9 Remove all traces of old sealant from the crankcase mating surfaces.

10 Check that all components and their bearings are in place in the upper and lower crankcase halves. If the transmission shafts have not been removed, remove the oil seal from the left-hand end of the output shaft and fit a new one – apply some grease to its lip **(see illustration 26.10)**. Check that the selector drum is in the neutral position.

11 Generously lubricate the crankshaft, balancer shaft, transmission shafts and selector drum and forks, particularly around the bearings, with clean engine oil, then use a rag soaked in high flash-point solvent to wipe over the mating surfaces of both crankcase halves to remove all traces of oil.

12 Apply a small amount of suitable sealant (such as Yamaha Bond 1215) to the mating surface of one crankcase half as shown **(see illustrations)**.

Caution: Do not apply an excessive amount of sealant as it will ooze out when the case halves are assembled and may obstruct oil passages. Do not apply the sealant on or too close (within 2 to 3 mm) to any of the bearing shells or surfaces.

13 If removed, fit the three locating dowels into the crankcase **(see illustration)**.

14 Check again that all components are in position, particularly that the bearing shells are located in their seats in the lower crankcase half. Fit the lower crankcase half onto the upper crankcase half, making sure the dowels locate correctly **(see illustration 19.6)**.

15 Check that the lower crankcase half is seated all the way round. The crankcase halves should fit together without being forced. If the casings are not correctly seated, remove the lower crankcase half and investigate the problem. Do not attempt to pull them together using the crankcase bolts as the casing could crack and be ruined.

16 Clean the threads of the crankcase bolts before fitting them, and lubricate the threads and under the heads of all bolts, the washers of the new bolts Nos. 1 to 6, and the new

19.16 Seat the new O-rings under the heads of bolts 7 to 12

19.17a You must use new M9 bolts with fitted washers

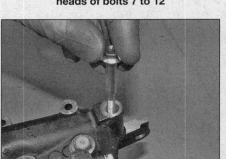

19.17b Fit thick-shanked M6 bolts in the wide holes numbered 15...

19.17c ... and 16

that if the tightening angle is exceeded on any bolt a new bolt must be fitted.

19 Now tighten the M8 bolts 7 to 14, evenly and a little at a time, in the correct numerical sequence, to 24 Nm **(see illustration 19.18a)**. Next tighten the M6 bolts 15 and 16 to 10 Nm. Finally tighten the remaining M6 bolts 17 to 27 in a criss-cross sequence to 10 Nm.

20 With all crankcase bolts tightened, check that the crankshaft and transmission shafts rotate smoothly and easily. Check that all gears can be selected and that the shafts rotate freely in every gear. If there are any signs of undue stiffness, rough spots, or of any other problem, the fault must be rectified before proceeding further.

21 Clean the threads of the balancer shaft end cap bolts, then apply some fresh threadlock. Fit the cap using a new gasket and tighten the bolts to 12 Nm **(see illustration)**.

22 Install all the removed assemblies in the reverse order of removal.

20 Main and big-end bearing information

1 Even though main and connecting rod bearings are generally replaced with new ones during an engine overhaul, the old bearings should be carefully examined as they can reveal valuable information about the condition of the engine.

2 Bearing failure occurs mainly because of lack of lubrication, the presence of dirt or other foreign particles, overloading the engine and/or corrosion. Regardless of the cause of bearing failure, it must be corrected before the engine is reassembled to prevent it from happening again.

3 When examining the bearings, match them with their corresponding journal on the crankshaft to help identify the cause of any problem.

4 Dirt and other foreign particles get into the engine in a variety of ways. They may be left in the engine during assembly or they may pass through filters or breathers, then get into the oil and from there into the bearings. Metal chips from machining operations and normal engine wear are often present.

O-rings for bolts Nos. 7 to 12, with clean engine oil **(see illustration)**.

17 Fit the bolts in their correct locations according to your template and secure them finger-tight. If you didn't make a template fit the bolts as follows:

● M9 bolts – fit the six bolts with washers in positions 1 to 6 **(see illustration and 19.18a)**.

● M8 bolts – fit the six 70mm bolts with O-rings in positions 7 to 12, and the two 65mm bolts in positions 13 and 14 **(see illustration 19.18a)**.

● M6 bolts – fit the two 65mm bolts with the thick shanks in positions 15 and 16 **(see illustrations)**, the eight 40mm bolts in positions 17, 18, 21 to 24, 26 and 27, and the three 60mm bolts in positions 19, 20 and 25 **(see illustration 19.18a)**.

18 First tighten bolts Nos. 1 to 6 in sequence to 24 Nm **(see illustration)**. Working in the same sequence, first loosen all the bolts, then tighten them all to 17 Nm. Finally using a degree disc, tighten the bolts further through 60° **(see illustration)**. Mark the top of each bolt with a marker pen once you have completed its second stage tightening to ensure none get omitted or done twice. Note

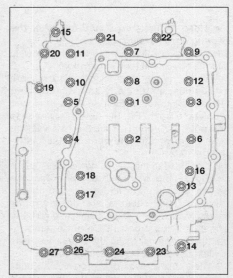

19.18a Crankcase bolt numbers and tightening sequence

19.18b Use a degree disc for the final tightening of the M9 bolts

19.21 Use a new gasket and apply threadlock to the bolts

21.4a Unscrew the bolts…

21.4b … and pull the cap off the connecting rod

21.4c Use the bolts to push the rod down if necessary

Abrasives are sometimes left in engine components after reconditioning operations, especially when parts are not thoroughly cleaned using the proper cleaning methods. Whatever the source, foreign objects often end up imbedded in the soft bearing material and are easily recognised. Large particles will not imbed in the bearing and will score or gouge the bearing and journal. The best prevention for this type of bearing failure is to clean all parts thoroughly and keep everything spotlessly clean during engine reassembly. Regular oil and filter changes are also essential.

5 Lack of lubrication or lubrication breakdown have a number of interrelated causes. Excessive heat (which thins the oil), overloading (which squeezes the oil from the bearing face) and oil throw-off (from excessive bearing clearances, a worn oil pump or high engine speeds) all contribute to a breakdown of the protective lubricating film. Blocked oil passages will starve a bearing of lubrication and destroy it. When lack of lubrication is the cause of bearing failure, the bearing material is wiped or extruded from the steel backing of the bearing. Temperatures may increase to the point where the steel backing and the journal turn blue from overheating.

6 Riding habits can have a definite effect on bearing life. Full throttle, low speed operation, or labouring the engine, puts very high loads on bearings, which tend to squeeze out the oil film. These loads cause the bearings to flex, which produces fine cracks in the bearing face (fatigue failure). Eventually the bearing material will loosen in pieces and tear away from the steel backing. Short trip riding leads to corrosion of bearings, as insufficient engine heat is produced to drive off the condensed water and corrosive gases produced. These products collect in the engine oil, forming acid and sludge. As the oil is carried to the engine bearings, the acid attacks and corrodes the bearing material.

7 Incorrect bearing installation during engine assembly will lead to bearing failure as well. Tight fitting bearings which leave insufficient bearing oil clearances result in oil starvation. Dirt or foreign particles trapped behind a bearing shell result in high spots on the bearing which lead to failure.

8 To avoid bearing problems, clean all parts thoroughly before reassembly, double check all bearing clearance measurements and lubricate the new bearings with clean engine oil during installation.

21 Connecting rods and bearings

Note: *On installation new connecting rod bolts must be used, so it is wise to obtain them before commencing work.*

Removal

1 Remove the engine from the frame (Section 4) and separate the crankcase halves (Section 19).
2 Remove the balancer shaft (Section 25) and the transmission output shaft (Section 26).
3 Using paint or a marker pen, mark the cylinder identity on the top of each piston and across the front of each connecting rod and cap. Cylinders are numbered 1 – left, 2 – right. Note that the number and letter already written across the back of the rod and cap are the rod size code and weight grade respectively, not the cylinder number.
4 Unscrew the connecting rod cap bolts and separate the caps, complete with the lower bearing shells from the crankpins **(see illustrations)**. If a cap appears stuck, thread the bolts part-way in, then push them or tap them lightly and evenly to push the rod down **(see illustration)**. Note that new bolts must be fitted.

21.5 Push each rod down off its crankpin

5 Detach the connecting rods from the crankpins and push them down the bore until they are clear **(see illustration)**. Lift the crankshaft out, taking care not to dislodge the main bearing shells **(see illustration 24.3)**.
6 Rest the crankcase on its side. Push each piston/connecting rod assembly to the top end of the cylinder bore and remove it, making sure the connecting rod does not mark the bore walls **(see illustration)**. Note the 'Y' mark on each connecting rod that must face to the left-hand side of the engine, and the circular mark on the top of each piston which points to the front of the engine. If this is not visible, mark the piston accordingly so that it can be installed the correct way round.
Caution: Do not try to remove the piston/ connecting rod from the bottom of the cylinder bore. The piston will not pass the crankcase main bearing webs. If the piston is pulled right to the bottom of the bore the oil control ring will expand and lock the piston in position. If this happens it is likely the ring will be broken.
7 Fit the related bearing shells (if removed), bearing cap, and bolts on each piston/ connecting rod assembly so that they are all kept together as a matched set. New bolts must be used on final assembly, but use the old bolts for the oil clearance check.
8 If required remove the pistons from the connecting rods (Section 22).

Inspection

9 Check the connecting rods for cracks and other obvious damage.

21.6 Push each piston and connecting rod out of its bore

21.10 Check for freeplay between the pin and the small-end

21.14 Remove the shells from the rods and caps

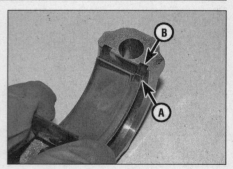

21.15 Locate the tab (A) in the notch (B)

10 Apply clean engine oil to the No. 1 piston pin, insert it into its connecting rod small-end and check for any freeplay between the two **(see illustration)**. If freeplay is excessive, measure the external diameter at the centre of the pin. Compare the result to the figure given in the Specifications. Replace the pin with a new one if it is worn beyond its specified limits. If the pin diameter is within specifications, replace the connecting rod with a new one. Repeat the measurements for the No. 2 pin and rod.

11 Refer to Section 20 and examine the connecting rod bearing shells. If they are scored, badly scuffed or appear to have seized, new shells must be fitted. Always replace the shells in the connecting rods as a set. If they are badly damaged, check the corresponding crankpin. Evidence of extreme heat, such as bluing, indicates that lubrication failure has occurred. Be sure to thoroughly check the oil pump and pressure relief valve as well as all oil holes and passages before reassembling the engine.

12 Have the rods checked by a Yamaha dealer if you are in doubt about their straightness.

Oil clearance check

Note: *It is essential that, throughout this procedure, the connecting rod does not rotate on the crankshaft. If the procedure is being carried out on a bench find some way of clamping the crankshaft so it cannot move, and also the connecting rod once it has been fitted onto its journal. The alternative is to fit the rod and piston back into its bore and lay*

the crankshaft in the crankcase to keep them held steady.

13 Whether new bearing shells are being fitted or the original ones are being re-used, the connecting rod big-end bearing oil clearance should be checked prior to reassembly. Bearing oil clearance is measured with a product known as Plastigauge.

14 Remove the bearing shells from the rods and caps, keeping them in order **(see illustration)**. Clean the backs of the shells, the bearing housings in both the connecting rod and cap, and the crankpin journal with a suitable solvent.

15 Press the bearing shells into their locations, locating the tab on each shell in the notch in the connecting rod or cap **(see illustration)**. Make sure the shells are fitted in the correct locations and take care not to touch any shell's bearing surface with your fingers.

16 Work on one rod at a time. Cut an appropriate size length of Plastigauge (it should be slightly shorter than the width of the crankpin) and place it on the crankpin journal to be checked **(see illustration 24.13)**. Do not place Plastigauge over the oil holes in the journal.

17 Apply molybdenum disulphide oil (a 50/50 mix of molybdenum disulphide grease and engine oil) to the threads and under the heads of the bolts. Fit the connecting rod and cap onto the crankpin. Make sure the cap is fitted the correct way around so the previously made markings align (see Step 3), and that the 'Y' mark on the rod is facing to the left-hand end of the crankshaft (see Step 6). Fit the bolts and tighten them finger-tight. Remember that it is essential that, throughout

this procedure, the connecting rod does not rotate on the crankshaft.

18 Tighten the bolts to the initial torque setting given in the Specifications with a torque wrench. Now tighten each bolt in turn and in one continuous movement through the specified angle using a degree disc (torque angle gauge) **(see illustration 21.34)**.

19 Slacken the bolts and remove the cap and rod from the crankshaft.

20 Compare the width of the crushed Plastigauge on the crankpin to the scale printed on the Plastigauge envelope to obtain the connecting rod big-end bearing oil clearance **(see illustration 24.17)**. Compare the reading to that given in the 1 Specifications 0. If the clearance is within the range specified and the bearings are in perfect condition, they can be reused.

21 Carefully clean away all traces of the Plastigauge from the crankpin journal and bearing shells using a fingernail or other object which will not score the bearing surfaces.

22 If the clearance is beyond the service limit, replace the bearing shells with new ones (see Steps 25 and 26) and check the oil clearance once again.

23 If the clearance is still greater than the service limit listed in the Specifications the crankpin journal is worn and the crankshaft should be replaced with a new one.

24 Repeat the procedure for the other connecting rod, then discard the old big-end bolts.

Bearing shell selection

25 Replacement bearing shells are supplied on a selected fit basis. Code numbers for the crankpin journals are stamped on the outside of the crankshaft web on the left-hand end of the crankshaft **(see illustration)**. The left-hand block of two numbers are the size codes for the crankpin journals (the right-hand block of three numbers are the size codes for the main bearing journals). The first number of the block is for the left-hand (No. 1 cylinder) journal, and so on. Each connecting rod size code number is marked in ink on the flat face of the connecting rod and cap **(see illustration)**.

26 A range of bearing shells are available. To select the correct shells for a particular journal, subtract the crankpin journal number on the crankshaft from the number on the

21.25a Big-end journal size codes (arrowed)

21.25b Connecting rod size code number (arrowed)

21.29 Circular mark (A), Y mark (B)

21.30a Lower the assembly into the bore...

connecting rod and compare the result with the table below to find the colour coding of the replacement shells, e.g. connecting rod number 5 minus crankpin journal number 2 = 3; No. 3 bearing shells are colour-coded brown. The colour code is marked on the side of each bearing shell (see illustration 24.23).

Number	Colour
1	blue
2	black
3	brown
4	green

Installation

Note: *New big-end bolts must be used on final assembly.*

27 If removed, fit the pistons onto the connecting rods (Section 22) – make sure the piston ring end gaps are correctly spaced (Section 23).

28 Make sure that the backs of the bearing shells, the bearing seats in the caps and rods and the crankpin journals are clean. If new shells are being fitted, remove any protective grease using paraffin (kerosene). Dry the shells, caps, rods and journals with a clean, lint-free cloth. Fit the shells, locating the tab on each shell in the notch in the cap or rod, and making sure the end of each shell is flush with the cap or rod

21.30b ...then carefully compress and feed each ring in

(see illustration 21.15). If the original bearing shells are to be fitted, make sure that they are in their correct locations. Take care not to touch any bearing surfaces with your fingers.

29 Lubricate the pistons, rings and cylinder bores with clean engine oil. When fitting each piston/rod assembly into its bore make sure the circular mark on the top of the piston points to the front and the 'Y' mark on the rod faces the left-hand side of the engine, and that each is returned to the cylinder it came from (see illustration).

30 Insert the No. 1 piston/connecting rod assembly into the top of its bore, taking care not to allow the connecting rod to mark the wall (see illustration). Carefully compress

21.30c Alternatively fit the ring compressor over the piston...

and feed each piston ring into the bore until the piston crown is flush with the top of the bore (see illustration). If available, a good piston ring compressor of the correct size makes installation a lot easier (though a poor fitting one makes it more difficult, and if it is too big it goes out-of-round when fully tightened, allowing the rings to stick out) – fit the compressor around the piston and over the rings and tighten it to compress the rings, then locate the assembly on the top of the bore and tap the top of the piston using a wooden or plastic tool (such as the handle end of a hammer) until the piston is completely in the bore (see illustrations). Repeat for No. 2 piston/connecting rod assembly.

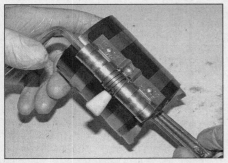

21.30d ...and tighten it to compress the rings

21.30e Insert the rod assembly into the top of the bore...

21.30f ...and carefully press the piston into the bore

21.32a Pull the rod up against the crankpin

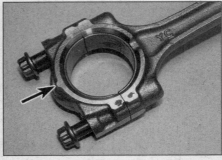

21.32b Projection (arrowed) must face the left side of the engine

21.34 Use a degree disc for the final tightening of the bolts

31 Turn the crankcase over. Make sure all the main bearing shells are in place, then lower the crankshaft into position **(see illustration 24.3)**.

32 Working on one connecting rod at a time, lubricate the crankpin and the shells in the connecting rod and cap with clean engine oil. Pull the rod onto the crankpin **(see illustration)**. Fit the cap onto the rod **(see illustration 21.4b)** – make sure the cap is fitted with the projection on its side facing to the left-hand side of the engine, the same way as the 'Y' mark on the rod, and so the previously made markings align (see Step 3) **(see illustration)**.

33 Apply molybdenum disulphide oil (a 50/50 mix of molybdenum disulphide grease and engine oil) to the threads and under the heads of the new big-end bolts. Fit the bolts and tighten them finger-tight **(see illustration 21.4a)**. Check that all components have been returned to their original locations using the marks made on disassembly.

34 Tighten the bolts to 20 Nm with a torque wrench. Now tighten each bolt in turn and in one continuous movement through 180° using a degree disc (torque angle gauge) **(see illustration)**. Fit the other rod onto the crankshaft in the same way.

35 Check that the crankshaft rotates smoothly and freely. If there are any signs of roughness or tightness, detach the rods and recheck the assembly. Sometimes tapping the bottom of the connecting rod cap will relieve tightness.

36 Install the balancer shaft (Section 25) and the transmission output shaft (Section 26).
37 Reassemble the crankcase halves (Section 19).

22 Pistons

Removal

1 Remove the engine from the frame (Section 4), and separate the crankcase halves (Section 19). Remove the piston/connecting rod assemblies (Section 21).
2 Before removing the pistons from the connecting rods, check that each is marked with its cylinder identity – each piston and rod must be matched on reassembly.
3 Carefully prise out the circlips on each side of the piston pin using needle-nose pliers or a small flat-bladed screwdriver inserted into the notch **(see illustration)** – new circlips must be used. Check for burring around the circlip grooves and remove any with a very fine file or knife blade, then push the piston pin out to free the piston from the connecting rod **(see illustration)**. When the piston has been removed from the rod, keep the piston and its pin together so that related parts do not get mixed up.
4 Using your thumbs or a piston ring removal and installation tool, carefully remove the rings from the pistons (Section 23). Note which way

up each ring fits and in which groove, as they must be installed in their original positions if being re-used. The upper surface of the two top rings (compression rings) should have a manufacturer's mark or letter at one end **(see illustration 23.1)**.
5 Scrape all traces of carbon from the tops of the pistons. A hand-held wire brush or a piece of fine emery cloth can be used once most of the deposits have been scraped away. Do not, under any circumstances, use a wire brush mounted in a drill motor; the piston material is soft and is easily damaged.
6 Use a piston ring groove cleaning tool to remove any carbon deposits from the ring grooves. If a tool is not available, a piece broken off an old ring will do the job. Be very careful to remove only the carbon deposits. Do not remove any metal and do not nick or gouge the sides of the ring grooves.
7 Once the carbon has been removed, clean the pistons with a suitable solvent and dry them thoroughly. Make sure the oil return holes at the back of the oil ring groove are clear. If the identification mark previously applied to the piston is cleaned off, be sure to re-mark it correctly.

Inspection

8 Inspect each piston for cracks around the skirt, at the pin bosses and at the ring lands. Normal piston wear appears as even, vertical wear on the thrust surfaces of the piston and slight looseness of the top ring in its groove. If the skirt is scored or scuffed, the engine may have been suffering from overheating and/or abnormal combustion, resulting in excessively high operating temperatures.
9 A hole in the top of the piston (only likely in extreme circumstances), or burned areas around the edge of the piston crown, indicate that pre-ignition or knocking under load have occurred. If you find evidence of any problems the cause must be corrected or the damage will occur again (see *Fault Finding* in the Reference section).
10 Check the piston-to-bore clearance by measuring the bore (Section 29) and the piston diameter. Make sure each piston is matched to its correct cylinder. Measure the piston 8 mm up from the bottom of the skirt and at

22.3a Prise out the circlip...

22.3b ...then push out the pin and remove the piston

22.10 Measuring the piston diameter with a micrometer

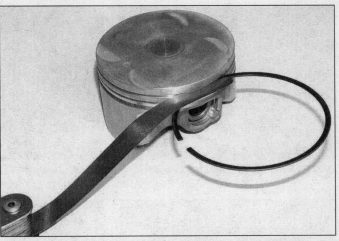

22.11 Measuring the piston ring-to-groove clearance with a feeler gauge

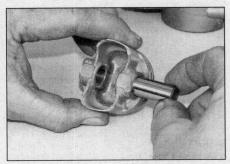

22.12a Insert the pin into the piston and check for freeplay

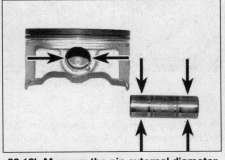

22.12b Measure the pin external diameter and the pin bore in the piston

22.15 Fit the circlip with the open end away from the removal notch

90° to the piston pin axis **(see illustration)**. Subtract the piston diameter from the bore diameter to obtain the clearance. If it is greater than the figure given in the Specifications, check whether it is the bore or piston that is worn beyond its service limit. If the bores are good, fit new pistons and rings. If the bores are worn, replace the crankcases, pistons and rings.

11 Measure the piston ring-to-groove clearance by laying each compression ring in its groove and slipping a feeler gauge in beside it **(see illustration)**. Make sure you have the correct ring for the groove (see Step 4). Check the clearance at three or four locations around the groove. If the clearance is greater than given in the Specifications, fit new piston rings then check the clearance again, and if it is still excessive fit a new piston. If new rings are being used anyway, measure the clearance using the new rings. If the clearance is greater than that specified, fit a new piston.

12 Apply clean engine oil to the piston pin, insert it part way into the piston and check for any freeplay between the two **(see illustration)**. Measure the pin external diameter at each end, and the pin bores in the piston **(see illustration)**. Subtract the pin

diameter from the bore diameter to obtain the clearance. If it is greater than the figure given in the Specifications, check whether it is the bore or pin that is worn beyond its service limit and fit new ones as required. Check for excessive play between the pin and the connecting rod small-end (Section 21).

Installation

13 Inspect and install the piston rings (Section 23).

14 Fit a new circlip into one side of the piston (never re-use old circlips). Lubricate the piston pin, the piston pin bore and the connecting rod small-end bore with clean engine oil.

15 Line up the piston on its connecting rod so that the mark on the top of the piston will point to the front and the 'Y' mark on the rod will face the left-hand side of the engine when they are installed **(see illustration 21.29)**. Insert the piston pin from the side without the circlip **(see illustration 22.3b)**. Secure the pin with the other new circlip. When fitting the circlips, compress them only just enough to fit them in the piston, and make sure they are properly seated in their grooves with the open end at least 3mm away from the removal notch **(see illustration)**.

16 Install the connecting rods (Section 21).

23 Piston rings

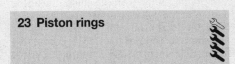

Note: *It is good practice to fit new piston rings when an engine is being overhauled.*

Inspection

1 The upper surface of the two top rings (compression rings) will sometimes have a manufacturer's mark or letter at one end **(see illustration)** – if the mark on each ring is different, note which mark is for the top ring and which is for the second.

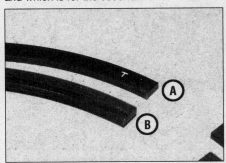

23.1 Top ring (A), middle or second ring (B)

23.2a Ease the ring into the cylinder...

23.2b ...and set it square using the piston

23.2c Measuring piston ring end gap

23.5a Fit the oil ring expander in its groove...

23.5b ...then fit the lower side rail...

23.5c ...and the upper side rail as described

2 To measure the ring end gap, which should be done for all rings except the expander section of the oil control ring, fit the ring into the top of the cylinder, square it up with the cylinder walls by pushing it down with the top of the piston, setting it near the bottom of the cylinder where wear is lowest **(see illustrations)**. Slip a feeler gauge between the ends of the ring and compare the measurement to the figure given in the Specifications at the beginning of this Chapter **(see illustration)**.

3 Excess end gap is not critical unless it exceeds the service limit. If so check that the bore is not worn (Section 29). If the bore is not worn, the rings are too – fit a new set.

4 Repeat the procedure for each ring and each cylinder in turn. Note that the end gaps differ between the top, second and oil ring.

When checking the oil ring, only the side-rails can be checked as the ends of the expander ring should contact each other. Remember to keep the rings together with their matched piston and cylinder.

Installation

5 Fit the oil control ring (lowest on the piston). It is composed of three separate components, namely the expander and the upper and lower side rails. First slip the expander into the ring groove, making sure the ends do not overlap **(see illustration)**. Next fit the lower side rail – do not use a piston ring installation tool on the oil ring side rails as they may be damaged **(see illustration)**. Instead, place one end of the side rail into the groove between the expander and the ring land. Hold it firmly in place and slide a finger around the piston

while pushing the rail into the groove. Next, fit the upper side rail in the same manner **(see illustration)**. Make sure the ends of the expander touch but do not overlap.

6 After the three oil ring components have been fitted, check to make sure that both the upper and lower side rails can be turned smoothly in the ring groove.

7 Fit the second ring into the middle groove in the piston with the mark (where present) uppermost – using a feeler gauge blade helps to slip the ring into place **(see illustrations)**. Do not expand the ring any more than is necessary – they are brittle and break easily.

8 Finally, fit the top ring in the same manner into the top groove in the piston **(see illustration)**.

9 Once the rings are correctly installed, check they move freely without snagging

23.7a Carefully feed the second ring into its groove...

23.7b ...using a feeler gauge blade if required

23.8 Finally, fit the top ring

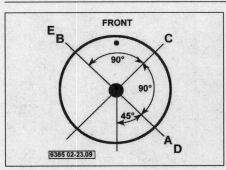

23.9 Piston ring installation details – stagger the ring end gaps as shown

A Top ring
B Second ring
C Upper side rail
D Oil ring expander
E Lower side rail

and stagger their end gaps as shown **(see illustration)**.

24 Crankshaft and main bearings

Removal

1 Remove the engine from the frame (Section 4), separate the crankcase halves (Section 19) and disconnect the piston/connecting rod assemblies from the crankshaft (Section 21). There is no need to remove the piston/connecting rod assemblies from the cylinders, but push them up the bores so that the connecting rod ends are clear of the crankshaft and wrap clean rag around the rod ends to prevent damage to the bores **(see illustration 21.5)**.

2 Remove the balancer shaft (Section 25).

3 Lift the crankshaft out of the upper crankcase half, taking care not to dislodge the main bearing shells **(see illustration)**.

4 If required, remove the main bearing shells from the crankcase halves **(see illustration)**. Keep the shells in order so that they can be returned to their original locations for the oil clearance check and if being reused.

Inspection

5 Clean the crankshaft with a suitable solvent,

24.3 Lift the crankshaft out of the crankcase

paying particular attention to flush out the oil passages. If available, blow the crank dry with compressed air, and also blow through the oil passages. Check the primary/balancer drive gear teeth for wear or damage **(see illustration)**. If any of the teeth are excessively worn, chipped or broken, the crankshaft must be replaced with a new one. Check the primary driven gear on the clutch housing **(see illustration 13.23)** and the driven gear on the balancer shaft **(see illustration 25.4)** for corresponding wear or damage. Also check the cam chain sprocket, the sprockets on the camshafts and the cam chain itself and replace them with new ones, if necessary (Section 8 and Section 9).

6 Refer to Section 20 and examine the main bearing shells. If they are scored, badly scuffed or appear to have seized, a complete new set of bearings must be installed. If they are badly damaged, check the corresponding crankshaft journals. Evidence of extreme heat, such as bluing, indicates that lubrication failure has occurred. Be sure to thoroughly check the oil pump and pressure relief valve as well as all oil holes and passages before reassembling the engine.

7 Give the crankshaft journals a close visual examination, paying particular attention where damaged bearings have been discovered. If the journals are scored or pitted in any way, a new crankshaft will be required. Note that undersized bearing shells are not available, precluding the option of re-grinding the crankshaft.

8 Place the crankshaft on V-blocks and check the runout at the middle main bearing journals

24.4 Remove the main bearing shells from their housings

using a dial gauge (see *Tools and Workshop Tips* in the Reference section). Compare the reading to the maximum given in the Specifications. If the runout exceeds the limit, fit a new crankshaft.

Oil clearance check

9 Whether new bearing shells are being fitted or the original ones are being re-used, the main bearing oil clearance should be checked before the engine is reassembled, and while you are doing it you should simultaneously check the balancer shaft bearing oil clearance. Oil clearance is measured with a product known as Plastigauge.

10 If not already done, remove the bearing shells from the crankcase halves (see Step 4 and Section 25). Clean the backs of the shells and the bearing seats in both crankcase halves, and the bearing journals on the crankshaft and balancer shaft.

11 Press the bearing shells into their seats, locating the tab on each shell in the notch in the crankcase **(see illustration)**. Make sure the shells are fitted in the correct locations and take care not to touch the bearing surfaces with your fingers.

12 Make sure the shells and crankshaft are clean and dry. Lay the crankshaft and balancer shaft in position in the upper crankcase.

13 Cut appropriate size lengths of Plastigauge (they should be slightly shorter than the width of the journals). Place a strand of Plastigauge on each journal **(see illustration)**. Do not place Plastigauge over the oil holes in the crankshaft. Make sure the shafts are not rotated.

24.5 Check the gear teeth

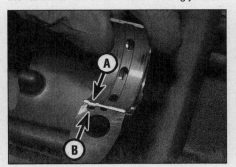

24.11 Locate the tab (A) in the notch (B)

24.13 Lay a strip of Plastigauge across each main bearing journal

24.17 Compare the width of the crushed Plastigauge to the printed scale provided

24.21 Crankshaft journal size codes (arrowed)

24.22 Main bearing size codes (arrowed)

14 If removed, fit the dowels into the crankcase **(see illustration 19.13)**. Carefully fit the lower crankcase half onto the upper half, making sure the dowels locate correctly and the Plastigauge is not disturbed **(see illustration 19.6)**. Check that the lower crankcase half is correctly seated all round – do not tighten the crankcase bolts if the casing is not correctly seated.

15 Refer to Steps 16 to 19 in Section 19 and fit and tighten the crankcase bolts Nos. 1 to 12 as described, noting that you do not have to use new bolts or O-rings for this procedure, and making sure the crankshaft and balancer shaft do not turn.

16 Now unscrew the bolts as described in Step 5 in Section 19, until they are loose, then remove them. Carefully lift off the lower crankcase half, making sure the Plastigauge is not disturbed.

17 Compare the width of the crushed Plastigauge on each journal to the scale provided with the Plastigauge container to obtain the bearing oil clearance **(see illustration)**. Compare the readings to the figures given in the Specifications, noting the clearance for the main bearings is different to that of the balancer shaft bearings. If the clearance is within the range specified and the bearings are in perfect condition, they can be reused.

18 Carefully clean away all traces of the Plastigauge from the journals and bearing shells using a fingernail or other object which will not score the bearing surfaces.

19 If the clearance is larger than specified, replace all the bearing shells with new ones (see Steps 21 to 23 for the main bearings, and Section 25 for the balancer shaft bearings) and check the oil clearance once again.

20 If the clearance is still larger than the specified figure the journals are worn and a new crankshaft and/or balancer shaft must be fitted.

Bearing shell selection

Note: *Refer to Section 25 for balancer shaft bearing selection.*

21 Replacement bearing shells are supplied on a selected fit basis. Code numbers for the crankshaft journals are stamped on the outside of the crankshaft web on the left-hand end of the crankshaft **(see illustration)**. The right-hand block of three numbers are the size codes for the main bearing journals (the left-hand block of two numbers are the size codes for the big-end bearing journals). The first number of the block is for the left-hand (No. 1) journal, and so on.

22 The crankcase bearing housing size codes are stamped into the back of the lower crankcase half, the left-hand block of numbers for the crankshaft, the right-hand block for the balancer shaft **(see illustration)**. The first number is for the left-hand (No. 1) bearing, and so on.

23 A range of bearing shells are available. To select the correct shells for a particular journal, subtract the crankshaft journal number on the crankshaft from the number on the crankcase,

and then subtract 2. Compare the result with the table below to find the colour code of the replacement shells, e.g. crankcase number 5 minus crankshaft journal number 2 minus 2 = 1; No. 1 bearing shells are colour coded blue. The colour code is marked on the side of each bearing shell **(see illustration)** – note that all shells carry two colours, one of which is always pink, representing the colour code of the bearing set for this engine.

Number	Colour
-1	purple
0	white
1	blue
2	black
3	brown
4	green

Installation

24 Make sure the backs of the bearing shells, the bearing seats in both crankcase halves, and the main bearing journals on the crankshaft are clean. If new shells are being fitted clean any protective grease off using paraffin (kerosene). Wipe the shells and crankcase halves dry with a lint-free cloth. Make sure all the oil passages and holes are clear, and blow them through with compressed air if it is available.

25 Press the bearing shells into their seats, locating the tab on each shell in the notch in the crankcase **(see illustration 24.11)**. Make sure the bearings are fitted in the correct locations and take care not to touch any bearing surfaces with your fingers. Lubricate the shells with clean engine oil.

26 Lower the crankshaft into position in the upper crankcase, making sure all bearing shells remain in place **(see illustration 24.3)**.

27 Refer to Section 21 and fit the connecting rods onto the crankshaft using new bolts.

28 Turn the crankshaft so the punch mark on the primary/balancer drive gear is pointing to the front and level with the crankcase mating surface **(see illustration)**.

29 Install the balancer shaft (Section 25).

30 Reassemble the crankcase halves (Section 19).

24.23 Main bearing shell colour code (arrowed)

24.28 Align the punch mark facing forwards as shown

25.2a Align the punch marks

25.2b Lift the balancer shaft out of the crankcase

25.3 Remove the shells from their housings

25 Balancer shaft and bearings

Removal

1 Remove the engine from the frame (Section 4) and separate the crankcase halves (Section 19).

2 Turn the crankshaft and balancer shaft to align the punch marks on their gears **(see illustration)** – this is the position they must be in on installation. Lift the balancer shaft out of the upper crankcase half, taking care not to dislodge the bearing shells **(see illustration)**.

3 If required, remove the balancer bearing shells from the crankcase halves **(see illustration)**. Keep the shells in order so that they can be returned to their original locations for the oil clearance check and if being reused.

Inspection

4 Clean the balancer shaft with a suitable solvent. Check the gear teeth for wear or damage **(see illustration)**. If any of the teeth are excessively worn, chipped or broken, the balancer shaft must be replaced with a new one. Check the drive gear on the crankshaft for corresponding wear or damage **(see illustration 24.5)**.

5 Refer to Section 20 and examine the bearing shells. If they are scored, badly scuffed or appear to have seized, a new set of bearings must be fitted. If they are badly

damaged, check the balancer shaft journals. Evidence of extreme heat, such as bluing, indicates that lubrication failure has occurred. Be sure to thoroughly check the oil pump and pressure relief valve as well as all oil holes and passages before reassembling the engine.

6 Give the journals a close visual examination, paying particular attention where damaged bearings have been discovered. If the journals are scored or pitted in any way, a new crankshaft will be required. Note that undersized bearing shells are not available, precluding the option of re-grinding the shaft.

7 Place the shaft on V-blocks and check the runout at the centre using a dial gauge (see *Tools and Workshop Tips* in the Reference section). Compare the reading to the maximum given in the Specifications. If the runout exceeds the limit, the balancer shaft must be replaced with a new one.

Oil clearance check

8 Whether new bearing shells are being fitted or the original ones are being re-used, the bearing oil clearance should be checked before the engine is reassembled. Refer to Section 24 for details of the procedure, which can be carried out at the same time as doing the main bearing oil clearance, but note that the specified clearance is different – refer to the Specifications. When the check has been made, if new shells are needed, refer below for shell selection details – do not use the selection procedure given for the main bearings.

Bearing shell selection

9 Replacement bearing shells are supplied on a selected fit basis. Code numbers for the balancer shaft journals are stamped on the outside of the right-hand weight **(see illustration)**. The left-hand number is the size code for the left-hand journal.

10 The crankcase bearing housing size codes are stamped into the back of the lower crankcase half, the right-hand block of numbers for the balancer shaft, the left-hand block for the crankshaft **(see illustration)**. The first number is for the left-hand (No. 1) bearing, and so on.

11 A range of bearing shells are available. To select the correct shells for a particular journal, subtract the balancer shaft journal number on the shaft from the number on the crankcase. Compare the result with the table below to find the colour code of the replacement shells, e.g. crankcase number 8 minus balancer shaft journal number 5 = 3; No. 3 bearing shells are colour coded brown. The colour code is marked on the side of each bearing shell **(see illustration 24.23)**.

Number	Colour
1	blue
2	black
3	brown
4	green
5	yellow

25.4 Check the gear teeth

25.9 Balancer shaft journal size codes (arrowed)

25.10 Balancer bearing size code(s) (arrowed)

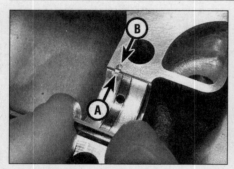

25.13 Locate the tab (A) in the notch (B)

25.14 Make sure the punch marks align as you engage the teeth

Installation

12 Make sure the backs of the bearing shells, the bearing seats in both crankcase halves, and the bearing journals on the shaft are clean. If new shells are being fitted clean any protective grease off using paraffin (kerosene). Wipe the shells and crankcase halves dry with a lint-free cloth. Make sure all the oil passages and holes are clear, and blow them through with compressed air if it is available.
13 Press the bearing shells into their seats, locating the tab on each shell in the notch in the crankcase **(see illustration)**. Make sure the bearings are fitted in the correct locations and take care not to touch any bearing surfaces with your fingers. Lubricate the shells with clean engine oil.
14 Make sure the alignment punchmark on

26.2 Lift the output shaft out of the crankcase

the crankshaft is facing forwards and level with the crankcase mating surface **(see illustration 24.28)**. Lower the balancer shaft into position in the upper crankcase with the punch mark facing back, making sure all bearing shells remain in place, engaging the gear teeth and making sure the punch marks align **(see illustration)**.
15 Reassemble the crankcase halves (Section 19).

26 Transmission shaft removal and installation

Removal

1 Remove the engine from the frame (Sec-

26.5a Undo the bolts (arrowed) and remove the plate

tion 4). Remove the gearchange mechanism (Section 15), then separate the crankcase halves (Section 19) – there is no need to remove the camshafts, cylinder head or alternator rotor, but you have to remove the alternator cover (see Chapter 8).
2 Note how the pin on the output shaft left-hand bearing locates in the cut-out in the upper crankcase half, and the circlip on the bearing and the lip on the seal locate in the grooves **(see illustration 26.11)**. Also note how the output shaft selector forks locate in the grooves on the 5th and 6th gear pinions, and how the guide pins on the forks locate in the grooves in the selector drum. Lift the output shaft out of the crankcase **(see illustration)**; if it is stuck, use a soft-faced hammer and gently tap on the ends of the shaft to free it.
3 Remove the oil seal from the left-hand end of the shaft – a new one must be used **(see illustration 26.10)**.
4 Remove the selector drum and forks (Section 28).
5 Undo the input shaft bearing housing retainer plate bolts and remove the plate **(see illustration)**. Thread two of the bolts into the two threaded holes in the bearing housing as shown until they contact the surface of the crankcase, then continue turning them evenly and a little at a time until the bearing housing is displaced, then withdraw the input shaft from the crankcase **(see illustrations)**. Remove the bolts.
6 To remove the left-hand input shaft bearing from the crankcase, see *Tools and Workshop Tips* in the Reference section **(see illustration)**.

Installation

7 Clean the threads of the bearing housing retainer plate bolts and apply a suitable thread locking compound.
8 Slide the input shaft into the crankcase far enough for the left-hand end of the shaft to locate in its bearing, and push the bearing housing on the right-hand end in as far as it

26.5c ...and when it is free slide the shaft out

26.6 Input shaft left-hand bearing (arrowed)

26.5b Screw the bolts into the threaded holes and against the crankcase, and keep turning them to push the bearing housing out...

26.8a Make sure the bolt holes are aligned then push the housing in

26.8b Fit the plate and evenly tighten the bolts to draw the bearing housing in

26.10 Fit a new oil seal, and check the circlip (arrowed) is fitted in its groove

will go **(see illustration)**. Fit the retainer plate and thread the bolts into the crankcase, then tighten them evenly and a little at a time to draw the bearing housing into its location in the crankcase **(see illustration)**. When the housing is seated tighten the bolts to 12 Nm.
9 Install the selector drum and forks (Section 28).
10 Smear the lip of the new output shaft seal with grease. Slide the seal onto the left-hand end of the shaft **(see illustration)**. Make sure the bearing circlip is in its groove in the bearing.
11 Lower the output shaft into position in the upper crankcase **(see illustration 26.2)** – make sure the selector forks locate in their pinion grooves and selector drum tracks correctly, the circlip on the bearing and the lip on the seal seat in the grooves, and the pin on the bearing locates correctly in the crankcase **(see illustration)**.
Caution: If the circlip is not correctly engaged, the crankcase halves will not seat correctly.
12 Make sure the output shaft is correctly seated and that the selector forks are located in the grooves in the appropriate gear pinions (Section 28).
13 Position the gears in the neutral position and check the shafts are free to rotate easily and independently (i.e. the input shaft can turn whilst the output shaft is held stationary) before proceeding further.
14 Reassemble the crankcase halves (Section 19).

27 Transmission shaft overhaul

1 Remove the transmission shafts from the crankcase (Section 26). Always disassemble the transmission shafts separately to avoid mixing up the components.

Input shaft disassembly

2 Slide the 2nd gear pinion off the left-hand end of the shaft, noting which way around it is fitted **(see illustration 27.26)**.
3 Note how the tabs on the lock washer fit into the slotted splined washer and remove the lockwasher **(see illustration 27.25)**.
4 Turn the slotted splined washer to offset the splines and slide it off the shaft **(see illustration 27.24a)**.
5 Slide the 6th gear pinion and its splined bush off the shaft, followed by the splined washer **(see illustrations 27.23c, b and a)**.
6 Remove the circlip securing the combined 3rd/4th gear pinion, then slide the pinion off the shaft noting which way round it fits **(see illustrations 27.22b and a)**. A new circlip must be fitted on reassembly.
7 Remove the circlip securing the 5th gear pinion, then slide the splined washer, the pinion and its bush off the shaft **(see illustrations 27.21b and a and 27.20b and a)**. A new circlip must be fitted on reassembly.
8 The 1st gear pinion is integral with the shaft **(see illustration)**.

9 The right-hand bearing and housing are an integral part of the shaft **(see illustration 27.8)**.

Shaft inspection

10 Wash all the components in solvent and dry them off.
11 Check the gear teeth for cracking, chipping, pitting and other obvious wear or damage. Any pinion that is damaged must be replaced with a new one.
12 Inspect the dogs and the dog holes in the gears for cracks, chips, and excessive wear especially in the form of rounded edges. Make sure mating gears engage properly. Replace mating gears as a set if necessary.
13 Check for signs of scoring or bluing on the pinions, bushes and shaft. This could be caused by overheating due to inadequate lubrication. Check that all the oil holes and passages are clear. Replace any worn or damaged parts with new ones.
14 Check that each pinion moves freely on the shaft or its bush but without undue freeplay. Check that each bush moves freely on the shaft but without undue freeplay.
15 The shaft is unlikely to sustain damage unless the engine has seized, placing an unusually high loading on the transmission, or the machine has covered a very high mileage. Check the surface of the shaft, especially where a pinion turns on it, and replace the shaft with a new one if it has scored or picked up, or if there are any cracks. Check the shaft runout using V-blocks and a dial gauge and replace the shaft with a new one if the runout exceeds that given in the Specifications.
16 Check the washers and replace any that are bent or worn with new ones.
17 Check the bearings referring to *Tools and Workshop Tips* in the Reference section. The input shaft left-hand bearing is housed in the crankcase, and is available, but if the right-hand bearing is worn a new shaft must be fitted. The output shaft bearings are available.

Input shaft reassembly

18 During reassembly, apply clean engine oil or molybdenum disulphide oil (a 50/50 mixture of molybdenum disulphide grease and engine oil) to the mating surfaces of the shaft, pinions and bushes.

26.11 Make sure the lip (A) and circlip (B) locate in the grooves and the pin (C) seats in the cut-out

27.8 The 1st gear pinion (arrowed) is integral with the shaft

27.20a Slide the 5th gear pinion bush...

27.20b ...the 5th gear pinion...

27.21a ...and the splined washer onto the shaft...

27.21b ...and secure them with the circlip...

27.21c ...making sure it locates correctly

left-hand end of the shaft, then fit the 5th gear pinion onto the bush with its dogs facing away from the integral 1st gear **(see illustrations)**.

21 Slide the splined washer onto the shaft, then fit the new circlip, making sure that it locates correctly in the groove in the shaft **(see illustrations)**.

22 Slide the combined 3rd/4th gear pinion onto the shaft with the smaller 3rd gear pinion facing the 5th gear pinion, aligning the oil holes **(see illustration)**. Fit the new circlip, making sure it locates correctly in its groove in the shaft **(see illustrations)**.

23 Slide the splined washer onto the shaft, followed by the splined 6th gear pinion bush, aligning the oil hole in the bush with the hole in the shaft **(see illustrations)**. Fit the 6th gear pinion, making sure its dogs face the 3rd/4th gear pinion **(see illustration)**.

19 Use new circlips and do not expand their ends any further than is necessary to slide them along the shaft. Install them so that their chamfered side faces the pinion they

secure (see Correct fitting of a stamped circlip illustration in *Tools and Workshop Tips* in the Reference section).

20 Slide the 5th gear pinion bush onto the

27.22a Align oil holes and slide the 3rd/4th gear pinion onto the shaft...

27.22b ...and secure it with the circlip...

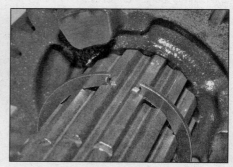

27.22c ...making sure it locates correctly

27.23a Fit the splined washer...

27.23b ...align the oil holes and fit the 6th gear pinion bush...

27.23c ...and slide on the 6th gear pinion

27.24a Fit the slotted splined washer...

27.24b ...then turn it to align the splines so it is locked

27.25 ...then slide on the tabbed lockwasher...

24 Slide the slotted splined washer onto the shaft and locate it in its groove, then turn it in the groove, so that the splines on the washer locate against the splines on the shaft and secure the washer in the groove (**see illustrations**).

25 Slide the lockwasher onto the shaft, so that the tabs on the lockwasher locate in the slots on the outside edge of the splined washer (**see illustration**).

26 Slide the 2nd gear pinion onto the shaft with its lipped side facing out (**see illustration**).

27 Check that all components have been correctly installed. The assembled shaft should look as shown (**see illustration**).

Output shaft disassembly

28 Slide the bearing off the right-hand end of the shaft (**see illustration 27.49**).

29 Slide the thrust washer off the shaft, followed by the 1st gear pinion and its bush (**see illustrations 27.48c, b and a**).

30 Slide the 5th gear pinion off the shaft (**see illustration 27.47**).

31 Remove the circlip securing the 3rd gear pinion, then slide the splined washer, the pinion and its splined bush off the shaft (**see illustrations 27.46d, c, b and a**). A new circlip must be fitted on reassembly.

32 Note how the tabs on the lock washer fit

into the slotted splined washer and remove the lockwasher (**see illustration 27.45**).

33 Turn the slotted splined washer to align it with the splines on the shaft and slide it off the shaft (**see illustration 27.44a**).

34 Slide the 4th gear pinion and its splined bush, followed by the splined washer, off the shaft (**see illustrations 27.43c, b and a**).

35 Remove the circlip securing the 6th gear pinion, then slide the pinion off the shaft (**see illustrations 27.42b and a**). A new circlip must be fitted on reassembly.

36 Remove the circlip securing the 2nd gear pinion, then slide the splined washer, the pinion and its bush off the shaft (**see illustrations 27.41d, c, b and a**).

37 If required, remove the collar and bearing from the left-hand end of the shaft, referring to *Tools and Workshop Tips* in the Reference section (**see illustration**). The bearing cannot be re-used, and a new circlip must be fitted into the groove in the new bearing.

Shaft inspection

38 Refer to Steps 10 to 17 above.

Output shaft reassembly

39 During reassembly, apply engine oil or molybdenum disulphide oil (a 50/50 mixture of molybdenum disulphide grease and engine

27.26 ...and the 2nd gear pinion

oil) to the mating surfaces of the shaft, pinions and bushes. When installing the new circlips, do not expand their ends any further than is necessary to slide them along the shaft. Install them so that their chamfered side faces the pinion they secure (see Correct fitting of a stamped circlip illustration in *Tools and Workshop Tips* in the Reference section).

40 If removed, fit the bearing and collar onto the left-hand end of the shaft, referring to *Tools and Workshop Tips* in the Reference section (**see illustration 27.37**). Fit a new circlip into the groove in the new bearing (**see illustration 26.10**).

27.27 The assembled gearbox input shaft

27.37 Remove the collar and bearing if required

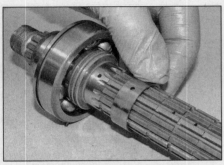

27.41a Slide the 2nd gear pinion bush...

27.41b ...the 2nd gear pinion...

27.41c ...and the splined washer onto the shaft...

27.41d ...and secure them with the circlip...

27.41e ...making sure it locates correctly

41 Slide the 2nd gear pinion bush onto the shaft, then slide on the 2nd gear pinion (dog holes facing away from the bearing) and the splined washer **(see illustrations)**. Fit the new circlip, making sure it is locates correctly in its groove on the shaft **(see illustrations)**.

42 Align the oil holes in the shaft and the 6th gear pinion, and slide the pinion onto the shaft with its selector fork groove facing away from the 2nd gear pinion, then fit the new circlip, making sure it locates correctly in its groove on the shaft **(see illustrations)**.

43 Slide the splined washer and the splined 4th gear pinion bush onto the shaft, making sure the oil hole in the bush aligns with the hole in the shaft, then fit the 4th gear pinion so that its dished side and dog holes face the 6th gear pinion **(see illustrations)**.

27.42a Align the oil holes and slide the 6th gear pinion onto the shaft...

27.42b ...and secure it with the circlip...

27.42c ...making sure it locates correctly

27.43a Fit the splined washer...

27.43b ...then align the oil holes and fit the 4th gear pinion bush...

27.43c ...and slide on the 4th gear pinion

27.44a Fit the slotted splined washer…

27.44b …then turn it to align the splines so it is locked…

27.45 …then slide on the tabbed lockwasher

27.46a Align the oil holes and fit the 3rd gear pinion bush…

27.46b …then slide on the 3rd gear pinion…

27.46c …and the splined washer…

27.46d …and secure them with the circlip…

44 Slide the slotted splined washer onto the shaft and locate it in its groove, then turn it in the groove so that the splines on the washer align against the splines on the shaft and secure the washer in the groove **(see illustrations)**.

45 Slide the lockwasher onto the shaft, so that the tabs on the lockwasher locate into the slots in the outer rim of the splined washer **(see illustration)**.

46 Slide the splined 3rd gear pinion bush onto the shaft, making sure the oil hole in the bush aligns with the hole in the shaft, then fit the 3rd gear pinion (dished side and dog holes facing away from the 4th gear pinion) and the splined washer **(see illustrations)**. Fit the new circlip, making sure it locates correctly in its groove in the shaft **(see illustrations)**.

47 Align the oil holes in the shaft and the 5th gear pinion, and slide the pinion onto the shaft with its selector fork groove facing the 3rd gear pinion **(see illustration)**.

48 Slide the 1st gear pinion bush onto the shaft, followed by the 1st gear pinion with its

27.46e …making sure it locates correctly

27.47 Align the oil holes and slide the 5th gear pinion onto the shaft

27.48a Fit the 1st gear pinion bush...

27.48b ...then slide the 1st gear pinion...

27.48c ...and the thrust washer onto the shaft...

27.49 ...and fit the bearing

27.50 The assembled gearbox output shaft

dog holes facing the 5th gear pinion, and the thrust washer **(see illustrations)**.

49 Fit the bearing onto the end of the shaft with its open side facing the 1st gear pinion **(see illustration)**.

50 Check that all components have been correctly installed. The assembled shaft should look as shown **(see illustration)**.

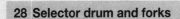

28 Selector drum and forks

Removal

1 Remove the engine from the frame (Section 4). Remove the gearchange mechanism (Section 15), then separate the crankcase halves (Section 19) – there is no need to remove the camshafts, cylinder head or alternator rotor, but you have to remove the alternator cover (see Chapter 8). Also remove the gear position switch and its contact plunger and spring (see Chapter 8).

2 Note that each selector fork is lettered for identification. The right-hand fork has an 'R', the centre fork a 'C', and the left-hand fork an 'L'. These letters face the right-hand (clutch) side of the engine. If no letters are visible, mark the forks yourself using a felt pen.

3 Note how the output shaft selector forks locate in the grooves on the 5th and 6th gear pinions and how the guide pins on the forks locate in the grooves in the selector drum, then remove the output shaft (Section 26).

4 Note how the input shaft selector fork locates in the groove on the 3rd/4th gear pinion and how the guide pin on the fork locates in the groove in the selector drum.

5 Undo the selector drum retainer plate screws and remove the plate **(see illustration)**.

6 Hold the output shaft selector forks (L and R), withdraw the shaft and remove the forks **(see illustration)**. Slide the forks back onto

28.5 Undo the screws (arrowed) and remove the retainer plate

the shaft in the correct order and the right way round.

7 Support the input shaft selector fork (C) and withdraw the fork shaft from the crankcase **(see illustration 28.18)**. Move the fork guide pin out of its track in the selector drum, then withdraw the selector drum from the left-hand side of the casing **(see illustration 28.16)**.

8 Move the selector fork around in its groove in the 3rd/4th gear pinion and remove it **(see illustration 28.15)**. Slide the fork back onto the shaft.

Inspection

9 Inspect the selector forks for any signs of

28.6 Withdraw the shaft and remove the forks

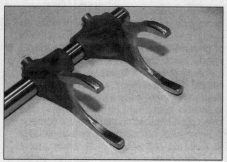

28.9 Check and measure the fork ends

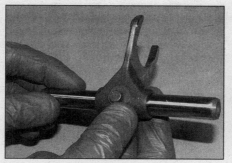

28.10 Check the fit of each fork on its shaft

28.12 Check the tracks and guide pins for wear and damage

28.15 Fit the C fork as described

28.16 Slide the drum into the crankcase

28.18 Hold the fork with the guide pin in its track then slide the shaft in

wear or damage, especially around the fork ends where they engage with the grooves in the pinions **(see illustration)** – measure the thickness of the fork ends and compare with the figure given in the Specifications to check whether they're worn. Check that each fork fits correctly in its pinion groove **(see illustration 28.15)**. Check closely to see if the forks are bent. If the forks are in any way damaged fit new ones.

10 Check that the forks fit correctly on their shaft **(see illustration)**. They should move freely with a light fit but no appreciable freeplay. Check that the fork shaft holes in the casing are not worn or damaged.

11 Check the selector fork shaft runout using V-blocks and a dial gauge and fit a new one if the runout exceeds the limit given in the Specifications at the beginning of this Chapter. A bent shaft will cause difficulty in selecting gears and make the gearchange action heavy.

12 Inspect the selector drum tracks and selector fork guide pins for signs of wear or damage **(see illustration)**.

13 Check the selector drum bearing referring to *Tools and Workshop Tips* in the Reference section. If the bearing is worn a new selector drum will have to be fitted as the bearing is not available separately. Also check that the gear position switch contact plunger is not damaged or worn away. If required, replace the plunger and spring with new ones.

Installation

14 Lubricate the moving surfaces of all components with engine oil before fitting them.

15 Locate the input shaft selector fork (C) ends in its groove in the 3rd/4th gear pinion, making sure the letter faces the right-hand (clutch) side of the engine, then slide the fork around and below the input shaft so that it

does not get in the way when installing the selector drum **(see illustration)**.

16 Slide the selector drum into the crankcase **(see illustration)**. Align the drum so the neutral detent in the right-hand end is positioned towards the top of the engine **(see illustration 15.8b)**.

17 Lubricate the fork shafts with clean engine oil.

18 Move the input shaft selector fork around in its groove and locate the fork guide pin into its track in the selector drum, then slide the fork shaft into the crankcase and through the fork **(see illustration)**.

19 Position the output shaft fork R in the crankcase, making sure the letter faces the right-hand (clutch) side of the engine and the fork guide pin locates in its tracks in the drum, and slide the shaft into the crankcase and through the fork, then repeat for the L fork **(see illustrations)**.

28.19a Fit the R fork...

28.19b ... and slide the shaft through it...

28.19c ... then fit the L fork and slide the shaft all the way in

28.20 Threadlock the retainer plate screws

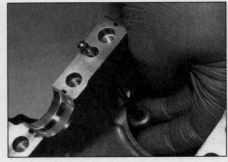

29.2a Push each oil jet out using a small screwdriver

29.2b Remove the O-ring (arrowed) from each jet

20 Clean the threads of the retainer plate screws and apply a suitable non-permanent thread locking compound. Fit the plate and tighten the screws to 10 Nm **(see illustration)**.
21 Install the transmission output shaft (Section 26).
22 Fit the spring and contact plunger into the end of the selector drum, then fit the gear position switch (see Chapter 8).
23 Reassemble the crankcases (Section 19).

29 Crankcases and cylinder bores

Crankcase halves

1 After the crankcases have been separated, remove the balancer shaft and crankshaft and their bearing shells, connecting rods and pistons, transmission shafts, selector drum and forks, and any other components or assemblies, referring to the relevant Sections of this and other Chapters (see Step 3 of Section 19).
2 Remove the three oil jets from the upper crankcase **(see illustration)**. Remove their O-rings – new ones must be used **(see illustration)**.
3 If required unscrew the oil gallery plugs from each side of the lower crankcase – new O-rings must be fitted on reassembly.
4 Clean the crankcases thoroughly with solvent and dry them with compressed air.

Blow out all oil passages and pipes with compressed air.
5 Remove all traces of old gasket sealant from the mating surfaces. Minor damage to the surfaces can be cleaned up with careful use of a fine sharpening stone.
Caution: Be very careful not to nick or gouge the crankcase mating surfaces, or oil leaks will result. Check both crankcase halves very carefully for cracks and other damage.
6 Before proceeding further, check the cylinder bores (see Steps 14 to 17).
7 Inspect the bearing seats for signs of damage, especially if an engine or transmission bearing has overheated or seized (Section 20). If bearing shells or a ball bearing cage are not a precise fit in their seats, ask your Yamaha dealer for a suitable bearing locking compound which will overcome small amounts of wear. Otherwise the crankcase halves will have to be replaced with a new set.
8 Small cracks or holes in aluminium castings can be repaired with an epoxy resin adhesive as a temporary measure. Permanent repairs can only be effected by argon-arc welding, and only a specialist in this process is in a position to advise on the economy or practical aspect of such a repair. Note that low temperature aluminium welding kits are available for minor repairs. If any damage is found that can't be repaired, replace the crankcase halves with a new set.
9 Damaged threads can be economically reclaimed by using a diamond section wire

insert which is easily fitted after drilling and re-tapping the affected thread.
10 Sheared studs or screws can usually be removed with stud or screw extractors; if you are in any doubt consult your Yamaha dealer or specialist motorcycle engineer.
11 Lightly grease the new O-rings for the oil gallery plugs and fit the plugs, tightening them to the specified torque (Specifications).
12 Lightly grease the new O-rings for the oil jets, then fit them onto the jets **(see illustration 29.2b)**. Push the jets into the upper crankcase **(see illustration)**.
13 Install the remaining components in the reverse order of removal.

Cylinder bores

14 Check the cylinder walls carefully for scratches and score marks.
15 Using telescoping gauges and a micrometer (see *Tools and Workshop Tips*), check the dimensions of each cylinder to assess the amount of wear, taper and ovality. Measure near the top (but below the level of the top piston ring at TDC), the centre and bottom (but above the level of the oil ring at BDC) of the bore. Measure both parallel to and across the crankshaft axis in each case and calculate the average cylinder dimension at each point **(see illustrations)**. Compare the results to the specifications at the beginning of this Chapter.
16 If the precision measuring tools are not available, take the crankcase to a Yamaha dealer or specialist motorcycle engineer for assessment and advice.

29.12 Push the jets down until they seat

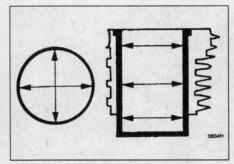

29.15a Measure the cylinder bore in the directions shown...

29.15b ...with a telescoping gauge

17 If the cylinders are worn or badly scratched, scuffed or scored, replace the crankcases with a new set. The cylinders cannot be rebored. If new crankcases are fitted, new pistons and rings must be used.

30 Running-in procedure

1 Make sure the engine oil and coolant levels are correct (see *Pre-ride checks*).
2 Make sure there is fuel in the tank.
3 Turn the ignition 'ON' and check that the warning lights for engine trouble, coolant temperature and immobiliser (where fitted) come on for a few seconds and then go off. The oil pressure warning light should also come on and stay on until the engine is started. Make sure that the transmission is in neutral and that the neutral light is on.
4 Start the engine, then allow it to run at a moderately fast idle until it reaches normal operating temperature. Make sure the oil pressure light goes out after starting the engine.
5 If a lubrication failure is suspected, stop the engine immediately and try to find the cause. If an engine is run without oil, even for a short period of time, severe damage will occur. After running the rebuilt engine for 600 miles (1000 km), change the engine oil and filter (see Chapter 1).
6 Check carefully that there are no oil or coolant leaks and make sure the transmission and controls, especially the brakes and clutch, work properly before road testing the machine.
7 Treat the machine gently for the first few miles to allow the oil to circulate throughout the engine and any new parts installed to seat.
8 Great care is necessary if the engine has been extensively overhauled – the bike will have to be run in as when new. This means more use of the transmission and a restraining hand on the throttle until at least 1000 miles (1600 km) have been covered. There is no point in keeping to any set road speed, the main idea is to keep from labouring the engine and to gradually increase performance up to the 1000 mile (1600 km) mark. These recommendations apply less when only a partial overhaul has been done, though it does depend to an extent on the nature of the work carried out and which components have been renewed. Experience is the best guide, since it is easy to tell when an engine is running freely. If in any doubt, consult a Yamaha dealer. The following maximum engine speed limitations, which Yamaha provide for new motorcycles, can be used as a guide.

Up to 600 miles (1000 km)	Do not exceed 5000 rpm for long periods
600 to 1000 miles (1000 to 1600 km)	Vary throttle position/ speed. Do not exceed 6000 rpm for long periods
Over 1000 miles (1600 km)	Normal riding. Do not exceed tachometer red line

9 Upon completion of the road test, and after the engine has cooled down completely, recheck the valve clearances (see Chapter 1) and check the engine oil and coolant levels (see *Pre-ride checks*).

Notes

Chapter 3
Cooling system

Contents

Degrees of difficulty

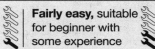

Easy, suitable for novice with little experience	**Fairly easy,** suitable for beginner with some experience	**Fairly difficult,** suitable for competent DIY mechanic	**Difficult,** suitable for experienced DIY mechanic	**Very difficult,** suitable for expert DIY or professional

Specifications

Coolant

Coolant type.. Pre-mixed coolant for motorcycle engines, or a mixture of 50% distilled water and 50% ethylene glycol anti-freeze with corrosion inhibitors for aluminium engines. Note that Yamaha specify that soft tap water can be used, but NOT hard water. If in doubt, use only distilled water.

Coolant capacity
Radiator and all passages .... 1.6 litres
Reservoir... 0.25 litre

Radiator

Cap valve opening pressure................................. 15.7 to 19.9 psi (1.08 to 1.37 Bar)

Coolant temperature (ECT) sensor

Resistance @ 20°C.. 2.51 to 2.78 K-ohms
Resistance @ 100°C....................................... 210 to 221 ohms

Thermostat

Opening temperature .... 80 to 84°C
Fully open... 95°C
Valve lift .... 8 mm (min)

Torque wrench settings

Coolant inlet union bolts................................... 10 Nm
Coolant temperature (ECT) sensor .... 16 Nm
Thermostat cover bolts .... 12 Nm
Water pump cover bolts.................................... 10 Nm

2.2a On MT-07 (FZ-07) models each cover is secured by two screws with collars

2.2b On XSR models each cover is secured to an inner bracket by two screws (arrowed), and two screws secure the inner brackets to the radiator

2.2c On MT-07TR models each cover is secured by two trim clips (arrowed)

1 General Information

1 The cooling system uses a water/antifreeze mixture to carry excess heat away from the engine. The cylinders are surrounded by a water jacket, through which the coolant is circulated by a water pump. The water pump is driven by the oil pump.

2 Heated coolant from the engine flows through the radiator, where it is cooled by the airflow across it. A thermostat fitted in the left-hand end of the cylinder head is closed when the engine is cold to prevent the coolant flowing, therefore accelerating the speed at which the engine reaches normal operating temperature, and opens as the engine warms up, allowing the coolant to flow.

3 A coolant temperature (ECT) sensor is fitted into the back of the cylinder head, and provides signals for the coolant temperature display on the instrument panel and for the ECU as part of the engine management system.

4 A relay-controlled cooling fan is fitted behind the radiator, to aid cooling in extreme conditions. The relay is controlled by a signal from the ECU.

5 Some coolant is routed through an oil cooler on the front of the engine.

6 The complete cooling system is partially sealed and pressurised, the pressure being controlled by a spring-loaded valve contained in the radiator cap. By pressurising the coolant the boiling point is raised, preventing premature boiling in adverse conditions. The overflow hose from the system is connected to a reservoir mounted on the front of the engine, into which excess coolant is expelled under pressure. The discharged coolant automatically returns to the radiator when the engine cools.

⚠️ **Warning: Do not remove the pressure cap from the radiator when the engine is hot. Scalding hot coolant and steam may be**

blown out under pressure and could cause serious injury. When the engine has cooled, place a thick rag such as a towel over the pressure cap; slowly rotate the cap anti-clockwise to the first stop. This procedure allows any residual pressure to escape. When the pressure has stopped escaping, press down on the cap while turning it anti-clockwise, and remove it.

7 Do not allow antifreeze to come into contact with your skin, or painted surfaces of the motorcycle. Rinse off any spills immediately with plenty of water. Antifreeze is highly toxic if ingested. Never leave antifreeze lying around in an open container or in puddles on the floor; children and pets are attracted by its sweet smell and may drink it. Check with the local authorities about disposing of used antifreeze. Many communities will have collection centres which will see that antifreeze is disposed of safely.

Caution: At all times use the specified type of antifreeze, and always mix it with distilled water in the correct proportion. The antifreeze contains corrosion inhibitors which are essential to avoid damage to the cooling system. A lack of these inhibitors could lead to a build-up of corrosion which will block the coolant passages inside the engine, resulting in overheating and severe engine damage. Distilled water should be used as opposed to tap water to avoid a

build-up of scale which would also block the passages. Alternatively purchase pre-mixed motorcycle coolant.

8 Read the *Safety first!* section of this manual carefully before starting work.

2 Radiator

Removal

⚠️ *Warning: The engine must be completely cool before carrying out this procedure.*

1 On MT-07 (FZ-07) models remove the left-hand fuel tank cover, on MT-07TR models remove the fairing side panels and inner panels, and on XSR models remove the left-hand air scoop (see Chapter 7).

2 On MT-07 (FZ-07) and XSR models remove the right-hand radiator cover to access the radiator mounting bolt, and the left-hand radiator cover if required **(see illustrations)**. On MT-07TR models remove the radiator covers if required **(see illustration)**.

3 Drain the cooling system (see Chapter 1).

4 Disconnect the horn wiring connectors, and if required remove the horn **(see illustration)**. Release the wiring and hose from the clip on the fan bracket **(see illustration)**.

5 Disconnect the cooling fan wiring

2.4a Disconnect the wiring, and if required unscrew the nut (arrowed) and remove the horn

2.4b Open the clip and release the wiring and hose

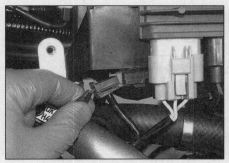

2.5 Cooling fan wiring connector

2.6a Disconnect the overflow hose

2.6b Release the clamp by squeezing the ears together using pliers

2.6c Slacken the clamp screw…

2.6d … and pull the hose off

2.7 Unscrew the bolt

connector, then feed the wiring to the radiator, noting its routing **(see illustration)**.

6 Disconnect the overflow hose from the filler neck **(see illustration)**. Release the clamp on the outlet hose on the bottom of the radiator on the right-hand side and slide it down the hose **(see illustration)**. Disconnect the inlet hose from the thermostat housing on the left-hand end of the cylinder head **(see illustrations)**.

7 Unscrew the radiator mounting bolt **(see illustration)**.

8 Move the right-hand side of the radiator forwards and disconnect the hose, then move the radiator to the right to free its grommets from the lugs and remove the radiator, drawing the inlet hose out and noting its routing **(see illustrations)**.

9 If required remove the cooling fan (Section 4).

10 Check the radiator for signs of damage and clear any dirt or debris that might obstruct airflow and inhibit cooling. Radiator fins can be straightened carefully with a flat-bladed screwdriver, but if the fins are badly damaged or broken the radiator must be replaced with a new one. Remove the collar for the mounting bolt, and check the condition of the three mounting grommets – fit new ones if necessary **(see illustration)**.

Installation

11 Installation is the reverse of removal, noting the following.

● Make sure the coolant hoses are in good condition.

● Make sure the collar for the mounting bolt is fitted in the grommet **(see illustration 2.10)**.

● When fitting the radiator feed the inlet

hose down to the thermostat housing, routing it above the wiring, and make sure the grommets seat over the lugs **(see illustration 2.8b)**.

● Make sure the coolant hoses are securely retained by their clamps – use new clamps if necessary (see Step 6).

● Make sure that the wiring is correctly routed and the connector is secure **(see illustration 2.5)**.

● Refill the cooling system as described in Chapter 1.

Radiator pressure cap

12 If problems such as overheating or loss of coolant occur, check the entire system as described in Chapter 1. The radiator cap opening pressure should be checked by a Yamaha dealer with the special tester required for the job. If the cap is defective, fit a new one.

2.8a Disconnect the hose…

2.8b … then slide the radiator off the lugs (arrowed)

2.10 Make sure the grommets are in good condition

3.1a Note the collar with the bolt

3.1b The peg locates in the hole

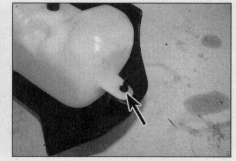

3.2 Cover is secured by a trim clip (arrowed)

3 Coolant reservoir

Removal

1 Unscrew the bolt and displace the reservoir, noting how the peg locates **(see illustrations)**.
2 If required release the trim clip and remove the cover **(see illustration)**.

Installation

3 Installation is the reverse of removal, noting the following:
● Make sure the breather hose and the overflow hose are correctly routed and secured.
● Fill the reservoir with the specified coolant up to the correct level (see *Pre-ride checks*).

4 Cooling fan and cooling fan relay

Cooling fan
Check

1 If the engine is overheating and the coolant temperature display flashes 'HI', yet the cooling fan isn't cutting in, first check the fan fuse in the fusebox (see Chapter 8).
2 If the fuse is good, on MT-07 (FZ-07) models remove the left-hand fuel tank cover, on MT-07TR models remove the left-hand fairing side panel and inner panel, and on XSR models remove the left-hand air scoop (see Chapter 7). Disconnect the fan wiring connector **(see illustration 2.5)**. Using a 12 volt battery and two jumper wires, connect the positive (+) battery lead to the blue wire terminal on the fan side of the wiring connector and the negative (–) lead to the black wire terminal. Once connected, the fan should operate. If it does not, and the wiring between the connector and the fan is good, then the fan is faulty.
3 If the fan motor works check the fan relay (see below). If the relay works check the wiring and connectors in the cooling fan circuit, referring to Chapter 8, Section 2 and to the wiring diagram for your model at the end of Chapter 8.

Removal and installation

⚠️ *Warning: The engine must be completely cool before carrying out this procedure.*

4 Remove the radiator (Section 2).
5 If not already done remove the horn **(see illustration 4.6)**.

6 Undo the fan screws and remove the fan **(see illustration)**.
7 Installation is the reverse of removal.

Cooling fan relay

8 On MT-07 (FZ-07) models remove the front fuel tank cover, on MT-07TR models remove the fuel tank cover, and on XSR models remove the left-hand fuel tank cover and air scoop (see Chapter 7).
9 Displace the relay unit, then displace the fan relay and disconnect the wiring connector **(see illustration)**. Set a multimeter to the ohms x 1 scale and connect the positive (+) probe to the red wire terminal on the relay, and the negative (-) probe to the blue wire terminal. There should be no continuity (infinite resistance).
10 Using a fully-charged 12 volt battery and two insulated jumper wires, connect the positive (+) battery terminal to the red/white wire terminal on the relay, and the negative (–) battery terminal to the green/yellow wire terminal. At this point the relay should be heard to click and the multimeter should read 0 ohms (continuity).
11 If this is the case, the relay is proved good. If there is continuity through the relay at all times, or if the relay does not click when battery voltage is applied and indicates

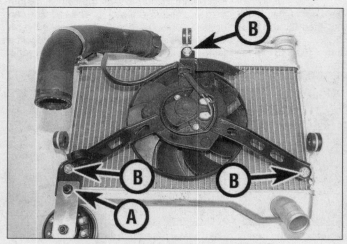

4.6 Horn nut (A), cooling fan screws (B)

4.9 Displace the relay unit (A) to access the fan relay (B)

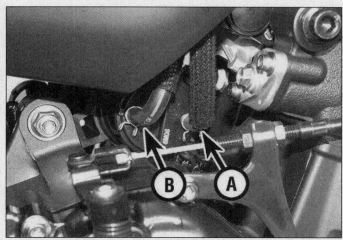

5.8a Disconnect the fuel tank breather hose (A) and the canister to throttle body hose (B) on the right-hand side

5.8b Disconnect the breather hose (arrowed), then draw the canister out of its holder

no continuity (infinite resistance) across its terminals, it is faulty.

12 If the relay is good, test the fan motor (if not already done), and the coolant temperature sensor (Section 5), then if necessary check the wiring and connectors between the relay, the fan motor and the ECU.

5 Coolant temperature display and ECT sensor

Temperature display

Check

1 The circuit consists of the sensor mounted in the back of the cylinder head and the coolant temperature display/warning light on the instrument cluster, according to model.

2 When the engine is cold (below 40°C), 'LO' will be shown. Between 40°C and 116°C the actual temperature will be displayed. If the engine is too hot 'HI' will be displayed flashing.

3 If the engine is over-heating turn it OFF immediately. When the engine has cooled, check the coolant level (see *Pre-ride checks*). If the level is low, check the cooling system for leaks (see Chapter 1, Section 12). If no leaks can be found fit a new pressure cap, and if that does not solve the problem fit a new thermostat (Section 6).

4 If the temperature display malfunctions, the operation of the sensor can be checked as described below.

5 If no problems are found, refer to Chapter 8, Section 16 for removal details, and if necessary take the instrument cluster to a Yamaha dealer for further assessment – Yamaha provide no specific test data for the instruments themselves. If there are any faults, a new cluster will have to be fitted, as no individual components are available.

Removal and installation

6 Refer to Chapter 8, Section 16, for removal and installation details.

Coolant temperature (ECT) sensor

Check

7 The sensor is mounted in the back of the cylinder head on the left-hand side. The resistance of the sensor changes with changes in temperature – see the Specifications. While in theory it is possible to bench-test the sensor at those temperatures, in practice the test is difficult to set up and perform. However you can test the resistance of the sensor in the bike with the engine cold, warm and hot.

8 On models with the EVAP canister release the hoses from each end, noting which fits where on the right-hand end, then draw the canister put of its holder **(see illustrations)**.

9 Disconnect the sensor wiring connector **(see illustration)**. With the engine cold connect the probes of a multimeter set to read resistance to the terminals in the sensor and take a reading.

10 Reconnect the wiring, start the engine and allow it warm up a bit, then stop it and take another reading. Do this again with the engine hot. Resistance should decrease as temperature increases – if the sensor fails it is most likely to give a zero, constant, or infinite resistance reading at all temperatures.

11 If the meter readings obtained are widely different the sensor is faulty.

Removal and installation

 Warning: The engine must be completely cool before carrying out this procedure.

12 Drain the cooling system (see Chapter 1).

13 Where fitted remove the EVAP system canister (see Step 8).

14 Disconnect the wiring connector from the sensor, then unscrew the sensor from

the head using a deep 17mm socket **(see illustration 5.9)**. Remove the sealing washer – a new one must be used.

15 Fit the sensor using a new sealing washer and tighten it to 16 Nm.

16 Fill the cooling system (see Chapter 1).

6 Thermostat

 Warning: The engine must be completely cool before carrying out this procedure.

1 The thermostat is automatic in operation and should give many years service without requiring attention. In the event of a failure, the valve will probably jam open, in which case the engine will take much longer than normal to warm up. Conversely, if the valve jams shut, the coolant will be unable to circulate and the engine will overheat. Neither condition is acceptable, and the fault must be investigated promptly.

Removal

2 Drain the cooling system (see Chapter 1).

3 Unscrew the thermostat cover bolts,

5.9 Coolant temperature sensor wiring connector (arrowed)

displace the cover and remove the thermostat (**see illustrations**).

Check

4 Examine the thermostat visually before carrying out the test. If it remains in the open position at room temperature, it should be replaced with a new one.

5 Suspend the thermostat by a piece of wire in a container of cold water. Suspend a thermometer capable of reading temperatures up to 110°C in the water so that the bulb is close to the thermostat (**see illustration**). Make sure neither the thermostat nor thermometer touches the container. Heat the water, noting the temperature when the thermostat opens, and compare the result with the specifications given at the beginning of the Chapter. Also check the amount the valve opens after it has been heated for a few minutes and compare the measurement to the specifications. If the readings obtained differ from those given, the thermostat is faulty and must be replaced with a new one.

6 In the event of thermostat failure, if the thermostat is permanently closed, as an emergency measure only it can be removed and the machine used without it (this is better than leaving it in as the engine will overheat). If it is permanently open you are better to leave it in. In both cases take care when starting the engine from cold as it will take much longer than usual to warm up. Ensure that a new unit is installed as soon as possible.

7 Check the condition of the seal and fit a new thermostat if it is damaged or deformed – it is not available separately.

Installation

8 Make sure the seal is correctly seated around the rim of the thermostat (**see illustration**).

9 Fit the thermostat with the breather hole facing in so it is at the highest point (**see illustration 6.3b**). Fit the cover and tighten the bolts to 12 Nm (**see illustration 6.3a**).

10 Fill the cooling system (see Chapter 1).

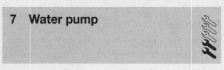

7 Water pump

Removal

1 Drain the engine oil and the coolant (see Chapter 1).

2 Remove the clutch cover (see Chapter 2).

3 Release the circlip securing the impeller shaft in the clutch cover (**see illustration**). Draw the impeller shaft out (**see illustration**).

Inspection

4 Check the pump impeller bearing in the inner side of the clutch cover – if it is noisy or rough when turned fit a new one (see below).

5 If there are signs of wear or other damage to the shaft or impeller, fit a new one. Check that the shaft is straight.

6.3a Unscrew the bolts (arrowed)

6.3b Move the cover aside and lift the thermostat out

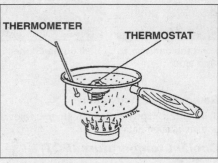

6.5 Thermostat testing set-up

6.8 Seal must be in good condition

6 Check the condition of the rubber damper on the inner face of the impeller. If it is damaged or deteriorated, replace it with a new one (**see illustrations**) – it is not available

on its own, but comes as a kit along with a mechanical seal. Wet the outer rim of the damper with water or coolant mix before pushing it into place.

7.3a Remove the circlip...

7.3b ... then remove the impeller shaft

7.6a Remove the damper using a screwdriver...

7.6b ...and push the new one in with your fingers

7.10a Drive the mechanical seal out using a punch ...

7.10b ... then remove any remnants as required

7 Inspect the pump cover for corrosion or a build-up of scale and clean with a scouring pad as necessary, then rinse in clean water.

8 Check the pump mechanical seal and oil seal – if there has been any evidence of seal failure (see Chapter 1), fit new ones (see below).

Seal and bearing renewal

Note: *Once removed, neither of the seals or the bearing can be re-used – they must be replaced with new ones.*

9 Remove the pump impeller from the clutch cover (Steps 1 to 3).

10 To remove the mechanical seal, drive it out using a suitable punch inserted through the bearing and oil seal and located against the inner rim of the seal – the inner sprung section of the seal will probably come out first, and the outer section will then have to removed in the same way, or pulled and gouged out using pliers **(see illustrations)**. Take care not to score the seal housing.

11 To remove the oil seal, first remove the mechanical seal (see Step 10). Lever the oil seal out using a flat-bladed screwdriver, noting which way round it fits **(see illustration)**.

12 To remove the bearing, first remove the mechanical seal and the oil seal (see Steps 10 and 11). Support the inner side of the clutch cover on blocks of wood so the bearing housing is off the work surface, then drive the bearing out using a 13mm socket seated against the inner race **(see illustration)**.

13 Clean any traces of sealant from around the mechanical seal seat with a suitable solvent.

14 Drive the new bearing into the pump body using a piece of wood across the bearing until

7.11 Lever the oil seal out using a screwdriver

it is seated, so its outer face is flush with the housing **(see illustration)**.

15 Push or drive the new oil seal into the body with its marked side facing away from

7.12 Drive the bearing out using a 13mm socket, supporting the cover as shown

7.14 Drive the new bearing in using a piece of wood until seated

7.15 Push the new seal in so it is flush in its housing

7.16a Grind a piece of tube if required so it is the correct size

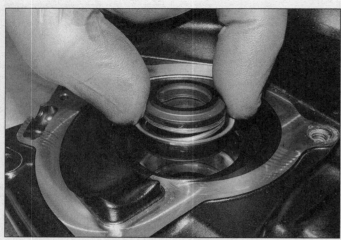

7.16b Position the new seal in the pump...

7.16c ...then seat the tube over it and drive or press it in

the bearing using a 14mm socket, and setting it so there is a 0.5 to 1.0 mm gap between the inner side of the seal and the bearing **(see illustration)**. Smear the seal lip with grease.

16 Press or carefully drive the new mechanical seal into the pump body using a piece of tube with an internal diameter of 28mm and an external diameter of 31.5mm (you can grind down a 32 or 34mm diameter tube to achieve this), so that it bears only on the outer rim of the seal but also fits inside the housing recess **(see illustrations)**. Alternatively Yamaha produce a special tool, Part No. 90890-04132 (European models) or YM-33221-A (US models), for installing the seal if required.

17 Refer to Step 6 and fit the new damper into the back of the impeller, then refer to Step 18 to fit the impeller.

Installation

18 Lubricate the impeller shaft and damper

with coolant and slide it into the clutch cover **(see illustration 7.3b)**. Seat the clutch cover so the impeller is on the work surface and push the cover down so the impeller compresses the mechanical seal and the circlip groove is exposed, and fit a new circlip into the groove with its smooth side facing the bearing **(see illustration 7.3a)**.

19 Install the clutch cover (see Chapter 2).

20 Refill the engine with oil and the cooling system with coolant to the correct levels (see Chapter 1).

---

8 Coolant hoses, pipes and unions

Removal

 Warning: Allow the engine to cool completely before disconnecting a coolant hose.

1 Before removing a hose, pipe or union, drain the coolant (see Chapter 1). When removing components of the cooling system, be prepared to catch any residual fluids.

2 Use a pair of pliers to squeeze the ends of the spring type clamps together, and a screwdriver to slacken the screw type hose clamps **(see illustrations 2.6b and c)**. Slide the clamp back along the hose and clear of the union spigot, then pull the hose off the union.

Caution: The radiator unions are fragile. Do not use excessive force when attempting to remove the hoses.

3 If a hose proves stubborn, release it by rotating it on its union before working it off. If all else fails, cut the hose with a sharp knife then slit it at each union so that it can be peeled off in two pieces. Whilst this means renewing the hose, it is preferable to buying a new radiator.

8.4a Unscrew the two bolts...

8.4b ... then pull the pipes out of the pump

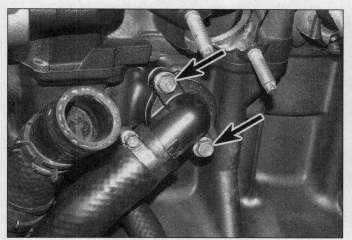

8.5 Coolant union bolts (arrowed)

8.7 Use new O-rings when fitting the pipes

4 To remove the water pump inlet and outlet pipes first disconnect the hoses, then unscrew the bolts and remove the pipes (**see illustrations**) – new O-rings must be used where the pipes fit into the pump cover.
5 Remove the union on the front of the engine by detaching the hose, then unscrewing the bolts (**see illustration**). Remove the O-ring – a new one must be used.

Installation

6 If the union on the front of the engine has been removed, fit a new O-ring into the groove and smear it with grease. Fit the union and tighten the bolts to 10 Nm.
7 Fit new O-rings smeared with grease onto the coolant pipes (**see illustration**). Fit the

pipes and tighten the bolts to 10 Nm (**see illustrations 8.4b and a**).
8 Slide the clamp onto the hose and then work the hose onto its union, up against the spigot where present.
9 Rotate the hose on its union to settle it in position before sliding the clamp into place, and tighten the screw type clamps where fitted.

Chapter 4
Engine management system

Contents

Degrees of difficulty

Easy, suitable for novice with little experience	**Fairly easy,** suitable for beginner with some experience	**Fairly difficult,** suitable for competent DIY mechanic	**Difficult,** suitable for experienced DIY mechanic	**Very difficult,** suitable for expert DIY or professional

Specifications

General information

Cylinder numbering	1 – left, 2 – right
Ignition timing	10° BTDC @ 1200 rpm
Spark plugs	see Chapter 1

Component test data

Crankshaft position sensor resistance	228 to 342 ohms
Coolant temperature (ECT) sensor	
Resistance @ 20°C	2.51 to 2.78 K-ohms
Resistance @ 100°C	210 to 221 ohms
Fuel level sensor resistance	
2014 to 2016 MT-07 (FZ-07), MT-07TR and XSR models	
Fuel tank full	9 to 11 ohms
Fuel tank empty	213 to 219 ohms
2017-on MT-07 (FZ-07) models	
Fuel tank full	19 to 21 ohms
Fuel tank empty	429 to 435 ohms
Fuel pump pressure (at idle)	43.5 to 56.6 psi (3.0 to 3.9 Bar)
Intake air flap solenoid valve resistance	approx. 46 ohms
Intake air pressure sensor output voltage	3.57 to 3.71 V
Intake air temperature sensor resistance	
Resistance @ 0°C	5.4 to 6.6 K-ohms
Resistance @ 80°C	290 to 390 ohms
Speed sensor output voltage (models without ABS)	
On	4.8V
Off	0.6V
Throttle position sensor	
Resistance (max)	2.64 to 6.16 K-ohms
Output voltage (at idle)	
2014 to 2016 MT-07 (FZ-07), MT-07TR and XSR models	0.63 to 0.73 V
2017-on MT-07 (FZ-07) models	0.21 to 0.22 V
Tip-over sensor output voltage	
Sensor upright	0.4 to 1.4 V
Sensor tilted at 65° or more	3.7 to 4.4 V

Fuel

Grade . . . . Unleaded, minimum 95 RON (Research Octane Number)
Fuel tank capacity (including reserve)
MT-07 (FZ-07) and XSR models . . . . 14 litres
MT-07TR models . . . . 17 litres
Reserve
MT-07 (FZ-07) and XSR models . . . . 2.7 litres
MT-07TR models . . . . 3.5 litres

Throttle bodies

Type . . . . Mikuni EHDW38

Fuel injector

Type/quantity 297500-2310/2
Resistance . . . . 12 ohms

Ignition coils

Primary resistance . . . . 1.19 to 1.61 ohms
Secondary resistance. . . . . 8.5 to 11.5 K-ohms
Minimum spark gap . . . . 6 mm

Torque wrench settings

Exhaust header pipe nuts. . . . . 20 Nm
Exhaust mounting bolts . . . . 20 Nm
Exhaust mounting bracket bolts . . . . 10 Nm
Footrest bracket bolts . . . . 30 Nm
Fuel pump mounting plate bolts . . . . 4 Nm
Fuel rail bolts . . . . 3.5 Nm
Fuel tank mounting bolts
Front . . . . 30 Nm
Rear . . . . 10 Nm

---

1 General information and precautions

General information

1 All models are fitted with a fully electronic engine management system that controls both the fuelling and ignition from one engine control unit, or ECU.

Fuel system

2 The fuel system consists of the fuel tank, inside which is located the fuel pump with integral filter and fuel level sensor, the fuel supply hose, the fuel injectors, the throttle body assembly, and the throttle cables. Air is drawn into the throttle bodies via an air filter, which is housed under the fuel tank.
3 The fuel pump is activated initially by the ignition switch, and fuel pressure is controlled by a regulator in the pump.
4 In the event of the machine falling over, a tip-over sensor cuts power to the fuel and ignition systems.
5 The fuel injection system is controlled by the engine control unit (ECU), which monitors data sent from the various system sensors and adjusts fuel delivery to the engine and ignition timing accordingly. The ECU has its own fault diagnosis function and displays fault codes and diagnostic codes on the LCD display in the instrument cluster.
6 The exhaust is an underslung two-into-one

design and incorporates a catalytic converter and an oxygen sensor.

Ignition system

7 The ignition system consists of the timing triggers on the alternator rotor, on the left-hand end of the crankshaft, a crankshaft position (CKP) sensor in the alternator cover, the engine control unit (ECU), 'stick' type ignition coils, and spark plugs.
8 The timing triggers on the alternator rotor generate signals in the CKP sensor as the crankshaft rotates. The CKP sensor sends those signals to the ECU, which, in conjunction with data sent from the various other system sensors, calculates the best ignition timing and supplies the ignition coils with the power necessary to produce a spark at the plugs. There is no provision for adjusting the ignition timing.
9 The system incorporates a starter safety circuit that will cut the ignition if the sidestand is extended whilst the engine is running and in gear, or if a gear is selected whilst the engine is running and the sidestand is extended. It also prevents the engine from being started if the engine is in gear unless the clutch lever is pulled in and the stand is up.
10 Models sold in certain markets are fitted with an immobiliser system, which will not allow the engine to be started unless the correct key is used. The immobiliser system has its own fault diagnosis function.
Note: *Individual engine management system components can be checked but not repaired*

if faulty. If system troubles occur, and the faulty component can be isolated, the only cure for the problem in most cases is to replace the part with a new one. Keep in mind that most electronic parts, once purchased, cannot be returned. To avoid unnecessary expense, make very sure the faulty component has been positively identified before buying a new part.

Precautions

 Warning: Petrol (gasoline) is extremely flammable, so take extra precautions when you work on any part of the fuel system. Don't smoke or allow open flames or bare light bulbs near the work area, and don't work in a garage where a natural gas-type appliance is present. If you spill any fuel on your skin, rinse it off immediately with soap and water. When you perform any kind of work on the fuel system, wear safety glasses and have a fire extinguisher suitable for a class B type fire (flammable liquids) on hand.

● Always perform service procedures in a well-ventilated area to prevent a build-up of fumes.
● Never work in a building containing a gas appliance with a pilot light, or any other form of naked flame. Ensure that there are no naked light bulbs or any sources of flame or sparks nearby.
● Do not smoke (or allow anyone else to smoke) while in the vicinity of petrol (gasoline), or of components containing

petrol. Remember the possible presence of vapour from these sources and move well clear before smoking.

● Check all electrical equipment belonging to the house, garage or workshop where work is being undertaken (see the *Safety first!* section of this manual). Remember that certain electrical appliances such as drills, cutters, etc, create sparks in the normal course of operation and must not be used near petrol (gasoline) or any component containing it. Again, remember the possible presence of fumes before using electrical equipment.

● Always mop up any spilt fuel and safely dispose of the rag used.

● Any stored fuel that is drained off during servicing work must be kept in sealed containers that are suitable for holding petrol (gasoline), and clearly marked as such; the containers themselves should be kept in a safe place. Note that this last point applies equally to the fuel tank if it is removed from the machine; also remember to keep its filler cap closed at all times.

● Read the *Safety first!* section of this manual carefully before starting work.

2 Fuel tank

⚠ **Warning: Refer to the precautions given in Section 1 before starting work.**

2.5 IAT sensor wiring connector

2.6 Pull the hoses off their unions, noting which fits where

Removal

Note: *To reduce the weight of the tank remove it when it is nearly empty, or if the tank is full siphon the fuel into a suitable container using a hand pump (available from tool suppliers).*

1 Make sure the ignition switch is OFF and the fuel filler cap is secure.

2 On MT-07 (FZ-07) models remove the seat and the fuel tank covers (see Chapter 7).

3 On MT-07TR models remove the fairing side panels and inner panels and the fuel tank cover (see Chapter 7).

4 On XSR models remove the seat, the fuel tank top and side covers, and the right-hand air scoop (see Chapter 7).

5 Disconnect the intake air temperature

(IAT) sensor wiring connector **(see illustration)**.

6 Disconnect the breather and overflow hoses **(see illustration)**.

7 Unscrew the bolts securing the rear of the tank **(see illustration)**. Slacken, but do not yet remove, the front bolt **(see illustration 2.10)**. Raise the rear of the tank and support it using a piece of wood as shown **(see illustration)**.

8 Place some rag under the fuel pump. Slide the fuel hose connector security cover across to expose the two release tabs, press the tabs in and pull the connector off the union **(see illustrations)**.

9 Disconnect the fuel pump wiring connector **(see illustration)**.

2.7a Unscrew the bolts on each side

2.7b Raise and support the tank as shown

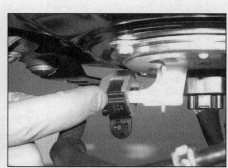

2.8a Slide the cover across to expose the tabs...

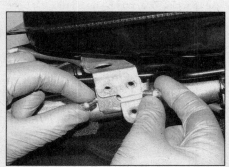

2.8b ...press the tabs in...

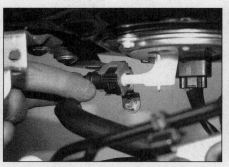

2.8c ...and pull the hose connector off

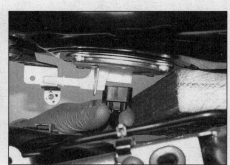

2.9 Disconnect the wiring

2.10 Unscrew the front bolt and remove the tank

2.11a Front mounting bracket

2.11b Rear mounting bracket

10 Remove the support and lower the tank. Unscrew the front bolt, then carefully lift the tank off the frame (see illustration). Support the tank on a block of wood so it does not rest on the underside of the fuel pump.

11 Inspect the tank brackets and grommets for signs of damage or deterioration and fit new ones if necessary (see illustrations). Note the collars in the grommets. When fitting the brackets make sure the arrow on the front bracket points towards the underside of the tank, and the arrow on the rear bracket points towards the rear of the tank.

Installation

12 Installation is the reverse of removal, noting the following:

● Make sure the hoses are properly connected and secured – push the fuel hose on until it is felt to click into place, then push the security cover into place (see illustration). Make sure the wiring connector is secure.

● Tighten the front mounting bolt to 30 Nm and the rear bolts to 10 Nm.

● Connect the hose with the blue mark to the rear union on the tank and the hose with the white mark to the front (see illustration 2.6).

● Start the engine and check that there are

no fuel leaks. If the tank has been emptied, make sure it is refilled before turning the ignition switch ON.

Repair

13 All repairs to the fuel tank should be carried out by a professional who has experience in this critical and potentially dangerous work. Even after cleaning and flushing of the fuel system, explosive fumes can remain and ignite during repair of the tank.

14 If the fuel tank is removed from the bike, it should not be placed in an area where sparks or open flames could ignite the fumes coming out of the tank. Be especially careful inside garages where a natural gas-type appliance is located, because the pilot light could cause an explosion.

3 Fuel pump and pressure regulator

⚠️ Warning: Refer to the precautions given in Section 1 before starting work.

Check

1 The fuel pump is located inside the fuel

tank. When the ignition is switched ON, it should be possible to hear the pump run for a few seconds until the system is up to pressure. If you can't hear anything, first check that the kill switch is set to run and the battery is not flat, then check the main, ignition and fuel injection system fuses.

2 Next, check the fuel pump relay (Section 8). If the fuses and relay are good, check the wiring and terminals in the circuit for physical damage or loose or corroded connections and rectify as necessary (see the Wiring Diagrams at the end of Chapter 8).

3 If the pump still will not run, make sure the ignition switch is OFF, then raise the fuel tank and disconnect the pump wiring connector (Section 2). Connect the positive (+) lead from a fully charged battery to the red/blue wire terminal in the pump side of the connector and the negative (-) lead to the adjacent black wire terminal – the pump should run. If it does there is a fault in the wiring circuit to the pump. If it doesn't, remove the pump and check the internal wiring connectors (see illustration). If the wiring is good the pump motor is faulty.

Fuel pressure check

Special tools: A fuel pressure gauge with an appropriate adapter is required for this procedure.

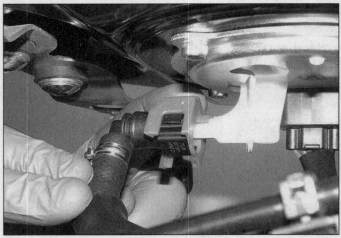

2.12 Make sure the hose is fully pushed on and the tabs have clicked into place before pushing the cover across

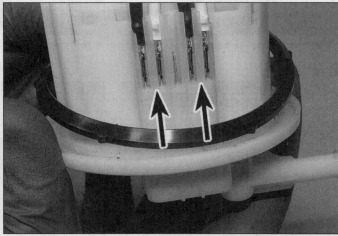

3.3 Check the internal wiring and connectors (arrowed)

4 Fuel pressure is governed by a regulator that is an integral part of the fuel pump.

5 Raise the fuel tank, then disconnect the fuel supply hose from it (Section 2). Connect the adapter and fuel pressure gauge between the fuel tank and the fuel hose. Yamaha can provide a gauge (Pt. No. 90890-03153 in Europe, YU-03153 in the US) and gauge adapter (Pt. No. 90890-03176 or YM 03176) for this purpose.

6 Start the engine and note the pressure recorded on the gauge – it should be similar to that given in the Specifications. Stop the engine.

7 If the pressure is not as specified, make sure the fuel hose has not become kinked. If the hose is in good condition, a new pump will have to be fitted – individual components are not available. Note that the fuel filter is an integral part of the fuel pump.

Removal

8 Siphon the fuel from the tank into a suitable container using a hand-pump, available from good tool and DIY stores.

9 Remove the fuel tank (Section 2), and lay it upside down on plenty of clean rag.

10 Unscrew the pump mounting plate bolts and remove the plate, noting how it fits **(see illustration)**.

11 Carefully lift the pump and manoeuvre it out of the tank **(see illustration)**.

12 Remove the sealing ring **(see illustration 3.13)** – a new one must be fitted.

Installation

13 Fit a new sealing ring flat side down onto the pump base **(see illustration)**.

14 Manoeuvre the pump into the aperture in the tank **(see illustration 3.11)**.

15 Align the pump so the fuel supply hose union points to the back, and align the stud on the underside of the pump with the mark on the tank, then fit the mounting plate, seating the cut-out in the ring around the stud **(see illustration)**. Tighten the bolts evenly and in a criss-cross sequence to 4 Nm.

3.10 Unscrew the pump bolts and remove the mounting plate

3.11 Carefully remove the pump

---

4 Fuel level display and sensor ⚙

Fuel level display

Check

1 The circuit consists of the sensor mounted inside the fuel tank and the fuel level display that is part of the multi-function display in the instrument cluster.

2 The fuel level display should function as follows. When the ignition switch is turned ON, all the segments of the display should appear in sequence as a test of the circuit. Then, depending upon how much fuel is in the tank, the requisite number of segments between 'F' (full) and 'E' (empty) will be shown.

3 When the fuel content in the tank falls to approx. 2.7 litres on MT-07 (FZ-07) and XSR models and 3.5 litres on MT-07TR models, the E segment on the display and the fuel warning symbol begin flashing and the odometer display automatically changes to fuel reserve trip meter mode.

4 If required, the trip meter can be reset using the left (MT models) or bottom (XSR models) button on the instrument cluster (refer to your owner's manual). Once the tank has been topped-up, the fuel reserve trip meter should reset automatically after the machine has travelled approx. 3 miles (5 km).

5 The fuel level display has its own self-diagnosis function. If it malfunctions, the display and the fuel symbol will flash eight times on a repeating cycle, with a three second gap between cycles. First check the fuel pump/level sensor wiring connector on the underside of the tank (Section 2), then check the wiring from the sensor to the instrument cluster, referring to Chapter 8. If all is good, check the sensor as described below.

6 If no problems are found, take the instrument cluster to a Yamaha dealer for further assessment – Yamaha provide no specific test data for the instruments themselves. If there are any faults, a new cluster will have to be fitted, as no individual components are available.

Removal and installation

7 Refer to Chapter 8, Section 16.

Fuel level sensor

8 Remove the fuel pump from the tank (see Section 3).

9 Using an ohmmeter or multimeter set to the ohms x 10 scale, measure the resistance

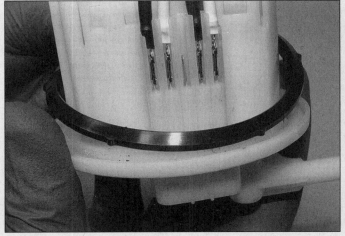

3.13 Make sure the seal is fitted with the flat side against the base

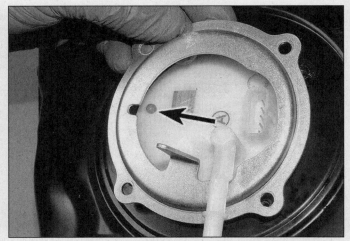

3.15 Align the pump and mounting plate as shown and fit the cut-out in the plate over the stud (arrowed)

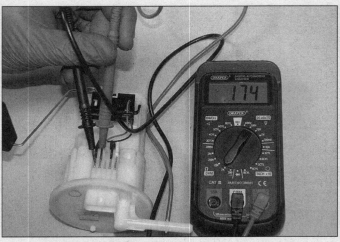

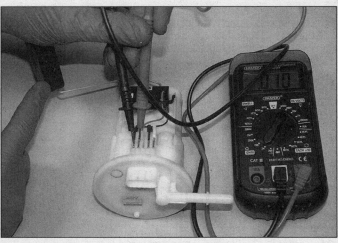

4.9a Measure the resistance in the empty position...

4.9b ...and the full position

between the sensor terminals on the pump as shown, first with the sensor float in the empty position, and then held up in the full position **(see illustrations)**.

10 If the measurements are not as given in the Specifications at the beginning of the Chapter, the sensor is faulty and a new pump will have to be fitted – individual components are not available (Section 3).

5 Air filter housing

Removal

1 Remove the air filter (see Chapter 1).
2 Remove the throttle bodies (Section 9).
3 On models without the EVAP canister undo the fuel tank drain and breather hose clamp screw on the front of the housing and move the hoses out of the way **(see illustration 5.4)**.
4 Remove the air filter housing **(see illustration)**.

Installation

5 Installation is the reverse of removal, noting the following:

5.4 Drain/breather hose clamp screw (arrowed), where fitted. Manoeuvre the housing out the left-hand side

● Check the condition of the mounting grommets in the frame and fit new ones if necessary. Make sure the collars are fitted into the inner side of the grommets.
● Make sure that the clamps are correctly positioned.

6 Fuel injection system description

1 The fuel injection system consists of two main component groups, the fuel circuit and the electronic control circuit.
2 The fuel circuit consists of the tank, the integrated pump/filter/pressure regulator, the throttle bodies and the injectors. Fuel is pumped under pressure from the tank to the fuel rail, from which the individual injectors are fed. Operating pressure is maintained by the pressure regulator in the pump. The injectors spray pressurised fuel into the throttle bodies where it mixes with air and vaporises, before entering the cylinder where it is compressed and ignited.
3 The electronic control circuit consists of the ECU, which operates and co-ordinates both the fuel injection and ignition systems, and the various sensors which provide the ECU with information on engine operating conditions.
4 The ECU monitors signals from the following sensors:
● Intake air temperature sensor
● Intake air pressure sensor
● Throttle position sensor
● Crankshaft position sensor
● Coolant temperature sensor
● Oxygen sensor
● Speed sensor
● Tip-over sensor
5 Based on the information it receives, the ECU calculates the appropriate ignition, fuel and throttle requirements of the engine. By varying the length of the electronic pulse it sends to each injector, the ECU controls the length of time the injectors are held open and thereby the amount of fuel that is supplied to the engine.
6 In the event of an abnormality in any of the sensor signals, the ECU will determine whether the engine can still be run safely. If it can, a back-up mode substitutes the sensor signal with a fixed signal, restricting performance but allowing the bike to be ridden home or to a dealer. When this occurs, the engine trouble warning light in the instrument cluster will come on and stay on. If the fault is serious, the fuel injection system will be shut down and the engine will not run. When this occurs, the engine trouble warning light will flash when the ignition switch is ON and the start button is being pressed. **Note:** *The warning light should come on for about 2 seconds after the ignition switch has been turned ON. If the warning light does not come on, check its LED circuit in the instrument cluster (see Chapter 8).*
7 After the engine has been stopped, the appropriate self-diagnostic fault code will appear on the instrument display on 2014 to 2016 MT-07 (FZ-07) models, and can be accessed using the Yamaha diagnostic tool or a generic OBD tool on 2017-on MT-07 (FZ-07) models and on all MT-07TR and XSR models (for which see Section 7). If more than one fault has occurred, the lowest code numerically will be displayed. See Section 7 for fault diagnosis.

7 Fuel injection system fault diagnosis

2014 to 2016 MT-07 (FZ-07) models

1 The system incorporates a self-diagnostic function whereby most faults, when they occur, are identified by a fault code, which is displayed on the instrument LCD after the engine has been stopped. The codes are stored in the ECU memory until a deletion operation is performed. In the case of a minor fault in the injection system, the engine trouble warning light in the instrument cluster will come on and stay on and the engine will continue to run, enabling the machine to be ridden, although performance will be reduced. In the case of a major fault the warning light will flash when the ignition switch is turned ON and the start button is pressed, and it will not be possible to run the engine. Certain faults will not activate the warning light and are not subject to a fault code, but will be recorded in the ECU as a diagnostic code – the diagnostic codes can only be accessed by a Yamaha dealer.

2 Compare the fault code displayed with those in the table below to identify the faulty component. Next refer to Section 8 for information on the component itself and its wiring and connectors and check the component as described.

3 Once the fault has been corrected, confirm that the fault code is no longer displayed by turning the ignition switch OFF and then ON again. If the code is no longer displayed on the clock LCD the repair is complete.

4 If the fault code is displayed again, or to delete a fault code from the ECU memory, take the bike to a Yamaha dealer.

Fuel system fault codes – 2014 to 2016 MT-07 (FZ-07) models

Fault code displayed	Faulty component – symptoms	Possible causes
12	Crankshaft position sensor – engine will stop and will not restart	Faulty wiring or wiring connector. Damaged or improperly installed sensor or timing rotor. Faulty ECU
13	Intake air pressure sensor – engine will run	Faulty wiring or wiring connector. Damaged or faulty sensor. Faulty ECU
14	Intake air pressure sensor hose system – engine will run	Kinked, clogged or detached hose. Faulty ECU
15	Throttle position sensor – engine will run	Faulty wiring or wiring connector. Damaged or improperly installed sensor. Faulty ECU
19	Sidestand switch – engine will not run	Faulty wiring or wiring connector. Faulty ECU
21	Coolant temperature (ECT) sensor – engine will run	Faulty wiring or wiring connector. Damaged or improperly installed sensor. Faulty ECU
22	Intake air temperature sensor – engine will run	Faulty wiring or wiring connector. Damaged or improperly installed sensor. Faulty ECU
24	Oxygen sensor – engine will run	Faulty wiring or wiring connector. Damaged or faulty sensor. Faulty ECU
30	Tip-over sensor – engine will not run, fuel system turned OFF	Machine overturned. Damaged or improperly installed sensor. Faulty ECU
33	Ignition coil, No. 1 cylinder	Faulty primary wiring or wiring connector. Coil not seated on plug. Damaged ignition coil. Faulty component in ignition cut-off safety circuit. Faulty ECU
34	Ignition coil, No. 2 cylinder	Faulty primary wiring or wiring connector. Coil not seated on plug. Damaged ignition coil. Faulty component in ignition cut-off safety circuit. Faulty ECU
37	Idle speed control (ISC) valve – engine will run	Faulty wiring or wiring connector. Damaged or improperly installed ISC valve. Faulty ECU. Faulty speed sensor (non-ABS models) or rear wheel sensor (ABS models). Faulty throttle bodies
39	Fuel injector	Faulty wiring or wiring connector
41	Tip-over sensor – engine will not run	Faulty wiring or wiring connector. Damaged sensor. Faulty ECU
42	Speed sensor (non-ABS models) or rear wheel sensor (ABS models)/gear position switch/clutch switch – engine will run	Damaged speed sensor/gear position switch. Faulty wiring or wiring connector. Faulty ECU
43	Power supply to the fuel pump or injectors – engine will run	Faulty wiring or wiring connector. Faulty ECU
44	Carbon monoxide (CO) density reading/writing error – engine will run	Error writing CO adjustment value to EEPROM. Faulty ECU
46	Power supply to fuel injection system – engine will run	Faulty charging system
50	ECU malfunction, fault code may not be displayed – engine will not run	ECU internal memory malfunction
51, 52, 53, 54, 55, 56	Immobiliser – refer to Section 19	
89 (on Yamaha diagnostic tool), ERR on instrument display	Instrument cluster, no communication between ECU and instrument cluster – engine will run	Faulty wiring or wiring connector. Faulty instrument cluster. Faulty ECU
Start unable warning	Engine warning light flashes when the ignition switch is ON and the start button is pushed	Error detected – refer to fault codes 12, 19, 30, 41 or 50

7.5a Diagnostic socket (arrowed) –
MT models (Tracer shown)

7.5b Diagnostic socket (arrowed) –
XSR models

2017-on MT-07 (FZ-07), MT-07TR and XSR models

5 The system incorporates a self-diagnostic function whereby most faults, when they occur, are identified by a fault code, which can be read using the dealer-only Yamaha Diagnostic System. It is possible to use a generic OBD/GST fault code reader but an adaptor lead kit (Yamaha part No. 90890-03249) will be required to link the tool with the bike's diagnostic socket **(see illustrations)** – to access the socket, on MT-07 (FZ-07) models remove the passenger seat, and on MT-07TR and XSR models remove the seat (see Chapter 7). Without access

Fault code	Faulty component – symptoms	Possible causes	Diagnostic code
P0335	Crankshaft position sensor – engine will stop and will not restart	Faulty wiring or wiring connector. Damaged or improperly installed sensor or timing rotor. Faulty ECU	-
P0107, P0108	Intake air pressure sensor – engine will run	Faulty wiring or wiring connector. Damaged or faulty sensor. Faulty ECU	03
P0122, P0123	Throttle position sensor – engine will run	Faulty wiring or wiring connector. Damaged or improperly installed sensor. Faulty ECU	01
P1601	Sidestand switch – engine will not run	Faulty wiring or wiring connector. Faulty ECU	20
P0117, P0118	Coolant temperature (ECT) sensor – engine will run	Faulty wiring or wiring connector. Damaged or improperly installed sensor. Faulty ECU	06
P0112, P0113	Intake air temperature sensor – engine will run	Faulty wiring or wiring connector. Damaged or improperly installed sensor. Faulty ECU	05
P0030, P0132, P2195	Oxygen sensor – engine will run	Faulty wiring or wiring connector. Damaged or faulty sensor. Faulty ECU	-
P0351	Ignition coil, No. 1 cylinder	Faulty primary wiring or wiring connector. Coil not seated on plug. Damaged ignition coil. Faulty component in ignition cut-off safety circuit. Faulty ECU	30
P0352	Ignition coil, No. 2 cylinder	Faulty primary wiring or wiring connector. Coil not seated on plug. Damaged ignition coil. Faulty component in ignition cut-off safety circuit. Faulty ECU	31
P0201 or P0202	Fuel injector No. 1 or 2	Faulty wiring or wiring connector	36 or 37
P0507	Idle speed control valve – engine will run	Faulty wiring or wiring connector. Damaged or improperly installed ISC valve. Faulty ECU. Faulty speed sensor (non-ABS models) or rear wheel sensor (ABS models). Faulty throttle bodies	54
P0511	Idle speed control (ISC) valve – engine will run	Faulty wiring or wiring connector. Damaged or improperly installed ISC valve. Faulty ECU.	-
P1604, P1605	Tip-over sensor – engine will not run	Faulty wiring or wiring connector. Damaged sensor. Faulty ECU	08
P0500	Rear wheel sensor/gear position switch/clutch switch – engine will run	Damaged speed sensor/gear position switch. Faulty wiring or wiring connector. Faulty ECU	07/21
P0657	Power supply to the fuel pump or injectors – engine will run	Faulty wiring or wiring connector Faulty ECU	09/50
P062F	Carbon monoxide (CO) density reading/writing error – engine will run	Error writing CO adjustment value to EEPROM. Faulty ECU	60
P0560	Power supply to fuel injection system – engine will run	Faulty charging system	-
P0601, P1602	ECU malfunction, fault code may or may not be displayed – engine may or may not run	ECU internal memory malfunction	-
U0155 (on Yamaha diagnostic tool), ERR on instrument display	Instrument cluster, no communication between ECU and instrument cluster – engine will run	Faulty wiring or wiring connector. Faulty instrument cluster. Faulty ECU	-
Start unable warning	Engine warning light flashes when the ignition switch is ON and the start button is pushed	Error detected in CKP sensor, tip-over sensor or ECU	-

Table 1 Fuel system fault codes – 2017-on MT-07 (FZ-07), MT-07TR and XSR models

to either tester, you must take the bike to a Yamaha dealer for assessment should a fault be indicated. The codes are stored in the ECU memory until a deletion operation is performed. In the case of a minor fault in the injection system, the engine trouble warning light in the instrument cluster will come on and stay on and the engine will continue to run, enabling the machine to be ridden, although performance will be reduced. In the case of a major fault the warning light will flash when the ignition switch is turned ON and the start button is pressed, and it will not be possible to run the engine. Certain faults will not activate the warning light and are not subject to a fault code, but will be recorded as a diagnostic code.

6 If a code reader is being used follow the instructions supplied with the tool, and compare the fault code displayed with those in Table 1 to identify the faulty component and the appropriate diagnostic code (Table 2). Also refer to Section 8 for information on the component itself and its wiring and connectors, as required.

7 Once the fault has been corrected, confirm that the fault code is no longer displayed, then delete the fault code.

Table 2 Fuel system diagnostic codes and data – 2017-on MT-07 (FZ-07), MT-07TR and XSR models

Diagnostic code	Action required	Data displayed
01	Check angle data displayed with throttle fully closed Check angle data displayed with throttle fully open	Fully closed – 11 to 21. Fully open – 96 to 106
03	Turn the engine stop switch ON and fully open the throttle	Value should change as throttle is opened
05	Check the temperature* in the air filter housing and compare with data displayed	-
06	Check the temperature** of the coolant and compare with data displayed – see Chapter 3 to check the operation of the sensor	-
07	Turn the rear wheel in the normal direction of rotation and check pulses generated are displayed. Check the rear wheel sensor wiring connector and sensor-to-rotor clearance (see Chapter 6)	0 to 999
08	Check the operation of the tip-over sensor	Sensor upright – 0.4 to 1.4V. Tilted more than 65° – 3.7 to 4.4V
09	Turn the engine stop switch ON and check for battery voltage Check the operation of the fuel injection system relay	Approx.12V
20	Check the operation of the sidestand switch. Select a gear position other than neutral – see Chapter 8 for access and further checks	Stand retracted – ON. Stand down – OFF
21	Check the operation of the gear position sensor and clutch switch	Gearbox in neutral – ON. In gear or clutch lever released – OFF. In gear with clutch lever pulled in and sidestand up – ON. In gear with the clutch lever pulled in and sidestand down – OFF
30 and 31	Check the operation of the appropriate ignition coil (see Section 16) – actuation will generate five sparks in the appropriate plug and the engine trouble warning light will come on.	-
36 and 37	Check the operation of the appropriate fuel injector (see Section 10) – actuation will generate five pulses in the appropriate injector and the engine trouble warning light will come on. Listen for the pulses using a sounding rod.	-
50	Check the operation of the fuel injection system (starter safety cut-off relay) – actuation closes the relay five times. You should be able to hear the relay click – see Chapter 8 for access and further checks	-
51	Check the operation of the cooling fan relay – actuation closes the relay five times. You should be able to hear the relay click – see Chapter 3 for access and further checks	-
52	Check the operation of the headlight relay – actuation closes the relay five times. You should be able to hear the relay click – see Chapter 8 for access and further checks	-
54	Check the operation of the ISC valve – actuation closes and opens the valve three times, each one taking approx. six seconds for the valve to close and open. You should be able to hear the valve – see Section 8 for access and further checks	-
60	EEPROM fault code/Check the carbon monoxide density in the exhaust gas	00 – no fault 01 – faulty cylinder No. 1; 02 – faulty cylinder No. 2; 11 – data error for ISC value; 12 – data error for oxygen sensor; 13 – OBD memory value
67	ISC (idle speed control) data has been erased, ISC (idle speed control) data does not need to be erased, ISC (idle speed control) data needs to be erased	00, 01, 02 To erase data set engine stop switch from OFF to ON three times in five seconds
87	Oxygen sensor data has been erased, Oxygen sensor data has not been erased	00, 01 To erase data set engine stop switch from OFF to ON three times in five seconds

Note: * *If possible, check the temperature next to the sensor, otherwise use the ambient temperature as the standard*
Note: ** *Check the temperature of the coolant as close as possible to the sensor*

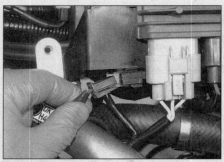

8.5a Disconnect the fan wiring connector (black)...

8.5b ... to make it easier to disconnect the CKP sensor wiring connector (white)

8.7 IAP sensor (arrowed)

8 Fuel injection system components

1 If a fault is indicated in any of the system components, first check the wiring and connectors between the appropriate component and the ECU – refer to Chapter 8, Section 2 and to the wiring diagram for your model at the end of Chapter 8. A continuity test of all wires will locate a break or short in any circuit. Inspect the terminals inside the wiring connectors and ensure they are not loose, bent or corroded. Spray the inside of the connectors with a proprietary electrical terminal cleaner before reconnection.

2 It is possible to undertake most checks on system components using a multimeter and comparing the results with the specifications at the beginning of the Chapter. **Note:** *Different meters may give slightly different results to those specified even though the component being tested is not faulty – do not consign a component to the bin before having it double-checked. However, some faults will only become evident when a component is tested with specialised equipment, in which case the checks should be undertaken by a Yamaha dealer.*

3 If after a thorough check the source of a fault has not been identified, it is possible that the ECU itself is faulty. Yamaha provides no test specifications for the ECU. In order to determine conclusively that the unit is defective, it should be substituted with a known good one (Section 18). If the problem is rectified, the original unit is confirmed faulty.

Crankshaft position (CKP) sensor

4 Make sure the ignition is OFF. On MT-07 (FZ-07) models remove the left-hand fuel tank cover, on MT-07TR models remove the left-hand fairing side panel and inner panel, and on XSR models remove the left-hand air scoop (see Chapter 7).

5 The crankshaft position sensor is located in the alternator cover on the left-hand side of the engine. Trace the wiring from the cover and disconnect it at the 2-pin connector, and for best access disconnect the cooling fan wiring connector first **(see illustrations)**.

6 Using an ohmmeter or multimeter set to the ohms x 100 scale, measure the resistance between the terminals on the sensor side of the connector – connect the positive (+) meter probe to the grey wire terminal in the connector and the negative (-) probe to the black/blue wire terminal. Compare the result with the value given in the Specifications. If the result is not as specified, replace the alternator stator/CKP sensor assembly with a new one (see Chapter 8) – the sensor is not available separately.

Intake air pressure (IAP) sensor

Check

Note: *A wiring harness, part No. 90890-03207 (YU-03207 in the US), that connects between the sensor and its wiring connector so the* sensor *remains connected to the engine management system, is needed.*

7 Make sure the ignition is OFF. Remove the fuel tank (Section 2). The intake air pressure sensor is on the left-hand side of the frame **(see illustration)**.

8 Check the condition of the vacuum hose between the underside of the sensor and the throttle bodies **(see illustration)**. If the hose is cracked or perished fit a new one. Make sure the hose is a tight fit on the sensor and the throttle bodies.

9 Disconnect the wiring connector from the sensor and fit the test harness. Using a voltmeter or multimeter set to the volts (DC) scale, measure the sensor output voltage as follows: insert the positive (+) probe of the meter into the pink/white wire open connector in the test harness, and the negative (-) probe into the black/blue wire connector. Turn the ignition switch ON and note the output voltage. Turn the ignition OFF.

10 If the voltage is not as given in the Specifications the sensor is faulty.

Removal and installation

11 Follow Step 7, then disconnect the sensor wiring connector and undo the sensor screw **(see illustration 8.7)**. Lift the sensor and disconnect the vacuum hose.

12 Check the condition of the vacuum hose (Step 8). Make sure the wiring connector terminals are clean.

Intake air temperature (IAT) sensor

13 Make sure the ignition switch is OFF. The sensor is mounted on the right-hand end of the front fuel tank bracket.

14 On MT-07 (FZ-07) models remove the front fuel tank cover, on MT-07TR models remove the fuel tank cover, and on XSR models remove the right-hand fuel tank cover (see Chapter 7).

15 Disconnect the wiring connector **(see illustration 2.5)**. Check the connector wiring and the IAT sensor terminal pins. Remove the screw and detach the sensor from the tank bracket **(see illustration)**.

16 With the sensor detached from the tank bracket, connect an ohmmeter or multimeter set to the K-ohms scale to the terminals on the sensor and measure the resistance.

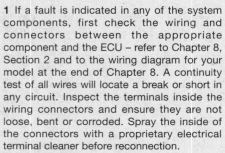

8.8 IAP sensor vacuum hose (arrowed – connection to throttle bodies)

8.15 Remove the IAT sensor from the tank bracket for testing. Retaining screw (arrowed)

Keeping the meter connected, gently heat the sensor tip with a hot air gun and check the meter reading – if you have a thermometer hold it next to the sensor tip as you heat it so you can check the temperature. Compare the meter readings obtained to the values given in the Specifications for zero and eighty degrees, setting the meter range accordingly. If the results are not close to the those given, the sensor is faulty and should be renewed.

Throttle position (TP) sensor

Check

17 Make sure the ignition is OFF.
18 The throttle position sensor is on the right-hand end of the throttle body assembly. Disconnect the wiring connector **(see illustration)** – access to it is quite restricted from the side but is possible, on XSR models after removing the right-hand side cover and inner cover (see Chapter 7). For best access remove the fuel tank (Section 2), then disconnect the engine breather hose from the front of the air filter housing **(see illustration 10.5a)**.
19 Using an ohmmeter or multimeter set to the K-ohms scale, connect the meter positive (+) probe to the blue wire terminal and the negative (-) probe to the black/blue wire terminal on the sensor and measure the sensor maximum resistance.
20 If the resistance is not as specified at the beginning of the Chapter, replace the sensor with a new one.

Removal and installation

Note: If the sensor is removed, its position must be set using Yamaha's diagnostic tool after it has been fitted.
21 Displace the throttle body assembly so you have access to the sensor screws (Section 9). If not already done disconnect the sensor wiring connector **(see illustration 8.18)**.
22 Mark the position of the screws in the holes as a guide for positioning the sensor on installation **(see illustration)**. Undo the screws and draw the sensor off, noting how the slot fits over the throttle shaft.
23 To fit the sensor, make sure the throttle is fully closed, then align the slot with the throttle

8.18 TP sensor wiring connector (arrowed)

8.22 TP sensor screws (arrowed)

8.25 Oxygen sensor (arrowed)

8.26 Oxygen sensor wiring connector

shaft and fit the sensor. Align the screws in the holes as marked, or align them centrally if a new sensor is being fitted, and tighten them.
24 Install the throttle body assembly (Section 9). Take the bike to a Yamaha dealer to have the position of the sensor correctly set using the Yamaha diagnostic tool.

Oxygen sensor

25 Make sure the ignition is OFF. The sensor is located in the right-hand side of the exhaust system **(see illustration)**. Inspect the sensor for damage.
26 Remove the right-hand frame cover (see Chapter 7). Trace the wiring to the connector and check that the wiring is not damaged or trapped, and that the connector is secure **(see illustration)**.
27 Check that the sensor is tight.

28 No test specifications for the sensor are available – if no physical damage can be found, it must be assumed that the sensor is defective and so a new one must be fitted.

Tip-over sensor

Note: A wiring harness, part No. 90890-03209 (YU-03209 in the US), that connects between the sensor and its wiring connector so the sensor remains connected to the engine management system, is needed.
29 Make sure the ignition is OFF. On MT-07 (FZ-07) models remove the seats and the centre seat cowl, and on MT-07TR and XSR models remove the seat (see Chapter 7).
30 On MT-07 (FZ-07) models displace the rear fusebox from its mount **(see illustration)**. On XSR models remove the seat bracket **(see illustration)**.

8.30a Release the clip and lift the fusebox off its mount

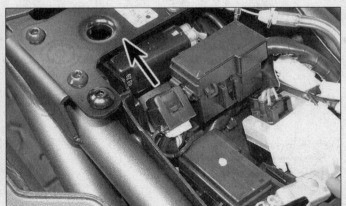

8.30b Remove the bracket (arrowed) to expose the sensor screws

8.31a Undo the screws and displace the sensor...

8.31b ... then disconnect the wiring

31 Undo the screws and lift the sensor off **(see illustrations)**.

32 Disconnect the wiring connector from the sensor and fit the test harness. Using a voltmeter or multimeter set to the volts (DC) scale, measure the sensor output voltage as follows: insert the positive (+) probe of the meter into the yellow/green wire open connector in the test harness, and the negative (-) probe into the black/blue wire connector.

33 Hold the sensor in its normal position with the UP mark facing up, then turn the ignition switch ON and note the output voltage. Now tilt the sensor 65° to one side and then 65° to the other, noting the output voltage. Turn the ignition OFF.

34 If the output voltage is not as specified when the sensor is upright and tilted over, replace it with a new one. Note the top surface of the sensor is marked UP – make sure this is uppermost when fitting the sensor.

Speed sensor (non-ABS models)

Note: *On ABS models refer to Chapter 6,*

Section 17 – the road speed information is collected from the rear wheel sensor.

Check

Note: *A wiring harness, part No. 90890-03208 (YU-03208 in the US), that connects between the sensor and its wiring connector so the sensor remains connected to the engine management system, is needed.*

35 Support the machine on an auxiliary stand so the rear wheel is off the ground. Make sure the ignition is OFF.

36 The speed sensor is located on the top of the crankcase to the rear of the starter motor. Remove the fuel tank to access the wiring connector (Section 2).

37 Disconnect the wiring connector from the sensor and fit the test harness. Using a voltmeter or multimeter set to the volts (DC) scale, measure the sensor output voltage as follows: insert the positive (+) probe of the meter into the white/yellow wire open connector in the test harness, and the negative (-) probe into the black/blue wire connector.

38 Turn the ignition switch ON. Turn the rear wheel in its normal direction of rotation and check the reading on the meter – it should be seen to fluctuate between 0.6 and 4.8 volts as the wheel is turned. Turn the ignition switch OFF.

39 If the voltage is not as specified, replace the sensor with a new one.

Removal and installation

40 Remove the fuel tank (Section 2). Disconnect the wiring connector. Unscrew the bolt and remove the sensor. Remove the O-ring – a new one must be fitted.

41 Use a new O-ring on installation, and make sure the wiring connector terminals are clean and that the pins are not damaged.

Fuel pump relay

42 The fuel pump relay is in the relay unit **(see illustration 8.43a)** – to access it, on MT-07 (FZ-07) models remove the front fuel tank cover, on MT-07TR models remove the fuel tank cover, and on XSR models remove the left-hand fuel tank cover and air scoop (see Chapter 7). The relay unit also contains the starter circuit safety cut-off relay and diodes.

43 Lift the relay assembly off its bracket and disconnect the wiring connector **(see illustrations)**.

44 Using an ohmmeter or continuity tester, connect the positive (+) probe to the red/white wire terminal on the relay and the negative (-) probe to the red/blue wire terminal **(see illustration)**. There should be no continuity.

45 Using a fully-charged 12V battery and some insulated jumper leads, connect the positive (+) battery terminal to the red/black wire terminal on the relay, and the negative (–) battery terminal to the blue/yellow wire terminal **(see illustration 8.44)**. There should now be continuity between the red and red/blue wire terminals.

46 If the relay does not operate as described, replace it with a new one.

Coolant temperature (ECT) sensor

47 Refer to Chapter, 3 Section 5.

Exhaust gas oxygen content

48 Have the exhaust gases analysed by a Yamaha dealer.

---

9   Throttle bodies

8.43a Displace the relay...

8.43b ... then release the catch and pull the connector off

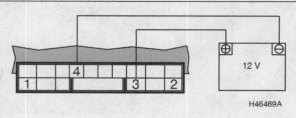

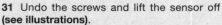

8.44 Test connections for the fuel pump relay

1 Red/white
2 Red/blue
3 Red/black
4 Blue/yellow

12 V

H46469A

⚠ Warning: Refer to the precautions given in Section 1 before starting work.

Removal

1 Remove the fuel tank (Section 2).

2 On MT-07 (FZ-07) and MT-07TR models remove the frame covers, and on XSR models remove the side covers and inner covers (see Chapter 7).

9.4a ISC valve connector (arrowed)

9.4b ECT sensor connector (arrowed)

9.6a Air flap diaphragm valve hose

3 Remove the fuel rail and injectors (Section 10).
4 Disconnect the throttle position sensor wiring connector **(see illustration 8.18)**. Disconnect the idle speed control valve wiring connector **(see illustration)**. Disconnect the ECT sensor wiring connector **(see illustration)**.
5 Disconnect the throttle cables (Section 12).
6 On 2014 to 2016 MT-07 (FZ-07) models disconnect the intake air flap diaphragm valve hose, where fitted disconnect the EVAP system hoses, and on all models disconnect the IAP sensor hose **(see illustrations)**.
7 On models with the EVAP canister release the hoses from each end, noting which fits where on the right-hand end, then draw the canister put of its holder **(see illustrations)**.

9.6b EVAP system hoses (arrowed)

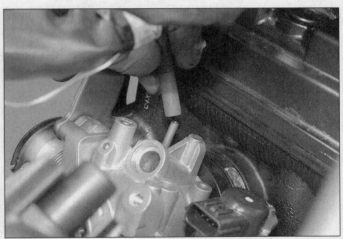

9.6c IAP sensor hose

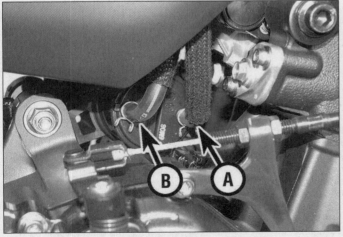

9.7a Disconnect the fuel tank breather hose (A) and the canister to throttle body hose (B) on the right-hand side

9.7b Disconnect the breather hose (arrowed), then draw the canister out of its holder

9.8 Slacken the clamp screws (arrowed)

9.9a Ease the throttle bodies back out of the ducts...

9.9b ... then draw them out to the left a bit...

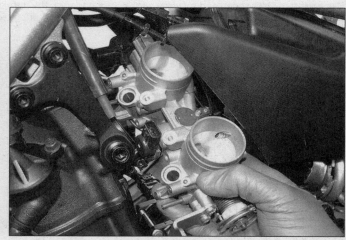

9.9c ... then turn and tilt them as shown and draw them all the way out

8 Slacken the clamps securing the throttle bodies to the intake ducts **(see illustration)**.
9 Ease the throttle body assembly off the intake manifolds and manoeuvre it out to the left-hand side as shown **(see illustrations)**.
10 If required slacken the clamps securing the intake ducts to the cylinder head and remove the ducts **(see illustration)**.

9.10 Note the orientation of the clamps and how they locate. Slacken the screws (arrowed) to remove the ducts

Caution: Stuff clean rag into each intake manifold to prevent anything from falling inside.

Disassembly

11 If required, remove the idle speed control valve (Section 11), and the throttle position sensor (Section 8).

Cleaning

Caution: The throttle bodies should only be cleaned if it has not been possible to synchronise them correctly, and only after checking all other service items mentioned in the synchronisation procedure (see Chapter 1). Use a suitable petroleum-based solvent for cleaning the throttle bodies – ask a Yamaha dealer if necessary.
12 Place the throttle bodies on a flat surface and treat them with care. Fit blanking caps onto the hose unions. If not already done remove the fuel injectors (Section 10).
13 Make sure that only metal components come into contact with the cleaning

solvent and always follow manufacturer's recommendations. Do not turn the bypass air (synchronisation) screws when cleaning the throttle bodies.
14 Apply the recommended cleaner to the throttle valves, then operate the throttle cable pulley to hold the valves open to clean inside the bodies – do not push on the valves themselves to open them. If necessary use a soft-bristle (non-metallic) brush to remove any stubborn deposits, and make sure no dirt enters any passage. Rinse the throttle bodies with the cleaner, then dry them with compressed air.

Inspection

15 Check the throttle bodies for cracks, distorted sealing surfaces and other damage. If any defects are found, fit a new throttle body assembly.
16 Operate the throttle cable pulley and check that the throttle butterfly valves open and close smoothly.
17 Check all the disconnected hoses (Step 4)

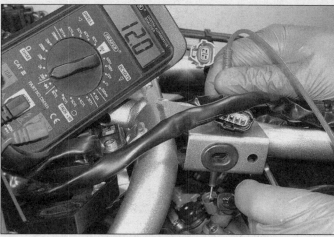

10.2 Checking injector resistance

10.5a Use pliers to release the clamps and detach the hose from the filter housing...

10.5b ... and the valve cover

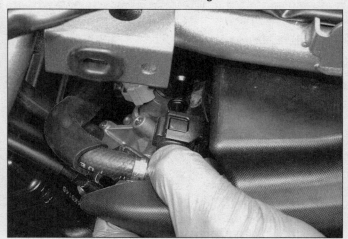

10.6 Disconnect the fuel hose from the rail

for cracks, splits and kinks and fit new ones if necessary.

Reassembly

18 If removed, install the idle speed control valve (Section 11), and the throttle position sensor (Section 8).

Installation

19 Installation is the reverse of removal, noting the following.

● Check for cracks or splits in the air ducts and intake ducts and fit new ones if necessary.

● Make sure the clamps are correctly aligned and seated on the intake ducts and the air ducts **(see illustrations 9.10 and 10.7)**.

● Lubricate the inside lip of each intake duct with a squirt of lubricant or a smear of light oil to aid installation of the throttle body assembly.

● Once the assembly is correctly aligned, press it firmly into place and tighten the clamps **(see illustrations 9.9a and 9.8)**.

● Refer to Section 12 to connect the throttle cables.

● Make sure the terminals in the wiring connectors are clean and that the connectors are secure.

● Make sure the fuel hose is secure on the fuel rail.

● Make sure all hoses are correctly and securely connected.

10 Fuel rail and injectors

⚠ **Warning: Refer to the precautions given in Section 1 before proceeding.**

Check

1 If the engine will run check the operation of each injector in turn using a sounding rod held against the injector being checked – you should hear a clicking sound as the injector opens and closes. If an injector is silent, either the injector or its wiring is faulty.

2 If the engine will not run remove the fuel tank (Section 2). Disconnect the wiring connectors from the injectors **(see illustration 10.7)**. To check the wiring, refer to Chapter 8 Section 2 and to the wiring diagram for your model at the end of Chapter 8 and check for continuity in the circuit to and from each injector. To check the injectors use an ohmmeter connected to the terminals in the injector socket to test the resistance **(see illustration)** – if it is not as given in the Specifications at the beginning of the Chapter the injector is faulty.

Removal

3 Remove the fuel tank (Section 2).

4 On MT-07TR models remove the side covers (see Chapter 7).

5 Disconnect the engine breather hose from the front of the air filter housing and the valve cover and remove it **(see illustrations)**.

6 Disconnect the fuel hose from the fuel rail in the same way as disconnecting it from the pump when removing the tank **(see illustration)**. Refer to Section 2 for hose removal.

10.7 Disconnect the injector wiring

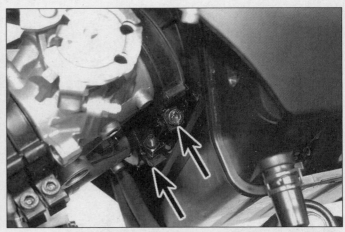

10.8a Slacken the clamp screws (arrowed)

10.8b Unscrew the bolt on each side

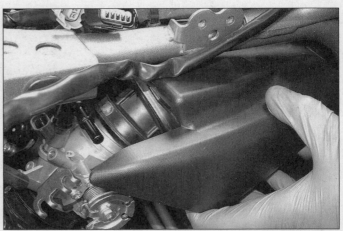

10.8c Ease the housing back off the throttle bodies

7 Disconnect the wiring connectors from the fuel injectors **(see illustration)**.

8 Slacken the clamps securing the air ducts to the throttle bodies **(see illustration)**. Unscrew the air filter housing bolts, noting the washer with the left-hand bolt, then draw the housing back off the throttle bodies **(see illustrations)**.

9 Unscrew the bolts securing the fuel rail, and as you remove each one retrieve the spacer that sits between the fuel rail mount and the throttle bodies using a telescopic magnet inserted from the side **(see illustrations)** – new washers should be used. Carefully lift the fuel rail and injectors off the throttle bodies

10.9a Unscrew the bolts (arrowed)…

10.9b … and retrieve the spacer from under the rail as you remove each bolt

10.9c Lift the rail and injectors off

10.9d If the seal is not in the injector port...

10.9e ... remove it from the injector

10.10a Carefully pull the injector out of the rail

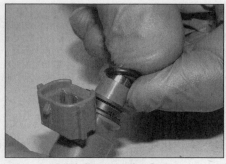

10.10b Remove the O-ring

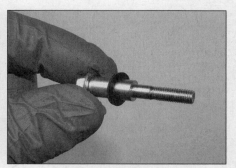

10.13 Fit new washers

(see illustration). Remove the seal from each injector port or from the lower end of each injector if they came away (see illustrations) – new ones must be used.

10 Pull the injector(s) out of the fuel rail as required (see illustration). Remove the O-ring from the upper end of each injector (see illustration) – new ones must be used.

11 Modern fuels contain detergents that should keep the injectors clean and free of gum or varnish from residue fuel. If an injector is suspected of being blocked, clean it through with injector cleaner, following the manufacturer's instructions.

Installation

12 Fit a new O-ring into the groove in the top of each injector (see illustration 10.10b). Align each injector so the wiring connector will face forwards, then carefully press the injectors into the rail (see illustration 10.10a). Avoid twisting the injectors as this may damage the O-rings.

13 Fit a new seal onto each injector (see illustration 10.9e). Fit new washers onto the fuel rail bolts (see illustration). Align the injectors with their ports and fit the fuel rail into place (see illustration 10.9c). Fit each spacer between the underside of the rail and the throttle body and insert each bolt while holding the spacer with a magnet (see illustration 10.9b). Make sure the injectors, spacers and rail are seated correctly, then tighten the bolts to 3.5 Nm.

14 Slide the air filter housing forwards, seating the ducts onto the throttle bodies (see illustration 10.8c). Check each duct is fully seated all round, then fit the housing bolts, and then tighten the clamp screws (see illustrations 10.8b and a).

15 Connect the injector wiring connectors (see illustration 10.7).

16 Push the fuel hose on until it is felt to click into place, then slide the security cover across (see illustration 10.6).

17 Fit the engine breather hose onto the valve cover and air filter housing and secure it with the clamps (see illustrations 10.5b and a).

18 On MT-07TR models fit the side covers.

19 Install the fuel tank (Section 2). Run the engine and make sure there are no fuel leaks before riding the bike.

11.4a Note how the plate locates around the valve

11 Idle speed control (ISC) valve

Check

1 If there is a fault indicated with the ISC valve remove it (see below), and check that the valve and its housing are clean.

2 If the valve is faulty fit a new one, then take the bike to a Yamaha dealer – the Yamaha diagnostic tool is required to set the learning values of the new valve.

Removal and installation

3 Remove the throttle bodies (Section 9).

4 Undo the screw and remove the retaining plate, then draw the valve out (see illustrations).

11.4b Lift the valve out

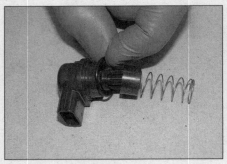

11.4c Remove the O-ring and fit a new one on installation

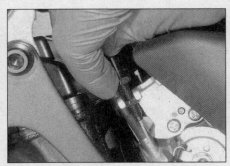

12.3a Slacken the nut…

12.3b … free the opening cable from the bracket…

A new O-ring is needed for the valve **(see illustration)**.

5 Fit a new O-ring onto the valve **(see illustration 11.4c)**. Insert the valve **(see illustration 11.4b)**. Fit the retaining plate, aligning its cut-out with the rib on the valve, and tighten the screw **(see illustration 11.4a)**.

6 Install the throttle bodies (Section 9).

12 Throttle cables

 Warning: Refer to the precautions given in Section 1 before proceeding.

Removal

1 On MT-07 (FZ-07) models remove the left-hand fuel tank cover(see Chapter 7). On MT-07TR models remove theleft-hand fairing side panel and inner panel(see Chapter 7). On XSR models remove the left-hand fuel tank cover, the left-hand air scoop, and the left-hand side cover and inner cover (see Chapter 7).

2 Note the differences between the front (throttle opening) cable and the rear (throttle closing) cable on the throttle body assembly and how they seat in the bracket. Note the differences between the upper (throttle opening) cable and the lower (throttle closing) cable on the front of the housing on the handlebar. If required, mark each cable according to its location at both ends. If new cables are being fitted, match them to the old cables to ensure they are correctly installed.

3 At the throttle body end, loosen the upper nut on the front cable until the lower nut clears the bracket and slip the cable out of the bracket, then detach the cable end from the pulley **(see illustrations)**. Loosen the hex on the rear cable and slip the cable out of the bracket, then detach the end from the pulley **(see illustrations)**.

4 Pull the rubber boot off the cable housing on the handlebar. Undo the housing screws and detach the housing halves, noting how the cable elbows locate **(see illustrations)**.

12.3c …and disconnect the cable end

12.3d Free the closing cable from the bracket…

12.3e …and disconnect the end

12.4a Pull the boot off

12.4b Undo the screws …

12.4c …and remove the housing

12.5 Disconnect the cable ends

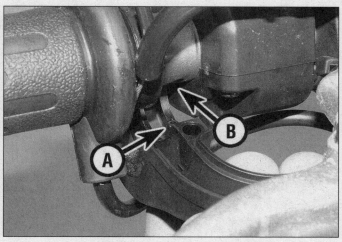

12.9 Locate the pin (A) in the hole (B)

5 Detach the inner cable ends from the pulley **(see illustration)**.

6 Withdraw the cables from the machine, noting their routing.

Installation

7 Feed the cables from the handlebar through to the throttle bodies, making sure they are correctly routed and arranged. The cables must not interfere with any other component and should not be kinked or bent sharply.

8 Lubricate the cable upper ends with multi-purpose grease. Fit the closing cable end into the rear socket in the twistgrip, feeding it around the underside of the pulley, and the opening cable end into the front **(see illustration 12.5)**.

9 Seat the cable elbows in the housing and join the housing halves, making sure the pin in the bottom half locates in the hole in the handlebar **(see illustration)**. Fit and tighten the screws, then slide the boot on **(see illustrations 12.4b and a)**.

10 Lubricate the cable lower ends with multi-purpose grease. Fit the closing cable into the rear socket in the throttle pulley and the rear of the bracket, then fit the opening cable into the front socket and front of the bracket **(see illustrations 12.3e, d, c and**

b). Seat each lower nut against its tabs on the bracket then tighten the nut on the front cable and the hex on the rear cable against the bracket **(see illustration 12.3a)**.

11 Follow the procedure in Chapter 1 to adjust the cable freeplay. Start the engine and check that the idle speed does not rise as the handlebars are turned. If it does, the throttle cables are routed incorrectly. Correct the problem before riding the motorcycle.

12 Install the body panels in reverse order of removal (see Chapter 7).

13 Exhaust system

⚠️ *Warning: If the engine has been running the exhaust system will be very hot. Allow the system to cool before carrying out any work.*
Caution: The header pipe flange nuts can become extremely corroded, to the point that no amount of wire brushing and penetrating fluid will release them, and extreme heat using an oxy-acetylene torch needs to be applied before the nuts

come undone. This equipment is not usually available to the home mechanic, if necessary try using a blow-torch instead, but if this does not work take the bike to a workshop equipped with oxy-acetylene, rather than trying to apply too much force which could end with sheared studs in the cylinder head. Also, when applying heat in this way take care not to overheat surrounding components and the alloy cylinder head itself.*

Removal

1 Remove the right-hand frame cover (see Chapter 7). On Moto Cage models remove the sump guard.

2 Disconnect the oxygen sensor wiring connector **(see illustration 8.26)**. Feed the wiring down to the sensor, noting its routing.

3 Unscrew the rider's right-hand footrest bracket bolts and remove the washers, then displace the bracket **(see illustration)**.

4 Unscrew the header pipe flange nuts and draw the flanges off the studs **(see illustration)**.

5 Support the silencer and undo the mounting bolt on each side **(see illustration)**.

6 Draw the header pipes off the cylinder

13.3 Unscrew the bolts and displace the bracket

13.4 Unscrew the four nuts

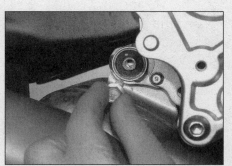

13.5 Unscrew the bolt on each side

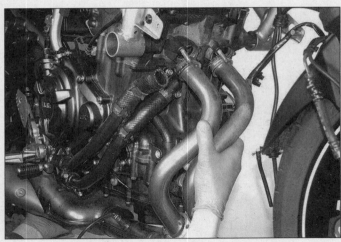

13.6 Removing the exhaust system

13.7 Lever the old gaskets out

head and manoeuvre the exhaust out from underneath the engine **(see illustration)**.

Note: *The exhaust contains a catalytic converter – handle it carefully to avoid damaging it.*

7 Remove the gasket from each exhaust port in the cylinder head **(see illustration)** – new ones must be fitted.

8 Check the condition of the rubber bush in each mounting bracket and fit new brackets if necessary. If the flange nuts are corroded replace them with new ones.

Installation

9 Clean the threads of the studs in the cylinder head and the mounting bolts, and the bracket bolts if removed, and smear copper grease over them.

10 Fit the mounting brackets if removed and tighten the bolts to 10 Nm.

11 Apply dabs of multi-purpose grease to the new gaskets to keep them in place, then fit a gasket into each exhaust port **(see illustration)**.

12 Manoeuvre the exhaust into position, locating each header pipe in its port **(see illustration 13.6)**. Fit the mounting bolts finger-tight **(see illustration 13.5)**.

13 Locate the header pipe flanges onto the studs, then fit the nuts and tighten them to 20 Nm **(see illustration 13.4)**.

14 Tighten the mounting bolts to 20 Nm.

15 Route the oxygen sensor wiring and reconnect the connector **(see illustration 8.26)**.

16 Fit the footrest bracket, locating the grommet in the inner side over the peg on the inner bracket, then fit the bolts with their washers and tighten them to 30 Nm **(see illustration)**. Fit the frame cover.

17 Run the engine and check that there are no exhaust gas leaks.

14 Intake air flap (2014 to 2016 MT-07 (FZ-07) models)

Function

1 The system uses the increased vacuum produced in the right-hand throttle body duct on throttle-off to close a flap in the duct in the rear of the air filter housing, reducing the amount of air going into the air filter housing. The vacuum flow is controlled by a solenoid valve, which receives a signal from the ECU. There is a one-way valve and a surge tank fitted between the throttle body and the solenoid valve.

Solenoid valve

Removal and installation

2 Remove the right-hand fuel tank cover (see Chapter 7).

3 Disconnect the wiring connector and the hoses, noting which fits where, then unscrew the nut and remove the valve **(see illustration)**.

4 When fitting the valve connect the diaphragm valve hose to the inner union and the one-way valve hose to the outer union.

Check

5 Remove the valve. Measure the resistance of the valve using a multimeter set to ohms and connected to the sensor terminals **(see illustration)**. If the resistance is not as given in the Specifications the valve is faulty.

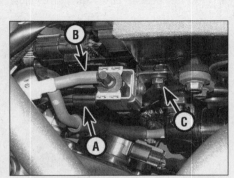

14.3 Solenoid valve wiring connector (A), hoses (B) and mounting nut (C)

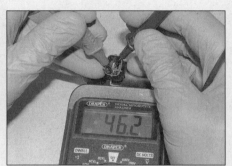

14.5 Checking solenoid valve resistance

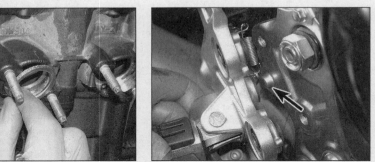

13.11 Fit the new gaskets

13.16 Seat the grommet over the peg (arrowed)

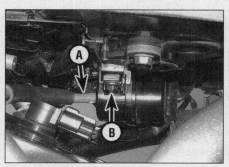

14.7 Surge tank hose (A) and mounting nut (B)

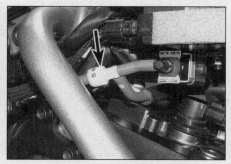

14.11 One-way valve (arrowed)

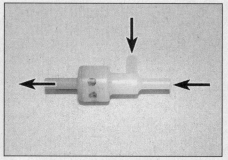

14.13 Airflow through one-way valve

Surge tank

Removal and installation

6 Remove the right-hand fuel tank cover (see Chapter 7).
7 Disconnect the hose, then unscrew the nut and remove the tank **(see illustration)**.
8 Fit the tank with the hose union pointing to the rear.

Check

9 Check the tank for dents and cracks.

One-way valve

Removal and installation

10 Remove the right-hand fuel tank cover (see Chapter 7).
11 Disconnect the hoses from the valve, noting which fits where **(see illustration)**.
12 When fitting the valve make sure the wider (blue) end faces to the rear and connect the throttle body hose to the rear union, connect the surge tank hose to the side union, and the solenoid valve hose to the front union.

Check

13 Remove the valve. Blow through the throttle body (blue) hose union – no air should flow through the valve. Block the surge tank hose union and blow through the solenoid valve hose union – air should flow through the valve and out the throttle body hose union **(see illustration)**. Block the solenoid valve hose union and blow through the surge tank hose union – air should flow through the valve and out the throttle body hose union.

14.15 Disconnect the hose

Diaphragm valve

Check

14 Remove the rider's seat (see Chapter 7).
15 Disconnect the hose from the valve **(see illustration)**. Apply a vacuum to the valve hose union using a Mityvac brake bleeding tool and check that the flap in the rear air duct closes. If it doesn't, remove the valve and fit a new one.

Removal and installation

16 Remove the rider's seat (see Chapter 7).
17 Disconnect the hose from the valve **(see illustration 14.15)**. Unhook the valve rod from the flap, then turn the valve 90° anti-clockwise to release it from the housing.
18 Fit the valve with the hose union pointing to the left, then turn it 90° clockwise to lock it so the hose union ends up pointing to the front.

15 Catalytic converter

General information

1 A catalytic converter is incorporated in the exhaust system to minimise the level of exhaust pollutants released into the atmosphere.
2 The catalytic converter consists of a canister containing a fine ceramic honeycomb impregnated with a catalyst material, over which the hot exhaust gases pass. The catalyst speeds up the oxidation of harmful carbon monoxide, unburned hydrocarbons and soot, effectively reducing the quantity of harmful products released into the atmosphere via the exhaust gases.
3 The catalytic converter is a closed-loop design – an oxygen sensor in the exhaust system enables the ECU to vary the intake fuel/air mixture dependent upon engine operating conditions.

Precautions

4 The catalytic converter is a reliable and simple device which needs no maintenance in itself, but there are some facts of which an owner should be aware if the converter is to function properly for its full service life.

● DO NOT use leaded or lead replacement petrol (gasoline) – the additives will coat the precious metals, reducing their converting efficiency and will eventually destroy the catalytic converter.
● Always keep the ignition and fuel systems well-maintained in accordance with the manufacturer's schedule – if the fuel/air mixture is suspected of being incorrect have the exhaust gas CO content checked by a Yamaha dealer.
● If the engine develops a misfire, do not ride the bike at all (or at least as little as possible) until the fault is cured.
● DO NOT use fuel or engine oil additives – these may contain substances harmful to the catalytic converter.
● DO NOT continue to use the bike if the engine burns oil to the extent of leaving a visible trail of blue smoke.
● Remember that the catalytic converter is FRAGILE – handle the exhaust mid-section carefully if removing it from the machine.

16 Ignition system check

⚠ **Warning: The energy levels in electronic systems can be very high. On no account should the ignition be switched on whilst the plugs or plug caps are being held. Shocks from the HT circuit can be most unpleasant. Secondly, it is vital that the engine is not turned over or run with any of the coils removed or disconnected, and that the plugs are soundly earthed (grounded) when the system is checked for sparking. The ignition system components can be seriously damaged if the HT circuit becomes isolated.**

1 As no means of adjustment is available, any failure of the system can be traced to failure of a system component or a simple wiring fault. Of the two possibilities, the latter is by far the most likely. In the event of failure, check the system in a logical fashion, as described below.
2 First check for a spark at each spark plug – use a new set of spark plugs to do this, and

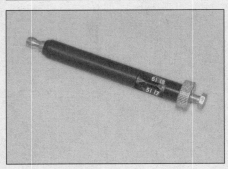

16.6 A typical ignition spark testing tool

17.3 To test the coil primary resistance, connect the probes as shown

● Faulty ignition coil(s) (Section 17).
● Faulty ignition switch or engine kill switch (see Chapter 8).
● Faulty crankshaft position (CKP) sensor (Section 8) or damaged triggers on alternator rotor (see Chapter 8).
● Faulty tip-over sensor or starting circuit cut-off relay (see Section 8 and Chapter 8).
● Faulty ECU (Section 18).

9 If the above checks don't reveal the cause of the problem, have the ignition system tested by a Yamaha dealer.

17 Ignition coils

Check

1 Remove the coil(s) (see below).
2 Inspect the coil(s) for cracks and other damage. Check that the wiring connectors and terminals are clean.
3 Measure the ignition coil primary circuit resistance as follows: set the meter to the ohms x 1 scale, then connect the positive (+) meter probe to the red/black wire terminal in the coil socket and the negative (-) probe to the orange (cyl 1) or grey/red (cyl 2) wire terminal **(see illustration)**. If the reading obtained is not within the range shown in the Specifications, it is likely that the coil is defective.
4 Measure the secondary circuit resistance as follows: remove the rubber cap from the bottom of the coil **(see illustration)**. Set the meter to the K-ohm scale, then connect the positive (+) meter probe to the red/black wire terminal in the coil socket and the negative (-) meter probe to the spark plug contact in the bottom of the coil **(see illustration)**. If the reading obtained is not within the range shown in the Specifications, it is likely that the coil is defective.
5 If a coil is confirmed to be faulty, fit a new

work on one cylinder at a time. Remove the fuel tank (Section 2).
3 Disconnect the wiring connector from the coil on the cylinder being tested, pull the coil off, then reconnect the wiring **(see illustrations 17.9a and b)**. Connect the coil to a new spark plug.
4 Hold the coil and earth the plug threads on the frame – shade the plug electrodes so the spark will be easy to see.

⚠️ *Warning: Do not remove the spark plugs from the engine to perform this check – atomised fuel being pumped out of the open spark plug hole could ignite, causing severe injury! Make sure the plug in the coil being tested is earthed – if it isn't the ECU could be damaged when the engine is turned over.*

5 Check that the kill switch is in the RUN position and the transmission is in neutral, then turn the ignition switch ON and turn the engine over on the starter motor. If the system is in good condition a regular, fat blue spark should be evident at the plug electrodes. If the spark appears thin or yellowish, or is non-existent, further investigation is necessary. Turn the ignition OFF and repeat the check for each coil.
6 The ignition system must be able to

produce a spark that is capable of jumping at least a 6 mm gap. Simple ignition spark gap testing tools are commercially available **(see illustration)** – follow the manufacturer's instructions, and set the gap at 6 mm.
7 If the test results are good the entire ignition system can be considered good. If the spark appears thin or yellowish, or is non-existent, further investigation is necessary.
8 Ignition faults can be divided into two categories, namely those where the ignition system has failed completely, and those that are due to a partial failure. The likely faults are listed below, starting with the most probable source of failure. Work through the list systematically, referring to the subsequent sections for full details of the necessary checks and tests. **Note:** *Before checking the following items ensure that the battery is fully charged and that all fuses are in good condition.*

● Faulty spark plug, dirty, worn or corroded plug electrodes, incorrect electrode gap (see Chapter 1).
● Loose, corroded or damaged wiring connections, broken or shorted wiring between any of the component parts of the ignition system.
● Faulty gear position, clutch or sidestand switch (see Chapter 8).

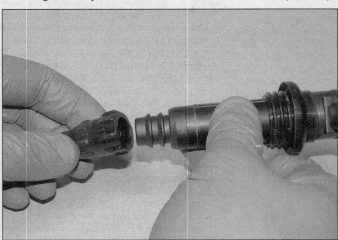

17.4a Pull the cap off

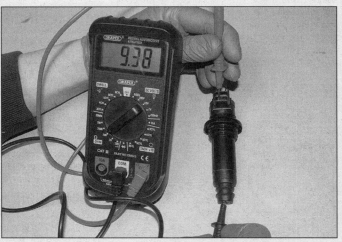

17.4b To test the coil secondary resistance, connect the probes as shown

17.9a Coil wiring connectors (arrowed)

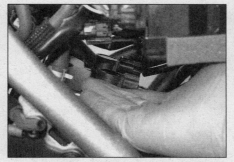

17.9b Ease the coil up – the seal can make them a tight fit...

17.9c ... and remove from the top

one – the coils are sealed units and cannot therefore be repaired.

Removal and installation

6 Remove the fuel tank (Section 2).

7 On 2014 to 2016 MT-07 (FZ-07) models remove the intake air flap solenoid valve and surge tank (Section 14).

8 Clean around the seal on each coil so no dirt can drop into the spark plug channel.

9 Disconnect the wiring connector from the coil, then pull the coil up off the plug **(see illustrations)**.

10 Installation is the reverse of removal. Make sure that each coil is pushed fully onto the top of its spark plug, and that the wiring connector is secure.

18 Engine Control Unit (ECU)

Check

1 If the tests shown in the preceding Sections have failed to isolate the cause of an ignition fault, it is possible that the ECU itself is faulty. No details are available for testing the ECU – it must taken to a Yamaha dealer for assessment.

2 On machines not fitted with an immobiliser system, it is possible to substitute a known good ECU in place of the suspect one for testing purposes. If an immobiliser system is

fitted, the only solution in the event of an ECU failure is to fit a new unit and go through the key registration procedure.

Removal and installation

3 On MT-07 (FZ-07) models remove the right-hand fuel tank cover, and on MT-07TR models remove the fuel tank cover (see Chapter 7). Disconnect the wiring connector, then unhook the rubber band and lift the ECU out **(see illustrations)**.

4 On XSR models remove the right-hand air scoop (see Chapter 7). Release the rubber holder from the tabs **(see illustration)**, then disconnect the wiring connector **(see illustrations 18.3a and b)** and slide the ECU out of the holder.

5 Installation is the reverse of removal. Make

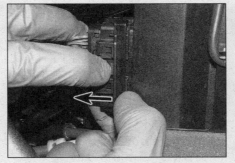

18.3a Press the catch in and push the release lever to the rear...

18.3b ... to release the connector

sure the wiring terminals are clean and none of the pins are bent, and make sure that the connector is correctly aligned with the socket before pushing the lever to draw the connector fully onto the terminals until the catch engages **(see illustration)**.

19 Immobiliser system

General information

1 The immobiliser system will only allow the machine to be started if a registered key is used to turn the ignition switch ON. The system consists of a transponder in the ignition key, the immobiliser unit (transceiver)

18.3c Unhook the band and remove the ECU

18.4 ECU (arrowed) – XSR models

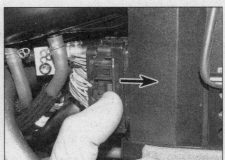

18.5 Align the connector then push the lever forwards to draw the connector onto the socket until it goes past the catch fitted on the front of the ignition switch, and the engine control unit (ECU).

2 When the ignition is switched ON, the ECU sends power through the immobiliser transceiver to the transponder. The transponder sends a coded signal back through the transceiver to the ECU. If the code sent by the transponder matches the code stored in the ECU memory, the immobiliser indicator light in the instrument cluster comes on for about a second, then goes out, and the ECU allows the engine to be started.

3 If the key code is not recognised, or if there is a fault in the system, the indicator light flashes. If the light flashes, or does not come on at all, refer to the Fault diagnosis and Troubleshooting Sections below.

4 The ECU can store the codes for up to three registered keys, two of which are standard-use keys with black casings, the other being the code re-registering key with a red casing. The three keys should be kept separately i.e. not on the same key-ring. The proximity of another key to the one being used in the switch can lead to the signal from the switch key transponder being jammed, and the bike will not start.

5 The transponder in the ignition key can be damaged if the key is dropped or knocked, gets too hot, is too close to a magnetic object, or is submerged in water. If this happens, a new key can be obtained from a Yamaha dealer and registered using the (red) code re-registering key. It is important, therefore, to keep the (red) code re-registering key in a safe place and never to use it on a daily basis.

6 Always make sure you have a spare standard-use key. If an existing key is damaged or lost, obtain a new key and register it with the immobiliser system as soon as possible.

7 If all the keys are lost, or if the ignition switch is faulty, the immobiliser transceiver and ECU must be replaced with new ones along with the new ignition switch (they come as a set – see Chapter 8).

Standard-use key registration procedure

Note: *This must be done when a standard-use key is lost and a new one is obtained. The procedure automatically renders the lost key useless – even if you don't replace the lost key with a new one and just have one standard-use key, following this procedure will re-register your remaining standard-use key and so doing will de-register the lost key.*

8 Obtain a new key from a Yamaha dealer, and have it cut to match the original key.

9 Have all three keys ready to hand – when a new standard-use key is registered, the code in the remaining standard-use key is cancelled, so this will also have to be registered.

10 Using the (red) code re-registering key, turn the ignition switch ON, then turn it OFF and remove the key. Within 5 seconds, turn the ignition ON with the new key. The immobiliser indicator light should flash on and off every half second. This indicates that the system is in registration mode. If at any time during the procedure the light stops flashing, more than 5 seconds have elapsed and the system is no longer in registration mode, in which case start again to register both keys.

11 While the light is still flashing, turn the ignition OFF, remove the new key (placing it well away from the transceiver) and within 5 seconds turn the ignition ON with the remaining standard-use key. When the light stops flashing the registration is complete. Turn the ignition OFF and remove the key.

12 Check that both standard-use keys can start the motorcycle.

Code re-registering key registration procedure

Note: *This must be done when a new ECU has been fitted, or when a new immobiliser system has been installed.*

13 Turn the ignition switch ON using the (red) code re-registering key. The immobiliser light will come on for a few seconds, then go out, indicating that the key has been registered.

14 Check that the key can start the motorcycle.

15 Now register the standard-use keys as described in Steps 8 to 12.

Installing a new ECU

16 Install the new ECU (Section 18).

17 Turn the ignition switch ON using the code re-registering key. This registers the key to the new ECU.

18 Check that the key can start the motorcycle.

19 Now register the standard-use keys as described in Steps 8 to 12.

Installing a new immobiliser transceiver

20 Remove the ignition switch, then remove the old immobiliser transceiver from it and fit the new one (see Chapter 8).

21 Turn the ignition switch ON using the code re-registering key. This registers the key to the transceiver.

22 Check that the key can start the motorcycle.

23 Now register the standard-use keys as described in Steps 8 to 12

Fault diagnosis

24 If there is a fault in the system, the immobiliser indicator light in the instrument cluster flashes and a fault code is shown in the LCD display (see table below).

Troubleshooting procedure

25 If fault code 51 or 52 is shown, first check that none of the other registered keys are close to the receiver. If they are, remove them and try the ignition again. The key transponder may be faulty – try starting the bike with another key.

26 If any fault code is shown, first check the fuses, wiring and connectors between the immobiliser receiver, ignition switch and the ECU (see Chapter 8, Sections 2 and 18, and to the Wiring diagrams at the end of Chapter 8). A continuity test of all wires will locate a break or short in any circuit. Inspect the terminals inside the wiring connectors and ensure they are not loose, bent or corroded. Spray the inside of the connectors with a proprietary electrical terminal cleaner before reconnection. Also make sure the battery is in good condition and that the ignition switch is not faulty (see Chapter 8).

27 If the immobiliser LED or the LCD display in the instrument cluster do not come on, refer to Chapter 8 and check the instrument cluster.

28 If all indications are that either the immobiliser transceiver or the ECU are faulty, it is worth having them checked by a Yamaha dealer before buying new parts.

Fault code	Symptoms	Possible causes
51	Signal from key not being received by immobiliser transceiver	Interference from other keys or magnet. Faulty key transponder. Faulty immobiliser transceiver
52	Code from key not recognised by immobiliser transceiver	Interference from other key. Unregistered key being used
53	Signal from immobiliser transceiver not being received by ECU	Faulty wiring or wiring connector. Faulty immobiliser transceiver. Faulty ECU
54	Codes do not match between immobiliser and ECU	Code re-registering key not registered. Faulty wiring or wiring connector. Faulty immobiliser transceiver. Faulty ECU
55	Key registration error	Same key being registered twice
56	Code not recognised by ECU	Interference. Faulty wiring or wiring connector. Faulty immobiliser transceiver. Faulty ECU

Chapter 5
Frame and suspension

Contents

Degrees of difficulty

Easy, suitable for novice with little experience	**Fairly easy,** suitable for beginner with some experience	**Fairly difficult,** suitable for competent DIY mechanic	**Difficult,** suitable for experienced DIY mechanic	**Very difficult,** suitable for expert DIY or professional

Specifications

Front forks

Fork oil type	Yamaha suspension oil G10 or equivalent 10W fork oil
Fork oil capacity	403 cc
Fork oil level*	162 mm
Fork spring free length	
Standard.	345.4 mm
Service limit	331.6 mm
Fork inner tube runout (max.)	0.2 mm

Oil level is measured from the top of the inner tube with the fork spring removed and the leg fully compressed.

Torque wrench settings

Clutch lever bracket clamp bolt	11 Nm
Clutch lever pivot bolt nut	7 Nm
Footrest bracket bolts	30 Nm
Fork clamp bolts	
Bottom yoke.	23 Nm
Top yoke.	26 Nm
Fork damper rod bolt	30 Nm
Fork top bolt.	23 Nm
Front brake lever pivot bolt	1 Nm
Front brake lever pivot bolt nut	6 Nm
Front brake master cylinder clamp bolts	10 Nm
Handlebar clamp bolts	28 Nm
Handlebar holder nuts	32 Nm
Inner bracket bolts	45 Nm
Rear brake pedal pivot bolt	22 Nm
Rear shock absorber mountng bolt nuts	
Front	44 Nm
Rear	40 Nm
Sidestand bracket bolts	63 Nm
Suspenion linkage bolts/nuts	see Section 12
Steering head bearing adjuster nut clamp bolt	
MT-07 (FZ-07) and XSR models	21 Nm
MT-07TR models	35 Nm
Swingarm pivot bolt nut	110 Nm

1 General Information

1 All models have a steel frame that uses the engine as a stressed member.

2 Front suspension is by a pair of 41 mm telescopic forks with internal coil springs and a conventional damper. The forks are not adjustable.

3 At the rear, a swingarm acts on a single shock absorber via a rising-rate linkage. The shock absorber has adjustable spring pre-load.

2 Frame

1 The frame should not require attention unless accident damage has occurred. In most cases, fitting a new frame is the only satisfactory remedy for such damage. A few frame specialists have the jigs and other equipment necessary for straightening the frame to the required standard of accuracy, but even then there is no simple way of assessing to what extent the frame may have been over-stressed.

2 After the machine has covered a high mileage, the frame should be examined closely for signs of cracking or splitting at the welded joints. Loose engine mount bolts can cause ovaling or fracturing of the mounts themselves. Minor damage can often be repaired by welding, depending on the extent and nature of the damage, but this is a task for an expert.

3 Remember that a frame that is out of alignment will cause handling problems. If misalignment is suspected as the result of an accident, first check the wheel alignment (see Chapter 6). To have the frame checked thoroughly it will be necessary to strip the machine completely.

3 Footrests, gearchange lever and rear brake pedal

Footrests

1 To remove the rider's footrests, remove the split pin from the pivot pin, then pull the pivot pin out and remove the footrest, noting how the return spring ends locate **(see illustration)**.

2 To remove the passenger footrests on MT-07 (FZ-07) and XSR models follow the procedure in Step 1, noting that a spring-loaded ball and detent plate are located between the footrest and its bracket to secure the footrest in the UP position when not in use **(see illustration)**. Take care not to loose the ball and spring when the footrest is removed.

3 To remove the passenger footrests on MT-07TR models unscrew the nut, withdraw the bolt and remove the footrest, noting that a spring-loaded ball and detent plate are located between the footrest and its bracket to secure the footrest in the UP position when not in use, and that there is a sleeve for the bolt in the pivot. Take care not to loose the ball and spring when the footrest is removed.

4 The footrest rubbers can be replaced with new ones if necessary by undoing the two screws on the underside of the footrest **(see illustration)**.

5 Installation is the reverse of removal. Use new split pins.

Gearchange lever and linkage

Removal

6 If you want to separate the gearchange lever from the linkage rod, measure and note the amount of exposed thread on each end of the linkage rod (this determines the height of the lever relative to the footrest), then slacken the linkage rod locknuts, turning the lower one clockwise as it has left-hand threads **(see illustration)**. Unscrew the rod and separate it from the lever and the arm – as the rod is reverse-threaded on the lower end it will simultaneously unscrew from both lever and arm when turned in the one direction **(see illustration)**.

7 Unscrew the gearchange lever pivot bolt and remove the wave washer, the outer thrust washer, the lever and the inner thrust washer **(see illustration)**.

3.1 Remove the split pin (A) and withdraw the pivot pin – note how the return spring ends (B) locate

3.2 Note the fitting of the ball, spring and plate (arrowed)

3.4 Footrest rubber screws (arrowed)

3.6a Hold the joint piece with one spanner and slacken the locknut with another

3.6b Unscrew and remove the rod

3.7 Note the arrangement of the washers

3.8 Linkage arm/shaft alignment

3.11 Unscrew the bolts and displace the bracket

3.12 Unhook the springs (arrowed)

8 Note the alignment of the line on the gearchange shaft with the punch mark on the gearchange linkage arm, then unscrew the pinch bolt and slide the arm off the shaft **(see illustration)**.
9 If the toe rubber is worn remove it and fit a new one.

Installation

10 Installation is the reverse of removal, noting the following:
● Align the punch mark on the linkage arm with the line on the shaft **(see illustration 3.8)**.
● Clean any old grease off the lever pivot and the pivot bolt, then apply fresh grease.
● The large inner thrust washer fits between the lever and the footrest bracket, and fit the wave washer outside the outer thrust washer **(see illustration 3.7)**.
● Adjust the gear lever height as required by screwing the linkage rod in or out of the lever and arm **(see illustration 3.6b)**. Tighten the locknuts **(see illustration 3.6a)**.

Rear brake pedal

11 Unscrew the rider's right-hand footrest bracket bolts and displace the footrest assembly **(see illustration)**.
12 Unhook the rear brake light switch spring and the pedal return spring **(see illustration)**.

13 Remove the split pin and washer from the clevis pin connecting the brake pedal to the master cylinder pushrod, then withdraw the clevis pin **(see illustration)**. A new split pin must be used on reassembly.
14 Unscrew the brake pedal pivot bolt and remove the wave washer, the outer thrust washer, the pedal and the inner thrust washer **(see illustration 3.13)**.
15 Installation is the reverse of removal, noting the following:
● Clean any old grease off the pedal pivot and pivot bolt and any old threadlock off the bolt threads, then apply fresh grease to the pivot and threadlock to the threads.
● The large inner thrust washer fits between the pedal and the footrest bracket, and fit the wave washer outside the outer thrust washer **(see illustration 3.7)**.
● Tighten the pivot bolt to 22 Nm.
● Make sure the springs are hooked up correctly **(see illustration 3.12)**.
● Secure the clevis pin with a new split pin and bend both ends of the split pin around the clevis pin **(see illustration 3.13)**.
● Fit the footrest bracket, locating the grommet in the inner side over the peg on the inner bracket, then fit the bolts with their washers and tighten them to 30 Nm **(see illustration)**.

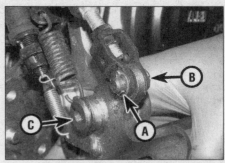

3.13 Straighten and remove the split pin (A) and withdraw the clevis pin (B). Brake pedal pivot bolt (C)

16 If required, follow the procedure in Chapter 1, Section 14, to adjust the rear brake light switch and pedal position.

4 Sidestand

1 Support the motorcycle securely in an upright position using an auxiliary stand. Tie the front brake on.
2 Unhook the spring with the stand in the raised position, and remove it with the link plate **(see illustration)**.

3.15 Seat the grommet over the peg (arrowed)

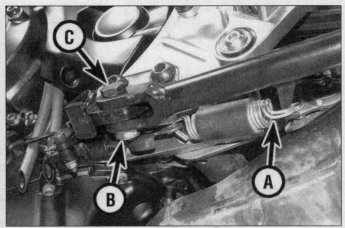

4.2 Using a spring hook to unhook the springs (A). Sidestand pivot nut (B) and bolt (C)

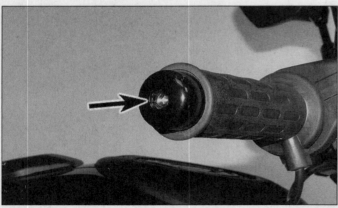

5.4a On MT-07 (FZ-07) and XSR models unscrew the end-weight (arrowed)

5.4b On MT-07TR models unscrew the end-weight bolt (arrowed) and remove the weight

3 Counterhold the bolt head, unscrew the nut and remove the washer, then draw the bolt out **(see illustration 4.2).** Push the pivot sleeve out, then draw the stand off the bracket and remove the washers that fit between the stand and each side of the bracket.

4 Installation is the reverse of removal, noting the following points:
● Apply lithium-based grease to the pivot sleeve/washer/bracket contact areas.
● Check the spring tension – it must hold the stand up when it is not in use. If the spring has sagged, replace it with a new one.
● Check the operation of the sidestand switch and starter safety circuit (see Chapter 1, Section 18).

5	**Handlebars and levers**	

Handlebars

Removal

Note: *The handlebars can be displaced from the top yoke without having to remove the throttle twistgrip, switch assemblies or levers (see Step 11). In all cases, take care to avoid straining the handlebar wiring. Support or tie the handlebar assembly using rags to cushion it and anything it sits against. Also cover the front brake master cylinder with rag in case of leakage.*

1 Remove the mirrors, and on MT-07TR and Moto Cage models remove the hand guard assemblies (see Chapter 7).
2 On MT-07 (FZ-07) and XSR models remove the instruments (see Chapter 8).
3 Disconnect the throttle cables (see Chapter 4).
4 Remove the end-weight from each end of the handlebar **(see illustrations).**
5 Slide the throttle twistgrip off the handlebar.
6 Displace the front brake master cylinder (see Chapter 6) – there is no need to disconnect the brake hose. Keep the reservoir upright to prevent fluid spillage and make sure no strain in placed on the hose.
7 Displace the switch housings (see Chapter 8).
8 Pull the left-hand grip off the handlebar – push a plastic tool or screwdriver covered with tape between the grip and the bar and use spray lubricant (see Caution) and/or compressed air to loosen the grip. If the grip has been bonded in place you may need to cut it free, in which case you will need a new one.
Caution: Wear eye protection when using a spray lube for this purpose – it can spray back into your face.
9 Disconnect the clutch cable from the clutch lever (see Chapter 2).
10 Loosen the clutch lever bracket pinch bolt and slide the lever off the handlebar **(see illustration).**
11 Support the handlebars, unscrew the clamps bolts and remove the clamps, then lift the handlebars off **(see illustration).**
12 If required unscrew the nuts on the underside of the top yoke and remove the washers, then lift the handlebar holder out of the top yoke, again removing the washers **(see illustration).**

Installation

13 If the holder was removed from the top yoke fit it back on with the upper washers, then fit the lower washers and tighten the nuts to 32 Nm **(see illustration 5.12).**
14 Position the handlebars centrally, aligning the punch mark on the back of the bar with the top edge of the left-hand end of the holder **(see illustration).**

5.10 Clutch lever bracket pinch bolt (arrowed)

5.11 Handlebar clamp bolts (arrowed)

5.12 Handlebar holder nut (arrowed)

5.14 Align the clamp mating surfaces with the punch mark (arrowed)

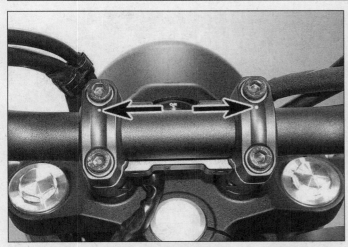

5.15 Fit the clamps with the punch marks (arrowed – XSR shown, on MT-07 models the mark on the front) or triangular mark (Tracer) to the front

5.16a Align the slit with the punch mark (arrowed)

15 Fit the handlebar clamps with the mark at the front **(see illustration)**. Tighten the front clamp bolts to 28 Nm, then tighten the rear clamp bolts to the same torque.

16 Install the remaining components in the reverse order of removal, noting the following.

● Align the slit in the clutch lever bracket with the punch mark on the underside of the handlebar **(see illustration 5.16a)**. Tighten the clamp bolt to 11 Nm.

● Align the front brake master cylinder clamp mating surfaces with the punch mark on the top of the handlebar, and fit the clamp with the UP mark facing up **(see illustration 5.16b)**. Note that there should be at least 11mm gap between the clamp and switch housing. Tighten the clamp bolts to 10 Nm, tightening the top bolt first.

● Make sure that the peg on the lower half of the right-hand switch housing and the front half of the left-hand housing locates in the hole in the underside and front of the handlebar respectively. Do not forget to reconnect the front brake light switch and clutch switch wiring connectors.

● Lubricate the right-hand bar end before sliding on the throttle twistgrip.

● Refer to Chapter 4 to connect the throttle cables.

● Check and adjust throttle and clutch cable freeplay (see Chapter 1).

● Check the operation of all switches, the front brake and clutch before taking the machine on the road.

Clutch lever

17 On MT-07TR and Moto Cage models remove the mirror and the hand guard bracket (see Chapter 7). On all models, create slack in the cable by threading the adjuster into the lever bracket (see Chapter 1, Section 10).

18 Unscrew the lever pivot bolt nut, then push the pivot bolt out of the bracket, displace the lever and disconnect the clutch cable **(see illustrations)**. Note there is a sleeve in the lever pivot – make sure it does not drop out.

19 Installation is the reverse of removal. Apply grease to the pivot bolt shaft and sleeve and to the contact areas between the lever and its bracket, and to the inner clutch cable end. Align the flats on the underside of the pivot bolt head with those in the bolt head seat **(see illustration)**. Tighten the nut to 7 Nm. Adjust the clutch cable freeplay (see Chapter 1).

5.16b Align the clamp mating surfaces with the punch mark (arrowed)

5.18a Unscrew the nut…

5.18b … withdraw the bolt…

5.18c … and disconnect the cable

5.19 When fitting the bolt align the flats on the underside of the head with those in the bracket

Front brake lever

20 On MT-07TR and Moto Cage models remove the mirror and the hand guard bracket (see Chapter 7).

21 Hold the lever pivot bolt with a screwdriver and unscrew the locknut **(see illustration)**. Unscrew the pivot bolt and remove the lever, noting how it locates against the master cylinder pushrod.

22 Installation is the reverse of removal. Apply silicone grease to the pivot bolt shaft and to the contact areas between the lever and its bracket and where the pushrod locates in the cup in the lever. Tighten the pivot bolt to 1 Nm, then hold the pivot bolt and tighten the locknut nut to 6 Nm **(see illustration 5.21)**.

6 Fork removal and installation

Removal

1 Support the motorcycle upright on level ground so that the front wheel is off the ground. On MT-07TR models, if required for best access and to avoid the possibility of damage, remove the fairing side panels and inner panels (see Chapter 7).

2 Remove the front wheel (see Chapter 6).

3 Remove the front mudguard (see Chapter 7).

4 Work on each fork leg individually. Note the routing of the cables, wiring and hoses around the forks.

5 Note the alignment between the top of the fork outer tube and the top yoke, then loosen the fork clamp bolt in the top yoke **(see illustration)**. If the fork leg is to be disassembled, or if the fork oil is being changed, loosen the fork top bolt.

6 Support the fork leg, then loosen the fork clamp bolts in the bottom yoke and remove the fork by twisting it and pulling it downwards **(see illustration)**. Note which fork fits on which side. On MT-07 (FZ-07) models lift the fork shroud off the bottom yoke to free the peg from the hole, and remove the O-ring **(see illustration)**.

5.21 Counter-hold the pivot bolt when unscrewing and tightening the locknut

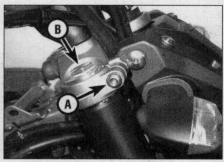

6.5 Slacken the clamp bolt (A) in the top yoke, then slacken the fork top bolt (B) if required

6.6a Slacken the clamp bolts (arrowed) in the bottom yoke and remove the fork

6.6b On MT-07 (FZ-07) models remove the shroud and its O-ring

Installation

7 Remove all traces of corrosion from the fork tubes and the yokes.

8 On MT-07 (FZ-07) models lubricate the fork shroud O-rings with oil, using new ones if necessary.

9 Slide the fork leg up through the bottom yoke – on MT-07 (FZ-07) models fit the O-ring and fork shroud over the top of the fork, pushing the peg on the shroud into the hole in the yoke **(see illustrations)** – then slide the fork into the top yoke, on MT-07 (FZ-07) models making sure the O-ring remains at the bottom of the shroud so its sits between it and the bottom yoke, and does not get pushed up inside the shroud as you slide the fork up, and

on all models making sure the wiring, cables and hoses are the correct side of the leg as noted on removal. Align the top of the fork tube with the top yoke, so the top bolt rim is raised above it **(see illustration)**.

10 Tighten the fork clamp bolts in the bottom yoke to 23 Nm **(see illustration 6.6a)**. If the fork has been dismantled or if the oil has been changed, tighten the top bolt to 23 Nm **(see illustration 6.5)**. Tighten the fork clamp bolt in the top yoke to 26 Nm **(see illustration 6.5)**.

11 Install the remaining components in the reverse order of removal.

12 Check the operation of the front forks and brakes before taking the machine on the road.

6.9a On MT-07 (FZ-07) models fit the O-ring over the fork...

6.9b ...fit the shroud trim clip into the hole in the yoke

6.9c Correct setting of the fork in the top yoke

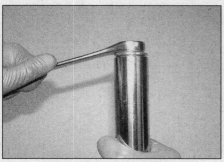

7.3 Unscrew the top bolt

7.4a Remove the spacer...

7.4b ... the washer...

7.4c ... and the spring

7.5a Tip the oil out...

7.5b ... then pump the fork

7 Fork oil change

1 After a high mileage the fork oil will deteriorate and its damping and lubrication qualities will be impaired. Always change the oil in both fork legs.

2 Remove the fork (Section 6) – make sure you loosen the top bolt while the leg is still clamped in the bottom yoke.

3 Unscrew the fork top bolt from the top of the inner tube – the bolt is under pressure from the fork spring, so if available use a ratchet tool so it does not need to be removed from the bolt as you unscrew it, and maintain some downward pressure on it, particularly as you come to the end of the threads, or alternatively hold the tool still and twist the fork tube to unthread it from the bolt **(see illustration)**.

4 Remove the spacer, then slide the inner tube down gently and remove the washer and the spring **(see illustrations)**.

5 Invert the fork over a suitable container and pump the inner tube several times to expel as much fork oil as possible **(see illustrations)**. Support the fork upside down in the container for a while to allow as much oil as possible to drain, then pump it again. If the fork oil contains metal particles inspect the fork bushes for wear (Section 8). Wipe any excess oil off the spring and spacer.

6 Stand the fork upright. Slowly pour in the correct quantity and grade of fork oil as given in the Specifications **(see illustration)**. Now pump the inner tube slowly at least ten times to distribute the oil evenly and expel all air. Slide the inner tube down gently until it seats on the bottom. Measure the oil level from the top of the tube **(see illustration)**. Add or subtract oil until it is at the level given in the Specifications at the beginning of this Chapter.

7 Pull the inner tube out, then fit the spring **(see illustration)**. Fit the washer on top of the spring, then fit the spacer **(see illustration 7.4b and a)**.

7.6a Fill the fork slowly to prevent air bubbles and overfilling

7.6b Measure the distance from the top of the tube to the oil

7.7 Fit the spring

7.8 Check the O-ring (arrowed)

8.2a Use a hammer and piece of wood to tap the protector off

8.2b Remove the axle clamp bolt

8 If the top bolt O-ring is damaged or has deteriorated fit a new one **(see illustration)**. Smear some fork oil onto the O-ring. Extend the inner tube and fit the top bolt into it, compressing the spring as you do, and thread it in, making sure it does not cross-thread. Keep downward pressure on the spring using a ratchet tool or by turning the tube while holding the bolt still, and tighten the top bolt as much as possible holding the inner tube by hand. Tighten the top bolt to the specified torque setting when the fork has been installed in the bike and is held in the bottom yoke, but before the top yoke clamp bolt is tightened.

9 Install the fork (Section 6).

8.3a Slacken the damper rod bolt as described

8.3b Steel rod with end ground as shown to fit in the top of the damper rod

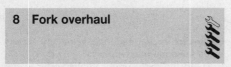

8 Fork overhaul

Special tool: *A dedicated fork bush and seal driver is a good tool to have for this procedure, though not essential – an alternative method is given.*

1 Remove the fork – make sure you loosen the top bolt while the leg is still clamped in the bottom yoke (Section 6). Always dismantle the fork legs separately to avoid interchanging parts and thus causing an accelerated rate of wear. Store all components in separate, clearly marked containers.

Disassembly

2 Remove the fork protector, noting how it locates **(see illustration)**. When working on

the right-hand fork remove the wheel axle clamp bolt **(see illustration)**.

3 Slacken the damper rod bolt in the base of the outer tube **(see illustration)**. If the damper rod turns with the bolt, turn the leg upside down and compress the fork so the pressure of the spring holds the damper while the bolt is loosened. Alternatively use an air impact wrench, if available. If the bolt cannot be loosened at this stage, Yamaha produce a service tool (Part No. 90890-01460) and T-bar (Part No. 90890-01326) which can be inserted down inside the inner tube once the spring has been removed – the tool has a tapered head that grips in the top end of the damper to hold it while the bolt is loosened. As an alternative you can try a broom handle tapered at the end, and it usually does the job, but on the fork photographed the rod continued to turn with the bolt. A home-made version of the

Yamaha tool was made by shaping the end of a steel rod **(see illustration)**; stand this on the ground with its shaped end upwards and slide the fork over the tool, pressing it down onto it while unscrewing the bolt.

4 Refer to Section 7 and drain the oil from the fork.

5 Remove the damper rod bolt and its copper sealing washer from the bottom of the outer tube, using a holding tool as described in Step 3 if necessary **(see illustrations 8.3a and b)**. A new sealing washer must be used on reassembly. Tip the damper rod and rebound spring out **(see illustration)**.

6 Carefully prise out the dust seal from the top of the outer tube **(see illustration)**. A new seal must be used on installation.

7 Carefully remove the retaining clip, taking care not to scratch the surface of the tube **(see illustration)**.

8.5 Tip the damper rod out

8.6 Prise out the dust seal using a flat-bladed screwdriver

8.7 Prise out the retaining clip using a flat-bladed screwdriver

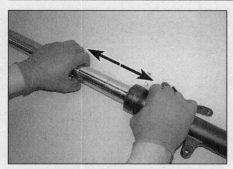

8.8a Repeatedly draw the tubes apart...

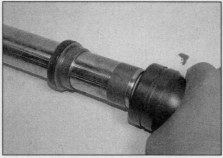

8.8b ... until the seal and bush are displaced

8.10a Retrieve the damper rod seat...

8 To separate the inner tube from the outer tube it is necessary to displace the oil seal and top bush from the top of the outer tube. The bottom bush on the inner tube will not pass through the top bush in the outer tube, and this can be used to good effect. Slide the inner tube in, then pull it quickly out so the bottom bush strikes the top bush **(see illustration)**. Repeat this operation until the seal and top bush are tapped out of the outer tube and the inner tube can be fully withdrawn **(see illustration)**.

9 Slide the oil seal, washer and top bush off the inner tube, noting which way round they fit. A new oil seal must be used, but unless you have a dedicated seal installation tool keep the old one to use as an interface when driving the new seal in to prevent damage.

10 Remove the damper rod seat – if it is not in the bottom of the inner tube, tip it out of the outer tube **(see illustration)**. Note the spring inside the seat **(see illustration)**.

Inspection

11 Clean all parts in solvent and blow them dry with compressed air, if available. Check the inner fork tube for score marks, scratches, rust spots and flaking of the chrome finish. Any such damage will result in premature seal failure. Fork inner tubes can be re-chromed using hard chrome, or replace them with new ones. Check the fork seal seat for nicks, gouges and scratches. If damage is evident, leaks will occur.

12 Check the inner tube for runout using V-blocks and a dial gauge **(see illustration)**. If the amount of runout exceeds the service limit given in the Specifications at the beginning of the chapter, the tube must be replaced with a new one.

 Warning: If the tube is bent or exceeds the runout limit, it should not be straightened; replace it with a new one.

13 Check the working surface of each bush for wear **(see illustration)** – the surface should be Teflon grey all over. If the Teflon has worn to expose the material below replace both bushes with new ones – Yamaha specify to use new ones as a matter of course, and as the expense is not great it is worth doing. To remove the bottom bush from the inner tube

8.10b ... and note the spring fitted in it

8.12 Checking the fork tube for runout

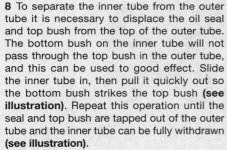

8.13a Check the working surface of each bush (arrowed) for wear

8.13b Lever the ends apart and slide the bush off

lever its ends apart using a screwdriver and slide it out of its seat **(see illustration)**.

14 Check the main spring for cracks and other damage. Measure the spring free length and compare the measurement to that given in the Specifications at the beginning of the Chapter **(see illustration)**. If it is defective or

sagged below the service limit, replace the spring in each fork with a new one – never replace only one spring.

15 Check the damper rod, and in particular the ring in its head, and the rebound spring for damage and wear **(see illustration)**. Check the damper rod seat and its spring for damage.

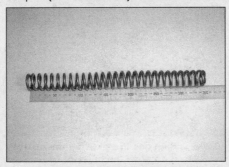

8.14 Measure the free length of the spring

8.15 Check the rod, rebound spring and ring (arrowed) for wear

8.17a Slide the damper rod into the top of the tube…

8.17b … so it protrudes from the bottom, then fit the seat…

8.17c … and push it into the bottom of the tube

Reassembly

16 If removed fit a new bottom bush into its seat on the inner tube – do not expand it any further than necessary to get it over the bottom of the tube **(see illustration 8.13b)**.

17 Fit the rebound spring onto the damper rod if removed **(see illustration 8.15)**. Make sure the piston ring is correctly seated in its groove with the castellated side facing the bottom of the rod. Slide the rod all the way down into the inner tube so it protrudes from the bottom **(see illustration)**. Check the spring is correctly located in the damper rod seat **(see illustration 8.10b)**. Fit the seat onto the bottom of the rod, then push the seat up inside the tube **(see illustrations)**.

18 Lubricate the bottom bush on the inner tube with new 10W fork oil. Insert the tube

8.18 Fit the inner tube into the outer tube

into the outer tube and slide it fully down until it contacts the bottom **(see illustration)**.

19 Lay the fork flat on the bench. Fit a new copper sealing washer onto the damper bolt and apply a few drops of a suitable

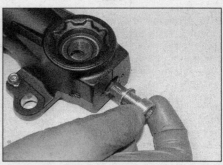

8.19 Fit a new sealing washer and apply threadlock

non-permanent thread locking compound **(see illustration)**. Fit the bolt into the bottom of the outer tube, thread it into the damper rod and tighten it to 30 Nm. If the rod rotates inside the tube as you tighten the bolt, use the same holding method as on disassembly, or wait until the fork is fully reassembled and tighten it then (the pressure of the spring on the rod will prevent it from turning).

20 Lubricate the top bush with fork oil and slide it down the inner tube and into the outer tube **(see illustration)**. Slide the washer down the tube and onto the bush **(see illustration)**. Carefully drive the bush onto its seat in the outer tube using a dedicated fork seal tool if available, or a suitable drift, against the washer (which acts as an interface to prevent damage to the softer bush), turning the fork so the bush enters squarely if using a drift **(see illustrations)**. Take care not to let the drift slip

8.20a Slide the bush on…

8.20b … then seat the washer on it

8.20c If using a proper fork seal installation tool fit the drive piece over the inner tube, into the top of the outer tube and onto the washer…

8.20d … then use the slide hammer piece to drive the bush in

8.20e You can also drive the bush into place using a suitable drift – the one shown was specially shaped

against the inner tube. You will know when the bush is seated as the tone of the impact changes, but lift the washer off to check **(see illustration)**.

21 Lubricate the lips of the new oil seal with fork oil, then slide it down the inner tube and into the outer tube – make sure the marked side of the seal faces out **(see illustration)**. Carefully drive the seal in and onto its seat using the same seal installation tool or drift **(see illustrations 8.20d and e)** – if using a drift slide the old seal onto the new one to act as an interface to prevent damage, then use a screwdriver to lift the old seal out when the new one is seated. The new seal is seated when the retaining clip groove is fully exposed **(see illustration)**.

22 Fit the retaining ring into its groove **(see illustration)**.

23 Lubricate the lips of the new dust seal then slide it down the fork tube and press it into position **(see illustration)**.

24 Refer to Section 7, Steps 6 to 8 and fill the fork with oil and finish reassembly.

25 If the damper rod bolt requires tightening (see Step 19), place the fork upside down on the floor, using a rag to protect it, then have an assistant compress the fork so that maximum spring pressure is placed on the damper rod head while tightening the bolt to 30 Nm.

26 Fit the axle clamp bolt loosely into the right-hand fork **(see illustration 8.2b)**. Fit the fork protector, aligning the tab with the cut-out **(see illustration)**.

27 Install the fork (Section 6).

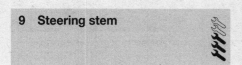

9 Steering stem

Removal

1 Support the motorcycle upright on level ground so that the front wheel is off the ground. Remove the fuel tank cover(s) (see Chapter 7), and for best access remove the fuel tank (see Chapter 4).

2 On MT-07 (FZ-07) models remove the headlight assembly (see Chapter 8). On

8.20f Lift the washer to check the bush (arrowed) is fully recessed

8.21b Check the retaining ring groove (arrowed) is fully exposed

8.23 Slide the dust seal down and press it into the outer tube

XSR models remove the complete headlight assembly (see Chapter 8).

3 Remove the front forks (see Section 6).

4 Unscrew the bolts securing the brackets to

8.21a Slide the oil seal on

8.22 Make sure the ring seats fully in its groove

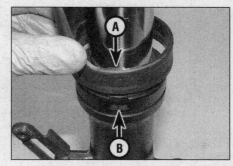
8.26 Seat the tab (A) in the cut-out (B)

the underside and topside of the bottom yoke **(see illustrations)**.

5 Slacken the steering head bearing adjuster nut clamp bolt **(see illustration)**. Lift the

9.4a Unscrew the bolts (arrowed)...

9.4b ... and the bolt (arrowed)

9.5a Slacken the clamp bolt

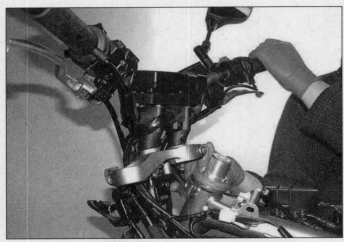

9.5b Displace the handlebar/yoke assembly ...

9.5c ...and tie it as shown

9.6a Slacken the adjuster nut using a C-spanner...

9.6b ... then unscrew it and remove the bottom yoke/steering stem

handlebar/top yoke assemblyup off the steering stem and tie it the right-hand side as shown **(see illustrations)**.

6 Supporting the bottom yoke, slacken the adjuster nut using a C-spanner, then unscrew it and carefully lower the bottom yoke and steering stem out of the frame **(see illustrations)**.

7 Remove the bearing cover, inner race and bearing from the top of the steering head **(see illustrations)**.

8 Remove the bearing and dust seal from the

9.7a Remove the cover...

9.7b ... and the inner race and upper bearing

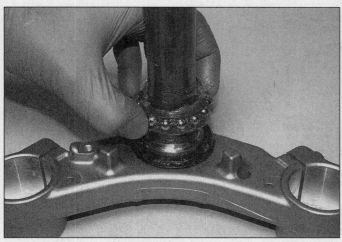

9.8a Remove the bearing …

9.8b …and the seal from the stem

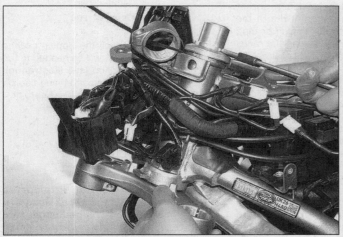

9.12 Tighten the adjuster nut as described

9.13 Fit the yoke assembly over the adjuster nut

base of the steering stem (see illustrations). It is advisable to fit a new dust seal.

9 Use a suitable solvent to remove all traces of old grease from the bearings and races and check them for wear or damage as described in Section 10. Do not remove the races from the steering head or the steering stem unless they are to be replaced with new ones – do not re-use the races if they have been removed.

Installation

10 Smear a liberal quantity of lithium-based grease onto the bearing races and work some grease well into both the upper and lower bearings. Fit the new dust seal over the lower bearing inner race on the steering stem, then fit the bearing (see illustrations 9.8b and a).

11 Fit the upper bearing and the inner race into the top of the steering head, then fit the bearing cover (see illustrations 9.7b and a).

12 Carefully lift the bottom yoke and steering stem up through the steering head and upper bearing, taking care not to dislodge it (see illustration 9.6b). Thread the adjuster nut onto the steering stem and tighten it enough

to hold the stem in the head without any play (see illustration).

13 Fit the top yoke assembly onto the steering stem and push it down until it seats (see illustration). Secure the brake hose to the bottom yoke (see illustrations 9.4a and b). Install the forks, mudguard and wheel, as their leverage and inertia need to be taken into account to properly set the bearings, then refer to the procedure in Chapter 1, and adjust the

10.2 Check the inner and outer races for wear and damage

bearings as described. Note that if new bearings have been fitted, you may need to carry out the procedure several times to allow them to settle.

14 Tighten the adjuster nut clamp bolt to 21 Nm on MT-07 (FZ-07) and XSR models, and to 35 Nm on MT-07TR models, then tighten the fork clamp bolts in the top yoke to 26 Nm.

15 Install the remaining components in the reverse order of removal. Carry out a check of the steering head bearing freeplay as described in Chapter 1, and if necessary re-adjust.

10 Steering head bearings

Inspection

1 Remove the steering stem (Section 9). Using a suitable solvent, remove all traces of old grease from the bearings and races.

2 Check for wear or damage – the races should be polished and free from indentations (see illustration). Inspect the bearing balls for

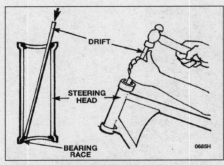

10.3a Drive the outer races from the steering head using a drift ...

10.3b ... located in the cut-outs provided (arrowed)

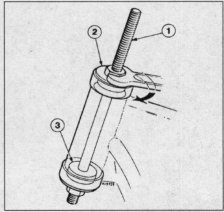

10.5 Drawbolt arrangement for fitting steering stem bearing races

1 Long bolt or threaded bar
2 Thick washer
3 Guide for lower race

signs of wear, damage or discoloration, and examine their retainer cages for distortion, cracks or splits. Spin the bearing balls by hand. They should spin freely and smoothly. If there are signs of wear on any of the above components, both upper and lower bearing assemblies must be replaced with a new set. Do not remove the races from the steering head or the steering stem unless they are to be replaced with new ones – do not re-use the races if they have been removed.

Renewal

3 The outer races are an interference fit in the steering head and can be tapped out with a suitable drift located in the cut-outs in the head **(see illustrations)**. Alternate between the cut-outs so that the race is driven out squarely. It may prove advantageous to curve the end of the drift slightly to improve access.

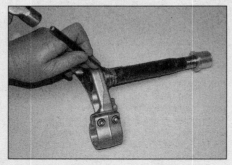

10.6a Displace and remove the bearing inner race ...

4 Alternatively, the races can be removed using a slide-hammer type bearing extractor – these can often be hired from tool shops.
5 The new outer races can be fitted using a drawbolt arrangement **(see illustration)**, or by using a suitable tubular drift or socket that bears only on the outer flat rim of the race, and does not touch the sloping bearing surface of the race itself. Freezing the races first to shrink them will make them easier to fit.
6 To remove the lower bearing race from the steering stem, first thread the adjuster nut onto the top of the stem to protect the threads, they lay the stem over on its side and drive a chisel between the base of the race and the bottom yoke, taking great care not to damage the yoke – heating the race first with a hot-air gun should expand it a little to ease removal **(see illustration)**. Work the chisel around the race to ensure it lifts squarely. Once there is clearance beneath the race, use two levers placed on opposite sides of the race to work it free, using blocks of wood to improve leverage and protect the yoke **(see illustration)**. If the race is firmly in place, carefully cut it off using a Dremel or angle grinder – you will probably not need to cut all the way through, as often the race may crack after a groove has been cut, or you can work a screwdriver or chisel in the groove to finally split it. Alternatively, take the steering stem to a Yamaha dealer.
7 Fit the new lower race onto the steering stem. A length of tubing with an internal diameter slightly larger than the steering stem that bears only on the inner top flat rim of the

race, and does not touch the sloping bearing surface of the race itself, will be needed to tap the new race into position **(see illustration)**. Heating the race first to expand it and cooling the stem in a freezer will make it easier to fit.
8 Install the steering stem (Section 9).

11 Rear shock absorber

 ⚠️ *Warning: Do not attempt to disassemble the shock absorber. It is nitrogen-charged under high pressure. Improper disassembly could result in serious injury. Take the shock to a Yamaha dealer or suspension specialist for servicing or disposal.*

Adjustment

1 The rear shock absorber has adjustable spring pre-load.
2 Spring pre-load is adjusted using a suitable C-spanner (one is provided in the bike's toolkit, along with an extension handle) to turn the adjuster ring at the front of the shock absorber **(see illustration)**.

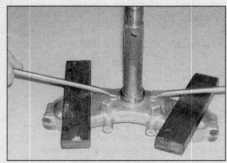

10.6b ... using one or more of the methods described, as necessary

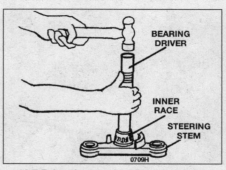

10.7 Drive the new bearing on using a suitable driver or a length of pipe

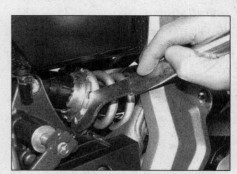

11.2 Adjusting spring pre-load

11.4 Bike supported using blocks of wood under the exhaust, with a front wheel clamp and ratchet straps for stability

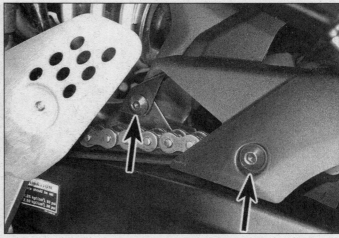

11.5a Chainguard screws (arrowed)

3 There are nine positions. Position 1 is the minimum (softest) setting, position 3 is the standard, and position 9 is the maximum (hardest). Align the setting required with the adjustment stopper. Turn the spring seat anti-clockwise (when looked at from the front) to increase pre-load and clockwise to decrease it.

Removal

4 Support the motorcycle upright on level ground on an auxiliary stand or stands (but not a rear paddock stand) – make sure that no weight is transmitted through any part of the rear suspension. If you have a ramp with a front wheel clamp you can use this and blocks of wood under the exhaust box – use a rear paddock stand to initially raise the rear of the bike, then put the blocks of wood under the exhaust, then remove the paddock stand. Also use ratchet straps to tie the bike to each side of the ramp for extra stability **(see illustration)**. If you don't have a ramp you can use a sturdy bar through the passenger footrest brackets, using rag to protect them, and support each end of the bar on a tall axle stand, with blocks of wood under the stand if necessary – use a rear paddock stand to initially raise the rear of the bike, then take it away after the bar is in place. Position a block of wood under the rear wheel so that it does not drop when the suspension is detached. Tie the front brake lever on so the bike can't roll forward.

5 Remove the chainguard – undo the two screws first, noting the sleeves, then release the front trim clip, then lift the guard enough to access the inner trim clip from the left-hand side **(see illustrations)**.

6 Unscrew the nut on the front mounting bolt, then withdraw the bolt with its spacer **(see illustrations)**.

7 Unscrew the nut on the rear mounting bolt, then withdraw the bolt and remove the shock absorber **(see illustrations)**.

11.5b Front trim clip (arrowed)

11.5c Lift the guard to access the inner trim clip (arrowed)

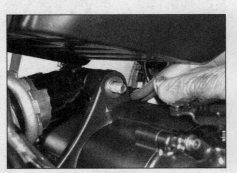

11.6a Unscrew the nut

11.6b Draw the spacer (arrowed) out with the bolt

11.7a Unscrew the nut, withdraw the bolt...

11.7b ... and remove the shock

11.10 Front mounting bush

12.3 Unscrew the nut and withdraw the bolt (arrowed) – on Tracer models the bolt goes in from the other side

12.4 Unscrew the nut and remove the washer, then withdraw the bolt (arrowed) and remove the linkage arm – on Tracer models the bolt goes in from the other side

Inspection

8 Inspect the body of the shock absorber for obvious physical damage and the coil spring for looseness, cracks or signs of fatigue.
9 Inspect the shock damper rod for signs of bending, pitting and oil leakage.
10 Inspect the pivot bush in the front mounting for wear **(see illustration)**.
11 Yamaha do not supply replacement parts for the shock, so if it is worn or damaged a new one must be fitted.

Installation

12 Installation is the reverse of removal, noting the following:
● Fit the shock absorber with the label facing down.
● Insert the rear bolt from the right-hand side

and the front bolt, with its spacer, from the left **(see illustrations 11.7a and 11.6b)**.
● Hold the bolt head and tighten the front nut to 44 Nm and the rear nut to 40 Nm.

12 Rear suspension linkage

Removal

1 Refer to Section 11 and support the bike as described in Step 4, then remove the chainguard as described in Step 5.
2 Unscrew the nut on the shock absorber rear mounting bolt, then withdraw the bolt and tie the rear end of the shock up out of the way using a cable-tie **(see illustration 11.7a)**.

3 Unscrew the nut on the bolt securing the linkage rod ends to the linkage arm, then withdraw the bolt **(see illustration)**.
4 Unscrew the nut and remove the washer on the bolt securing the linkage arm to the swingarm, then withdraw the bolt and remove the arm **(see illustration)**.
5 To remove the linkage rod, remove the frame covers (see Chapter 7) and the front sprocket cover (see Chapter 6). Release the wiring tie and disconnect the sidestand switch wiring connector, then release the wire from the clip **(see illustrations)**. Draw the fuel tank drain and breather hoses out of the guide on the sidestand bracket **(see illustration)**. Unscrew the sidestand bracket bolts and remove the stand assembly **(see illustration)**. Unscrew the swingarm pivot bolt nut and remove the washer **(see illustration 13.8b)**. Unscrew

12.5a Release the tie (arrowed) and disconnect the connector...

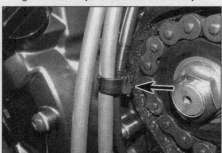

12.5b ... and release the wire from the clip (arrowed)

12.5c Lift the hoses out of the guide

12.5d Remove the sidestand assembly

12.5e Unscrew the two bolts...

12.5f ... draw the inner bracket out...

12.5g ... then pivot it round and support it so the linkage rod bolt (arrowed) is exposed

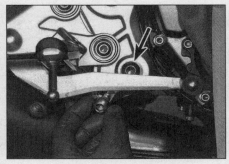

12.5h Unscrew the two bolts...

12.5i ... and displace and support the bracket to expose the nut (arrowed)

the left-hand inner bracket bolts, then draw the bracket away from the bike, bringing the swingarm pivot bolt with it, just far enough until there is enough clearance between the bracket and the swingarm to pivot the inner bracket anti-clockwise as shown to expose the linkage rod bolt (see illustrations) – place some rag between the bracket and the swingarm and secure the bracket using a cable-tie through a bolt hole. Unscrew the right-hand inner bracket bolts and displace the bracket, again using rag and a cable-tie for protection and support, to expose the linkage rod bolt nut (see illustrations).

6 Unscrew the nut, and on MT-07TR models remove the washer, on the linkage rod bolt, then withdraw the bolt and remove the rod (see illustrations).

Inspection

7 Remove the rubber cover from the linkage arm (see illustration). Withdraw the sleeve from each pivot of the arm, and from the linkage rod (see illustrations). Thoroughly clean all components with a suitable solvent, removing all traces of dirt, corrosion and grease.

8 Inspect all components closely, looking for obvious signs of wear such as heavy scoring, or for damage such as cracks or distortion. Inspect the bolt holes in the linkage rod ends for elongation.

9 Check the condition of the needle bearings in the linkage arm and rod. Refer to *Tools and Workshop Tips* in the Reference section for more information on bearings. Slip each sleeve back into its bearing and check that there is not an excessive amount of freeplay between them.

10 If the seals are obviously in bad condition, or if you are fitting new bearings, lever the

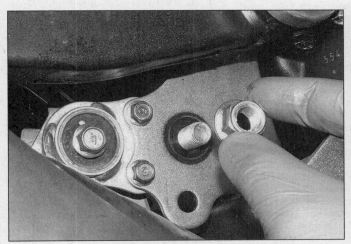

12.6a Unscrew the nut...

12.6b ... withdraw the bolt and remove the rod

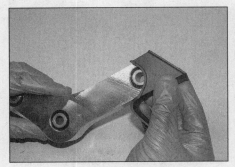

12.7a Remove the cover

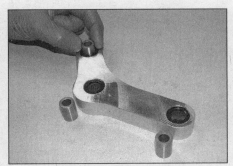

12.7b Withdraw the sleeves from the linkage arm ...

12.7c ... and the linkage rod

12.10 Lever the seals out

12.13 You should be able to press the new seals in with your thumbs

12.14 Make sure the linkage rod bolt head is locked between the flats as shown

seals out (see illustration). Once removed they cannot be reused – new ones must be fitted.

11 Worn bearings can be driven or drawn out of their bores, but note that once removed they cannot be reused – new bearings must be fitted. The new bearings should be pressed or drawn into their bores rather than driven into position. In the absence of a press, a suitable drawbolt tool can be made up as described in *Tools and Workshop Tips* in the Reference section. When fitting the new bearings make sure they are central in their bores.

12 Lubricate the bearings, sleeves and seal lips with multi-purpose lithium grease.

13 Press and/or drive the new seals squarely into place with the marked side facing out (see illustration).

Installation

14 Installation is the reverse of removal, noting the following:

● If not already done, remove the rubber cover from the linkage arm and withdraw the sleeve from each pivot of the arm and from the linkage rod, then clean the sleeves, seals and bearings, and apply multi-purpose lithium grease (see illustrations 12.7a, b and c). Refit the sleeves and cover.

● Insert the linkage rod bolt from the left (see illustration 12.6b), aligning two of the flats on its head with the projections on the frame so the head is locked (see

illustration). Tighten the linkage rod bolt nut to 52 Nm on MT-07 (FZ-07) and XSR models, and to 62 Nm on MT-07TR models (see illustration 12.6a). Clean the threads of the inner bracket bolts and apply some threadlock, position the brackets, pushing the swingarm pivot bolt through when doing the left-hand bracket and keeping the flats on the head seated against the flats in the inner bracket so it is locked, and tighten the bolts finger-tight (see illustrations 12.5e and h). Fit the washer and nut onto the right-hand end of the swingarm pivot bolt and tighten the nut to 110 Nm (see illustration 13.8b). Now tighten the inner bracket bolts on each side to 45 Nm. Clean the threads of the sidestand bracket bolts and apply some threadlock, fit the bracket and tighten the bolts to 63 Nm (see illustration 12.5d). Reconnect and secure the sidestand switch connector, then secure the wire in the clip with the fuel tank hose with the blue dot, and fit both the hoses into the guide (see illustrations 12.5a, b and c).

● Insert the linkage arm to swingarm and linkage rod bolts from the right on MT-07 (FZ-07) and XSR models, and from the left on MT-07TR models (see illustrations 12.4 and 12.3). Fit the washer onto the linkage arm-to-swingarm bolt (see illustration 12.4). Tighten the linkage arm bolt nuts to 40 Nm on MT-07 (FZ-07) and XSR models, and on MT-07TR models tighten the

linkage arm-to-linkage rod bolt nut to 60 Nm and the linkage arm-to-swingarm bolt nut to 50 Nm.

13 Swingarm

Removal

1 Refer to Section 11 and support the bike as described in Step 4, then remove the chain guard as described in Step 5.

2 Release the rear brake hose, and where fitted the ABS rear wheel sensor wire, from the swingarm (see illustration).

3 Remove the rear wheel (see Chapter 6). Lay the caliper assembly over the rider's right-hand heel guard so it is out of the way. Lay the drive chain over the left-hand heel guard with some rag between them.

4 On MT-07 (FZ-07) and XSR models slide the chain adjusters out of the swingarm, noting which way up they fit (see illustration). Mark each adjuster according to the side it fits as the end plates are different for each side.

5 Remove the front sprocket cover (see Chapter 6).

6 Remove the frame covers (see Chapter 7).

7 Unscrew the nut and remove the washer on the bolt securing the linkage arm to the swingarm, then withdraw the bolt (see illustration).

13.2 Undo the hose guide screws (arrowed)

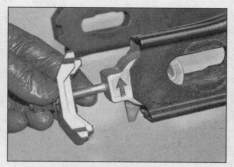

13.4 Remove the chain adjusters

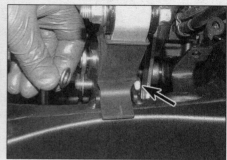

13.7 Unscrew the nut and remove the washer, then withdraw the bolt (arrowed) and remove the linkage arm – on Tracer models the bolt goes in from the other side

13.8a Slacken the two inner bracket bolts

13.8b Unscrew the nut and remove the washer

13.9a Withdraw the bolt...

13.9b ... and remove the swingarm

8 Slacken the right-hand inner bracket bolts **(see illustration)**. Unscrew the nut and remove the washer on the right-hand end of the swingarm pivot bolt **(see illustration)**. Push the pivot bolt in slightly so the head is accessible on the opposite side. Note how the flat edges of the pivot bolt head locate against the flat edges in the recess in the inner bracket.

9 Support the swingarm, then withdraw the pivot bolt and remove the swingarm **(see**

illustrations). If the bolt is difficult to remove knock it through using a long drift, but be careful not to damage the threaded end.

Inspection

10 If required remove the chain slider **(see illustration)**. If it is badly worn or damaged fit a new one.

11 Thoroughly clean the swingarm, removing all traces of dirt, corrosion and grease. Check

the swingarm for cracks or distortion due to accident damage.

12 Remove the bearing cover from each side of each pivot **(see illustration)** – the covers have seals fitted in them, but the seals may stay on the swingarm when removing the covers, in which case remove them from the swingarm **(see illustration)**. Clean the covers and check the condition of the seals. Also check the condition of the seal on the inner

13.10 Release the pegs from the holes and remove the slider

13.12a Remove the covers...

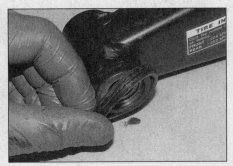

13.12b ... and the seals

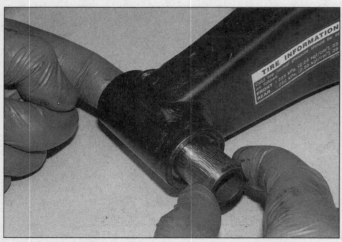

13.13 Withdraw the sleeves to check the bearings

13.14 Check the bearing(s) in each pivot

side of each pivot. Replace the seals with new ones if necessary (see below).

13 Withdraw the sleeve from each pivot **(see illustration)**. Clean all old grease off the sleeves and the bearings in each pivot.

14 Inspect the bearings for signs of wear such as pitting and heavy scoring **(see illustration)**. Replace them with new ones if necessary (see below).

15 Remove any old grease and corrosion from the swingarm pivot bolt. Check the bolt is straight by rolling it on a flat surface such as a piece of plate glass.

Seal and bearing renewal

16 If not already done remove the bearing covers and their seals (Step 12), and withdraw the sleeve from each pivot **(see illustration 13.13)**.

17 Three identical needle roller bearings

are fitted, one in the right-hand pivot and two in the left-hand **(see illustration 13.14)**. There is also a seal on the inner side of each pivot – these seals are deep rimmed and set against the bearings, meaning they are very difficult to lever out in the conventional way. Referring to the information in *Tools and Workshop Tips* in the Reference section if required, first remove the bearing from the right-hand side and the outer bearing from the left-hand side using a knife-edge puller with slide-hammer attachment **(see illustrations)**. Note that once removed, the bearings cannot be reused. Now drive or press the seal out of the inner end of the right-hand pivot and the bearing and seal out of the left-hand pivot using a deep socket or piece of tube with an outside diameter of 27.5 to 27.7 mm – socket OD sizes vary according to manufacturer and type, but we found that a 21 mm ordinary

socket or a 19 mm impact socket was about right.

18 Inspect the bearing seats and remove any scoring or corrosion carefully with steel wool or a suitable scraper.

19 The new bearings must be pressed or drawn into their bores, rather than driven into position, using the same 27.5 to 27.7 mm OD socket or tube. In the absence of a press, a suitable drawbolt arrangement can be made up as described in *Tools and Workshop Tips* in the Reference section, making sure the outer diameter of the washer that draws the bearing in is 27.5 to 27.7 mm – this can be achieved by grinding the perimeter of a larger washer **(see illustrations 13.20b and c)**. Make sure the right-hand bearing is set to a depth of 15 mm from the outer end of the pivot, and the left-hand outer bearing is set to a depth of 3 mm from the outer end of the pivot and

13.17a Seat the knife edge behind the bearing then expand it to lock it...

13.17b ... and jar the bearing out using the slide-hammer attachment

13.19 Make sure each bearing is set to the correct depth as dscribed

13.20a Push the seal in as far as it will go by hand...

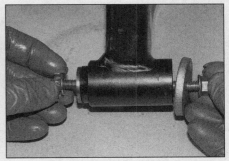

13.20b ... then set up a drawbolt arrangement as shown...

the inner bearing is 9 mm from the inner end **(see illustration)**. Lubricate the bearings with lithium-based grease.

20 Press or draw a new seal into the inner end of each pivot in the same way as the bearings, with its marked side facing out, setting them against the bearing so the outer end is recessed to a depth of 1 mm from the end, i.e. by the depth of the chamfered section **(see illustrations)**.

Installation

21 If removed, fit the chain slider **(see illustration 13.10)**.
22 Grease the sleeves, the inside of the bearing covers and the seal lips with lithium-based grease. Slide the sleeves into the bearings **(see illustration 13.13)**. If not in place fit the seals into the outer covers with the chamfered lipped side facing into the cover **(see illustration)**. Fit the covers **(see illustration)**.
23 Lubricate the swingarm pivot bolt with lithium-based grease.
24 Manoeuvre the swingarm into position **(see illustration 13.9b)**. Slide the pivot bolt all the way through from the left-hand side **(see illustration 13.9a)** – locate the flat edges

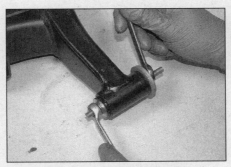

13.20c ... to the draw the seal in...

13.20d ... setting it as described and shown

on the bolt head against the flat edges in the inner bracket so it is locked **(see illustration)**.
25 Fit the washer and nut onto the pivot bolt and tighten the nut to 110 Nm **(see illustration 13.8b)**. Tighten the inner bracket bolts to 45 Nm **(see illustration 13.8a)**. Check that the swingarm moves up and down freely.
26 Align the linkage arm and insert the bolt from the right on MT-07 (FZ-07) and XSR models, and from the left on MT-07TR models **(see illustration 13.7)**. Fit the washer and tighten the nut to 40 Nm on MT-07 (FZ-07)

and XSR models, and to 50 Nm on MT-07TR models.
27 On MT-07 (FZ-07) and XSR models slide the chain adjusters into the swingarm, making sure each is fitted in the side from which it was removed, and the arrows on the side of the adjuster and the inner face of the end plate point up **(see illustration 13.4)**.
28 Install the remaining components in the reverse order of removal. Check and adjust the drive chain slack (see Chapter 1), and check the operation of the rear suspension before taking the machine on the road.

13.22a Fit the seals with the chamfered side facing into the cover

13.22b Fit the cover onto the outer end of each pivot

13.24 Make sure the bolt head flats locate correctly

Chapter 6
Brakes, wheels and final drive

Contents

Degrees of difficulty

Easy, suitable for novice with little experience	**Fairly easy,** suitable for beginner with some experience	**Fairly difficult,** suitable for competent DIY mechanic	**Difficult,** suitable for experienced DIY mechanic	**Very difficult,** suitable for expert DIY or professional

Specifications

Brakes

Brake fluid type	DOT 4
Front brake pad friction material wear limit	0.5 mm (4.5 mm new)
Front disc diameter	282 mm
Front disc thickness	
Standard	4.5 mm
Service limit	4.0 mm
Front disc maximum runout	0.1 mm
Front caliper bore ID	30.23 mm and 27.0 mm
Front master cylinder bore ID	15.0 mm
Rear brake pad friction material wear limit	1.0 mm (6.0 mm new)
Rear disc diameter	245 mm
Rear disc thickness	
Standard	5.0 mm
Service limit	4.5 mm
Rear disc maximum runout	0.15 mm
Rear caliper bore ID	38.18 mm
Rear master cylinder bore ID	12.7 mm

Wheels

Rim size	
Front	17 x MT3.50
Rear	17 x MT5.50
Wheel runout (max)	
Axial (side-to-side)	0.5 mm
Radial (out-of-round)	1.0 mm

Tyres

Tyre pressures	see *Pre-ride checks*
Tyre sizes – MT-07 (FZ-07) and MT-07TR*	
Front	120/70-ZR17 (58W)
Rear	180/55-ZR17 (73W)
Tyre sizes – XSR700*	
Front	120/70-R17 (58V)
Rear	180/55-R17 (73V)

Refer to your owner's manual or a Yamaha dealer for approved tyre brands.

Final drive

Chain type	DAIDO 525VZ endless
No. of links	
MT-07 (FZ-07) and XSR models	108
MT-07TR models	114
Chain slack	see Chapter 1
Chain stretch service limit (see text)	239.3 mm
Sprocket sizes (no. of teeth)	Front 16, Rear 43

Torque wrench settings

ABS modulator bolts	7 Nm
ABS rotor screws	8 Nm
ABS sensor mounting screw	7 Nm
Brake hose banjo bolts	30 Nm
Footrest bracket bolts	30 Nm
Front brake caliper mounting bolts	40 Nm
Front brake caliper bleed valves	5 Nm
Front brake disc bolts	18 Nm
Front brake master cylinder clamp bolts	10 Nm
Front sprocket nut	95 Nm
Front wheel axle	65 Nm
Front wheel axle pinch bolt	23 Nm
Inner bracket bolts	45 Nm
Rear brake caliper bleed valve	5 Nm
Rear brake caliper front slider pin	27 Nm
Rear brake caliper rear mounting bolt/slider pin	22 Nm
Rear brake pad retaining pin	17 Nm
Rear brake disc bolts	30 Nm
Rear brake master cylinder bolts	23 Nm
Rear sprocket nuts	80 Nm
Rear wheel axle nut	
MT-07 (FZ-07) and XSR models	105 Nm
MT-07TR models	150 Nm
Sidestand bracket bolts	63 Nm
Swingarm pivot bolt nut	110 Nm

1 General Information

1 All models are fitted with cast alloy wheels designed for tubeless tyres only.
2 Both front and rear brakes are hydraulically-operated disc brakes. The front brakes are twin floating discs with opposed four-piston calipers. The rear brake is a single disc with a single-piston sliding caliper. ABS was an option on 2014 to 2016 MT-07 (FZ-07) models, and is fitted as standard on all other models.
3 Drive from the gearbox to the rear wheel is by chain and sprockets.
Caution: Disc brake components rarely require disassembly. Do not disassemble *components unless absolutely necessary. If an hydraulic brake line is loosened, the entire system must be disassembled, drained, cleaned and then properly filled and bled upon reassembly. Do not use solvents on internal brake components. Solvents will cause the seals to swell and distort. Use only clean DOT 4 brake fluid or denatured alcohol for cleaning. Use care when working with brake fluid as it can injure your eyes and it will damage painted surfaces and plastic parts.*

2.1a Unscrew the bolts...

2.1b ... and displace the caliper

2 Front brake pads

1 Undo the caliper bolts, on ABS models noting how the bolts on the right-hand caliper secure the wheel sensor wire holders, and draw the caliper off the disc **(see illustrations)**. Do not operate the brake lever while the caliper is off the bracket.
2 Pull the pad pin clips out, then push the pin

2.2a Remove the clips…

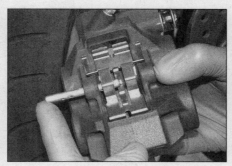

2.2b …the pin…

2.2c …the spring…

2.2d …and the pads

2.7 You should be able to push the pistons in using finger pressure

2.13 Clean and check the shim

out and remove the pad spring and the pads **(see illustrations)**.

3 Inspect the surface of each pad for contamination and check that the friction material has not worn down to the service limit (see Chapter 1, Section 14). If either pad is worn down to, or beyond the limit, is fouled with oil or grease, or is heavily scored or damaged, both pads in each caliper must be replaced with new ones. It is not possible to degrease the friction material – if the pads are contaminated in any way fit new ones.

4 Check that each pad has worn evenly at each end, and that each has the same amount of wear as the other. If uneven wear is noticed, one of the pistons is probably sticking in the caliper, in which case the caliper must be overhauled (Section 3).

5 If the pads are in good condition clean them carefully, using a fine wire brush that is completely free of oil and grease, to remove all traces of road dirt and corrosion. Using a pointed instrument, dig out any embedded particles of foreign matter. Spray the pads with brake system cleaner.

6 Spray the inside of the caliper with brake system cleaner, paying particular attention to the exposed section of the pistons to remove any dirt or debris that could cause the seals to be damaged. Remove any traces of corrosion that might cause sticking of the pads in the caliper.

7 If new pads are being fitted, push the pistons all the way back into the caliper to create room for them (but see Step 9 for machines fitted with ABS) **(see illustration)**. Push the pistons using finger pressure or a

piece of wood as leverage, or place the old pads back in the caliper and use a large, flat-bladed screwdriver inserted between them. Alternatively obtain a piston retracting tool from a good tool supplier.

8 On models without ABS, as the pistons are pushed into the caliper, brake fluid will be displaced back into the reservoir on the master cylinder. Depending on the initial level, it may be necessary to remove the reservoir cap, plate and diaphragm, and remove some fluid (see *Pre-ride checks*).

9 On ABS models it is necessary to open the caliper bleed valve to enable the pistons to be pushed back into the caliper. Remove the bleed valve cap, then attach a length of clear hose to the valve and place the open end in a suitable container **(see illustrations 11.6a and b)**. Open the valve and push the pistons in as described in Step 7. Take great care not to draw any air into the system. If in doubt, bleed the brake afterwards (Section 11). When the pistons are fully retracted tighten the bleed valve, remove the hose and fit the cap.

10 If a piston appears to be sticking in the caliper, the caliper must be overhauled (Section 3).

11 Check the condition of the brake disc (Section 4).

12 Clean the pad pin and remove any corrosion – if the pin is badly corroded fit a new one. Check the condition of the pad pin clips and fit new ones if necessary

13 Clean the shim on the back of each pad, and make sure it is correctly seated **(see illustration)**.

14 Smear the pad pin lightly with copper-based grease.

15 Fit the pads into the caliper with the friction material on each pad facing the other, then fit the spring with the arrow pointing in the direction of normal disc rotation, insert the pad pin with the clip holes facing up, making sure it locates correctly over the spring and through the pads **(see illustrations 2.2d, c and b)**. Fit the R-clips **(see illustration 2.2a)**.

16 Slide the caliper onto the disc **(see illustration 2.1b)**. Fit the bolts, not forgetting to secure the wheel sensor wire holders with the bolts for the right-hand caliper on ABS models, and tighten them to 40 Nm **(see illustration 2.1a)**.

17 Pump the brake lever several times to bring the pads into contact with the discs.

18 Check the fluid level in the master cylinder reservoir (see *Pre-ride checks*).

19 Check the operation of the brake before riding the motorcycle.

3 Front brake calipers

 Warning: If a caliper is in need of an overhaul all old brake fluid should be flushed from the system. Overhaul must be done in a spotlessly clean work area to avoid contamination and possible failure of the brake hydraulic system components. Do not, under any circumstances, use

3.2a Brake hose banjo bolt – right-hand caliper

3.2b Seal the banjo using a nut and bolt and the sealing washers ...

3.2c ... or using a dedicated tool

petroleum-based solvents to clean brake parts. Use clean DOT 4 brake fluid, dedicated brake cleaner or denatured alcohol only, as described. To prevent damage from spilled brake fluid, always cover paintwork when working on the braking system.

Note: *If the caliper is being overhauled (usually due to sticking pistons or fluid leaks) read through the entire procedure first and make sure that you have obtained all the new parts required, including some new DOT 4 brake fluid.*

Removal

1 To displace the caliper (e.g. for wheel removal) undo the caliper bolts, on ABS models noting how the bolts on the right-hand caliper secure the wheel sensor wire holders,

3.3 Hold the pistons on one side fully in and displace the pistons on the other side as described

and draw the caliper off the disc **(see illustrations 2.1a and b)**. Secure the calipers to the bike with a bungee or cable-tie so they are out of the way and not hanging by the hose. Do not operate the brake lever while the caliper is off the bracket.

2 To remove the caliper (but see Step 3 if the caliper is being overhauled), note the alignment of the brake hose banjo fitting(s) with the caliper, then unscrew the banjo bolt and detach the hose(s), noting the positions of the sealing washers **(see illustration)**. Be prepared with a rag to catch any drops of brake fluid. Seal the banjo union(s) with a suitable nut and bolt and the two sealing washers or using a dedicated tool, or support it upright and cover it in rag **(see illustrations)**. Note that new sealing washers must be used on reassembly. Undo the caliper bolts, on ABS models noting how the bolts on the right-hand caliper secure the wheel sensor wire holders, and draw the caliper off the disc **(see illustrations 2.1a and b)**. Remove the brake pads if required (Section 2).

3 If the caliper is being overhauled it must be done in two stages, one side of the caliper first, then the other. First remove the brake pads (Section 2). Push the pistons on one side of the caliper in and hold them so they can't move, then use the brake lever to pump the opposite pistons most of the way out (as far as the point where the disc runs), but make sure they don't come all the way out **(see illustration)**. Refit the caliper and tighten the bolts enough to hold it, then disconnect the hose(s) as described in Step 2.

Overhaul

Note: *If a piston sticks in its bore and cannot be displaced, the caliper will have to be replaced with a new one.*

4 Remove the displaced pistons and drain the fluid out of the caliper **(see illustration)**. Clean the exterior of the caliper with brake system cleaner.

5 Remove the dust seals and the piston seals from the piston bores using a wooden or plastic tool to avoid scratching the bores **(see illustration)**. New seals must be fitted on reassembly. Note that the pistons and their corresponding seals are different sizes (see Specifications).

6 Clean the pistons and bores with clean DOT 4 brake fluid. Blow compressed air through the fluid passages in the caliper to ensure they are clear (make sure the air is filtered and unlubricated).

Caution: Do not, under any circumstances, use a petroleum-based solvent to clean brake parts.

7 Inspect the caliper bores and pistons for signs of corrosion, nicks and burrs and loss of plating **(see illustration)**. If surface defects are present, the pistons and/or caliper assembly must be replaced with a new one. If the caliper is in bad shape the master cylinder should also be checked.

8 Compare the new seals and measure them if necessary to ensure that the correct seals are fitted in the correct bores.

9 Lubricate the new piston seals with clean DOT 4 brake fluid, then fit them into the

3.4 Remove the pistons

3.5 Remove the seals and discard them

3.7 Check the surfaces of the pistons and bores – the plating on this piston is lifting off

3.9a Lubricate the new piston seals with brake fluid...

3.9b ...then fit them into their grooves

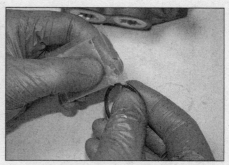

3.10a Lubricate the new dust seals with silicone grease ...

3.10b ... then fit them into their grooves

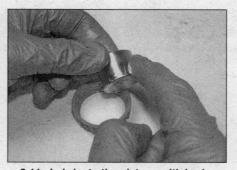

3.11a Lubricate the pistons with brake fluid ...

3.11b ...and push them all the way in

lower grooves in the caliper bores **(see illustrations)**.

10 Lubricate the new dust seals with silicone grease, then fit them into the upper grooves in the caliper bores **(see illustrations)**.

11 Lubricate the pistons with brake fluid and fit them, closed-end first, into the caliper bores **(see illustration)**. Using your thumbs, push the pistons all the way in, making sure they enter the bores squarely and do not displace the seals **(see illustration)**. Wipe away any excess fluid as it will attract dirt.

12 Reconnect the brake hose, then hold the pistons in on the side that was just overhauled and pump the opposite pistons out, and repeat the overhaul procedure.

3.15 Always use new sealing washers

Installation

13 If the caliper assembly was just displaced, slide the caliper onto the disc **(see illustration 2.1b)** – if necessary ease the pads apart slightly using a large flat-bladed screwdriver or similar tool, making sure you do not damage the friction material surface. Fit the bolts, not forgetting to secure the wheel sensor wire holders with the bolts for the right-hand caliper on ABS models, and tighten them to 40 Nm **(see illustration 2.1a)**. Operate the brake lever several times to bring the pads into contact with the discs.

14 Otherwise refer to Section 2 to fit the brake pads and install the caliper.

15 Connect the brake hose(s) to the caliper, using new sealing washers on each side of

4.2 Using a micrometer to measure disc thickness

the banjo fitting(s) **(see illustration)**. Align the fitting(s) as noted on removal **(see illustration 3.2a)**. Tighten the banjo bolt to 30 Nm.

16 Top-up the brake fluid reservoir with new DOT 4 brake fluid and bleed the system as described in Section 11.

17 Check that there are no fluid leaks and thoroughly test the operation of the brake before riding the motorcycle.

---

4 Front brake discs

Inspection

1 Inspect the surface of each disc for score marks and other damage. Light scratches are normal after use and will not affect brake operation, but deep grooves and heavy score marks will reduce braking efficiency and accelerate pad wear. If a disc is badly grooved it must be replaced with a new one.

2 The disc must not be allowed to wear down to a thickness less than the service limit given in the Specifications. Check the thickness of the disc with a micrometer **(see illustration)**. If the thickness is less than the service limit, fit a new one.

3 To check disc runout, support the bike upright so that the front wheel is raised off the ground. Mount a dial gauge to a fork leg, with the plunger on the gauge touching the surface

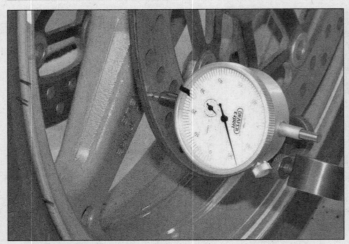

4.3 Set up a dial gauge with the probe contacting the brake disc, then rotate the wheel to check for runout

4.5 Unscrew the bolts (arrowed) and remove the disc

of the disc about 10 mm (1/2 in) from the outer edge **(see illustration)**. Rotate the wheel and watch the gauge needle, comparing the reading with the limit listed in the Specifications. If the runout exceeds the service limit, check the wheel bearings for play (see Chapter 1). If the bearings are worn, fit new ones (Section 16) and repeat this check. If disc runout is still excessive, fit a new one.

Removal

4 Remove the front wheel (Section 14).
Caution: Don't lay the wheel down and allow it to rest on either disc – they could become warped. Set the wheel on wood blocks so the wheel rim supports the weight of the wheel.
5 If you are not replacing the disc with a new one, mark the relationship of the disc to the wheel so that it can be installed in the same position. Unscrew the disc bolts, loosening them evenly and a little at a time in a criss-cross pattern to avoid distorting the disc, then remove the disc from the wheel **(see illustration)**. Note that Yamaha specify to use new bolts when fitting the disc.

Installation

6 Before fitting the disc, make sure there is no dirt or corrosion where it seats on the hub, particularly right in the angle of the seat. If the disc does not sit flat when it is bolted down, it will appear to be warped when checked or when the front brake is used.
7 Fit the disc onto the wheel – align the previously applied register marks if you are refitting the original disc.
8 Clean the threads of the disc bolts, then apply a suitable non-permanent thread locking compound. Fit the bolts and tighten them evenly and a little at a time in a criss-cross pattern to 18 Nm. If a new disc has been fitted remove any protective coating from its working surfaces. Clean the disc using acetone or brake system cleaner.If new discs have been fitted, fit new brake pads.

9 Install the front wheel (Section 14).
10 Operate the brake lever several times to bring the pads into contact with the discs. Check the operation of the brake carefully before riding the motorcycle.

5 Front brake master cylinder

⚠️ *Warning: If the brake master cylinder is in need of an overhaul all old brake fluid should be flushed from the system. Overhaul must be done in a spotlessly clean work area to avoid contamination and possible failure of the brake hydraulic system components. Do not, under any circumstances, use petroleum-based solvents to clean brake parts. Use clean DOT 4 brake fluid, dedicated brake cleaner or denatured alcohol only, as described. To prevent damage from spilled brake fluid, always cover paintwork when working on the braking system.*
Note: *If the master cylinder is being overhauled (usually due to sticking or poor action, or fluid leaks) read through the entire*

procedure first and make sure that you have obtained all the new parts required, including some new DOT 4 brake fluid.

Removal

1 Remove the mirror, on MT-07TR models remove the hand guard bracket, and on Moto Cage models remove the hand guard (see Chapter 7).
2 Disconnect the brake light switch wiring connectors **(see illustration)**.
3 If the master cylinder is being completely removed or overhauled, slacken then lightly retighten the reservoir cover screws **(see illustration 11.5a)**. Note the alignment of the brake hose banjo fitting, then unscrew the banjo bolt and detach the hose, noting the positions of the sealing washers **(see illustration)**. Be prepared with a rag to catch any drops of brake fluid. Seal the banjo union with a suitable nut and bolt and the two sealing washers or using a dedicated tool, or support it upright and cover it in rag **(see illustration 3.2b or c)**. Note that new sealing washers must be used on reassembly.
4 Remove the brake lever (see Chapter 5).
5 Note the alignment of the handlebar clamp with the punch mark on the handlebar, then unscrew the clamp bolts and remove the

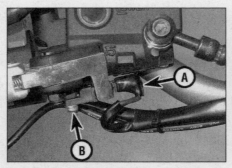

5.2 Brake light switch wiring connectors (A) and screw (B)

5.3 Brake hose banjo bolt (arrowed)

5.5 Master cylinder clamp bolts (arrowed)

5.8 Remove the pushrod and boot from the end of the master cylinder piston...

5.9a ...then depress the piston, remove the circlip...

clamp **(see illustration)**. If the master cylinder is just being displaced, secure it upright with a cable-tie to avoid straining the brake hose.

6 If the master cylinder is being overhauled undo the reservoir cover screws and remove the cover, the diaphragm plate and the diaphragm. Drain the brake fluid into a suitable container. Wipe any remaining fluid out of the reservoir with a clean rag.

7 If required, undo the screw securing the brake light switch, noting the washers, and remove the switch **(see illustration 5.2)**.

Overhaul

8 Remove the pushrod and boot **(see illustration)**.

9 The piston assembly is secured by a circlip. Remove the circlip using circlip pliers, then draw out the piston and spring assembly **(see illustrations)**.

10 Clean inside the master cylinder with fresh DOT 4 brake fluid. If compressed air is available, blow it through the fluid passages to ensure they are clear (make sure the air is filtered and unlubricated).

Caution: Do not, under any circumstances, use a petroleum-based solvent to clean brake parts.

11 Check the master cylinder bore for corrosion, scratches, nicks and score marks. If damage or wear is evident, the master cylinder must be replaced with a new one. If the master cylinder is in poor condition, then the calipers should be checked as well.

12 The pushrod and boot, circlip, piston (with seals) and spring are included in the master cylinder rebuild kit. Use all of the new parts, regardless of the apparent condition of the old ones.

13 Fit the narrow end of the spring over the inner end of the piston **(see illustration)**. Lubricate the piston and seals with clean brake fluid and fit the assembly into the master cylinder, wide end of the spring first **(see illustration 5.9b)**.

14 Push the piston in and fit the new circlip, making sure it is properly located in the groove **(see illustration)**.

15 If not already assembled, fit the boot onto the pushrod so that its outer (narrow) lip locates in the groove **(see illustration 5.8)**. Locate the pushrod against the outer end of

5.9b ...and draw out the piston and spring

the piston and press the inner (wide) lip of the boot into place.

16 Check the fluid reservoir top, diaphragm plate and diaphragm and replace them with new ones if they are damaged or deteriorated.

Installation

17 If removed, fit the brake light switch onto the bottom of the master cylinder, making sure the pin locates in the hole, and tighten the screw, making sure the washers are fitted **(see illustration 5.2)**.

18 Position the master cylinder on the handlebar, aligning the clamp joint on the outer side with the punch mark on the top of the handlebar, making sure there is more than 11 mm gap between the clamp and the switch housing **(see illustration)**. Fit the back of the clamp with its UP mark facing up, then fit the clamp bolts and tighten them

5.14 Push the piston into the bore and fit the circlip

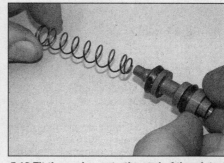

5.13 Fit the spring onto the end of the piston

to 10 Nm, tightening the top bolt first **(see illustration 5.5)**.

19 If disconnected align the brake hose banjo fitting with the master cylinder, then fit the banjo bolt using a new sealing washer on each side and tighten it to 30 Nm **(see illustration 5.3)**.

20 Install the brake lever (see Chapter 5).

21 Connect the brake light switch wiring connectors **(see illustration 5.2)**.

22 On MT-07TR models fit the hand guard bracket, on Moto Cage models fit the hand guard, and on all models fit the mirror (see Chapter 7).

23 If the master cylinder was overhauled, fill the master cylinder reservoir with new DOT 4 brake fluid and bleed the air from the system as described in Section 11.

24 Check that there are no fluid leaks and thoroughly test the operation of the brake before riding the motorcycle.

5.18 Align the mating surfaces of the clamp with the punch mark (arrowed) on the handlebar

6.1 Release the clip (arrowed)

6.2 Remove the plug then unscrew the pin (arrowed)

6.3 Unscrew the bolts/slider pins

6 Rear brake pads

1 On models with ABS release the clip joining the brake hose and wheel sensor wire **(see illustration)**.
2 Unscrew the pad retaining pin plug, then unscrew the pad pin **(see illustration)**.
3 Unscrew the caliper mounting bolts/slider pins **(see illustration)**.
4 Lift the caliper up off the disc and remove the pads **(see illustrations)**. Do not operate the brake pedal while the caliper is off the disc.
5 The pads have two-piece anti-chatter

shim sets clipped to the back – if required for cleaning, ease the shims and their insulators off **(see illustration)**.Replacement pads should come with new shim sets fitted. Make sure they do, especially if fitting after-market pads – if not they can be obtained separately if required, or use the ones from the old pads.
6 Inspect the surface of each pad for contamination and check that the friction material has not worn down to the service limit (see Chapter 1, Section 14). If either pad is worn down to, or beyond the limit, is fouled with oil or grease, or is heavily scored or damaged, fit a new set of pads. It is not possible to degrease the friction material – if the pads are contaminated in any way fit new ones.

7 If the pads are in good condition clean them carefully, using a fine wire brush that is completely free of oil and grease, to remove all traces of road dirt and corrosion. Using a pointed instrument, dig out any embedded particles of foreign matter. Spray the pads with brake system cleaner.
8 Spray the inside of the caliper with brake system cleaner, paying particular attention to the exposed section of the piston to remove any dirt or debris that could cause the seals to be damaged.
9 If new pads are being fitted, push the piston all the way back into the caliper to create room for them (but see Step 11 for machines fitted with ABS). Push the piston using finger pressure or a piece of wood as leverage, or place the old pads back in the caliper and use a large, flat-bladed screwdriver inserted between them **(see illustration)**. Alternatively obtain a piston retracting tool from a good tool supplier.
10 On standard (non-ABS) models, as the piston is pushed into the caliper, brake fluid will be displaced back through the master cylinder and into the reservoir. Depending on the initial level, it may be necessary to remove the reservoir cap, plate and diaphragm, and siphon out some fluid (see *Pre-ride checks*).
11 On ABS models it is necessary to open the caliper bleed valve to enable the piston to be pushed back into the caliper. Remove the bleed valve cap, then attach a length of clear hose to the valve and place the open end in a suitable container **(see illustrations 11.17a and b)**. Open the valve and push the piston in as described in Step 9. Take great care not to draw any air into the system. If in doubt, bleed the brake afterwards (Section 11). When the piston is fully retracted tighten the bleed valve, remove the hose and fit the cap.
12 If the piston appears to be sticking in the caliper, the caliper must be overhauled (Section 7).
13 Check the condition of the brake disc (see Section 8).
14 Clean and check the condition of the rubber boots, and replace them with new ones if necessary – the sleeve fitted in the rear boot must be transferred to the new boot **(see**

6.4a Lift the caliper off ...

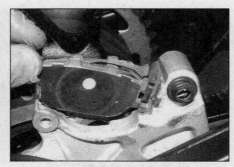

6.4b ...then remove the pads

6.5 Remove the shim and its backing from each pad

6.9 You should be able to push the piston in using finger pressure

6.14a Clean and check the boot and sleeve (arrowed) in the caliper...

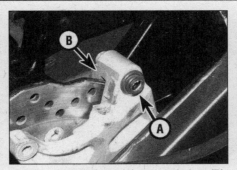

6.14b ...and the boot (A) and pad plate (B) on the bracket

6.15 Make sure the pad spring (arrowed) is correctly fitted

illustrations). Clean the face of the pad plate on the bracket, and make sure it is correctly in place. Clean the pad pin and the caliper slider pins and remove any corrosion.

15 If removed clip the anti-chatter shim sets in place – smear some silicone grease between the inner insulator and the shim, and make sure the outer face of the shim is clean (see illustration 6.5). If removed, clean and fit the pad spring (see illustration).

16 Clean the rear mounting bolt/slider pin threads and apply some fresh threadlock. Apply silicone grease to the slider sections of the bolts/pins and to the rubber boots. Position the pads in the bracket with the friction material facing the disc and so the leading edges locate against the pad plate (see illustration 6.4b). Seat the caliper over the pads and onto the bracket (see illustration 6.4a). Fit the mounting bolts/slider pins and tighten the front one to 27 Nm and the rear one to 22 Nm (see illustration 6.3).

17 Apply a smear of copper-based grease to the pad pin. Push the pads up against the spring to align the holes, insert the pad pin and tighten to 17 Nm (see illustration). Fit the pad pin plug (see illustration 6.2).

18 On models with ABS, fit the ABS sensor wiring and brake hose clip (see illustration 6.1).

19 Operate the brake pedal several times to bring the pads into contact with the disc.

20 Check the fluid level in the master cylinder reservoir (see Pre-ride checks).

21 Check the operation of the brake carefully before riding the motorcycle.

7 Rear brake caliper

⚠ **Warning: If the caliper is in need of an overhaul all old brake fluid should be flushed from the system. Overhaul must be done in a spotlessly clean work area to avoid contamination and possible failure of the brake hydraulic system components. Do not, under any circumstances, use petroleum-based solvents to clean brake parts. Use clean DOT 4 brake fluid, dedicated brake cleaner or denatured alcohol only, as described. To prevent damage from spilled brake fluid, always cover paintwork when working on the braking system.**

Note: If the caliper is being overhauled (usually due to a sticking piston or fluid leaks) read through the entire procedure first and make sure that you have obtained all the new parts required, including some new DOT 4 brake fluid.

Removal

1 On models with ABS release the clip joining the brake hose and wheel sensor wire (see illustration 6.1).

2 If the caliper is being completely removed or overhauled, note the alignment of the brake hose banjo fitting with the caliper, then unscrew the banjo bolt and detach the hose, noting the positions of the sealing washers (see illustration). Be prepared with a rag to catch any drops of brake fluid. Seal the banjo union with a suitable nut and bolt and the two sealing washers or using a dedicated tool, or support it upright and cover it in rag (see illustrations 3.2b and c). Note that new sealing washers must be used on reassembly.

3 Remove the brake pads (see Section 6) – this covers removing the caliper.

4 If required remove the rear wheel (see Section 15), then remove the caliper bracket.

Overhaul

5 Clean the exterior of the caliper with brake system cleaner.

6 To remove the piston you need either a piston removal tool, a good pair of external circlip removal pliers, or a supply of compressed air.

⚠ **Warning: Never place your fingers in front of the piston in an attempt to catch or protect it when applying compressed air, as injury could result.**

7 If you are using a dedicated tool or circlip pliers (as shown), grip the inner wall of the piston then twist and pull the piston out, keeping it square to the bore wall until it is free (see illustration). Do not try to remove

6.17 Push the pads up to align the holes

7.2 Brake hose banjo bolt (arrowed)

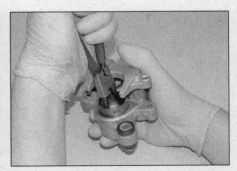

7.7 Using circlip pliers to extract a piston

7.8 Fit the wood or rag, then apply the compressed air as described until the piston is displaced

7.10 Remove the seals and discard them

7.13 Dust seal (A), piston seal (B)

the piston by levering it out or by using pliers or other grips that may scratch the outer wall, unless you are prepared to fit a new piston.

8 If you are using compressed air make sure the bleed valve is tight. Place a piece of wood or a wad of rag between the piston and the caliper, then apply compressed air gradually and progressively, starting with a fairly low pressure, to the fluid inlet in the caliper and allow the piston to ease out of the bore **(see illustration)**.

9 If the piston sticks in its bore and cannot be displaced, the caliper will have to be replaced with a new one.

10 Remove the dust seal and the piston seal from the piston bore using a wooden or plastic tool to avoid scratching the bores **(see illustration)**. New seals must be fitted on reassembly.

11 Clean the piston and bore with clean DOT 4 brake fluid. Blow compressed air through the fluid passages in the caliper to ensure they are clear (make sure the air is filtered and unlubricated).

Caution: Do not, under any circumstances, use a petroleum-based solvent to clean brake parts.

12 Inspect the caliper bore and piston for signs of corrosion, nicks and burrs and loss of plating **(see illustration 3.7)**. If surface defects are present, the piston or caliper assembly must be replaced with a new one. If the caliper is in bad shape the master cylinder should also be checked.

13 Compare the new seals to ensure that they are fitted correctly – the outer dust seal is thinner than the inner piston seal **(see illustration)**.

14 Lubricate the new piston seal with clean DOT 4 brake fluid, then carefully fit it into the lower groove in the caliper bore **(see illustration)**.

15 Lubricate the new dust seal with silicone grease and fit it into the upper groove in the caliper bore **(see illustration)**.

16 Lubricate the piston with brake fluid and fit it, closed-end first, into the caliper bore **(see illustration)**. Using your thumbs, push the piston all the way in, making sure it enters the bore squarely and do not displace the seals. Wipe away any excess lubricant as it will attract dirt.

Installation

17 If removed, fit the caliper bracket and install the rear wheel (see Section 15).

18 Refer to Section 6, Step 6 onwards to clean and check all components and to fit the brake pads, ignoring any Steps that do not apply following a caliper overhaul.

19 Connect the brake hose to the caliper, using new sealing washers on each side of the banjo fitting **(see illustration 3.15)**. Align the fitting as noted on removal **(see illustration 7.2)**. Tighten the banjo bolt to 30 Nm.

20 On models with ABS, fit the ABS sensor wiring and brake hose clip **(see illustration 6.1)**.

21 Top-up the brake fluid reservoir with new DOT 4 brake fluid and bleed the system as described in Section 11.

22 Check that there are no fluid leaks and thoroughly test the operation of the brake before riding the motorcycle.

8 Rear brake disc

Inspection

1 Refer to Section 4 of this Chapter. To check the disc runout, support the bike upright so that the rear wheel is raised off the ground. Mount the dial gauge to the swingarm.

Removal

2 Remove the rear wheel (Section 15).

Caution: Don't lay the wheel down and allow it to rest on the disc or the sprocket – they could become warped. Set the wheel on wood blocks so the wheel rim supports the weight of the wheel.

3 If you are not replacing the disc with a new one, mark the relationship of the disc to the wheel so that it can be installed in the same position. Unscrew the disc bolts, loosening them evenly and a little at a time in a criss-cross pattern to avoid distorting the disc, then remove the disc from the wheel

7.14 Fit the new piston seal into its groove

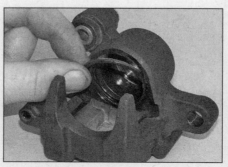

7.15 Fit the new dust seal into its groove

7.16 Fit the piston and push it all the way in

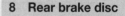

8.3 Rear brake disc bolts (arrowed)

9.2 Brake hose banjo bolt (arrowed)

9.3a Master cylinder bolts (arrowed)

(see illustration). Note that Yamaha specify to use new bolts when fitting the disc.

Installation

4 Before fitting the disc, make sure there is no dirt or corrosion where the disc seats on the hub, particularly right in the angle of the seat. If the disc does not sit flat when it is bolted down, it will appear to be warped when checked or when the rear brake is used.

5 Fit the disc onto the wheel; align the previously applied register marks if you are reinstalling the original disc.

6 Clean the threads of the disc bolts, then apply a suitable non-permanent thread locking compound. Fit the bolts and tighten them evenly and a little at a time in a criss-cross pattern to 30 Nm. If a new disc has been fitted remove any protective coating from its working surfaces. Clean the disc using acetone or brake system cleaner. If a new disc has been fitted, fit new brake pads.

7 Install the rear wheel (Section 15).

8 Operate the brake pedal several times to bring the pads into contact with the disc. Check the operation of the brake carefully before riding the motorcycle.

9 Rear brake master cylinder

⚠ **Warning: If the brake master cylinder is in need of an overhaul all old brake fluid should be flushed from the system. Overhaul must be done in a spotlessly clean work area to avoid contamination and possible failure of the brake hydraulic system components. Do not, under any circumstances, use petroleum-based solvents to clean brake parts. Use clean DOT 4 brake fluid, dedicated brake cleaner or denatured alcohol only, as described. To prevent damage from spilled brake fluid, always cover paintwork when working on the braking system.**

Note: If the master cylinder is being overhauled (usually due to sticking or poor action, or fluid leaks) read through the entire procedure first and make sure that you have

9.3b Unscrew the bolts and displace the bracket

obtained all the new parts required, including some new DOT 4 brake fluid.

Removal

1 On XSR models remove the right-hand frame cover (see Chapter 7).

2 Note the alignment of the brake hose banjo fitting, then unscrew the banjo bolt and detach the hose, noting the positions of the sealing washers (see illustration). Be prepared with a rag to catch any drops of brake fluid. Seal the banjo union with a suitable nut and bolt or using a dedicated tool, or support it upright and cover it in rag (see illustrations 3.2b or c). Note that new sealing washers must be used on reassembly.

3 Slacken the master cylinder bolts (see illustration). Unscrew the footrest bracket bolts and remove the washers, then displace

9.4 Remove the split pin and washer (A) then withdraw the clevis pin (B)

the bracket so you have access to the inner side (see illustration).

4 Remove the split pin and washer from the clevis pin connecting the brake pedal to the master cylinder pushrod and withdraw the pin (see illustration). A new split pin must be used on reassembly

5 Unscrew the nut or bolt securing the fluid reservoir, and on MT-07 (FZ-07) and MT-07TR models remove the bracket and release the reservoir hose from the clip (see illustrations).

6 Unscrew the master cylinder bolts, noting how they also secure the brake light switch/brake pedal spring bracket to the inside of the footrest bracket, and remove the master cylinder and reservoir.

Overhaul

7 Remove the reservoir cap, diaphragm plate

9.5a On MT-07 (FZ-07) and MT-07TR models unscrew the nut and remove the bracket

9.5b On XSR models unscrew the bolt

9.8 Detach the reservoir hose

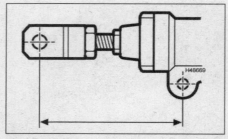

9.10a Before disturbing the clevis position measure from its eye to the centre of the lower mounting bolt hole as a guide to refitting

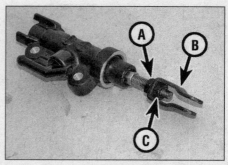

9.10b Slacken the locknut (A) and thread the clevis (B) and its nut (C) off

and diaphragm and drain the brake fluid into a suitable container. Wipe any remaining fluid out of the reservoir with a clean rag.

8 Release the clip securing the reservoir hose to the union on the master cylinder and detach the hose **(see illustration)**.

9 The reservoir hose union is a firm press fit in the master cylinder – unless there are signs that the seal is leaking, do not remove the union. If necessary, prise the union out, taking care not to damage the sealing surface of the master cylinder. If the union breaks in the process, both the seal and union are available as separate items – a new seal must be fitted.

10 Note the position of the clevis on the pushrod, then slacken the locknut **(see illustrations)**.

11 Pull back the boot from the end of the master cylinder to reveal the retaining circlip **(see illustration)**. Depress the pushrod and use circlip pliers to remove the circlip, then

draw out the pushrod, the piston and spring **(see illustrations)**. Note how the spring is clipped to the inner end of the piston. Thread the clevis and nuts off the pushrod – they must be transferred to the new pushrod.

12 Clean inside the master cylinder with fresh DOT 4 brake fluid. If compressed air is available, blow it through the fluid passages to ensure they are clear (make sure the air is filtered and unlubricated).

Caution: Do not, under any circumstances, use a petroleum-based solvent to clean brake parts.

13 Check the master cylinder bore for corrosion, scratches, nicks and score marks. If damage or wear is evident, the master cylinder must be replaced with a new one. If the master cylinder is in poor condition, then the caliper should be checked as well.

14 The pushrod and boot, circlip, piston (with seals) and spring are included in the master

cylinder rebuild kit. Use all of the new parts, regardless of the apparent condition of the old ones.

15 Fit one end of the spring over the inner end of the piston, clipping it into place over the metal tabs **(see illustration)**. Lubricate the piston and seals with clean brake fluid and fit the assembly into the master cylinder **(see illustration 9.11d)**.

16 Thread the locknut, clevis and nut onto the end of the pushrod. Smear some silicone grease onto the upper end of the pushrod. Press the pushrod into the master cylinder so that it compresses the spring, then fit the new circlip into its groove in the master cylinder **(see illustrations 9.11c and b)**.

17 Push the boot into place with its wider end located inside the groove in the master cylinder **(see illustration 9.11a)**.

18 Position the clevis as noted on removal (see Step 8), then tighten the locknut **(see illustration 9.10b)**. Note that the clevis position sets brake pedal height and final adjustments can be made after installation (see Chapter 1, Section 14).

19 If removed, lubricate a new reservoir hose union seal with clean brake fluid, then press the seal into the master cylinder. Make sure the union is facing towards the top of the master cylinder, then press it firmly into place **(see illustration 9.8)**.

20 Check the reservoir, cap, diaphragm plate and diaphragm and fit new ones as required if they are damaged or deteriorated. Check the reservoir hose for cracks or splits and replace it with a new one if necessary. Check the hose

9.11a Pull the boot out...

9.11b ...then release the circlip...

9.11c ...and remove the pushrod assembly...

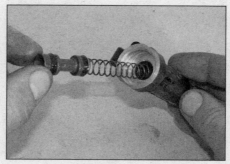

9.11d ...and the piston and the spring

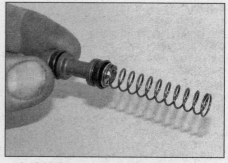

9.15 Make sure the spring is correctly fitted on the piston

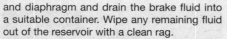

clips and use new ones if they are strained or corroded. Push the reservoir hose fully onto its union and secure it with the clip **(see illustration 9.8)**.

Installation

21 Position the master cylinder onto the footrest bracket with the brake light switch/pedal spring bracket between them, then align the bolt holes and tighten the bolts finger-tight. Secure the fluid reservoir loosely to the frame **(see illustration 9.5a or b)**.

22 Align the clevis with the brake pedal and insert the clevis pin, then fit the washer and a new split pin, bending its ends around as shown **(see illustration 9.4)**.

23 Fit the footrest bracket, locating the grommet in the inner side over the peg on the inner bracket, then fit the bolts with their washers and tighten them to 30 Nm **(see illustration)**. Tighten the master cylinder bolts to 23 Nm **(see illustration 9.3a)**.

24 Fit the brake hose banjo bolt using a new sealing washer on each side of the banjo union **(see illustration 3.15)**. Align the hose on the master cylinder, then tighten the bolt to 30 Nm **(see illustration 9.2)**.

25 On XSR models refit the right-hand frame cover (see Chapter 7).

26 Fill the fluid reservoir with new DOT 4 brake fluid and bleed the air from the system as described in Section 11.

27 Check that there are no fluid leaks and thoroughly test the operation of the brake before riding the motorcycle.

10 Brake hoses and fittings

Inspection

1 Brake hose and pipe condition should be checked regularly and the hoses replaced with new ones at the specified interval (see Chapter 1).

2 Twist and flex the hoses while looking for cracks, bulges and seeping hydraulic fluid. Check extra carefully around the areas where the hoses connect with the banjo fittings and unions, as these are common areas for hose failure.

3 Check the banjo fittings and unions connected to the brake hoses. If the fittings are rusted, scratched or cracked, fit new hoses.

Renewal

4 The brake hoses have banjo fittings on each end **(see illustrations 3.2a, 5.3, 7.2 and 9.2)**. On machines fitted with ABS, there are sections of pipe joined to the hoses that connect to the modulator **(see illustration 10.6 and 17.29)** – remove the right-hand frame cover (see Chapter 7) and the fuel tank for access (see Chapter 4). For full details on the ABS system see Section 17.

9.23 Seat the grommet over the peg (arrowed)

5 Flush the old brake fluid from the system (Section 11).

6 Cover the surrounding area with plenty of rags to catch any drops of brake fluid. Note the alignment of the banjo fitting with the master cylinder and brake caliper, and on ABS models the modulator. Release the hose(s) and pipe from the front mudguard, bottom yoke and swingarm, and from any other clips and guides as required according to model, noting the routing. Unscrew the banjo bolt at each end of the hose. On ABS models also unscrew the bolt securing the rear hose/pipe union block – do not unscrew the nuts at the hose/pipe unions as the hoses/pipes come as an assembly **(see illustration)**.

7 Position the new hose or hose/pipe, making sure it is correctly aligned and not twisted or otherwise strained, and ensure that it is correctly routed through any clips or guides and is clear of all moving components.

8 Check that the banjo fittings align correctly **(see illustrations 3.2a, 5.3, 7.2 and 9.2, and 17.29)**, then fit the banjo bolts, using a new sealing washer on each side of the fitting. On the double hose fitting on the front caliper, an additional sealing washer should be fitted between the two banjo unions.

9 Tighten the banjo bolts to 30 Nm.

10 Refill the system with new brake fluid and bleed out all air (Section 11). Check that there are no fluid leaks and thoroughly test the operation of the brake before riding the motorcycle.

11 Brake system bleeding and fluid change

Special tool: *The brake bleeding equipment described in Step 3 will be required – ready-made bleeding kits are cheaply available from automotive stores. On models with ABS Yamaha specify to pulse test the ABS system after any work, including after bleeding the system, and this requires the system to be plugged into Yamaha's diagnostic tool.*

Bleeding

1 Bleeding a brake is the process of removing aerated brake fluid from the master cylinder,

10.6 Hose/pipe union block bolt (arrowed)

the hose(s)/pipe(s) and the brake caliper(s). Bleeding is necessary whenever a brake system hydraulic connection is loosened, after a component or hose is replaced with a new one, when a master cylinder or caliper is overhauled, or when there is a spongy feel to the lever and it travels all the way back to the handlebar, and where braking force is less than it should be, and it is not due to any mechanical fault in the system (i.e. a sticking piston in the caliper, or a pad that is not moving as it should due to corrosion, for example on the pad pin). Leaks in the system may also allow air to enter, but leaking brake fluid will reveal their presence and warn you of the need for repair.

2 Brake bleeding is considered by some as a bit of a black art – seasoned professionals sometimes have trouble getting a good firm feel in the brake lever, while a first timer may have no trouble at all. One of the problems, particularly with the front brakes, is that you are working against natural principles – science dictates that air bubbles in a liquid will rise to the top, but the process entails pumping the brake fluid and any air bubbles it contains down, from the master cylinder at the top to the bleed valve in the caliper at the bottom, so while the fluid is moving down the air bubbles will want to rise. Air bubbles can also get trapped, particularly where there are high points in its path, and when there are extra components and pipes as on ABS models.

3 To bleed the brakes using the conventional method, you will need some new DOT 4 brake fluid, a length of clear flexible hose, a small container partially filled with clean brake fluid, some rags, and an 8 mm ring spanner to fit the brake caliper bleed valve. Bleeding kits that include the hose, a one-way valve and a container are available relatively cheaply from a good auto store, and simplify the task. You may also need a block of wood as a support for the fluid container **(see illustration 11.19)**.

4 Cover painted components to prevent damage in the event that brake fluid is spilled. *Caution: Brake fluid attacks painted finishes and plastics – to prevent damage from spilled fluid, always cover paintwork when working on the braking system, and clean up any spills immediately using brake cleaner.*

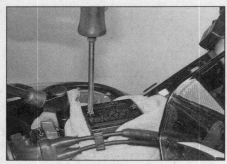

11.5a Undo the screws...

11.5b ...and remove the cover, plate and diaphragm

11.6a Pull the cap off the bleed valve

11.6b Fit the ring spanner over the valve then connect the hose

11.7 Keep the reservoir topped up

Front brake system

5 Turn the handlebars so the reservoir is level. Undo the reservoir cover screws and remove the cover, diaphragm plate and diaphragm **(see illustrations)**. Slowly pump the brake lever a few times to dislodge any fine air bubbles from the small hole in the bottom of the reservoir. Now hold the lever in to force any large air bubbles out of the large hole – you can tie the lever to the handlebar and leave it pressurised for a while to prevent having to hold it, then release it and slowly pump it a few times. You can tell when all the air is gone as the large hole appears completely dark, whereas if there is any air left it will appear to have a silvery rim that is actually the edge of an air bubble.

6 Pull the dust cap off the bleed valve on the caliper **(see illustration)**. If using a ring spanner (which is preferable to an open-ended one) fit it onto the valve. Attach one end of the bleeding hose to the bleed valve and, if not using a kit, submerge the other end in the clean brake fluid in the container **(see illustration)**.

7 Check the fluid level in the reservoir – keep it topped up and do not allow the level to drop below the bottom of the window during the procedure **(see illustration)**.

8 Slowly pump the brake lever a few times, then hold it in and open the bleed valve a quarter turn **(see illustration)**. When the valve is opened, brake fluid will flow out of the bleed valve into the clear tubing, and the lever will move to the handlebar. If there is air in the system there will be air bubbles in the brake fluid coming out of the valve.

9 Tighten the bleed valve, then release the brake lever. Repeat the process until no air bubbles are visible in the brake fluid, and the lever is firm when applied, topping the reservoir up when necessary. On completion tighten the bleed valve and remove the equipment, then fit the dust cap.

10 Transfer the equipment to the bleed valve on the other caliper. Repeat the bleeding procedure.

11 When the system has been successfully bled there should be a good and progressively firm feel as the lever is applied, and the lever should not be able to travel all the way back to the handlebar.

12 When you've completed bleeding, top-up the reservoir to the line cast inside the reservoir body, then fit the diaphragm, diaphragm plate, and cover **(see illustrations 11.7, 11.5b and a)**. Check for spilled brake fluid and clean up as required.

13 Check that there are no fluid leaks and thoroughly test the operation of the brake before riding the motorcycle.

14 On ABS models Yamaha specify to take the bike to a Yamaha dealer to pulse test the system.

11.8 Bleed the front brake as described

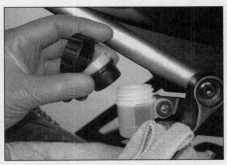

11.15 Unscrew the cap and remove the plate and diaphragm

11.17a Pull the cap off the bleed valve

11.17b Fit the ring spanner over the valve then connect the hose

Rear brake system

15 Unscrew the nut or bolt securing the fluid reservoir, and on MT-07 (FZ-07) and MT-07TR models remove the bracket **(see illustration 9.5a)**. Unscrew the cap and remove the diaphragm plate and diaphragm **(see illustration)**.

16 Slowly pump the brake pedal a few times to dislodge any air bubbles from the holes in the bottom of the reservoir.

17 Pull the dust cap off the bleed valve on the caliper **(see illustration)**. If using a ring spanner (which is preferable to an open-ended one) fit it onto the valve. Attach one end of the bleeding hose to the bleed valve and, if not using a kit, submerge the other end in the clean brake fluid in the container **(see illustration)**.

18 Check the fluid level in the reservoir – keep it topped up and do not allow the level to drop below the lower level line during the procedure **(see illustration)**.

19 Slowly pump the brake pedal a few times, then hold it down and open the bleed valve a quarter turn **(see illustration)**. When the valve is opened, brake fluid will flow out of the bleed valve into the clear tubing, and the pedal will move down. If there is air in the system there will be air bubbles in the brake fluid coming out of the valve.

20 Tighten the bleed valve, then release the brake pedal. Repeat the process until no air bubbles are visible in the brake fluid, and the pedal is firm when applied, topping the reservoir up when necessary.

21 When the system has been successfully bled there should be a good and progressively firm feel as the pedal is applied, and the pedal should not be able to travel all the way down to its stop.

22 When you've completed bleeding tighten the bleed valve and remove the equipment, then fit the dust cap. Top-up the reservoir to between the level marks, then fit the diaphragm, diaphragm plate, and cap, then secure it on its mount **(see illustrations 11.18, 11.15 and 9.5a)**. Check for spilled brake fluid and clean up as required.

23 Check that there are no fluid leaks and thoroughly test the operation of the brake before riding the motorcycle.

24 On ABS models Yamaha specify to take the bike to a Yamaha dealer to pulse test the system.

Both systems

25 If it is not possible to produce a firm feel to the lever or pedal, the fluid may be full of many tiny air bubbles rather than a few big ones. To remedy this apply some pressure to the system, for the front brake by tying the front brake lever lightly back to the handlebar, and for the rear by tying a weight to the brake pedal – do not apply too much pressure or the cup and seals in the master cylinder and caliper may fail. Let the fluid stabilise for a few hours, after which the tiny bubbles should either have risen to the top in the reservoir, or have formed into one or more big bubbles that can be more easily bled out by repeating the bleeding procedure.

26 If you are still having trouble look for any high point in the system in which a pocket of air may become trapped. Displace and agitate the hose or pipe so the bubble can be dislodged (but take care not to bend a pipe) – tapping it may help. If necessary displace the master cylinder and/or the caliper(s), and free the brake hose(s) from guides and move the parts around to dislodge the air and encourage it towards a bleed valve – refer to the relevant Sections as required to displace components. On models with ABS it is not practical to disturb the modulator as the pipes have to be detached, allowing more air to enter the system – if you cannot get the system to bleed correctly take the bike to a Yamaha dealer.

27 If bleeding the system using the conventional tools and methods stated does not give satisfactory results, or if otherwise

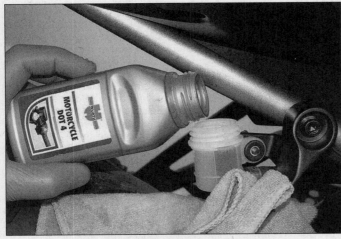

11.18 Keep the reservoir topped up

11.19 Bleed the rear brake as described

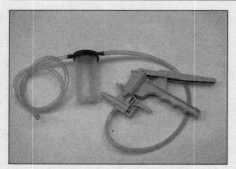

11.27 Vacuum-type brake bleeding tool

preferred, you can use a commercially available vacuum-type brake bleeding tool, such as the Mity-vac, following the manufacturer's instructions **(see illustration)**. This type of tool literally sucks the fluid out by creating a vacuum at the bleed valve. Users of such tools often get confused by the amount of air that appears to be in the brake fluid – more often than not this is caused by the vacuum sucking air past the bleed valve threads (air provides less resistance to the vacuum than the brake fluid) where it mixes with the fluid being drawn out. If this is the case the vacuum applied may be too great, or the bleed valve may have been loosened too much. One way to get round this is to remove the bleed valve and thread some PTFE tape around its threads, but note that doing so will be a bit messy, so have some rag to hand.

Fluid change

28 Changing the brake fluid is a similar process to bleeding the brakes and requires the same materials plus a suitable tool (such as a syringe, or alternatively lots of absorbent rag or paper) for siphoning the fluid out of the reservoir.
29 Cover painted components and fit the equipment to the relevant caliper following the

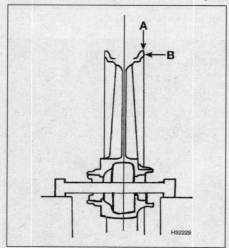

12.2 Check the wheel for radial (out-of-round) runout (A) and axial (side-to-side) runout (B)

appropriate Steps in the bleeding procedure given above. Remove the reservoir cover or cap, diaphragm plate and diaphragm (Step 5 or 15). Remove the fluid from the reservoir into a suitable container, either by sucking it up using a tool as shown, drawing it out into a syringe, or soaking it up in some paper towel. Wipe the reservoir clean. Fill the reservoir with new brake fluid **(see illustration 11.7 or 11.18)**. Squeeze or press the brake lever or pedal and open the bleed valve **(see illustrations 11.8 and 11.19)**. When the valve is opened, brake fluid will flow out of the caliper into the clear tubing, and the lever will move toward the handlebar, or the pedal will move down.
30 Tighten the bleed valve, then slowly release the brake lever or pedal. Keep the reservoir topped-up with new fluid at all times or air may enter the system and greatly increase the length of the task. Repeat the process until new fluid can be seen emerging from the caliper bleed valve.
31 On completion tighten the bleed valve and remove the equipment, then fit the dust cap. Top-up the reservoir to the mark, then fit the diaphragm, diaphragm plate, and cover or cap. Check for spilled brake fluid and clean up as required.
32 Check that there are no fluid leaks and thoroughly test the operation of the brake before riding the motorcycle.
33 On ABS models Yamaha specify to take the bike to a Yamaha dealer to pulse test the system.

Draining the system for overhaul

34 Draining the brake fluid is again a similar process to bleeding the brakes. The quickest and easiest way is to use a commercially available vacuum-type brake bleeding tool (see Step 27) – follow the manufacturer's instructions. Otherwise follow the procedure described above for changing the fluid, but quite simply do not put any new fluid into the reservoir – the system fills itself with air instead.
35 When it comes to refilling the system start by adding new fluid from a sealed container to the reservoir, then perform the bleeding procedure as described above until the fluid comes out of the bleed valve, and keep at it until you are certain there is no more air left in the system.

12 Wheel inspection and repair

1 In order to carry out a proper inspection of the wheels, it is necessary to support the bike securely in an upright position so that the wheel being inspected is raised off the ground. Clean the wheels thoroughly to remove mud and dirt that may interfere with the inspection procedure or mask defects. Make a general check of the wheels (see Chapter 1) and tyres (see *Pre-ride checks*).

2 Attach a dial gauge to the fork or the swingarm and position its tip against the side of the wheel rim **(see illustration)**. Spin the wheel slowly and check the axial (side-to-side) runout at the rim.
3 In order to accurately check radial (out of round) runout with the dial gauge, remove the wheel from the machine, and the tyre from the wheel. With the axle clamped in a vice and the dial gauge positioned on the top of the rim, the wheel can be rotated to check the runout.
4 An easier, though slightly less accurate, method is to attach a stiff wire pointer to the fork or the swingarm and position the end a fraction of an inch from the edge of the wheel rim where the wheel and tyre join. If the wheel is true, the distance from the pointer to the rim will be constant as the wheel is rotated. If wheel runout is excessive, check the wheel bearings very carefully before renewing the wheel.
5 The wheels should also be inspected for cracks, flat spots on the rim and other damage. Look very closely for dents in the area where the tyre bead contacts the rim. Dents in this area may prevent complete sealing of the tyre against the rim, which leads to deflation of the tyre over a period of time.
6 If damage is evident, or if runout in either direction is excessive, the wheel will have to be replaced with a new one. Never attempt to repair a damaged cast alloy wheel.

13 Wheel alignment check

1 Misalignment of the wheels due to a bent frame or forks can cause strange and possibly serious handling problems. If the frame or forks are at fault, repair by a frame specialist or replacement with new parts are the only options.
2 To check wheel alignment you will need an assistant, a length of string or a perfectly straight piece of wood and a ruler. A plumb bob or spirit level for checking that the wheels are vertical will also be required.
3 In order to make a proper check of the wheels it is necessary to support the bike in an upright position on an auxiliary stand. First ensure that the chain adjuster markings coincide on each side of the swingarm (see Chapter 1, Section 4). Next, measure the width of both tyres at their widest points. Subtract the smaller measurement from the larger measurement, then divide the difference by two. The result is the amount of offset that should exist between the front and rear tyres on both sides of the machine.
4 If a string is used, have your assistant hold one end of it about halfway between the floor and the rear axle, with the string touching the back edge of the rear tyre sidewall.
5 Run the other end of the string forward and pull it tight so that it is roughly parallel to the floor **(see illustration)**. Slowly bring the string into contact with the front edge of the rear tyre sidewall, then turn the front wheel until it is

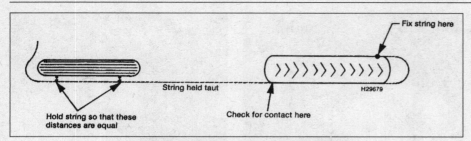

13.5 Wheel alignment check using string

parallel with the string. Measure the distance from the front tyre sidewall to the string.

6 Repeat the procedure on the other side of the motorcycle. The distance from the front tyre sidewall to the string should be equal on both sides.

7 As previously mentioned, a perfectly straight length of wood or metal bar may be substituted for the string **(see illustration)**.

8 If the distance between the string and tyre is greater on one side, or if the rear wheel appears to be out of alignment, have your machine checked by a Yamaha dealer.

9 If the front-to-back alignment is correct, the wheels still may be out of alignment vertically.

10 Using a plumb bob or spirit level, check the rear wheel to make sure it is vertical. To do this, hold the string of the plumb bob against the tyre upper sidewall and allow the weight to settle just off the floor. If the string touches both the upper and lower tyre sidewalls and is perfectly straight, the wheel is vertical. If it is not, adjust the stand until it is.

11 Once the rear wheel is vertical, check that the front wheel is vertical also. If both wheels are not perfectly vertical, the frame and/or major suspension components are bent.

14 Front wheel

Removal

1 Support the motorcycle on a rear paddock stand, then raise the front using a jack under the sump, with a piece of wood between

them to spread the load, so the forks are fully extended and the front wheel is just on the ground.

2 Displace the front brake calipers (Section 3).

3 Slacken the axle pinch bolt on the bottom of the right-hand fork, then unscrew the axle **(see illustration)**.

4 Support the wheel, then withdraw the axle and remove the wheel from between the forks **(see illustration)**.

5 Remove the spacer from each side of the wheel, noting how they fit inside the bearing seals **(see illustration)**.

Caution: Don't lay the wheel down and allow it to rest on either brake disc – they could become warped. Set the wheel on wood blocks so the wheel rim supports the weight of the wheel, or keep the wheel upright. Don't operate the brake lever with the wheel removed.

6 Wipe any old grease off the bearing seals and check the condition of the seals and the wheel bearings (Section 16).

7 Clean the axle and remove any corrosion using steel wool. Check the axle is straight by rolling it on a flat surface such as a piece of plate glass. If available, place the axle in V-blocks and check for runout using a dial gauge. If the axle is bent, fit a new one.

8 Clean the axle spacer(s) and remove any corrosion with steel wool. The spacer(s) should be perfectly smooth where it locates in its seal.

Installation

9 Apply lithium-based grease to the insides of the bearing seals. Fit a spacer into the seal on each side on non-ABS models and

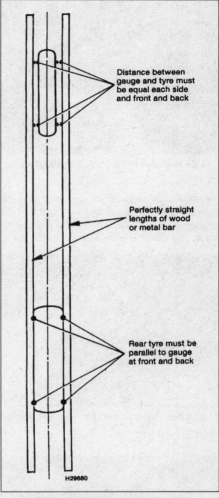

13.7 Wheel alignment check using a straight-edge

into the left side on ABS models **(see illustration 14.5)**.

10 Apply a thin coat of lithium-based grease to the axle. Position the wheel between the forks, making sure the directional arrow on the tyre points in the direction of normal rotation and the spacers remain in place.

14.3 Slacken the clamp bolt (arrowed) then unscrew the axle

14.4 Withdraw the axle and remove the wheel

14.5 Remove the spacer from each side on models without ABS, and from the left on ABS models

15.3a Remove the axle nut and washer ...

15.3b ... and the adjuster plate

15.4 Withdraw the axle and the adjuster plate

11 Align and support the wheel and slide the axle in from the right-hand side and into the bottom of the left-hand fork **(see illustration 14.4)**; tighten the axle lightly at this stage.

Tighten the pinch bolt on the bottom of the right-hand fork lightly **(see illustration 14.3)**.
12 Install the brake calipers, making sure the pads sit squarely on each side of the discs

(Section 3). Apply the front brake to bring the pads back into contact with the discs. Take the bike off its stand and check the action of the forks by applying the brake and pressing down on the handlebars.
13 Tighten the axle to 65 Nm then tighten the pinch bolt to 23 Nm.
14 Check the operation of the front brake before riding the motorcycle.

15.5 Slip the chain off the rear sprocket

15.6 Draw the wheel back a bit then displace the caliper bracket from its peg on the swingarm

15 Rear wheel and sprocket coupling

Removal

1 Support the motorcycle on a rear paddock stand. Place a support under the wheel that just takes up the gap without pushing up on it.
2 Create some slack in the chain (see Chapter 1).
3 Unscrew the axle nut and remove the washer and the left-hand adjuster plate **(see illustrations)**.
4 Support the wheel, then withdraw the axle with the right-hand adjuster plate, and rest the wheel on the support **(see illustration)**. The left and right adjuster plates differ so do not muddle them up.
5 Disengage the chain from the rear sprocket and lay it on some rag over the swingarm **(see illustration)**.
6 Draw the wheel back and displace the brake caliper bracket, noting how it locates on the swingarm, and support it out of the way **(see illustration)**.
7 Remove the spacer from the each side of the wheel, noting how they fit inside the bearing seals **(see illustrations)**.
Caution: Don't lay the wheel down and allow it to rest on the disc or the sprocket – they could become warped. Set the wheel on wood blocks so the wheel rim supports the weight of the wheel, or keep the wheel upright. Don't operate the brake pedal with the wheel removed.
8 Check for any rotational play in the sprocket coupling – play indicates worn rubber dampers, and a new set must be fitted. If required lift the sprocket coupling out of the hub and remove the dampers **(see**

15.7a Remove the small spacer from the right-hand side ...

15.7b ... and the large spacer from the left

15.8a Lift the sprocket coupling out...

15.8b ...and remove the dampers

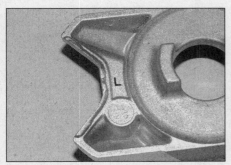

15.16 Each adjuster plate is marked R or L to denote the side it fits

15.17 Position of adjuster plate and axle head

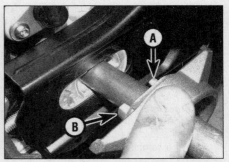

15.18a On MT-07 (FZ-07) and XSR models fit the plate with the small rib (A) at the front and the large one (B) at the back...

15.18b ... and make sure the plate and axle head seat as shown

15.20 Fit the adjuster plate as shown on MT-07TR

16.4 Lever out the grease seals

illustrations). Check the coupling for cracks or any obvious signs of damage. Also check the sprocket studs for looseness, wear or damage.

9 Wipe any old grease off the bearing seals and check the condition of the seals and the wheel bearings in both the wheel and the sprocket coupling (Section 16).

10 Clean the axle and remove any corrosion using steel wool. Check the axle is straight by rolling it on a flat surface such as a piece of plate glass. If available, place the axle in V-blocks and check for runout using a dial gauge. If the axle is bent, replace it with a new one.

11 Clean the spacers and remove any corrosion with steel wool. The spacers should be perfectly smooth where they locate in the seals.

Installation

12 If removed fit the rubber dampers, using a new set if necessary (see illustration 15.8b). Make sure the spacer is in place in the sprocket coupling bearing, then press the sprocket coupling firmly into the hub, making sure it is fully and evenly seated (see illustration 15.8a).

13 Apply lithium-based grease to the insides of the bearing seals. Fit the small spacer into the right-hand side of the wheel and the big spacer into the left, making sure they fit inside the bearing seals (see illustrations 15.7a and b).

14 Manoeuvre the wheel and the caliper

bracket into place, making sure that the slot in the bracket engages with the rib on the inside of the swingarm (see illustration 15.6).

15 Fit the drive chain around the sprocket (see illustration 15.5).

16 On MT-07 (FZ-07) and XSR models slide the adjuster plate marked R onto the axle with the smaller rib on the inner face at the front and the larger one at the back – the ribs locate in the corresponding slots in the chain adjuster (see illustration). The ribs on the left-hand adjuster plate (marked L) are the same size.

17 On MT-07TR models slide the adjuster plate with the wider front section onto the axle with its raised section seating against the flat side of the axle head (see illustration).

18 Lubricate the axle with a smear of grease. Align the wheel, making sure the spacers and caliper bracket remain in place, and slide the axle through from the right-hand side (see illustration 15.4) – make sure the adjuster plate and axle head seat correctly (see illustrations, or 15.17).

19 On MT-07 (FZ-07) and XSR models seat the left-hand adjuster plate marked L over the end of the axle and seat the ribs on the inner face in the slots in the adjuster, then fit the washer and the axle nut (see illustrations 15.3b and a).

20 On MT-07TR models seat the left-hand adjuster plate over the end of the axle with the raised section facing out and towards the adjuster bolt, then fit the washer and the axle nut (see illustration).

21 Follow the procedure in Chapter 1 and adjust the chain tension, then tighten the axle nut to 105 Nm on MT-07 (FZ-07) and XSR models, and to 150 Nm on MT-07TR models.

22 Apply the rear brake to bring the pads into contact with the disc. Check the operation of the rear brake before riding the motorcycle.

16 Wheel and sprocket coupling bearings

Front wheel bearings

Note: *Always fit the wheel bearings in sets, never individually.*

1 Remove the wheel (Section 14). Lay the wheel rim on wood blocks. A caged ball bearing is fitted in each side of the wheel.

2 Inspect the seals and bearings – check that each bearing inner race turns smoothly and that the outer race is a tight fit in the hub (see Tools and Workshop Tips 9 Section 1 in the Reference Section). Do not remove the bearings unless they are going to be replaced with new ones.

3 If new components are needed, on ABS models it is advisable to remove the sensor rotor (Section 17) to prevent the possibility of damage.

4 Lever out the bearing seal from each side of the hub using a flat-bladed screwdriver or a seal hook (see illustration). Take care not to damage the hub. New seals must be fitted on reassembly.

5 Move the bearing spacer aside to expose the inner race on the lower bearing **(see illustration)**. Using a metal rod (preferably a brass punch) inserted through the centre of the upper bearing and spacer and onto the lower bearing's inner race (do not locate the drift on the top of the spacer) drive the lower bearing from the hub, moving the spacer around and relocating the drift so it's driven out squarely **(see illustration)**. The bearing spacer will also come out. Turn the wheel over so that the remaining bearing faces down. Drive the bearing out of the wheel using a socket on the inner race and an extension bar. If you can't move the spacer, or if you can't get sufficient purchase with the drift, remove the bearings using an internal expanding puller with slide-hammer attachment, which can be obtained commercially – select the correct attachment and locate it between the inner race of the upper bearing and the spacer, then tighten the inner bolt to expand and lock the puller **(see illustration)**. Attach the slide-hammer, hold the wheel firmly down and jar the bearing out **(see illustration)**.

6 Thoroughly clean the hub area of the wheel and inspect the bearing housings for damage. If a housing is damaged, consult a Yamaha dealer or wheel specialist before reassembling the wheel.

7 Fit the new bearings with the marked side facing out. Drive the first bearing in using a bearing driver or suitable socket that bears only on the outer race, and make sure the

bearing fits squarely and all the way onto its seat **(see illustration)**. Alternatively draw it in using a drawbolt arrangement (see Tools and Workshop Tips 9 Section 1).

8 Turn the wheel over then fit the bearing spacer and the other new bearing.

9 Fit the new seals, marked side facing out, into the hub using finger pressure or a suitable driver that bears on the outer rim, setting them flush with the hub **(see illustration)**. Smear the seal lips with grease.

10 If removed on ABS models fit the sensor rotor (Section 17).

11 Clean the discs using acetone or brake system cleaner, then install the wheel (Section 14).

Rear wheel bearings

12 Remove the wheel (Section 15). Set the wheel on wood blocks. Lift the sprocket coupling out of the wheel and remove the rubber dampers **(see illustrations 15.8a and b)**. A caged ball bearing is fitted in each side of the wheel.

13 Inspect the seal and bearings – check that each bearing inner race turns smoothly and that the outer race is a tight fit in the hub (see Tools and Workshop Tips 9 Section 1 in the Reference Section). Do not remove the bearings unless they are going to be replaced with new ones.

14 If new components are needed, on ABS models it is advisable to remove the sensor rotor (Section 17), to prevent the possibility of damage.

15 Lever out the bearing seal from the right-side of the hub, using a flat-bladed screwdriver or a seal hook **(see illustration 16.4)**. Take care not to damage the hub. A new seal must be fitted on reassembly.

16 Move the bearing spacer aside to expose the inner race on the lower bearing **(see illustration 16.5a)**. Using a metal rod (preferably a brass punch) inserted through the centre of the upper bearing and spacer and located on the lower bearing's inner race (do not locate the drift on the top of the spacer) drive the lower bearing from the hub, moving the spacer around and relocating the drift so it's driven out squarely **(see illustration 16.5b)**. The bearing spacer will also come out. Turn the wheel over so that the remaining bearing faces down. Drive the bearing out of the wheel using a socket on the inner race and an extension bar. If you can't move the spacer, or if you can't get sufficient purchase with the drift, remove the bearings using an internal expanding puller with slide-hammer attachment, which can be obtained commercially – select the correct attachment and locate it between the inner race of the upper bearing and the spacer, then tighten the inner bolt to expand and lock the puller **(see illustration 16.5c)**. Attach the slide-hammer, hold the wheel firmly down and jar the bearing out **(see illustration 16.5d)**.

17 Thoroughly clean the hub area of the wheel and inspect the bearing housings for damage. If a housing is damaged, consult

16.5a Move the spacer to the side to expose the inner race...

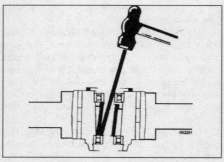

16.5b ...then locate the drift on it and drive the bearing out

16.5c Locate the knife edge of the puller in the gap between the bearing and the spacer, then expand it...

16.5d ...and use the slide-hammer to dislodge the bearing

16.7 A socket can be used to drive the new bearing in

16.9 Fit the grease seal and press or tap it into place

16.26 Lever out the grease seal

16.27 Drive the spacer out of the centre of the bearing

16.28 Drive the bearing out from the inside

16.30 A socket can be used to drive in the new bearing

16.31 Fit the spacer into the bearing

16.32 Press or drive the seal into the coupling

a Yamaha dealer or wheel specialist before reassembling the wheel.

18 Fit the new bearings with the marked side facing out. Drive the first bearing in using a bearing driver or suitable socket that bears only on the outer race, and make sure the bearing fits squarely and all the way onto its seat **(see illustration 16.7)**. Alternatively draw it in using a drawbolt arrangement (see Tools and Workshop Tips 9 Section 1).

19 Turn the wheel over then fit the bearing spacer and the other new bearing.

20 Fit the new seal, marked side facing out, into the right-hand side of the hub using finger pressure or a suitable driver that bears on the outer rim, setting it flush with the hub **(see illustration 16.9)**. Smear the seal lips with grease.

21 Fit the rubber dampers into the wheel. Make sure the spacer is in place in the sprocket coupling bearing, then press the coupling firmly into the hub, making sure it is fully and evenly seated **(see illustrations 15.8b and a)**.

22 If removed, on ABS models fit the sensor rotor (Section 17).

23 Clean the disc using acetone or brake system cleaner, then install the wheel (Section 15).

Sprocket coupling bearing

24 Remove the rear wheel (Section 15). Lift the sprocket coupling out of the wheel and remove the rubber dampers **(see illustrations 15.8a and b)**.

25 Inspect the seal and bearing – check that the bearing inner races turn smoothly and that the outer race is a tight fit in the coupling (see Tools and Workshop Tips 9 Section 1 in the Reference Section). Do not remove the bearing unless it is being replaced with a new one.

26 If new components are needed lever out the bearing seal using a flat-bladed screwdriver or a seal hook **(see illustration)**. Take care not to damage the rim of the coupling. Discard the seal – a new one must be fitted.

27 Drive the spacer out of the centre of the bearing using a socket that bears only on the spacer and not on the bearing inner race **(see illustration)**.

28 Support the coupling on blocks of wood, sprocket side down, and drive the bearing out from the inside using a bearing driver or socket **(see illustration)**.

29 Thoroughly clean the sprocket coupling and inspect the bearing housing for damage. If the housing is damaged, consult a Yamaha dealer or wheel specialist before reassembling the wheel.

30 Fit the new bearing with the marked side facing out. Drive the bearing in using a bearing driver or suitable socket that bears only on the outer race, and make sure the bearing fits squarely and all the way onto its seat **(see illustration)**.

31 Push the spacer into the inner side of the bearing **(see illustration)** – if you can't push it all the way in support the outer side of the

bearing on a socket that bears on the inner race, then drive the spacer into the bearing from the inner side.

32 Fit the new seal, marked side facing out, into the coupling using finger pressure or a suitable driver that bears on the outer rim, setting it flush with the hub **(see illustration)**. Smear the seal lips with grease.

33 Fit the rubber dampers into the wheel **(see illustration 15.8b)**. Press the sprocket coupling firmly into the hub, making sure it is fully and evenly seated **(see illustration 15.8a)**.

34 Clean the brake disc using acetone or brake system cleaner then install the wheel (Section 15).

17 Anti-lock brake system (ABS)

Special tool: *To access and read ABS fault codes and for information on the fault represented the dealer-only Yamaha diagnostic tool is required.*

ABS operation

1 The anti-lock brake system (ABS) prevents the wheels from locking up under hard braking or on uneven road surfaces. A sensor on each wheel transmits information about the speed of rotation to the ABS control unit; if the unit senses that a wheel is about to lock, it releases brake pressure to that wheel momentarily, preventing a skid.

2 The anti-lock system is self-checking

and is activated when the ignition switch is turned on – you may hear a clicking as the self-diagnosis routine is performed, or feel a pulse in the lever or pedal if applied. The ABS indicator light in the instrument cluster will come on when the ignition is turned on, and if the system is all good will go off when the bike is ridden above 6 mph (10 kmh). If the ABS indicator light does not come on initially there is a fault in the system – see below.

3 If the indicator light remains on or flashes, or comes on or flashes while the machine is being ridden, there is a fault in the system and the ABS function will be switched off – the brakes will still function but in normal mode. A fault code will be registered and stored in the ECU. If a fault is indicated stop the bike and turn the ignition off, then turn it back on again and ride the bike – if the light goes out the fault has cleared itself and can be considered a temporary glitch in the system. If the fault persists, next check the ABS fuses (see Chapter 8). If the fuses are good check the wheel speed sensor and modulator wiring connectors are securely connected and corrosion free **(see illustrations 17.6, 17.16 and 17.27a and b)**, and check the wiring for any obvious breaks or damage – refer to

Chapter 8 for information on electrical fault finding and for the wiring diagram for your model. Also check that the wheel speed sensor heads and rotors are clean and free of corrosion, and that there is no debris caught between the sensor rotor pulsers and that the rotor is not damaged or deformed in any way – see below for sensor and rotor removal and installation. If no problems can be found you need to retrieve the fault code.

4 To retrieve any stored fault codes, the diagnostic tool is required (see Special Tool above). If you have access to the tool follow the instructions supplied with it. The fault codes, what they relate to and the possible causes are tabled below. Otherwise take the bike to a Yamaha dealer and get them to diagnose and repair the fault.

Note: *The ABS indicator may diagnose a fault if tyre sizes other than those specified by Yamaha are fitted, if the tyre pressures are incorrect, if the machine has been run continuously over bumpy roads, if the front wheel comes off the ground whilst riding (wheelie) or if the machine is on an auxiliary stand with the engine running and the rear wheel turning.*

ABS components

Note: *Take great care not to damage the*

17.5a Undo the screw on each side and move the headlight forwards

wheel sensor head or sensor rotor surface, or use magnetic tools near them, and take care not to subject them to any sort of impact. Replace the rotor screws with new ones if removed.

Front wheel sensor

5 On MT-07 (FZ-07) models undo the screw on each side of the headlight assembly and move the top of the headlight forwards (it will pivot on the bottom mount) **(see illustration)**. Open the upper section of the

Fault code table		
Fault codes (preceded by ABS)	**Faulty component or system**	**Possible causes**
11, 13, 15, 17, 25, 26, 45	Front wheel speed sensor circuit	Faulty wiring or wiring connector
	Front wheel speed sensor	Faulty sensor
	Front wheel sensor rotor	Damaged sensor rotor
12, 14, 16, 18, 27, 46	Rear wheel speed sensor circuit	Faulty wiring or wiring connector
	Rear wheel speed sensor	Faulty sensor
	Rear wheel sensor rotor	Damaged sensor rotor
21	Control unit/modulator solenoid	Faulty control unit/modulator. Faulty wiring or wiring connector
24	Brake light circuit	Faulty wiring or wiring connector. Faulty LED. Faulty switch. Faulty relay
31, 32	Control unit/modulator relay	ABS solenoid fuse. Faulty wiring or wiring connector. Faulty relay. Faulty control unit/modulator
33, 34	Control unit/modulator motor	ABS motor fuse. Faulty wiring or wiring connector. Faulty relay. Faulty control unit/modulator
41	Front wheel can lock	Brake drag. Brake fluid or hose problem. Pulse test result incorrect. Faulty control unit/modulator
42, 47	Rear wheel can lock	Brake drag. Brake fluid or hose problem. Pulse test result incorrect. Faulty control unit/modulator
43	Front wheel speed sensor signal	Incorrect sensor installation Faulty wiring or wiring connector Damaged sensor rotor
44	Rear wheel speed sensor signal	Incorrect sensor installation. Faulty wiring or wiring connector. Damaged sensor rotor
51, 52	Power supply voltage high	Battery or charging system fault
53, 54	Power supply voltage low	Battery or charging system fault. Faulty wiring or wiring connector
55, 56	Control unit/modulator power circuit	Faulty control unit/modulator
63	Front wheel speed sensor power	Faulty wiring or wiring connector. Faulty control unit/modulator
64	Rear wheel speed sensor power	Faulty wiring or wiring connector. Faulty control unit/modulator

17.5b Open the top rubber flap and disconnect the turn signal connectors…

17.5c … then disconnect the sidelight connector

17.5d Open the bottom flap…

17.5e … and disconnect the wheel sensor connector (arrowed)

17.6 Wheel sensor connector (arrowed)

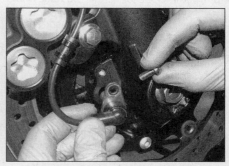

17.8 Undo the screw and remove the sensor

rubber connector cover and disconnect the turn signal wiring connectors **(see illustration)**. Move the headlight some more and disconnect the sidelight wiring connector **(see illustration)** – the headlight can stay in that position supported on the bottom pivot with the headlight wiring connected. Open the lower section of the connector cover to access the wheel sensor wiring connector **(see illustrations)**.

6 On MT-07TR models remove the right-hand fairing side panel and inner panel, and on XSR models remove the right-hand air scoop and fuel tank cover (see Chapter 7). Disconnect the wheel sensor wiring connector **(see illustration)**.

7 Release the sensor wiring from the clips and feed the wire down to the sensor, noting its routing.

8 Undo the sensor screw and remove the sensor **(see illustration)**.

9 Make sure the tip of the sensor and its mounting surfaces are clean and show no signs of damage or distortion. Fit the sensor and tighten the screw to 7 Nm.

10 Feed the wiring up to the connector, routing and securing it as noted on removal.

11 Install the remaining components in reverse order of removal. On MT-07 (FZ-07) models pull the centre peg of the rubber connector cover up through the holes in the flaps **(see illustration 17.5d)** so the bottom rim of the peg is seated on the top to keep the flaps closed **(see illustration)**.

Front sensor rotor

12 Remove the front wheel (Section 14).

13 Undo the screws securing the rotor and

lift it off **(see illustration)**. Yamaha specify to use new screws.

14 Make sure there is no dirt or corrosion where the ring seats on the hub – if the ring does not sit flat the signals from the sensor could be distorted. Make sure the sensor rotor is clean and shows no signs of damage or distortion. Fit new screws and apply a non-permanent thread locking compound, and tighten them to 8 Nm.

15 Install the front wheel (see Section 14).

Rear wheel sensor

16 Remove the right-hand frame cover (see Chapter 7).

17 Disconnect the wheel sensor wiring connector **(see illustration)**. Release the sensor wiring guides and feed the wire down to the sensor, noting its routing.

17.11 Correct fitting of the connector cover

17.13 Wheel sensor rotor screws (arrowed)

17.17 Rear wheel speed sensor wiring connector

17.18 Undo the screw (arrowed) and remove the sensor

17.27a Press the catch in...

17.27b ... and push the release lever ...

18 Undo the sensor screw and remove the sensor **(see illustration)**.
19 Make sure the tip of the sensor and its mounting surfaces are clean and show no signs of damage or distortion. Fit the sensor and tighten the screw to 7 Nm. Feed the wiring up to the connector, routing and securing it as noted on removal.
20 Refit the frame cover.

Rear sensor rotor

21 Remove the rear wheel (see Section 15).
22 Undo the screws securing the rotor and lift it off **(see illustration 17.13)**. Yamaha specify to use new screws.
23 Make sure there is no dirt or corrosion where the ring seats on the hub – if the ring does not sit flat the signals from the sensor could be distorted. Make sure the sensor rotor is clean and shows no signs of damage or distortion. Fit new screws and apply a non-permanent thread locking compound, and tighten them to 8 Nm.
24 Install the rear wheel (see Section 15).

Control unit/modulator

Note: *Before removing the modulator drain all old brake fluid from the brake system, then fill with new fluid on installation (see Section 11). The modulator cannot be dismantled for overhaul, and no component parts are available. If it fails, it must be replaced with a new one.*
25 The modulator is mounted under the front of the fuel tank on the right-hand side.
26 To just access the wiring connector, on MT-07 (FZ-07) models remove the front fuel tank cover, on MT-07TR models remove the

17.27c ... to release the connector

fuel tank cover, and on XSR models remove the right-hand air scoop (see Chapter 7). To remove the modulator remove the fuel tank (see Chapter 4).
27 Press the catch behind the connector release lever in then push the lever to release the connector **(see illustrations)**.
28 Cover the area around the modulator with clean rag to prevent damage to paintwork in the event that brake fluid is spilled.
29 Note the alignment of each brake hose banjo fitting, then unscrew the banjo bolts and detach the hoses, noting the positions of the sealing washers **(see illustration)**. Be prepared with a rag to catch any drops of brake fluid. Note that new sealing washers must be used on reassembly.
30 Unscrew the modulator mounting bolts **(see illustrations)**. Carefully lift the modulator out. Check the condition of the rubber mountings, and note the collars fitted in them.
31 Seal the end of each hose and plug the

17.29 Modulator hose alignment and banjo bolts (arrowed)

holes in the modulator using rubber bungs or loosely fit new (and clean) M10 x 1.0 bolts to prevent dirt entering the system.
32 Installation is the reverse of removal, noting the following:
● Make sure the collars are fitted in the grommets in the bracket, and tighten the mounting bolts to 7 Nm.
● Make sure the brake hoses are correctly aligned, use new sealing washers, and tighten the banjo bolts to 30 Nm **(see illustration 17.29)**.
● Align the wiring connector then push the lever to draw it on until it clicks over the catch **(see illustration)**.
● Follow the procedure in Section 11 to refill and bleed the brake system. Check that there are no fluid leaks and test the operation of the brakes before riding the motorcycle. Yamaha specifies to take the motorcycle to a Yamaha dealer to pulse test the system.

17.30a Unscrew the bolt (arrowed)...

17.30b ... and the bolts (arrowed)

17.32 Push the lever until it clicks over the catch

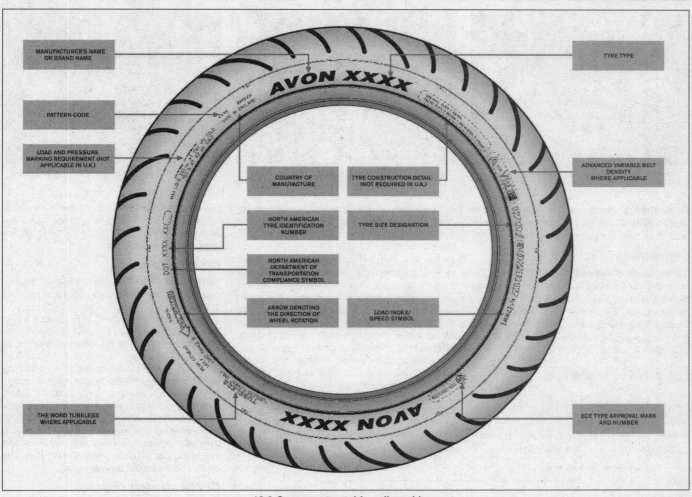

18.3 Common tyre sidewall markings

MANUFACTURER'S NAME OR BRAND NAME

PATTERN CODE

LOAD AND PRESSURE MARKING REQUIREMENT (NOT APPLICABLE IN U.K.)

COUNTRY OF MANUFACTURE

TYRE CONSTRUCTION DETAIL (NOT REQUIRED IN U.K.)

NORTH AMERICAN TYRE IDENTIFICATION NUMBER

TYRE SIZE DESIGNATION

NORTH AMERICAN DEPARTMENT OF TRANSPORTATION COMPLIANCE SYMBOL

ARROW DENOTING THE DIRECTION OF WHEEL ROTATION

LOAD INDEX/ SPEED SYMBOL

THE WORD TUBELESS WHERE APPLICABLE

TYRE TYPE

ADVANCED VARIABLE BELT DENSITY WHERE APPLICABLE

ECE TYPE APPROVAL MARK AND NUMBER

18 Tyres

General information

1 The wheels fitted on all models are designed to take tubeless tyres only. Tyre sizes are given in the Specifications at the beginning of this chapter.

2 Refer to *Pre-ride checks* at the beginning of this manual for tyre maintenance and pressures.

Fitting new tyres

3 When selecting new tyres, refer to the tyre information in the Owner's Manual. Ensure that front and rear tyre types are compatible, and of the correct size and speed rating; if necessary, seek advice from a Yamaha dealer or motorcycle tyre specialist **(see illustration)**.

4 It is recommended that tyres are fitted by a motorcycle tyre specialist and that this is not attempted in the home workshop. This is particularly relevant in the case of tubeless tyres because the force required to break the seal between the wheel rim and tyre bead is substantial, and is usually beyond the capabilities of an individual working with normal tyre levers. Additionally, the specialist will be able to balance the wheels after tyre fitting.

5 Note that punctured tubeless tyres can in some cases be repaired. Seek the advice of a Yamaha dealer or a motorcycle tyre specialist concerning tyre repairs and safe road speeds thereafter.

19 Front sprocket cover

Removal

1 Note the alignment of the line on the gearchange shaft with the punch mark on the gearchange linkage arm – if necessary make your own alignment mark before removing the arm so that it can be correctly aligned with the shaft on installation. Unscrew the pinch bolt and slide the arm off the shaft **(see illustration)**.

2 Unscrew the bolts and remove the cover, releasing the hoses from the guide **(see**

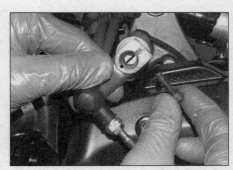

19.1 Note the alignment then unscrew the bolt and slide the arm off

19.2a Unscrew the bolts

19.2b Release the hoses as you remove the cover

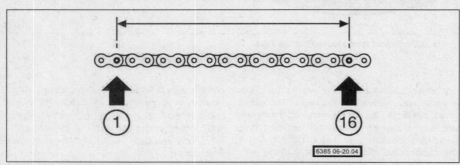

19.2c Note how the guide plate locates

illustrations). Remove the guide plate **(see illustration)**. Clean all old chain lube and dirt from the cover, the guide plate and the engine.

Installation

3 Installation is the reverse of removal. Make sure the guide plate locates correctly **(see illustration 19.2c)**. Make sure the hoses locate correctly in the guide **(see illustration 19.2b)**. Align the punch mark on the gearchange linkage arm with the line on the shaft **(see illustration 19.1)**.

20 Chain and sprockets

Note: *The chain and sprockets should always be replaced as a set – running a new chain on* old sprockets or vice versa will rapidly increase chain and sprocket wear. Refer to Chapter 1 for details of routine chain maintenance and checks.
Note: *The original equipment chain fitted to these models is endless, i.e. it comes as a completed loop and does not have a staked-type master (joining) link which can be disassembled. It is recommended that the same type of endless chain is used when fitting a new one. If you do decide to fit an aftermarket chain that comes open-ended and has a staked-type master link, make sure the chain is the correct size and has the correct number of links for your model (see Specifications), and use either the Yamaha service tool, (part. No. 90890-01550 in Europe or YM-01550 in the US), or one of several commercially-available drive chain cutting/ staking tools (but the cheap ones are best* avoided), to join the links of the new chain, following the instructions provided and the information given in Tools and workshop tips in the Reference section.

Chain cleaning

1 Refer to Chapter 1 for details of routine cleaning with the chain installed on the sprockets.
2 If the chain is extremely dirty remove it (see below) and soak it in paraffin (kerosene) for approximately five or six minutes, then clean it using a soft brush.
Caution: Don't use petrol, solvent or other cleaning fluids that might damage its internal sealing properties. Don't use high-pressure water. Remove the chain, wipe it off, then blow dry it with compressed air immediately. The entire process shouldn't take longer than ten minutes – if it does, the O-rings in the chain rollers could be damaged.

Chain stretch check

3 Chain condition can be determined by the amount it has stretched between a specified number of links. To assess the chain accurately, remove it (see below), then clean it (see above). The chain must be free of any kinks and binding links must be loosened-up before the check is made.
4 Stretch a section of the chain across a flat surface so it is taut and measure the distance between sixteen of the pins as shown **(see illustration)**.
5 Measure the chain in several places to compensate for uneven wear along its length, then calculate the average and compare it to the limit specified at the beginning of the Chapter. If the chain stretch exceeds the service limit, the chain must be replaced with a new one.

Chain and sprocket removal

6 Remove the front sprocket cover (Section 19).
7 Unstake the rim of the front sprocket nut from the indents in the shaft **(see illustration)**. Engage a high gear and have an assistant sit on the seat and apply the rear brake, then unscrew the sprocket nut and remove the washer **(see illustration)**. A new nut should be used.

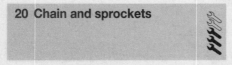

20.4 Measure chain section as shown to determine stretch

6385 06-20.04

20.7a Unstake the rim using a punch or cold chisel

20.7b Unscrew the nut and remove the washer

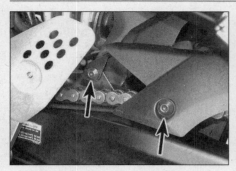

20.8a Undo the two screws (arrowed), noting the sleeves...

20.8b ... then release the front trim clip (arrowed)...

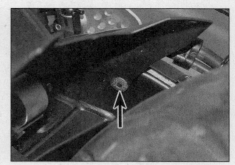

20.8c ... and the trim clip (arrowed) on the inner side

20.9a Release the tie (arrowed) and disconnect the connector...

20.9b ... and release the wire from the clip (arrowed)

20.9c Draw the hoses out of the guide

8 Remove the rear wheel (Section 15). Remove the chainguard (see illustrations).

9 Remove the frame covers (see Chapter 7). Release the wiring tie and disconnect the sidestand switch wiring connector, then release the wire from the clip (see illustrations). Draw the fuel tank drain and breather hoses out of the guide on the sidestand bracket (see illustration). Unscrew the sidestand bracket bolts and remove the stand assembly (see illustration). Slacken the swingarm pivot bolt nut and thread it most of the way off, leaving it held by a few threads (see illustration). Unscrew the left-hand inner bracket bolts, then draw the bracket away from the bike, bringing the swingarm pivot bolt with it, just far enough until there is enough clearance between the bracket and the frame to remove the chain (see illustrations).

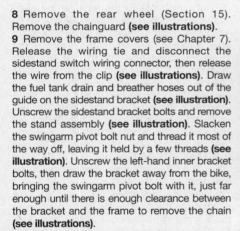

20.9d Remove the sidestand assembly

20.9e Slacken the nut most of the way

20.9f Unscrew the two inner bracket bolts...

20.9g ... then pull the bracket away from the frame

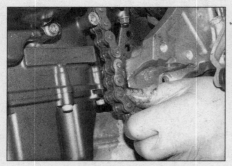

20.10a Slip the chain out and off the sprocket...

20.10b ... and off the back of the swingarm

20.11 Draw the sprocket off the shaft

10 Draw the lower run of the chain out from between the inner bracket and the frame, disengage it from the sprocket and draw it off the swingarm **(see illustrations)**.

11 Slide the front sprocket off the shaft **(see illustration)**.

12 Rest the rear wheel sprocket side up on some blocks of wood placed under the tyre. Unscrew the rear sprocket nuts and remove the washers, then lift the retainer and the sprocket off the studs **(see illustration)**.

Chain and sprocket installation

> ⚠️ *Warning: It is recommended that you always fit the OE type of endless chain. NEVER fit a drive chain that uses a clip-type master (split) link. If a riveted link chain is being fitted use ONLY the correct service tools to secure the master link – if you do not have access to such tools, have the chain replaced by a Yamaha dealer.*

13 Fit the rear sprocket over the studs and onto the hub with the marked side facing out **(see illustration 20.12)**. Fit the retainer and the washers, then tighten the nuts evenly and in a criss-cross sequence to 80 Nm.

14 Slide the front sprocket onto the shaft with the marked side facing out **(see illustration 20.11)**.

15 Route the drive chain over the end of the swingarm, around the front sprocket and between the inner bracket and the frame **(see illustrations 20.10b and a)**.

16 Clean the threads of the inner bracket bolts and apply some threadlock. Reposition the bracket, pushing the swingarm pivot bolt through and keeping the flats on the head seated against the flats in the inner bracket so it is locked, and tighten the bolts finger-tight **(see illustration and 20.9f)**. Tighten the swingarm pivot bolt nut to 110 Nm **(see illustration 20.9e)**. Now tighten the inner bracket bolts to 45 Nm. Clean the threads of the sidestand bracket bolts and apply some threadlock, fit the bracket and tighten the bolts to 63 Nm **(see illustration 20.9d)**. Reconnect and secure the sidestand switch connector, then secure the wire in the clip with the fuel tank hose with the blue dot, and fit both the hoses into the guide **(see illustrations 20.9a, b and c)**.

17 Install the rear wheel (Section 15) – take up some of the slack in the chain but tighten the axle nut finger-tight only at this stage.

18 Fit the front sprocket washer with its OUT mark facing out **(see illustration)**. Fit the new nut **(see illustration 20.7b)**. Hold the rear brake on and tighten the nut to 95 Nm. Stake the rim of the nut into the indent in the end of the shaft using a punch **(see illustration)**.

19 Install the front sprocket cover (Section 19).

20 Adjust and lubricate the chain (see Chapter 1).

20.12 Rear sprocket nuts (arrowed)

20.16 Make sure the chain is clear of the bracket as you seat it back against the frame

20.18a Fit the washer with the OUT mark on the outside

20.18b Stake the rim of the nut into the indent

Chapter 7
Bodywork

Contents

Degrees of difficulty

| Easy, suitable for novice with little experience | Fairly easy, suitable for beginner with some experience | Fairly difficult, suitable for competent DIY mechanic | Difficult, suitable for experienced DIY mechanic | Very difficult, suitable for expert DIY or professional |

1 General Information

1 This Chapter covers the procedures necessary to remove and install the bodywork. Since many service and repair operations on these motorcycles require the removal of the body panels, the procedures are grouped here and referred to from other Chapters.

2 In the case of damage to the bodywork, it is usually necessary to remove the broken component and replace it with a new (or used) one. Note that there are however some companies that specialise in 'plastic welding' and there are a number of DIY bodywork repair kits available.

3 When attempting to remove any body panel, first study it closely, noting any fasteners and associated fittings, to be sure of returning everything to its correct place on installation. Once the evident fasteners have been removed, try to withdraw the panel as described but DO NOT FORCE IT – if it will not release, check that all fasteners have been removed and try again.

4 When installing a body panel, first study it closely, noting any fasteners and associated fittings removed with it, to be sure of returning everything to its correct place. Check that all fasteners are in good condition, including the rubber mounts; replace any faulty fasteners with new ones before the panel is reassembled. Check also that all mounting brackets are straight and repair them or replace them with new ones if necessary before attempting to install the panel.

5 Tighten the fasteners securely, but be careful not to overtighten any of them or the panel may break (not always immediately) due to the uneven stress.

2 MT-07 (FZ-07) models

Note: *Procedures also apply to the Moto Cage model. For hand guards refer to Section 3.*

Trim clips

1 Release and remove a trim clip by pushing the centre pin in then drawing the body out **(see illustrations)**.

2 To fit a trim clip push the centre pin out so it protrudes from the top of the body **(see illustration)**. Fit the body into the hole, then push the centre pin so it is flush to lock the body in place.

2.1a Push the centre-pin (arrowed) into the body …

2.1b … then draw the body of the clip out

2.2 Reset the clip by pushing the centre pin out of the body as shown

2.3 Unscrew the two bolts, noting the collars

2.5 Locate the tab in the slot

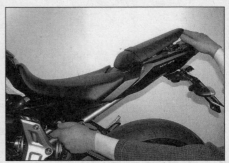

2.6 Insert and turn the key, then lift the rear of the seat and remove it

Seats

Rider's seat

3 Lift each rear corner of the seat, unscrew the bolt and remove the collar **(see illustration)**.

4 Draw the seat back, noting how the tab on the bracket across the frame locates in the slot in the underside of the seat.

5 Installation is the reverse of removal – make sure the tab locates correctly in the slot **(see illustration)**.

Passenger seat

6 Unlock the seat using the ignition key in the lock on the underside – turn the key anti-clockwise **(see illustration)**.

7 Lift the back of the seat and draw it back, noting how the hooks at the front locate.

8 Installation is the reverse of removal – make sure the hooks at the front locate under the bridges on the top of the frame **(see illustration)**. Push the back of the seat down to engage the lock.

Seat cowls

9 Remove the seats.

10 Undo the two screws securing the centre cowl, then release the tabs along each side and remove the cowl **(see illustrations)**.

11 Undo the two screws securing the tail cowl, then slide the cover back to release the tab on each side, and note how the projection on the tail light locates in the rear of the cover **(see illustrations)**.

12 Release and remove the three trim clips on the underside of the side cowl **(see illustrations)** – note that each side is removed individually.

2.8 Locate the hooks under the bridges

2.10a Undo the screws…

2.10b … then release the tabs

2.11a Undo the screws…

2.11b … and remove the tail cowl as described

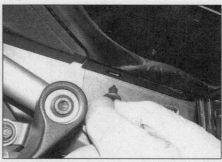

2.12a Release the front trim clip for the side being removed (right-hand side shown)…

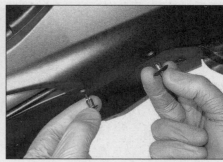

2.12b … and the rear trim clips (left side shown)

2.13a Unscrew the front bolt

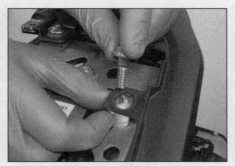

2.13b Unscrew the rear bolt and remove the spacer

2.14 Pull the peg out of the grommet

13 Unscrew the bolts on the top, noting the spacer between the cowl and the frame on the rear bolt **(see illustrations)**.

14 Pull the cowl away to free the peg at the back from the grommet and remove the cowl **(see illustration)**.

15 Installation is the reverse of removal.

Frame covers

16 Undo the two screws **(see illustration)**.

17 Carefully pull the bottom of the cover away to release it from the peg in the top of the inner bracket **(see illustration)**.

18 Installation is the reverse of removal. Make sure the grommets in the screw holes are in good condition and the sleeves are fitted in them.

Fuel tank covers

19 To remove the top cover undo the screw, then draw the cover back to release the tab at the front **(see illustrations)**.

2.16 Remove the screws

2.17 Pull the cover off the peg

2.19a Undo the screw…

2.19b … and release the tab

2.20a Undo the front screw…

2.20b … the middle screw…

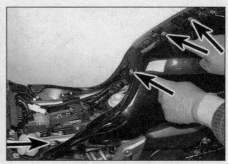

2.20c … and the four top screws

2.20d Pull the front peg out …

2.20e … then the middle peg

2.20f Pull the rear grommet off the peg

2.20g Release the tabs at the back…

20 To remove the side covers, first remove the top cover. Release and remove the trim clip on the underside of the side cover at the back **(see illustration 2.12a)**. Undo the screw at the front, noting the washer, the screw on the side in the middle, and the four screws along the top **(see illustrations)**. Carefully pull the lower edge of the cover away just far enough to free the two pegs along the bottom at the front and in the middle from the grommets, and the grommet at the rear from the peg, then push on the centre cover to release the tabs along the top, starting at the back and moving forwards **(see illustrations)**. If required the covers can be disassembled into their component parts by undoing the screws on the inside.

21 To remove the centre cover first remove the top and side covers. Release and remove the trim clip at the back and undo the two screws at the front **(see illustrations)**. Release the tabs at the front from the slots in the top cover and remove the cover **(see illustration)**.

22 To remove the front cover first remove the top, side and centre covers. Release and remove the trim clip at the back **(see illustration)**. Undo the top screws and the side screws and remove the cover **(see illustration)** – note the sleeves fitted in the top grommets and the collars fitted in the side grommets **(see illustration)**.

2.20h … in the middle…

2.20i … and at the front

2.21a Release the trim clip...

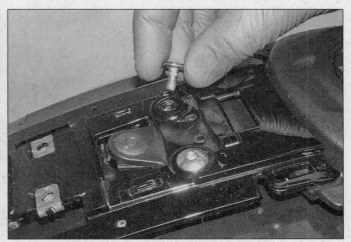

2.21b ... and undo the screws...

2.21c ... then release the front tabs

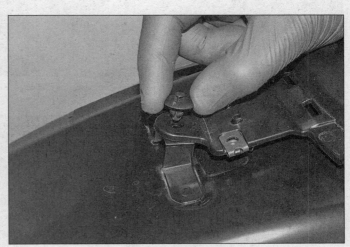

2.22a Release the trim clip...

2.22b ... then undo the screws

2.22c There is a collar in each side mount

2.25a Undo the screw...

2.25b ... pull the peg from the grommet...

2.25c ... and release the tabs

2.25d Note the collar

2.26a Release the hose/pipe/wire

2.26b Undo the bolts and screws (arrowed) on each side...

2.26c ... and manoeuvre the mudguard out

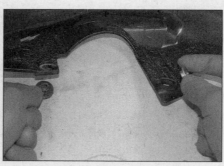

2.26d Note the collars and how they fit

23 Installation is the reverse of removal, except when fitting the side covers push the pegs into the grommets first, then engage the tabs along the top with the front and centre covers.

Front mudguard

24 Remove the front wheel (see Chapter 6).
25 Remove each side section by undoing the screw, then pull the peg from the grommet and slide the section forwards to release the tabs

along the top from the centre section (see illustrations). Note the collar for the screw fitted on the inner side (see illustration).
26 To remove the centre section first remove the side sections. Release the brake hose or pipe and wire (according to model) from the clip on the top of the centre section (see illustration). Unscrew the front bolt and the rear screw on each side, noting how the left-hand screw secures the brake hose holder, then manoeuvre the centre section out (see illustrations). Note the collar for each front bolt fitted in the outside, and the collar for each rear screw fitted in the inside (see illustration).
27 If required remove the brackets from the forks (see illustration).
28 Installation is the reverse of removal. When fitting the brackets onto the forks push the bottom down towards the fork as you tighten the bolts. Make sure the collars are fitted (see illustrations 2.26d and 2.25d).

Mirrors

29 See Section 3.

3 MT-07TR models

Trim clips

1 See Section 2.

Seat

2 Unlock the seat using the ignition key in the lock on the left-hand side (see illustration) – turn the key anti-clockwise. Lift the rear of the seat

2.27 Each bracket is secured by two bolts

3.2 Unlock the seat then draw it back

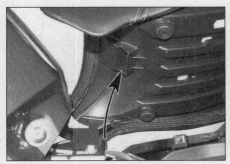

3.3a Locate the tab in the slot

3.3b Locate the hooks under the bridges

3.5a Undo the screws...

3.5b ... then pull the cover off the peg

3.6a Two bolts secure each grab-rail

3.6b Note how the tab locates

and draw it back, noting how the hooks in the middle locate under the bridges on the frame and the tab on the bracket across the frame locates in the slot in the underside at the front.

3 Installation is the reverse of removal. Make sure the tab on the bracket locates correctly in the slot at the front of the seat and the hooks in the middle locate under the bridges on the frame (see illustrations). Push down on the rear of the seat to engage the catch.

Side covers, grab-rails and seat cowls

4 Remove the seat.

5 To remove a side cover undo the three screws, then carefully pull the cover away to release the grommet from the peg, noting how the pin at the back locates in the hole in the seat cowl (see illustrations).

6 To remove a grab-rail unscrew the bolts and remove the rail, noting how the tab locates (see illustrations).

7 To remove the seat cowls first remove the side covers and grab-rails. Undo the four screws securing each side cowl, then carefully pull the front away to release the peg from the grommet (see illustrations). Undo the six screws securing the tail cowl, then release the

3.7a Undo the side screws...

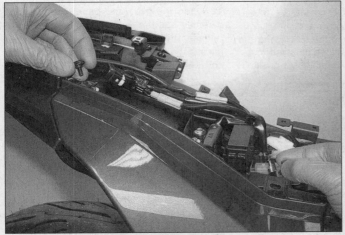

3.7b ... and the top screws...

3.7c ... then pull the peg from the grommet

3.7d Undo the front screw on each side...

3.7e ... and the rear screws on each side...

3.7f ... then release the tabs...

3.7g ... and the catch

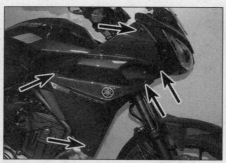

3.10a Side panel screws (arrowed)

3.10b Release the lower front tab...

3.10c ...and the upper front tabs

3.11a Undo the screw...

3.11b ... then release the tabs

tabs on each side and pull the catch at the back from the slot (see illustrations).

8 Installation is the reverse of removal.

Frame covers

9 See Section 2.

Fairing side panels and inner panels

10 Undo the five side panel screws, noting the washers (see illustration). Carefully pull the panel away to release the tabs along the front from the inner panel (see illustrations).

11 Set the windshield in its highest position.

Undo the front panel screw, then release the tabs and remove the panel (see illustrations).

12 Undo the five inner panel screws, then carefully pull the rear of the panel away to release the peg from the grommet, then release the tab at the front from the headlight cover (see illustrations).

3.12a Undo the front screw...

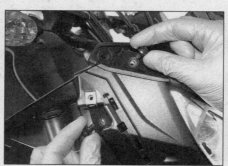

3.12b ... the upper screws...

3.12c ... and the lower screws...

3.12d … then pull the peg from the grommet

3.15 Release the trim clip

3.16a Undo the top screws…

13 Installation is the reverse of removal. Make sure the grommets are in good condition.

Fuel tank cover

14 Remove the seat and the fairing side panels and inner panels.

15 Release and remove the trim clip at the back **(see illustration)**.

16 Undo the two screws on the top and the two on each side, noting the collars in the grommets **(see illustrations)**. Carefully lift the cover off the tank **(see illustration)**.

17 If required the cover can be disassembled into its component parts by undoing the screws on the inside **(see illustration)**.

18 Installation is the reverse of removal.

Windshield

19 Undo the four screws and lift the windshield off **(see illustration)**.

20 To remove the windshield carrier remove the fairing side panels and inner panels, then refer to Chapter 8, Section 8 and remove the headlight cover. Unscrew the windshield

3.16b … and the screws on each side

3.16c Lift the cover off

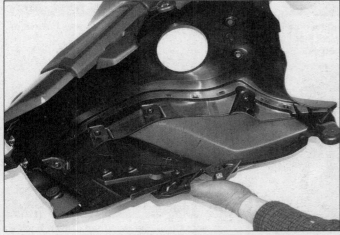

3.17 Screws on the inside join the various panels together

3.19 Windshield screws (arrowed)

3.25a Slacken the base hex...

3.25b ... then unscrew the mirror

3.28 Hand guard bracket screws (arrowed)

height adjuster knobs, then slide the carrier down out of the slot.

21 Installation is the reverse of removal. Make sure the rubber well-nuts are in good condition and correctly in place.

Front mudguard

22 Remove the front wheel (see Chapter 6).
23 Release the brake pipe and wire from the clip on the top **(see illustration 2.26a)**. Undo the two screws on each side, noting how the left-hand rear screw secures the brake hose holder, then manoeuvre the mudguard out. Note the collar for each screw fitted in the inside.
24 Installation is the reverse of removal.

Mirrors

25 Slacken the hex at the base then unscrew the mirror **(see illustrations)** – the right-hand

mirror has a left-hand thread and so must be unscrewed clockwise, the left-hand mirror has a conventional thread and so is unscrewed anti-clockwise.

26 Installation is the reverse of removal – position the mirror as required then tighten the base hex.

Hand guards

27 Remove the mirror.
28 To remove the brackets undo the two screws, noting the collars **(see illustration)**.
29 To remove the right-hand guard remove the fuel tank (see Chapter 4), and to remove the left-hand guard remove the fuel tank cover. Disconnect the front turn signal wiring connector, release the wiring from its ties and guides and feed it out, noting its routing **(see illustrations)**. Undo the handlebar brace

screws and remove the brace, then undo the hand guard clamp screw, noting how the clamp acts as a guide for the wiring, and remove the guard **(see illustrations)**.
30 Installation is the reverse of removal.

4 XSR models

Trim clips

1 See Section 2.

Seat

2 Unlock the seat using the ignition key in the lock on the left-hand side **(see illustration)** – turn the key anti-clockwise. Lift the rear of the seat and draw it back, noting how the tab

3.29a Right-hand turn signal wiring connector (arrowed)

3.29b Left-hand turn signal connector is inside the shroud (arrowed) – cut the cable ties to open it

3.29c Handlebar brace screws (arrowed)

3.29d Undo the screw (arrowed) and remove the clamp and the guard...

3.29e ... noting how the wiring is routed

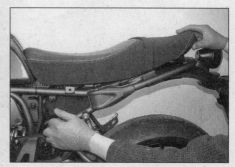

4.2 Unlock the seat then draw it back

4.3 Locate the tab in the slot

4.4 Undo the screws and remove the cover

4.5a Undo the screws...

on the bracket across the frame locates in the slot in the underside at the front.

3 Installation is the reverse of removal. Make sure the tab on the bracket locates correctly in the slot at the front of the seat **(see illustration)**. Push down on the rear of the seat to engage the catch.

Side covers and inner covers

4 Remove the side cover by undoing the four screws **(see illustration)**.

5 Undo the inner cover screws, then carefully pull the top of the panel at the front to release the peg from the grommet **(see illustrations)**.

6 Installation is the reverse of removal.

Frame covers

7 Undo the two screws **(see illustration)**.

8 Carefully pull the cover away to release it from the peg in the top of the inner bracket **(see illustration 2.17)**.

9 Installation is the reverse of removal. Make

sure the grommets in the screw holes are in good condition and the sleeves are fitted in them.

Air scoops

10 Remove the air scoop by undoing the three screws **(see illustration)**.

11 Installation is the reverse of removal.

Fuel tank covers

12 To remove the top cover undo the screws **(see illustration)**. Turn the handlebars to the

4.5b ... then pull the peg from the grommet

4.7 Frame cover screws (arrowed)

4.10 Undo the screws and remove the air scoop

4.12a Undo the six screws along each side and the two in the middle, noting which type fits where

4.12b Make sure the buttons are clear...

4.12c ... then remove the top cover

left so the instrument buttons are clear, then lift the cover off, noting how the two pegs on the underside locate in the holes in the centre cover **(see illustrations)**.

13 To remove the side covers, first remove the top cover. Release and remove the trim clip at the front **(see illustration)**. Undo the two screws on the top **(see illustration)**. Release the cover from the tabs along the side of the centre cover **(see illustration)**.

14 To remove the centre cover first remove the top and side covers. Undo the four screws and remove the centre cover **(see illustration)**.

15 Installation is the reverse of removal.

Front mudguard

16 Remove the front wheel (see Chapter 6).

17 Release the brake pipe and wheel sensor wire from the clip **(see illustration)**. Unscrew the nuts on the underside and remove the washers and screws and remove the mudguard from the brace, noting the collars for the screws in the mudguard.

18 Undo the two screws on each side, noting how the left-hand rear screw secures the brake hose holder, then manoeuvre the brace out **(see illustration)**.

Mirrors

19 See Section 3.

4.13a Release the trim clip

4.13b Undo the two screws...

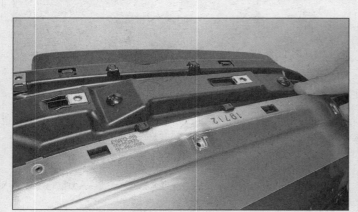

4.13c ... then slide the cover out from under the tabs

4.14 Centre cover screws (arrowed)

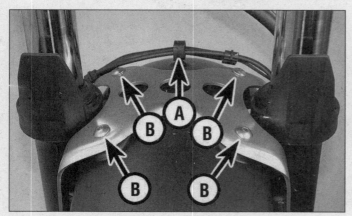

4.17 Open the clip (A), then unscrew the nuts on the underside and remove the screws (B) on the top

4.18 Undo the screws (arrowed) on each side

Chapter 8
Electrical system

Contents

Degrees of difficulty

Easy, suitable for novice with little experience	Fairly easy, suitable for beginner with some experience	Fairly difficult, suitable for competent DIY mechanic	Difficult, suitable for experienced DIY mechanic	Very difficult, suitable for expert DIY or professional

Specifications

Battery

Capacity	12V, 8.6Ah
Type	Yuasa YTZ10S
Charge condition	
Fully charged	12.8V
Half-charged	12.4V
Discharged	12V or less
Charging time	Until fully charged (12.8V) (see Section 4)

Charging system

Alternator nominal output	14V, 410W @ 5000 rpm
Alternator stator coil resistance	0.128 to 0.192 ohms
Current leakage	1mA (max)
Regulated voltage output (no load)	14.1 to 14.9V

Starter relay

Resistance	4.18 to 4.62 ohms @ 20°C

Starter motor

Brush length	
Standard	12 mm
Service limit	6.5 mm
Mica undercut	0.7 mm

Fuses

Main	30A
Ignition	10A
Fuel injection (EFI)	10A
Headlight	15A
Signal (horn, brake/tail light, sidelight, licence plate light)	10A
Parking lighting (turn signals and hazard lights)	7.5A
Cooling fan	10A
Back-up (clock, immobiliser)	7.5A
Auxiliary	2A
ABS (control unit)	7.5A
ABS MTR (motor)	30A
ABS SOL (solenoid)	15A

Bulbs

Headlight	
MT-07 (FZ-07) and XSR models	60/55W x 1 halogen (H4)
MT-07TR models	55W x 2 halogen (H7)
Sidelight	
MT-07 (FZ-07) and XSR models	5W
MT-07TR models	LED
Brake/tail light	LED
Turn signal lights	
UK models	10W amber
US models	
Front with running light	21/5W
Rear	21W
Licence plate light	5W
Instrument cluster illumination and warning lights	LED

Torque wrench settings

Alternator cover bolts	12 Nm
Alternator rotor bolt	70 Nm
Alternator stator bolts	10 Nm
CKP sensor bolts	10 Nm
Footrest bracket bolts	30 Nm
Oil pressure switch	15 Nm
Starter motor long bolts	5 Nm
Starter motor mounting bolts	10 Nm

1 General Information

1 All models have a 12 volt electrical system charged by a three-phase alternator, mounted on the left-hand end of the crankshaft, with a separate regulator/rectifier.

2 The regulator maintains the charging system output within the specified range to prevent overcharging, and the rectifier converts the ac (alternating current) output of the alternator to dc (direct current) to power the lights and other components and to charge the battery. The alternator rotor is mounted on the left-hand end of the crankshaft.

3 The starting system includes the starter motor, the battery, the relay and the various wires and switches. If the engine stop switch is in the RUN position and the ignition switch is ON, the starter relay allows the starter motor to operate only if the transmission is in neutral (neutral switch on) or, if the transmission is in gear, if the clutch lever is pulled into the handlebar and the sidestand is up. The starter motor is mounted on the top of the crankcase. **Note:** *Keep in mind that electrical parts, once purchased, cannot be returned. To avoid unnecessary expense, make very sure the faulty component has been positively identified before buying a replacement part.*

2 Electrical system fault finding

 Warning: To prevent the risk of short circuits, the battery negative (-ve) terminal should be disconnected before any of the bike's other electrical components are disturbed. Don't forget to reconnect the terminal securely once work is finished or if battery power is needed for circuit testing.

1 A typical electrical circuit consists of an electrical component, the switches, relays, etc, related to that component and the wiring and connectors that link the component to the battery and the frame.

2 Before tackling any troublesome electrical circuit, first study the wiring diagram thoroughly to get a complete picture of what makes up that individual circuit. Trouble spots, for instance, can often be narrowed down by noting if other components related to that circuit are operating properly or not. If several components or circuits fail at one time, chances are the fault lies either in the fuse or in a common earth (ground) connection, as several circuits are often routed through the same fuse and earth (ground) connections.

3 Electrical problems often stem from simple causes, such as loose or corroded connections or a blown fuse. Prior to any electrical fault finding, always visually check the condition of the fuse, wires and connections in the problem circuit. Intermittent failures can be especially frustrating, since you can't always duplicate the failure when it's convenient to test. In such situations, a good practice is to clean all connections in the affected circuit, whether or not they appear to be good. All of the connections and wires should also be wiggled to check for looseness which can cause intermittent failure.

4 If you don't have a multimeter it is highly

2.4a A digital multimeter can be used for all electrical tests

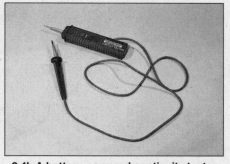

2.4b A battery-powered continuity tester

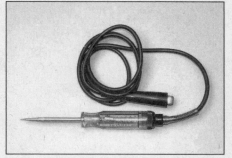

2.4c A simple test light is useful for voltage tests

advisable to obtain one – they are not expensive and will enable a full range of electrical tests to be made **(see illustration)**. Go for a modern digital one with LCD display as they are easier to use. A continuity tester and/or test light are useful for certain electrical checks as an alternative, though are limited in their usefulness compared to a multimeter **(see illustrations)**.

Continuity checks

5 The term continuity describes the uninterrupted flow of electricity through an electrical circuit. Continuity can be checked with a multimeter set either to its continuity function (a beep is emitted when continuity is found), or to the resistance (ohms/Ω) function, or with a dedicated continuity tester. Both instruments are powered by an internal battery, therefore the checks are made with the ignition OFF. As a safety precaution, always disconnect the battery negative (-) lead before making continuity checks, particularly if ignition system checks are being made.

6 If using a multimeter, select the continuity function if it has one, or the resistance (ohms) function. Touch the meter probes together and check that a beep is emitted or the meter reads zero, which indicates continuity. If there is no continuity there will be no beep or the meter will show infinite resistance. After using the meter, always switch it OFF to conserve its battery.

7 A continuity tester can be used in the same way – its light should come on or it should beep to indicate continuity in the switch ON

position, but should be off or silent in the OFF position.

8 Note that the polarity of the test probes doesn't matter for continuity checks, although care should be taken to follow specific test procedures if a diode or solid-state component is being checked.

Switch continuity checks

9 If a switch is at fault, trace its wiring to the wiring connectors. Separate the connectors and inspect them for security and condition. A build-up of dirt or corrosion here will most likely be the cause of the problem – clean up and apply a water dispersant such as WD40, or alternatively use a dedicated contact cleaner and protection spray.

10 If using a multimeter, select the continuity function if it has one, or the resistance (ohms) function, and connect its probes to the terminals in the connector **(see illustration)**. Simple ON/OFF type switches, such as brake light switches, only have two wires whereas combination switches, like the handlebar switches, have many wires. Study the wiring diagram to ensure that you are connecting to the correct pair of wires. Continuity should be indicated with the switch ON and no continuity with it OFF.

Wiring continuity checks

11 Many electrical faults are caused by damaged wiring, often due to incorrect routing or chaffing on frame components. Loose, wet or corroded wire connectors can also be the cause of electrical problems.

12 A continuity check can be made on a single length of wire by disconnecting it at each end and connecting the meter or continuity tester probes to each end of the wire **(see illustration)**. Continuity should be indicated if the wire is good. If no continuity is shown, suspect a broken wire.

13 To check for continuity to earth in any earth wire connect one probe of your meter or tester to the earth wire terminal in the connector and the other to the frame, engine, or battery earth (-) terminal. Continuity should be indicated if the wire is good. If no continuity is shown, suspect a broken wire or corroded or loose earth point (see below).

Voltage checks

14 A voltage check can determine whether power is reaching a component. Use a multimeter set to the dc (direct current) voltage scale to check for power from the battery or regulator/rectifier, or set to the ac (alternating current) voltage scale to check for power from the alternator. A test light can be used to check for dc voltage. The test light is the cheaper component, but the meter has the advantage of being able to give a voltage reading.

15 Connect the meter or test light in parallel, i.e. across the load **(see illustration)**.

16 First identify the relevant wiring circuit by referring to the wiring diagram at the end of this manual. If other electrical components share the same power supply (i.e. are fed from the same fuse), take note whether they are

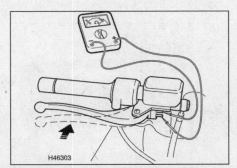

2.10 Continuity should be indicated across switch terminals when lever is operated

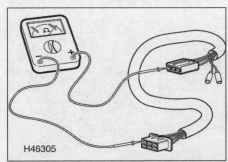

2.12 Wiring continuity check. Connect the meter probes across each end of the same wire

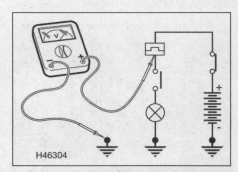

2.15 Voltage check. Connect the meter positive probe to the component and the negative probe to earth

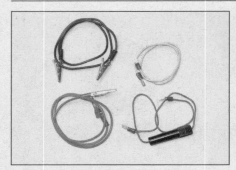

2.23 A selection of insulated jumper wires

3.2 Unscrew the four bolts and remove the bracket

3.3 Disconnect the negative terminal first, then the positive terminal (arrowed)

working correctly – this is useful information in deciding where to start checking the circuit.

17 If using a meter, check first that the meter leads are plugged into the correct terminals on the meter (red to positive (+), black to negative (-)). Set the meter to the appropriate volts function (dc or ac), where necessary at a range suitable for the battery voltage – 0 to 20 vdc. Connect the meter red probe (+) to the power supply wire and the black probe to a good metal earth (ground) on the motorcycle's frame or directly to the battery negative terminal. Battery voltage, or the specified voltage, should be shown on the meter with the ignition switch, and if necessary any other relevant switch, ON.

18 If using a test light (see illustration 2.4c), connect its positive (+) probe to the power supply terminal and its negative (-) probe to a good earth (ground) on the motorcycle's frame. With the switch, and if necessary any other relevant switch, ON, the test light should illuminate.

19 If no voltage is indicated, work back towards the power source continuing to check for voltage. When you reach a point where there is voltage, you know the problem lies between that point and your last check point.

Earth (ground) checks

20 Earth connections are made either directly to the engine or frame (such as the starter motor or ignition coil which only have a positive feed) or by a separate wire into the earth circuit of the wiring harness. Alternatively

a short earth wire is sometimes run from the component directly to the motorcycle's frame.

21 Corrosion is a common cause of a poor earth connection, as is a loose earth terminal fastener.

22 If total or multiple component failure is experienced, check the security of the main earth lead from the negative (-) terminal of the battery, the earth lead bolted to the engine, and the main earth point(s) on the frame. If corroded, dismantle the connection and clean all surfaces back to bare metal. Remake the connection and prevent further corrosion from forming by smearing battery terminal grease over the connection.

23 To check the earthing of a component, use an insulated jumper wire to temporarily bypass its earth connection (see illustration) – connect one end of the jumper wire to the earth terminal or metal body of the component and the other end to the motorcycle's frame. If the circuit works with the jumper wire installed, the earth circuit is faulty.

24 To check an earth wire first check for corroded or loose connections, then check the wiring for continuity (Step 13) between each connector in the circuit in turn, and then to its earth point, to locate the break.

3 Battery

Caution: Be extremely careful when handling or working around the battery. The electrolyte is very caustic and an

explosive gas (hydrogen) is given off when the battery is charging.

Removal and installation

1 On MT-07 (FZ-07) models remove the rider's seat, and on MT-07TR and XSR models remove the seat (see Chapter 7).

2 On MT-07 (FZ-07) and XSR models remove the seat bracket (see illustration). On XSR models release the diagnostic coupler from the battery cover, then undo the two screws and remove the cover.

3 Undo the negative (-) terminal screw first and disconnect the lead from the battery (see illustration). Lift up the insulating cover to access the positive (+) terminal, then undo the screw and disconnect the lead.

4 Release the rubber strap, noting how the positive lead passes through it, then lift the battery out (see illustrations).

5 Installation is the reverse of removal. Clean the battery terminals and lead ends with a wire brush, fine sandpaper or steel wool. Reconnect the leads, connecting the positive (+) terminal first.

Inspection and maintenance

6 The battery is a VRLA (valve-regulated lead acid) maintenance free (sealed) type, therefore requiring no regular maintenance. However, the following checks should still be performed.

7 Check the state of charge by measuring the voltage at the battery terminals (see illustration). Connect the voltmeter positive (+) probe to the battery positive (+) terminal, and

3.4a Unhook the strap...

3.4b and carefully lift the battery out – it is quite heavy

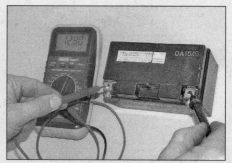

3.7 Checking battery voltage – connect the meter as shown

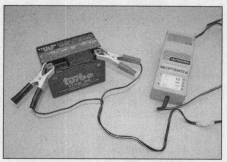

4.2a Battery connected to a charger

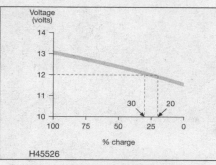

4.2b Open-circuit voltage will determine the percentage charge...

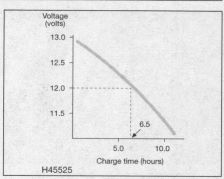

4.2c ...and the charging time required

the negative (–) probe to the battery negative (–) terminal. When fully charged there should be 12.8 volts present. If the voltage falls below 12 volts remove the battery (see above), and recharge it as described below in Section 4.

8 Check the battery terminals and leads are tight and free of corrosion. If corrosion is evident, clean the terminals as described in Step 5, then protect them from further corrosion.

9 Keep the battery case clean to prevent current leakage, which can discharge the battery over a period of time (especially when it sits unused). Wash the outside of the case with a solution of baking soda and water. Rinse the battery thoroughly, then dry it.

10 Look for cracks in the case and replace the battery with a new one if any are found. If acid has been spilled on the frame or battery box, neutralise it with a baking soda and water solution, then dry it thoroughly.

11 If the motorcycle sits unused for long periods of time, disconnect the leads from the battery terminals, negative (–) terminal first. Refer to Section 4 and charge the battery once every month to six weeks.

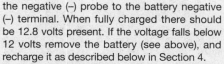

4 Battery charging

Caution: Be extremely careful when handling or working around the battery. The electrolyte is very caustic and an explosive gas (hydrogen) is given off when the battery is charging.

1 Check the charger is rated for a 12V battery.

2 Remove the battery (Section 3). If not already done, refer to Section 3, Step 7, and check the open circuit voltage of the battery. Refer to the chart **(see illustrations)** and read off the charging time required according to the voltage reading taken.

3 Connect the charger to the battery BEFORE switching the charger ON. Make sure that the positive (+) lead on the charger is connected to the positive (+) terminal on the battery, and the negative (-) lead is connected to the negative (-) terminal.

4 The battery should be charged at a rate of around 0.8 to 1.0 amp for up to 12 hours if it is completely flat, or until the voltage across the terminals reaches 12.8V – disconnect the charger and allow the battery to stabilise for 30 minutes after charging before taking a voltage reading. The actual time required depends on the initial voltage present. Exceeding this can cause the battery to overheat, buckling the plates and rendering it useless. It is best to use a dedicated motorcycle battery charger, preferably one of the 'intelligent' ones that constantly monitors the state of charge and controls its output accordingly. If a normal car type charger is used check that after a probable initial peak, the charge rate falls to a safe level consistent with the charge rate specified on the battery. If the battery becomes hot during charging stop. Further charging will cause damage. Many bike-specific chargers are designed for the maintenance and recovery of heavily discharged MF batteries. They are not too expensive, and are a worthwhile investment, especially if the bike is not used over winter. Follow the manufacturer's instructions.

5 If the recharged battery discharges rapidly when left disconnected it is likely that an internal short caused by physical damage or sulphation has occurred. A new battery will be required. A sound battery will tend to lose its charge at about 1% per day.

6 Install the battery (Section 3).

7 If the motorcycle sits unused for long periods of time, charge the battery once every month to six weeks and leave it disconnected. Note that many chargers contain a means of trickle charging the battery, allowing it to remain connected.

5 Fuses

1 The electrical system as a whole is protected by the main fuse, and individual circuits are protected by other fuses of different ratings (see Specifications). The main fuse is housed in the starter relay, which is under the rider's seat. All other fuses are housed in two fuseboxes, also under the rider's seat **(see illustration)**.

2 On MT-07 (FZ-07) models remove the rider's seat to access the main fuse and the fuses in the front fusebox, and also remove the passenger seat and the centre seat cowl to access the fuses in the rear fusebox (see Chapter 7). On MT-07TR and XSR models remove the seat to access all fuses (see Chapter 7).

3 To access the main fuse disconnect the starter relay wiring connector, then release and remove the cover **(see illustrations)**

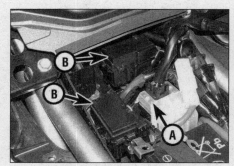

5.1 Main fuse (A), fuseboxes (B)

5.3a Disconnect the wiring...

5.3b ... and remove the cover

5.3c Main fuse (A), spare fuse (B)

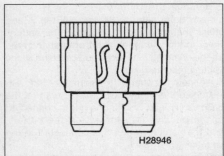

5.4 Unclip the fusebox lid to access the fuses within

5.5a Use suitable pliers to remove a fuse

H28946

5.5b A blown fuse can be identified by a break in its element

Note: *If the ignition is switched ON for any checks, remember to switch it OFF again before proceeding further or removing any electrical component from the system.*

Note: *Refer to Electrical system fault finding (Section 2) and to the Wiring Diagrams at the end of the Chapter when making electrical tests on any part of the system.*

1 If a bulb fails first check the bulb itself (see relevant Section), the bulb terminals in the holder, and the wiring connector. Next check the fuse (Section 5). If none of the lights work, check battery voltage – low voltage indicates either a faulty battery or a defective charging system. Refer to Section 3 for battery checks and Section 29 for charging system tests. If there is a problem with more than one circuit at the same time, or with all circuits, it is likely to be a fault relating to a multi-function component, such as the fuse or the ignition switch. When checking for a blown filament in a bulb, it is advisable to back up a visual check with a continuity test of the filament as it is not always apparent that a bulb has blown. When testing for continuity, remember that on single terminal bulbs it is the metal body of the bulb that is the earth (ground). Refer to Section 2 for details on testing electrical circuits.

Headlight

2 If a headlight beam fails to work, check the bulb and the bulb terminals and the wires in the connector first (Section 7). If the headlight does not work at all check the headlight fuse (Section 5), then check the relay (see below). Next check for battery voltage on the loom side of the connector with a test light or multimeter – connect the negative probe of the multimeter to a good earth and the positive probe to first the high beam (yellow wire) terminal and then the low beam (green wire) terminal with the ignition switch ON (see Wiring Diagrams at the end of this Chapter). Don't forget to select either high or low beam as appropriate at the handlebar switch while conducting this test.

3 If no voltage is indicated at either terminal, check the wiring and connectors between the headlight connector, the dimmer switch, the headlight relay and the fusebox, referring to Wiring Diagrams at the end of the chapter.

4 If voltage is indicated, check for continuity between the black wire connector terminal and earth (ground). If there is no continuity, check the earth (ground) circuit for an open or poor connection.

5 To check the headlight relay, on MT-07 (FZ-07) models remove the left-hand fuel tank side cover, on MT-07TR models remove the fuel tank cover, and on XSR models remove the left-hand air scoop and fuel tank side cover (see Chapter 4). Displace the regulator/rectifier (**see illustration**). Lift the relay off its mount and disconnect the wiring connector (**see illustration**).

– the fuse is on the right-hand side of the relay, and a spare is on the left (**see illustration**).

4 To access the fusebox fuses unclip the relevant fusebox lid – the identity, location and specified rating of each fuse is marked on the inside of each fusebox lid, and each fuse is marked with its rating (**see illustration**). A spare fuse of each rating is housed in the fusebox.

5 The fuses can be removed and checked visually. If you can't pull the fuse out with your fingertips, use a suitable pair of pliers (**see illustration**). A blown fuse is easily identified by a break in the element (**see illustration**), or can be tested for continuity using an ohmmeter or continuity tester – if there is no continuity, it has blown. Each fuse is clearly marked with its rating and must only be replaced by a fuse of the same rating. If a spare fuse is used, always replace it with a new one so that a spare of each rating is carried on the bike at all times.

⚠️ **Warning: Never put in a fuse of a higher rating or bridge the terminals with any other substitute, however temporary it may be. Serious damage may be done to the circuit, or a fire may start.**

6 If the new fuse blows, you need to check the relevant circuit and its components carefully for evidence of a short-circuit. Look for bare wires and chafed, melted or burned insulation.

7 Sometimes fuses blow for no specific reason, in which case replacing it with a new one is the only action required. Also corrosion of the fuse ends and fusebox terminals may occur and cause poor fuse contact. If this happens, remove the corrosion with a wire brush or emery paper, then spray the fuse end and terminals with electrical contact cleaner.

6.5a Unscrew the bolts (arrowed) and let the regulator/rectifier hang on its connectors

6.5b Removing the relay

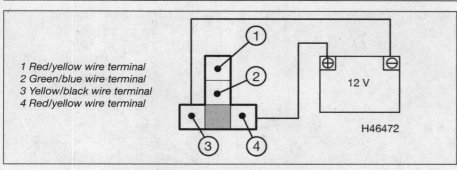

1 Red/yellow wire terminal
2 Green/blue wire terminal
3 Yellow/black wire terminal
4 Red/yellow wire terminal

12 V

H46472

6.6 Headlight relay test terminal identification

6 Using a continuity tester or a multimeter set to the resistance (ohms) range, test for continuity between the No. 1 red/yellow (positive meter probe) and No. 2 green/blue (negative meter probe) wire terminals on the relay **(see illustration)**. There should be no continuity (infinite resistance). Now, using insulated jumper wires and a fully charged 12V battery, connect the battery positive (+) terminal to the No. 4 red/yellow wire terminal on the relay and the battery negative (-) terminal to the No. 3 yellow/black wire terminal. Continuity (0 ohms) should now be shown on the meter. Note that it is important to differentiate between the two red/yellow wires.

7 If the relay does not operate as described, fit a new one.

Sidelight (Europe models)

MT-07 (FZ-07) and XSR models

8 If the sidelight fails to work, check the bulb and the bulb terminals and the wires in the bulbholder first (Section 7), and then check the signal fuse (Section 5).

9 Next check for battery voltage at the blue/red wire terminal on the loom side of the sidelight wiring connector, with the ignition switch ON.

10 If no voltage is indicated check the wiring between the sidelight and the fusebox (Section 18).

11 If voltage is indicated, check for continuity between the wiring connector terminals on the bulb side of the wiring connector and the corresponding terminals in the bulbholder; no continuity indicates a break in the circuit. If continuity is present, check for continuity between the black wire terminal and earth (ground). If there is no continuity, check the earth (ground) circuit for a broken or poor connection.

MT-07TR models

12 The sidelight is an LED. If the light fails to work, first check the signal fuse (Section 5), then the wiring connector (Section 8). If the LED fails a new headlight must be fitted.

Tail light

13 The tail lights are LEDs. If no fault can be found after making the following checks a new tail light must be fitted.

14 If the tail light fails to work, check the signal fuse (Section 5). Next, refer to Section 10 and disconnect the tail light wiring connector. Check for battery voltage at the blue/red wire terminal on the loom side of the connector, with the ignition switch ON.

15 If no voltage is indicated, check the wiring between the tail light connector and the fusebox.

16 If voltage is indicated, check for continuity between the black wire terminal and earth (ground). If there is no continuity, check the earth (ground) circuit for a broken or poor connection.

Brake light

17 The tail lights are LEDs. If no fault can be found after making the following checks a new tail light must be fitted.

18 If the brake light fails to work, check the signal fuse (Section 5). Next, refer to Section 10 and disconnect the tail light wiring connector. Check for battery voltage at the yellow wire terminal on the loom side of the connector, with the ignition switch ON and the brake lever or pedal applied.

19 If no voltage is indicated, check the brake light switches (see Section 14), then the wiring between the brake/tail light and the switches, then from the switches to the fusebox.

20 If voltage is indicated, check for continuity between the black wire terminal and earth (ground). If there is no continuity, check the earth (ground) circuit for a broken or poor connection.

Licence plate light

21 If the licence plate light fails to work, check the bulb and the bulb terminals and the wires in the bulbholder first (see Section 9), and then check the signal fuse (Section 5). Next, remove the (passenger) seat, and on MT-07 (FZ-07) models the centre seat cowl (see Chapter 7) and disconnect the licence plate light wiring connector **(see illustrations)**. Check for battery voltage at the blue or blue/red (according to model) wire terminal on the loom side of the connector, with the ignition switch ON.

22 If no voltage is indicated, check the wiring between the connector and the fusebox.

23 If voltage is indicated, check for continuity between the black wire terminal and earth (ground). If there is no continuity, check the earth (ground) circuit for a broken or poor connection.

Turn signal lights

24 If one light fails to work, check the bulb and the bulb terminals (Section 12), then the wiring connector. If none of the turn signals work, check the parking/lighting fuse (Section 5).

25 If the fuse is good, check the turn signal relay (Section 11).

Instrument cluster lights

26 See Section 17.

6.21a Licence plate light wiring connector – MT-07 (FZ-07) models

6.21b Licence plate light wiring connector – MT-07TR models

6.21c License plate light wiring connector (arrowed) – XSR models

7.2 Remove the cover

7.3a Release the clip...

7.3b ...and remove the bulb

7.8a Release the wire...

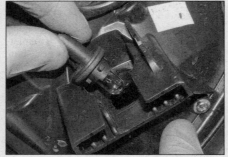

7.8b ... then release the bulbholder

7.9 Pull the bulb out of the holder

7 Headlight and sidelight bulbs

Caution: The headlight bulb is of the quartz-halogen type. Do not touch the bulb glass as skin acids will shorten the bulb's service life. If the bulb is accidentally touched, it should be wiped carefully when cold with a rag soaked in methylated spirit and dried before fitting.

MT-07 (FZ-07) models

Headlight bulb

1 Remove the headlight (Section 8).

2 Remove the rubber cover from the back of the headlight **(see illustration)**.
3 Release the bulb retaining clip, noting how it fits, then remove the bulb from the back of the headlight **(see illustrations)**.
4 Fit the new bulb, bearing in mind the information in the Caution above. Make sure the tabs on the bulb flange are aligned with the slots in the back of the headlight, and secure the bulb in position with the retaining clip.
5 Fit the cover.
6 Install the headlight (Section 8). Check the operation of the headlight.

Sidelight bulb (Europe models)

7 Remove the headlight (Section 8).
8 Release the wire from the guide, then turn the bulbholder anti-clockwise and draw it out of the headlight **(see illustrations)**.
9 Carefully pull the bulb out of its holder **(see illustration)**.
10 Align the new bulb with its socket and press it into place. Fit the bulbholder into the headlight and turn it clockwise to lock the tabs. Fit the wire in the guide.
11 Install the headlight. Check the operation of the sidelight.

MT-07TR models

Headlight bulbs

12 Remove the cover from the relevant beam by turning it anti-clockwise **(see illustration)**.
13 Disconnect the wiring connector **(see illustration)**.

7.12 Remove the cover

7.13 Pull the wiring connector off

7.14a Release the clip...

7.14b ...and remove the bulb

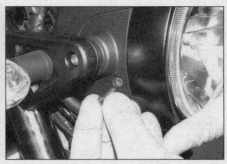

7.20a Remove the screw on each side of the shell

14 Release the bulb retaining clip, noting how it fits, then remove the bulb from the back of the headlight **(see illustrations)**.

15 Fit the new bulb, bearing in mind the information in the Caution above. Make sure the tabs on the bulb flange are aligned with the slots in the back of the headlight, and secure the bulb in position with the retaining clip.

16 Connect the wiring.

17 Align the tabs on the cover with the slots in the headlight and fit the cover, then turn it clockwise to lock it.

18 Check the operation of the headlight.

Sidelight

19 The sidelight is an LED – if it fails fit a new headlight (Section 8).

XSR models

Headlight bulb

20 Undo the screw on each side and displace the headlight from the shell, then disconnect the headlight and sidelight wiring connectors and remove the headlight **(see illustrations)**.

21 Remove the rubber cover from the back of the headlight **(see illustration)**.

22 Release the bulb retaining clip, noting how it fits, then remove the bulb **(see illustrations)**.

23 Fit the new bulb, bearing in mind the information in the Caution above. Make sure the tabs on the bulb flange are aligned with the slots in the back of the headlight, and

secure the bulb in position with the retaining clip.

24 Fit the dust cover so that the TOP mark is uppermost **(see illustration 7.21)**.

25 Reconnect the wiring. Fit the headlight into the shell, locating the tab on the top behind the rib on the shell **(see illustration)**. Fit the screws. Check the operation of the headlight.

Sidelight bulb (Europe models)

26 Undo the screw on each side and displace the headlight from the shell, then disconnect the headlight and sidelight wiring connectors and remove the headlight **(see illustrations 7.20a, b and c)**.

27 Pull the sidelight bulbholder from the

7.20b Disconnect the headlight wiring...

7.20c ... and the sidelight wiring

7.21 Remove the cover

7.22a Release the clip...

7.22b ...and remove the bulb

7.25 Tab at top locates behind lug inside the shell

7.27a Pull the bulbholder out…

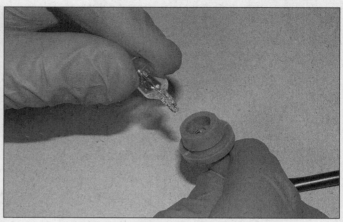

7.27b …and pull the bulb from the holder

headlight and pull the bulb out of its holder **(see illustrations)**.

28 Align the new bulb with its socket in the bulbholder and press it into place. Fit the bulbholder into the headlight.

29 Reconnect the wiring **(see illustrations 7.20c and b)**. Fit the headlight into the shell, locating the tab on the top behind the rib on the shell **(see illustration 7.25)**. Fit the screws **(see illustration 7.20a)**. Check the operation of the sidelight.

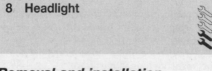

8 Headlight

Removal and installation

MT-07 (FZ-07) models

1 Undo the screw on each side of the headlight assembly and move the top of the headlight forwards (it will pivot on the bottom mount) **(see illustration)**. Open the upper section of the rubber connector cover and disconnect the turn signal wiring connectors **(see illustration)**. Move the headlight some more and disconnect the sidelight and headlight wiring connectors, then lift the headlight off the bottom mount, noting how it locates over the rubbers, and remove it **(see illustrations)**.

2 If required remove the turn signal

8.1a Undo the screw on each side and move the headlight forwards

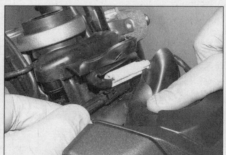

8.1b Open the top rubber flap and disconnect the turn signal connectors…

8.1c … then disconnect the sidelight connector…

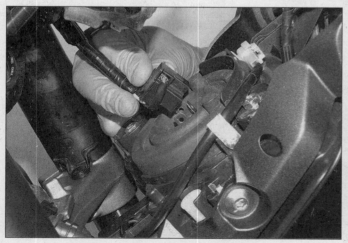

8.1d … and the headlight connector…

8.1e … and draw the headlight off the bottom mount

8.2a Undo the three screws...

8.2b ... to remove each turn signal holder. Note the collars in the side mount grommets

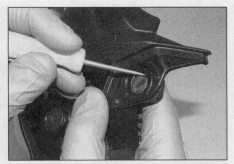

8.2c Carefully feed the rim of each top wellnut through...

8.2d ... to release the centre cover

8.3 Correct fitting of the rubber connector cover

8.5 Disconnect the headlight connector

holders, then remove the centre cover **(see illustrations)**.

3 Installation is the reverse of removal. Check the rubber supports are in place **(see illustration 8.1e)**. Make sure the wiring is securely connected. Pull the centre peg of the rubber connector cover up through the hole in the top flap so the bottom rim of the peg is seated on the top of the flap to keep it closed **(see illustration)**. Check the operation of the headlight and sidelight. Check the headlight aim.

MT-07TR models

4 Remove the fairing side panels and inner panels (see Chapter 7).
5 Refer to Section 15 and displace the instruments so you can access the back, and

8.6a Undo the screw on the underside...

8.6b ... and the screws on each side...

disconnect the headlight wiring connector **(see illustration)**.

6 Undo the headlight cover screws and remove the cover **(see illustrations)**.

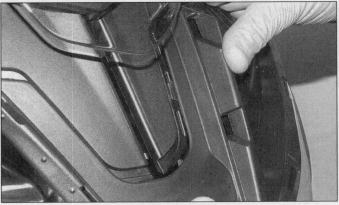

8.6c ... then release the tabs...

8.6d ... and remove the cover

8.7a Headlight is secured by two bolts on each side

8.7b Feed the wiring out as you remove the headlight, noting its routing

8.9 Undo the screw on the bottom and on each side at the top

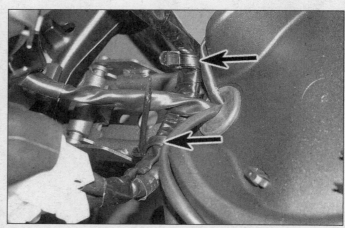

8.10a Release the ties (arrowed)...

7 Unscrew the headlight bolts and remove the headlight (see illustrations).

8 Installation is the reverse of removal. Make sure all the wiring is correctly connected and secured. Check the operation of the headlight and sidelight. Check the headlight aim.

XSR models
Complete headlight assembly removal

9 Undo the three screws securing the headlight stay to the top and bottom yokes and pivot the headlight forwards (see illustration).

10 Release the ignition switch wiring ties from the stay, then disconnect the headlight sub-loom wiring connector and lift the headlight assembly off the bottom bracket, noting how it locates (see illustrations).

8.10b ... and disconnect the wiring ...

8.10c ... then lift the headlight stay off the bracket, noting how it locates

8.12 Turn signal connectors (arrowed)

8.13a Unscrew the bolt on each side…

8.13b … lift the shell off the peg…

Headlight and shell removal

11 Undo the screw on each side and displace the headlight from the shell, then disconnect the headlight and sidelight wiring connectors and remove the headlight **(see illustrations 7.20a, b and c)**.

12 Disconnect the turn signal wiring connectors **(see illustration)**.

13 Unscrew the bolt securing each side of the shell **(see illustration)**. Lift the shell off the peg on the bracket and draw the turn signal wiring out through the holes in the back of the shell **(see illustrations)**. Disconnect the headlight/turn signal sub-loom wiring connector and remove the shell **(see illustration 8.10b)**. Note the sleeve in each side grommet. If required release the sub-loom from the clip inside the shell and remove it **(see illustration 8.12)**.

14 If required remove the headlight brackets/turn signal assemblies from the stay **(see illustration)**.

Installation

15 Installation is the reverse of removal. Make sure all the wiring is correctly connected and secured. Check the operation of the headlight, sidelight and turn signals. Check the headlight aim.

Headlight aim adjustment

Note: *An improperly adjusted headlight may cause problems for oncoming traffic or provide poor, unsafe illumination of the road ahead. Before adjusting the headlight aim, be sure to consult with local traffic laws and regulations – for UK models refer to MOT Test Checks in the Reference section.*

8.13c … and draw the turn signal wiring out

16 The headlight beam can adjusted both horizontally and vertically. Before making any adjustment, check that the tyre pressures are correct. Make any adjustments to the headlight aim with the machine on level ground, with the fuel tank half full and with an assistant sitting on the seat. If the bike is usually ridden with a passenger on the back, have a second assistant to do this.

MT-07 (FZ-07) models

17 The headlight adjusters are located on the back of the headlight, with the vertical adjuster on the lower left-hand side and the horizontal adjuster on the upper right-hand side **(see illustrations)** – turn the adjuster screws using a Phillips screwdriver inserted in the channel so it engages the teeth in the rim.

18 Turn the vertical adjuster clockwise to

8.14 Headlight bracket bolts (arrowed)

move the beam down, and anti-clockwise to move it up.

19 Turn the horizontal adjuster clockwise to move the beam to the right, and anti-clockwise to move it to the left.

MT-07TR models

20 The headlight adjusters are located on the back of the headlight on each side, and each beam can be adjusted individually **(see illustration)**. You can turn the adjusters using a Phillips screwdriver.

21 Turn the vertical adjuster clockwise to move the beam down, and anti-clockwise to move it up.

22 Turn the horizontal adjuster clockwise to move the beam to the right, and anti-clockwise to move it to the left.

XSR models

23 The headlight adjusters are located on the side of the headlight, with the vertical

8.17a Adjusting vertical alignment

8.17b Adjusting horizontal alignment

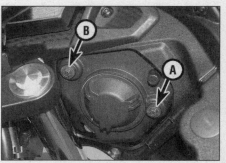

8.20 Vertical adjuster screw (A), horizontal adjuster screw (B) – right-hand unit

8.23a Adjusting vertical alignment

8.23b Adjusting horizontal alignment

adjuster on the lower right-hand side and the horizontal adjuster on the lower left-hand side **(see illustrations)**. You can turn the adjusters using a Phillips screwdriver.

24 Turn the vertical adjuster clockwise to move the beam up, and anti-clockwise to move it down.

25 Turn the horizontal adjuster clockwise to move the beam to the right, and anti-clockwise to move it to the left.

9 Licence plate light

1 On XSR models remove the cover from the underside of the tail unit **(see illustrations)**.
2 On all models undo the licence plate light nuts, remove the washers on MT-07 (FZ-07) and XSR models, and displace the light **(see illustrations)**.
3 Pull the bulbholder out, then pull the bulb out of the holder **(see illustrations)**.
4 Align the new bulb with its holder and push it in, then push the holder into the light.
5 Make sure the collars are in place in the rubber grommets **(see illustration)**. Fit the light and secure it with the nuts, not forgetting the washers on MT-07 (FZ-07) and XSR models. Check the operation of the light.
6 On XSR models fit the tail cover **(see illustrations 9.1b and a)**.

10 Tail light

MT-07 (FZ-07) models

1 Remove the seat cowls (see Chapter 7).
2 Disconnect the wiring connector, and release the wiring **(see illustration)**.
3 Undo the tail light screws and remove the

9.1a Undo the screws (arrowed)...

9.1b ... and remove the cover

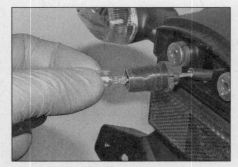

9.2a Undo the nuts ...

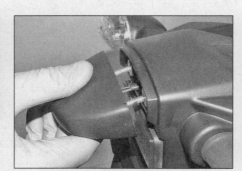

9.2b ... and displace the light

9.3a Pull the bulbholder out...

9.3b ...then pull the bulb from the holder

9.5 Collars fit in the grommets

10.2 Disconnect and release the wiring

10.3 Undo the two screws, noting the sleeves

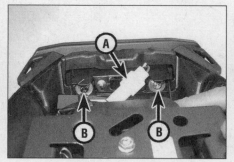

10.6 Tail light wiring connector (A) and screws (B)

10.10a Release the outer cable from the bracket and disconnect the cable end from the lever

10.10b Release the catch and lift the fusebox off

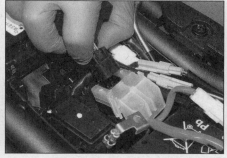

10.10c Disconnect the relay connector...

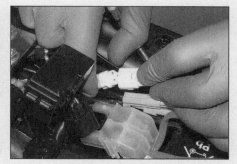

10.10d ... then lift the tail light connector out and disconnect it

light **(see illustration)**. Note the sleeves in the grommets.

4 Installation is the reverse of removal. Check the grommets are in good condition and the sleeves are fitted in them. Check the operation of the tail light and brake light.

MT-07TR models

5 Remove the seat cowls (see Chapter 7).
6 Disconnect the wiring connector **(see illustration)**.
7 Undo the tail light screws and remove the light **(see illustration 10.6)**. Note the collars in the grommets.
8 Installation is the reverse of removal. Check the grommets are in good condition and the collars are fitted in them. Check the operation of the tail light and brake light.

XSR models

9 Remove the seat (see Chapter 7).
10 Disconnect the seat lock cable **(see illustration)**. Displace the rear fusebox **(see illustration)**. Disconnect the starter relay wiring connector, then disconnect the tail light wiring connector **(see illustrations)**.
11 Undo the four exposed top cover screws, then undo the tail section mounting screws, drop the tail section to expose the fifth top cover screw and undo it, then remove the top cover, noting the routing of the tail light wiring, and allow the bottom section to rest on the wheel **(see illustrations)**.
12 Release the tail light wiring, then unscrew the nuts and remove the tail light **(see illustration)**. Note the collars in the rubber damper.

13 Installation is the reverse of removal. Check the collars are fitted in the damper. Check the operation of the tail light and brake light.

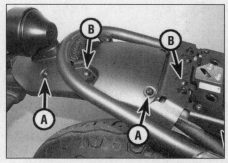

10.11a Undo the top cover screws (A) and the tail section screws (B) on each side...

10.11b ... and the top cover screw in the middle...

10.11c ... and remove the cover and tail light

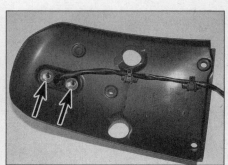

10.12 Release the wiring from the ties. Tail light nuts (arrowed)

11.3 Turn signal relay (arrowed)

12.1 Undo the screw and remove the lens

12.2 Release and remove the bulb

11 Turn signal circuit check

1 Most turn signal problems are the result of a burned-out bulb or corroded socket. This is especially true when the turn signals function properly in one direction, but fail to flash in the other direction. First check the bulbs and the sockets (Section 12) and the wiring connectors (Section 13). If none of the signals work check the parking/lighting fuse (Section 5).

2 If all is good, on MT-07 (FZ-07) models remove the left-hand fuel tank side cover, on MT-07TR models remove the fuel tank cover, and on XSR models remove the left-hand air scoop (see Chapter 7), and check the turn signal relay as follows.

3 Pull the relay off the mounting bracket and disconnect the wiring connector (see illustration).

4 Using a voltmeter, check for battery voltage between the blue/red wire terminal in the connector and earth (ground) with the ignition ON. If no voltage is indicated, refer to the appropriate wiring diagram at the end of this Chapter and check the wiring between the relay and fusebox for continuity.

5 If voltage is indicated, reconnect the relay connector. Check for a fluctuating voltage between the brown/white wire terminal in the connector and earth (ground).

6 If no voltage is indicated, replace the relay with a new one.

7 If voltage is indicated, check the wiring between the relay, turn signal switch and turn signal lights for continuity, then check the switch (Section 19).

12 Turn signal bulbs

1 Undo the turn signal lens screw and remove the lens (see illustration).

2 Push the bulb into the holder and twist it anti-clockwise to remove it (see illustration).

3 Make sure that the terminals inside the bulbholder are clean and free from corrosion.

4 Line up the pins of the new bulb with the slots in the holder, then push the bulb in and turn it clockwise until it locks into place – note that the amber bulbs fitted in Europe, and dual filament bulbs fitted on US models for the front running lights, have offset pins to prevent replacement with clear lens or single filament bulbs, and so can only be fitted one way in their holders.

5 Fit the lens – do not overtighten the screw as the lens or threads could be damaged.

13 Turn signal assemblies

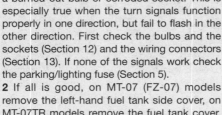

13.2a Right-hand turn signal wiring connector (arrowed)

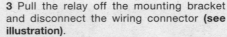

13.2b Left-hand turn signal connector is in the cover (arrowed) – cut the cable-ties to open it

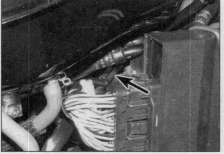

13.2c Slacken the screws (arrowed)...

13.2d ... and release the wiring

Front

1 On MT-07 (FZ-07) models undo the screw on each side of the headlight assembly and move the top of the headlight forwards (it will pivot on the bottom mount) (see illustration 8.1a). Open the upper section of the rubber connector cover and disconnect the turn signal wiring connectors (see illustration 8.1b). Undo the turn signal holder screws and remove the holder (see illustration 8.2a). Note the collars in the side mount grommets.

2 On MT-07TR (FZ-07) models remove the fuel tank to access the wiring connector for the right-hand turn signal (see Chapter 4) (see illustration). To access the wiring connector for the left-hand turn signal remove the fuel tank cover (see Chapter 7), then cut the cable-ties on the connector cover behind the relay unit and open the cover (see illustration). Release the wiring and feed it to the turn signal, noting its routing, and slacken the hand guard clamp screws to release the wiring from the clamp (see illustrations).

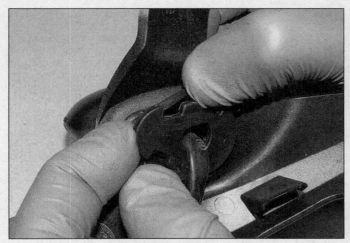

13.4a Remove the plate...

13.4b ...and remove the turn signal

3 On XSR models remove the headlight and shell (Section 8).

4 Unclip the mounting plate from the inner end of the turn signal stem, then ease the signal assembly out, noting how it locates **(see illustrations)**.

5 Installation is the reverse of removal. Make sure the mounting plate tabs locate in the slots in the turn signal. Check the operation of the turn signals.

Rear

6 On MT-07 (FZ-07) models remove the centre section of the seat cowl (see Chapter 7). Disconnect and release the turn signal wiring **(see illustration)**. Undo the screws securing the tail bracket to the underside and remove the tail section, drawing the wiring down and noting its routing. Undo the screws and remove the turn signal/licence plate holder from the brackets.

7 On MT-07TR models remove the seat (see Chapter 7). Disconnect and release the turn signal wiring **(see illustration)**. Undo the front screws securing the tail bracket to the underside and slacken the rear ones, then release the plastic cover and feed the wiring down, noting its routing **(see illustrations)**. Undo the eight screws and remove the turn signal/licence plate holder from the brackets **(see illustrations)**.

8 On XSR models remove the cover from the underside of the tail unit **(see illustrations 9.1a and b)**. Remove the seat (see Chapter 7). Disconnect the seat lock cable **(see illustration 10.10a)**. Displace the rear fusebox **(see illustration 10.10b)**. Disconnect the starter relay wiring connector **(see illustration 10.10c)**, then disconnect the turn

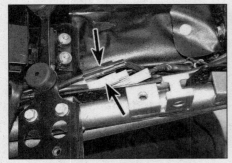

13.6 Turn signal wiring connectors (arrowed)

13.7a Turn signal wiring connectors (arrowed)

13.7b Undo the front screws, slacken the rear ones

13.7c Remove the plastic cover to access the wiring

13.7d Undo the screws (arrowed) on each side...

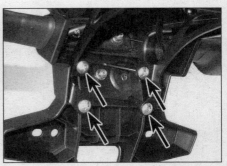

13.7e ...and the screws (arrowed)

13.8a Turn signal wiring connectors (arrowed)

13.8b Undo the screws and release the wiring

13.8c Secure the tail section back up

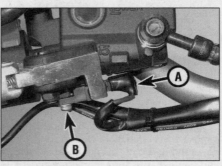

14.2 Front brake light switch wiring connectors (A) and screw (B)

14.4a Rear brake light switch (arrowed)

14.4b Rear brake light switch wiring connector (arrowed)

14.11 Unscrew the bolts and displace the bracket

14.12 Unhook the spring (A) then push the tabs (B) in to release the switch

signal wiring connectors **(see illustration)**. Undo the four exposed top cover screws, then undo the tail section mounting screws, drop the tail section to expose the fifth top cover screw and undo it, then remove the

top cover, noting the routing of the tail light wiring **(see illustrations 10.11a, b and c)**. Release the turn signal wiring clips and draw the wiring down through the hole, then secure the tail section back to the

frame with one or two screws **(see illustrations)**.
9 Unclip the mounting plate from the inner end of the turn signal stem, then ease the signal assembly out **(see illustrations 13.4a and b)**.
10 Installation is the reverse of removal. Make sure that the wiring is properly routed, secured and connected. Check the operation of the turn signals.

14 Brake light switches

Check

1 Before checking the switches, check the brake light circuit (Section 6).
2 The front brake light switch is mounted on the underside of the brake master cylinder. Disconnect the wiring connectors from the switch **(see illustration)**.
3 Using a continuity tester, connect its probes to the terminals of the switch **(see illustration 2.10)**. With the brake lever at rest, there should be no continuity. With the brake lever applied, there should be continuity. If the switch does not behave as described, replace it with a new one (the switch is not adjustable).
4 The rear brake light switch is mounted on the inside of the rider's right-hand footrest bracket **(see illustration)**. To access the switch wiring connector remove the right-hand frame cover (see Chapter 7). Trace the wiring from the switch and disconnect it at the two-pin connector **(see illustration)**.
5 Using a continuity tester, connect the probes to the two terminals on the switch side of the wiring connector. With the brake pedal at rest, there should be no continuity. With the brake pedal applied, there should be continuity. If the switch does not behave as described, replace it with a new one.

Removal and installation

Front brake light switch

6 Disconnect the wiring connectors from the switch **(see illustration 14.2)**.
7 Undo the switch screw and remove the switch.
8 Installation is the reverse of removal. Check the operation of the switch.

Rear brake light switch

9 Remove the right-hand frame cover (see Chapter 7).
10 Disconnect the switch wiring connector **(see illustration 14.4b)**. Feed the wiring down to the switch, noting its routing.
11 Unscrew the footrest bracket bolts and remove the washers, then displace the bracket so you have access to the back **(see illustration)**.
12 Detach the lower end of the switch spring from the brake pedal arm, then release the adjuster nut tabs on the underside of the bracket and pull the switch out **(see illustration)**.

13 Installation is the reverse of removal. When fitting the footrest bracket, locate the grommet in the inner side over the peg on the inner bracket, then fit the bolts with their washers and tighten them to 30 Nm **(see illustration)**. Check the operation of the switch and adjust as necessary (see Chapter 1 Section 14).

15 Instrument removal and installation

MT-07 (FZ-07) models

1 Unscrew the instrument bracket bolts, displace the instruments, pull the rubber cover back and disconnect the wiring connector **(see illustrations)**.
2 If required undo the screws on the underside and lift the instruments off the bracket **(see illustration)**.
3 Installation is the reverse of removal. Make sure the wiring connector is secure. Check the operation of the instruments before riding the motorcycle.

MT-07TR models

4 Release and remove the two trim clips and undo the two screws securing the instrument surround panel **(see illustration)**.
5 Displace the instrument assembly, release the headlight wiring connector and disconnect the instrument wiring connector **(see illustrations)**.
6 If required undo the screws on the underside and lift the instruments out of the surround panel **(see illustration)**.
7 Installation is the reverse of removal. Make sure the wiring connector is secure. Check the operation of the instruments before riding the motorcycle.

XSR models

8 Unscrew the instrument bracket bolts, displace the instruments, pull the rubber cover

14.13 Seat the grommet over the peg (arrowed)

15.1a Unscrew the bolts …

15.1b … displace the instruments and disconnect the wiring

15.2 Instrument screws (arrowed)

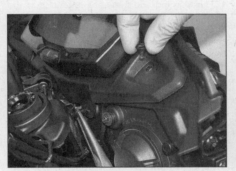

15.4 Release the trim clip and undo the screw on each side

15.5a Release the headlight connector …

15.5b … and disconnect the instrument connector

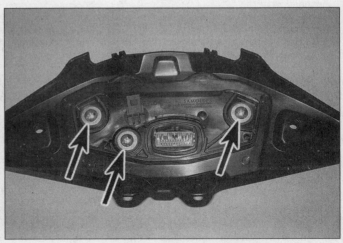

15.6 Instrument screws (arrowed)

15.8a Unscrew the bolts...

15.8b ... displace the instruments and disconnect the wiring

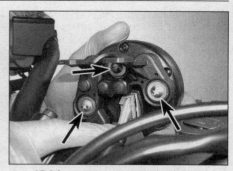

15.9 Instrument screws (arrowed)

back and disconnect the wiring connector **(see illustrations)**.

9 If required undo the screws on the underside and lift the instruments off the bracket **(see illustration)**.

10 Installation is the reverse of removal. Make sure the wiring connector is secure. Check the operation of the instruments before riding the motorcycle.

16 Instrument check

1 If all instrument and display functions fail at the same time, check the ignition fuse (Section 5) and the wiring and connectors, referring to Section 15 and the Wiring Diagrams at the end of this Chapter.

2 The warning and indicator functions (oil pressure, fuel level, gear position, engine trouble warning, neutral, high beam and turn signals) are all illuminated by LEDs (Section 17).

3 The oil pressure, fuel level, coolant temperature and speedometer displays are controlled by the appropriate sensor. If a display fails or is thought to be faulty, refer to the test details for the sensor as follows:

● Oil pressure switch – refer to Section 25 for test details.

● Gear position sensor – refer to Section 20 for test details

● Coolant temperature sensor – refer to Chapter 3 for test details.

● Fuel level sensor – refer to Chapter 4 for test details.

● Speed sensor – refer to Chapter 4 for test details.

4 If a display is proved to be faulty, a new instrument unit will have to be fitted (Section 15).

5 No test details are available for the tachometer.

17 Warning and indicator lights

1 The warning and indicator functions of the instruments are all illuminated by LEDs.

2 The LEDs illuminate when the functions are selected by the appropriate switch or sensor. If an indicator does not illuminate, first check the switch or sensor, then test the LED as described below.

3 The oil pressure warning light should come on when the ignition is switched ON, and then go off briefly, then come on again, and then go off when the engine is started. If the light does not go off when the engine is started, or comes on while the engine is running, stop the engine immediately and check the oil level (see *Pre-ride checks*). If the level is good, check the pressure switch, and if the switch is good carry out an oil pressure check (see Chapter 2).

4 The engine trouble warning light and coolant temperature warning light should come on for a few seconds when the ignition is switched

ON as a check of the LED, and then go off. The same applies to the immobiliser light, where fitted.

5 On models with ABS, the ABS light should come on for a few seconds when the ignition is switched ON as a check of the LED, and go off when the bike reaches a speed of 6 mph (10 kmh). If the light does not come on, does not go off, or starts flashing, refer to Chapter 6.

6 If an LED is thought to be faulty (after checking the appropriate switch or sensor and wiring) have the instrument cluster checked by a Yamaha dealer.

7 If an LED has failed a new instrument cluster will have to be fitted.

18 Ignition switch

 Warning: To prevent the risk of short circuits, disconnect the battery negative (–) lead before making any ignition switch checks.

Check

1 On MT-07 (FZ-07) models remove the fuel tank (see Chapter 4) – the ignition switch, and where fitted the immobiliser, wiring connectors are next to the frame **(see illustration)**.

2 On MT-07TR (FZ-07) models remove the fuel tank cover (see Chapter 7), then cut the cable-ties on the connector cover behind the relay unit and open the cover **(see illustration 13.2b)** – the ignition switch, and where fitted the immobiliser, wiring connectors are inside the cover.

3 On XSR models undo the three screws securing the headlight stay to the top and bottom yokes and pivot the headlight forwards **(see illustration 8.9)** – the ignition switch, and where fitted the immobiliser, wiring connectors are inside the rubber boot on the right-hand side **(see illustration)**.

4 Disconnect the ignition switch connectors. Using a multimeter or a continuity tester, make the checks on the switch side of the connector. Check the continuity of the connector terminal pairs (see Wiring Diagrams

18.1 Ignition switch and immobiliser wiring connectors (arrowed)

18.3 Ignition switch and immobiliser wiring connectors

18.11a Slacken the clamp bolt on each side…

18.11b … and the adjuster nut clamp bolt

at the end of this Chapter). Continuity should exist between the terminals connected by a solid line on the diagram when the switch key is turned to the indicated position.

5 If the switch fails any of the tests, replace it with a new one.

Removal

Note: *The ignition switch is not listed as being available on its own, but comes with a new seat lock and fuel tank cap, and on models with an immobiliser system it comes with a new immobiliser receiver and ECU (the receiver and ECU are available separately and individually, but the switch is not, with obvious implications to the cost!).*

6 Disconnect the battery negative (–) lead.

7 Remove the fuel tank cover(s) (see Chapter 7), and for best access remove the fuel tank (see Chapter 4).

8 Refer to Step 1, 2 or 3 above, according to model, and disconnect the ignition switch

19.2a Open the bottom flap…

19.2b … right-hand switch wiring connector (A), left-hand switch wiring connector (B)

and immobiliser wiring connectors. Feed the wiring back to the switch, noting its routing.

9 On MT-07 (FZ-07) models remove the instruments and the headlight assembly and on XSR models remove the instruments and the complete headlight assembly (Section 15 and Section 8).

10 Release the cables, wiring and hose from the guide(s) on the top yoke, noting their routing. Displace the handlebars (see Chapter 5).

11 Slacken the fork clamp bolts in the top yoke and the steering head bearing adjuster nut clamp bolt (see illustrations). Lift the top yokeup off the steering stem.

12 Two single-use shear-head security bolts mount the ignition switch to the underside of the top yoke. The heads of the bolts must be tapped around using a suitable drift such as a cold chisel, or drilled off, before the switch can be removed. To do this, mount the yoke in a vice equipped with padded soft jaws to avoid damaging the yoke. Remove the bolts, noting how the guide bracket is secured, then withdraw the switch from the top yoke. New bolts must be used.

13 Where fitted, remove the immobiliser transceiver.

Installation

14 Installation is the reverse of removal, noting the following:

● Obtain the correct type shear-head bolts from a Yamaha dealer – do not use another type of bolt. Do not forget to fit the cable guide. Tighten the bolts until their heads shear off.

● Make sure the wiring is securely connected and correctly routed.

19.3 Right-hand switch wiring connector (arrowed) – shown with fuel tank in place

● Tighten the steering head bearing adjuster nut clamp bolt and then the fork clamp bolts to the torque settings given in the Specifications at the beginning of Chapter 5.

19 Handlebar switches

Check

1 Generally speaking, the handlebar switch units are reliable and trouble-free. Most problems are caused by dirty or corroded contacts, but wear and breakage of internal parts is a possibility that should not be overlooked. If breakage does occur, the entire switch unit and related wiring harness will have to be replaced with a new one, as individual parts are not available. The switches can be checked for continuity using a multimeter or a continuity tester.

2 On MT-07 (FZ-07) models undo the screw on each side of the headlight assembly **(see illustration 8.1a)**. Move the top of the headlight forwards (it will pivot on the bottom mount), then open the upper section of the rubber connector cover and disconnect the turn signal wiring connectors **(see illustration 8.1b)**. Move the headlight some more and disconnect the sidelight wiring connector **(see illustration 8.1c)** – the headlight can stay in that position supported on the bottom pivot with the headlight wiring connected. Open the lower section of the connector cover to access the handlebar switch wiring connectors **(see illustrations)**.

3 On MT-07TR (FZ-07) models remove the fuel tank to access the wiring connector for the right-hand switches (see Chapter 4) **(see illustration)**. To access the wiring connector for the left-hand switches remove the fuel tank cover (see Chapter 7), then cut the cable-ties on the connector cover behind the relay unit and open the cover **(see illustration 13.2b)**.

4 On XSR models undo the three screws securing the headlight stay to the top and bottom yokes and pivot the headlight forwards **(see illustration 8.9)** – the handlebar switch wiring connectors are inside the rubber connector cover below the ignition switch **(see illustration)**.

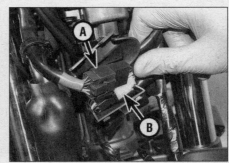

19.4 Open the rubber cover – right-hand switch wiring connector (A), left-hand switch wiring connector (B)

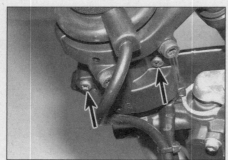

19.10a Right-hand switch housing screws (arrowed)

19.10b Left-hand switch housing screws (arrowed)

5 Disconnect the wiring connector for the switch being checked. Check for continuity between the terminals of the switch harness with the switch in the various positions (i.e. switch OFF – no continuity, switch ON – continuity) – see Section 2 and the Wiring Diagrams 10 at the end of this Chapter.

6 If the continuity check indicates a problem exists, refer to Section 19 and displace the switch from the handlebar. Spray the inside of the switch with electrical contact cleaner, and check for any broken or damaged components.

7 If they are accessible, the contacts can be scraped clean with a penknife or polished with steel wool. If wiring connections are weak or broken, they could be re-soldered. If any components are damaged or broken a new switch must be fitted.

Removal

8 If the switch unit is to be removed from the motorcycle, rather than just displaced from the handlebar, follow Step 2, 3 or 4 according to model and disconnect the appropriate wiring connector. Feed the wiring back to the switch, freeing it from any clips and ties and noting its routing. On MT-07TR models slacken the hand guard clamp screws to release the wiring from the clamp **(see illustrations 13.2c and d)**.

9 Disconnect the wiring connector(s) from the brake light switch (if removing the

right-hand switch unit) or the clutch switch (if removing the left-hand switch unit) **(see illustration 14.2 or 22.2)**.

10 Undo the switch housing screws, noting which fits where if they are different **(see illustrations)**.

11 Separate the two halves of the switch unit and lift it off, noting how the pin in the lower or front half locates in the hole in the handlebar.

Installation

12 Installation is the reverse of removal. Make sure the locating pin locates in the hole in the handlebar. Make sure the wiring is securely connected and correctly routed. Do not forget to connect the brake light switch and clutch switch wiring, and check the operation of all switches before riding the motorcycle.

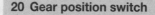

20 Gear position switch

Check

1 The switch is located on the left-hand side of the engine. The wiring connector is on the top of the crankcase next to the starter motor **(see illustration)** – you can access it from the right-hand side, but if necessary displace the clutch cable bracket and disconnect the cable

end from the clutch release arm first (see Chapter 2).

2 Disconnect the connector and check for continuity between each wire terminal in the switch side of the connector and the crankcase as follows: with the transmission in neutral there should be continuity in the light blue wire; with the transmission in 1st gear there should be continuity in the pink wire, in 2nd gear the white wire, in 3rd gear the grey wire, in 4th gear the orange wire, in 5th gear the white/red wire, and in 6th gear the yellow/white wire. If not, displace the switch (see below – there is no need at this stage to release the connector from the bracket), and check that the sprung contact plunger and the contacts on the inner face of the switch are not damaged or worn **(see illustration)**, and the plunger is not seized in the end of the selector drum **(see illustration 20.7)**.

3 If the switch is good, check the wire between the connector, the starter circuit cut-off relay and the instrument cluster for continuity (see Wiring Diagrams at the end of this Chapter). Refer to Section 23 for details of checking the diodes in the cut-off relay.

4 If the wiring is good, check the starter circuit cut-off relay (Section 23) and other components in the starter circuit as described in the relevant Sections of this Chapter. If all components are good, check the wiring between the various components (see Wiring Diagrams at the end of this Chapter).

Removal and installation

5 The switch is located on the left-hand side of the engine. Remove the sprocket cover to access the switch (see Chapter 6, Section 19). On models with the EVAP canister release the hoses from each end, noting which fits where on the right-hand end, then draw the canister put of its holder **(see illustrations 27.3a and b)**. Disconnect the wiring and release the connector from the bracket, then draw it out to the switch, noting its routing **(see illustration 20.1)**.

6 Undo the screws and remove the switch **(see illustration)** – a new O-ring must be used.

20.1 Gear position switch wiring connector

20.2 Check the contacts for wear

20.6 Removing the switch

20.7 Remove the plunger and spring

20.8 Fit the O-ring into the groove

21.2 Release the tie (arrowed) then disconnect the connector

7 Withdraw the contact plunger and its spring from the end of the selector drum **(see illustration)**.
8 Installation is the reverse of removal – use a new O-ring and smear it with grease **(see illustration)**. Clean the threads of the screws and apply some fresh threadlock. Make sure the wiring is correctly routed and the connectors are secure. Check the operation of the switch.

21 Sidestand switch

Check

1 The sidestand switch is mounted on the sidestand bracket. The switch is part of the safety circuit, which prevents or stops the engine running if the transmission is in gear whilst the sidestand is down, and prevents the engine from starting if the transmission is in gear unless the sidestand is up and the clutch lever is pulled in.
2 Remove the front sprocket cover to access the switch wiring connector (see Chapter 6). Release the wiring tie then disconnect the connector **(see illustration)**.
3 Check the operation of the switch using a multimeter or continuity tester. Connect the meter probes to the terminals on the switch side of the connector. With the sidestand up there should be continuity (with a low

resistance) between the terminals, and with the stand down there should be no continuity (infinite resistance).
4 If the switch is good, check the starter circuit cut-off relay (Section 23) and other components in the starter circuit as described in the relevant Sections of this Chapter.
5 If all components are good, check the wiring between the various components (see Section 2 and the Wiring Diagrams at the end of this Chapter).

Renewal

6 The sidestand switch is mounted on the sidestand bracket.
7 Disconnect the switch wiring connector (see Step 2). Feed the wiring down to the switch, noting its routing.
8 Undo the nuts and remove the screws, the hose/wiring guide and the switch **(see illustration)**.
9 Installation is the reverse of removal. Check the operation of the switch (see Step 1).

22 Clutch switch

Check

1 The clutch switch is mounted on the underside of the clutch lever bracket. The switch is part of the safety circuit, which prevents or stops the engine running if the

transmission is in gear whilst the sidestand is down, and prevents the engine from starting if the transmission is in gear unless the sidestand is up and the clutch lever is pulled in. The switch is not adjustable.
2 Disconnect the switch wiring connector **(see illustration)**. Check the operation of the switch using a multimeter or continuity tester. Connect the meter probes to the terminals on the switch. With the lever pulled in there should be continuity (zero resistance) between the terminals, and with the lever out there should be no continuity (infinite resistance).
3 If the switch is good, check the starter circuit cut-off relay (Section 23) and other components in the starter circuit as described in the relevant Sections of this Chapter. If all components are good, check the wiring between the various components (see Section 2 and the Wiring Diagrams at the end of this Chapter).

Renewal

4 Disconnect the wiring connector **(see illustration 22.2)**. Undo the screw securing the switch and remove it **(see illustration)**.
5 Installation is the reverse of removal.

23 Starter circuit cut-off relay

1 The starter circuit cut-off relay and its associated diodes are in the relay unit **(see**

21.8 Sidestand switch screws (arrowed) – note the positioning of the hoses and wiring in the guide

22.2 Clutch switch wiring connector (arrowed)

22.4 Clutch switch screw (arrowed)

23.1 Relay unit (arrowed)

23.3a Lift the relay off its mount…

23.3b … then lift the rubber boot to access the connector

illustration). The relay and diodes are part of the safety circuit, which prevents or stops the engine running if the transmission is in gear whilst the sidestand is down, and prevents the engine from starting if the transmission is in gear unless the sidestand is up and the clutch lever is pulled in. The relay unit also contains the fuel pump relay, which controls power to the fuel pump and injectors, and is covered in Chapter 4 Section 8.

2 To check the operation of the relay, on MT-07 (FZ-07) models remove the front fuel tank cover, on MT-07TR models remove the fuel tank cover, and on XSR models remove the left-hand fuel tank cover and air scoop (see Chapter 7).

3 Disconnect the battery negative (–) lead (Section 3). Displace the relay and disconnect the wiring connector **(see illustrations)**. Move the relay to the bench to test its operation and diodes.

4 Using a continuity tester or a multimeter

set to the resistance (ohms) range, test for continuity between the No. 1 (positive meter probe) and No. 2 (negative meter probe) wire terminals on the relay **(see illustration)**. There should be no continuity (infinite resistance). Now, using insulated jumper wires and a fully charged 12V battery, connect the battery positive (+) terminal to the No. 3 wire terminal on the relay and the battery negative (-) terminal to the No. 4 wire terminal. Continuity (0 ohms) should now be shown on the meter.

5 If the relay does not operate as described, replace it with a new one.

6 The diodes contained within the relay assembly can be checked by performing a continuity test (see Section 2) – diodes should show continuity in one direction and no continuity when the meter or tester probes are reversed. Connect the multimeter (set to ohms) or continuity tester across the wire terminals for the diode being tested and perform the tests

(see illustration). If any diode shows continuity in both directions it is faulty, and the relay assembly must be replaced with a new one.

Positive probe (+)	Negative probe (-)	Result
1	2	Continuity
2	1	No continuity
1	3	Continuity
3	1	No continuity
1	4	Continuity
4	1	No continuity
5	3	Continuity
3	5	No continuity

7 If the cut-out relay and diodes are good, but the starting system fault still exists, check all other components in the starting circuit (i.e. the gear position switch, sidestand switch, clutch switch, starter switch and starter relay) as described in the relevant Sections of this Chapter. If all components are good, check the wiring between the various components (see Section 2 and the Wiring Diagrams at the end of this Chapter).

8 Installation is the reverse of removal.

24 Horn

1 The horn is mounted on the bottom of the radiator on the left-hand side.

Check

2 If the horn doesn't work, first check the signal fuse (Section 5).

3 Pull the wiring connectors off the horn terminals **(see illustration)**. Using two jumper wires and a fully charged 12V battery, apply voltage directly to the terminals on the horn. If the horn sounds, check the switch (Section 19) and the wiring between the switch and the horn (see Section 2 and the Wiring Diagrams at the end of this Chapter).

4 If the horn sounds weak or distorted, the tone can be adjusted by turning the screw on the back.

5 If the horn doesn't sound, or can't be adjusted, replace it with a new one.

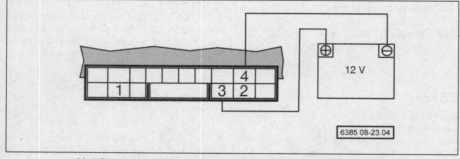

12 V

6385 08-23.04

23.4 Starter circuit cut-off relay check – terminal identification

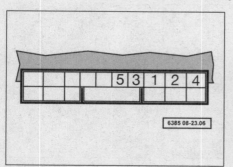

5 3 1 2 4

6385 08-23.06

23.6 Starter circuit cut-off relay diode check – terminal identification

24.3 Horn wiring connectors and mounting nut (arrowed)

25.1 Oil pressure switch (arrowed)

25.3 Undo the screw to release the wire

26.2 Starter relay (arrowed)

Removal and installation

6 Pull the wiring connectors off the terminals, then unscrew the nut and remove the horn **(see illustration 24.3)**.

7 Fit the horn and tighten the nut. Connect the wiring connectors and check the operation of the horn.

25 Oil pressure switch

1 The switch is on the front of the engine on the right-hand side **(see illustration)**.

Check

Note: *Refer to electrical system fault finding in Section 2 and to the Wiring Diagrams.*

2 The oil pressure warning light should come on when the ignition is switched ON, and then go off briefly, then come on again, and then go off when the engine is started. If the light does not go off when the engine is started, or comes on while the engine is running, stop the engine immediately and check the oil level (see *Pre-ride checks*). If the level is correct check the switch as described below, and if the switch is good carry out an oil pressure check (see Chapter 2).

3 If the oil pressure warning light does not come on when the ignition is turned ON, but all other instrument functions work, pull the rubber cover off the oil pressure switch and undo the screw securing the wiring connector **(see illustration)**. With the ignition

switched ON, earth (ground) the wire on the crankcase and check that the warning light comes on. If the light comes on, the switch is faulty. To confirm the switch is faulty check for continuity between the terminal and the crankcase – with the engine off there should be continuity, with the engine running there should be no continuity.

4 If the light still does not come on, check for voltage at the wire terminal with the ignition ON. If there is no voltage present check there is continuity in the wire between the switch and the instrument connector, referring to Section 15 for access. Repair the wiring if necessary. If the wiring is all good and the switch is good the instrument PCB could be faulty.

5 If the warning light does not go out when the engine is started or comes on whilst the engine is running, yet the oil pressure is satisfactory, detach the wire from the oil pressure switch (see above). With the wire detached and the ignition switched ON the light should be out. If it is illuminated, the wire between the switch and instrument cluster is earthed (grounded) at some point. If the wiring is good, the switch must be assumed faulty and replaced with a new one.

Removal

6 Drain the engine oil (see Chapter 1).

7 Pull the rubber cover off the switch, then undo the screw securing the wiring connector **(see illustrations 25.3)**.

8 Unscrew and remove the switch – be prepared to catch any residual oil with a rag.

Installation

9 Apply a suitable sealant (such as Three bond 1215) to the upper portion of the switch threads near the switch body, leaving the bottom 3 to 4 mm of thread clean. Thread the switch into the crankcase and tighten to 15 Nm.

10 Attach the wiring connector and secure it with the screw, then fit the rubber cover **(see illustration 25.3)**.

11 Replenish the engine oil (see Chapter 1). Run the engine and check that the switch operates correctly and without leakage.

26 Starter relay

Check

1 If the starter circuit appears to be faulty, first check the main fuse and ignition fuses (Section 5).

2 On MT-07 (FZ-07) models remove the rider's seat, and on MT-07TR and XSR models remove the seat (see Chapter 7). The starter relay is located to the rear of the battery **(see illustration)**.

3 Disconnect the relay wiring connector, then remove the relay cover, then reconnect the wiring connector **(see illustrations)**. Unscrew the bolt securing the black starter motor lead **(see illustration)**. Position the lead away from the relay terminal.

26.3a Disconnect the wiring...

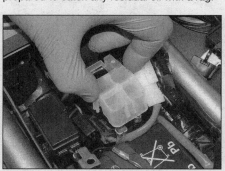

26.3b ... then unclip and remove the cover

26.3c Starter motor lead terminal (A) and battery lead terminal (B)

4 With the ignition switch ON, the engine kill switch in the RUN position and the transmission in neutral, press the starter switch. The relay should be heard to click.

5 If the relay doesn't click, switch the ignition OFF, remove the relay (see Steps 10 to 12) and test it as follows.

6 Using a continuity tester or a multimeter set to the resistance (ohms) range, test for continuity between the relay's starter motor (black) and battery (red) lead terminals (see illustration 26.3c). There should be no continuity (infinite resistance). Now, using insulated jumper wires and a fully charged 12V battery, connect the battery positive (+) terminal to the red/white wire terminal on the relay and the battery negative (-) terminal to the blue/white wire terminal (see illustration). With voltage applied, the relay should be heard to click and continuity (0 ohms) should now be shown on the meter.

7 If the relay does not click when battery voltage is applied and indicates no continuity (infinite resistance) across its terminals, it is faulty.

8 The starter relay coil resistance can be checked by connecting a multimeter set to the ohms x 1 range across the red/white and blue/white terminals of the relay wire connector; the value should be as given in the Specifications.

9 If the relay is good, check for battery voltage at the red/white wire terminal on the loom side of the relay wiring connector when the starter button is pressed with the ignition switched ON. If voltage is present, check the other components in the starter circuit as described in the relevant Sections of this Chapter. If no voltage is present, check the wiring between the various components (see Section 2 and the Wiring Diagrams).

Renewal

10 On MT-07 (FZ-07) models remove the rider's seat, and on MT-07TR and XSR models remove the seat (see Chapter 7). Disconnect the battery negative (-) lead (Section 3).

11 Disconnect the relay wiring connector then remove the relay cover (see illustrations 26.3a and b). Unscrew the starter motor and battery lead bolts and detach the leads (see illustration 26.3c).

12 Remove the relay, and if it is being replaced with a new one remove the fuse and its spare – the new relay should come with new fuses already fitted, in which case keep the others as spares.

13 Installation is the reverse of removal. Make sure the terminal bolts are tight.

27 Starter motor removal and installation

Removal

1 The starter motor is mounted on the crankcase, behind the cylinder block.

2 Disconnect the battery negative (–) lead (Section 3). For best access remove the throttle bodies and the air filter housing (see Chapter 4).

3 On models with the EVAP canister release the hoses from each end, noting which fits where on the right-hand end, then draw the canister put of its holder (see illustrations).

4 On models without the EVAP canister release the fuel tank drain and breather hoses from the clips (see illustration).

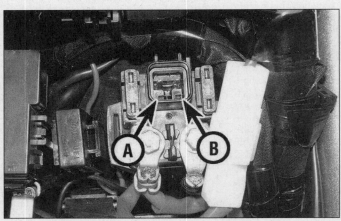

26.6 Red/white wire terminal (A), blue/white wire terminal (B)

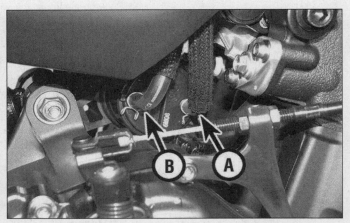

27.3a Disconnect the fuel tank breather hose (A) and the canister to throttle body hose (B) on the right-hand side

27.3b Disconnect the breather hose (arrowed), then draw the canister out of its holder

27.4 Release the hoses

27.5 Connector/hose clip bracket screw (arrowed)

27.6 Unscrew the nut and detach the lead

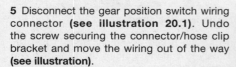

27.7 Unscrew the two bolts

5 Disconnect the gear position switch wiring connector **(see illustration 20.1)**. Undo the screw securing the connector/hose clip bracket and move the wiring out of the way **(see illustration)**.

6 Peel back the terminal boot, unscrew the nut securing the lead to the starter motor terminal and detach the lead **(see illustration)**.

7 Unscrew the two starter motor mounting bolts **(see illustration)**. Draw the starter motor out of the crankcase **(see illustration 27.11)** – use a screwdriver to initially lever it out if required. On models with the EVAP canister remove the canister holder from the starter motor, noting their relative alignment.

8 Remove the O-ring on the end of the starter motor **(see illustration 27.9)** – a new one must be used.

Installation

9 Fit a new O-ring onto the end of the starter motor, making sure it is seated in its groove, and smear it with grease **(see illustration)**.

10 On models with an EVAP canister fit the canister holder over the starter motor, making sure they are correctly aligned.

11 Manoeuvre the motor into position and slide it into the crankcase **(see illustration)**. Make sure that the starter motor teeth mesh correctly with those of the starter idler gear.

12 Fit the mounting bolts and tighten them to 10 Nm **(see illustration 27.7)**.

13 Connect the lead to the starter motor terminal and secure it with the nut **(see**

27.9 Fit a new O-ring and smear it with grease

27.11 Manoeuvre the motor into place as shown

illustration 27.6). Fit the boot over the terminal.

14 Install all remaining components in reverse order of removal.

15 Connect the battery negative (–) lead.

28 Starter motor overhaul

Check

1 Remove the starter motor (Section 27). Cover the body in some rag and clamp the motor mounting lugs in a soft-jawed vice – do not overtighten it.

2 Using a fully-charged 12 volt battery and two insulated jumper wires, connect the

positive (+) terminal of the battery to the protruding terminal on the starter motor, and the negative (–) terminal to one of the motor's mounting lugs. At this point the starter motor should spin. If this is the case the motor is proved good, though it is worth disassembling it and checking it if you suspect it of not working properly under load. If the motor does not spin, disassemble it for inspection.

Disassembly

3 Remove the starter motor (Section 27).

4 Note the alignment marks between the main housing and the front and rear covers, or make your own if they aren't clear **(see illustration)**.

5 Unscrew the two long bolts and remove the front cover from the motor **(see illustrations)**.

28.4 Note the alignment marks between the housing and the covers

28.5a Unscrew the bolts...

28.5b ...and remove the front cover...

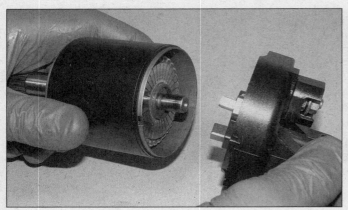

28.6 ...and the rear cover

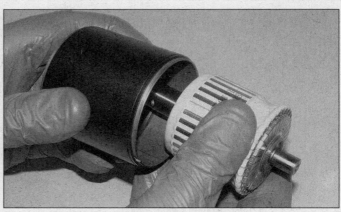

28.7 Withdraw the armature

28.9 Measure the length of each brush

6 Remove the rear cover **(see illustration)**.

7 Withdraw the armature from the main housing **(see illustration)** – it is held in by the attraction of the magnets, so take care not to lose your grip on the armature before the magnets lose theirs.

Inspection

8 At this stage check for continuity between the terminal bolt and the positive brush in the rear cover – there should be continuity (zero resistance). Check for continuity between the terminal bolt and the cover – there should be no continuity (infinite resistance). Also check for continuity between the negative and positive brushes – there should be no continuity (infinite resistance). If there is no continuity when there should be or viceversa,

fit a new brush assembly (Step 10) – the brushes, springs, holder, terminal bolt and O-ring and screw are all included.

9 The parts of the starter motor that are most likely to require attention are the brushes. Measure the length of each brush and compare the results to the length given in the Specifications **(see illustration)**. If worn fit a new brush assembly (Step 10). If the brushes are not worn excessively, nor cracked, chipped, or otherwise damaged, they can be reused.

10 To remove the brush assembly undo the screw and remove the negative brush and spring **(see illustration)**. Unscrew the nut from the terminal bolt and remove the plain washer, the insulator and the terminal shield **(see illustrations)**. Remove the brush holder,

28.10a Undo the screw and remove the negative brush...

28.10b ... and the spring

28.10c Unscrew the nut and remove the washer...

28.10d ... the insulator...

28.10e ... and the shield

28.10f Remove the brush holder from the rear cover

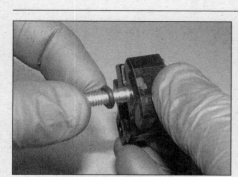

28.10g Remove the O-ring from the bolt...

28.10h ... then remove the bolt/brush assembly...

28.10i ... and the spring

then remove the O-ring from the terminal bolt, and remove the terminal bolt/positive brush, and the brush spring **(see illustrations)**.

11 Inspect the commutator bars on the armature for scoring, scratches and discoloration. The commutator can be cleaned and polished with crocus cloth, but do not use sandpaper or emery paper. After cleaning, wipe away any residue with a cloth soaked in electrical system cleaner or denatured alcohol.

12 Using an ohmmeter or a continuity test light, check for continuity between the commutator bars **(see illustration)**. Continuity should exist between each bar and all of the others. Also, check for continuity between the commutator bars and the armature shaft **(see illustration)**. There should be no continuity (infinite resistance) between the commutator and the shaft. If the checks indicate otherwise, the armature is defective and a new starter motor must be obtained – the armature is not available separately.

13 Check the front end of the armature shaft for worn, cracked, chipped and broken teeth. If the shaft is damaged or worn, a new starter motor must be obtained – the armature is not available separately.

14 Inspect the front and rear covers for signs of cracks or wear. Check the oil seal and the needle bearing in the front cover and the bush in the rear cover for wear and damage **(see illustration)** – the seal, bearing, bush and covers are not listed as being available separately so if necessary a new starter motor must be fitted.

28.12a There should be continuity between the bars...

28.12b ...and no continuity between the bars and the shaft

15 Inspect the magnets in the main housing and the housing itself for cracks.

16 Check the sealing rings on the housing, for signs of damage, deformation and deterioration and fit new ones if necessary **(see illustration)**.

Reassembly

17 If the brush holder assembly was removed, fit the positive brush spring into its housing, then fit the terminal bolt and seat the brush on the spring, with the wire in the slot **(see illustrations 28.10i and h)**. Fit the O-ring all way down onto the base of the terminal bolt **(see illustration 28.10g)**. Fit the terminal bolt through the hole in the rear cover and seat the brush holder **(see illustrations 28.10f)** – make sure the O-ring seats between the bolt and the cover so the bolt is insulated **(see illustration)**. Fit the terminal shield with

the cut-out for the lead to the left, then fit the insulator and the washer and secure them with the nut **(see illustrations 28.10e, d and c)**. Fit the spring and the negative brush and secure it with the screw **(see illustrations 28.10b and a)**.

18 To check for correct installation do the continuity checks described in Step 8.

19 If removed fit the sealing rings onto each end of the main housing **(see illustration 28.16)**.

20 Grasp the housing and carefully allow the armature to be drawn in, making sure the cut-out in the housing is at the same end as the commutator bars **(see illustration 28.7)**.

21 Apply a smear of grease to the short end of the shaft. Fit the rear cover, aligning the tab so it locates in the cut-out in the housing rim, and making sure the brushes remain

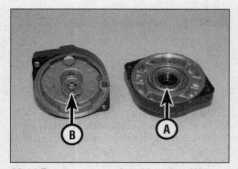

28.14 Front cover seal and bearing (A), rear cover bush (B)

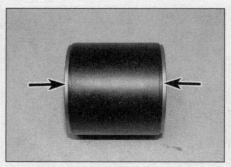

28.16 Main housing sealing rings (arrowed)

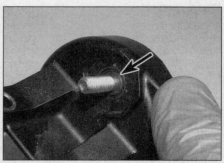

28.17 Seat the O-ring (arrowed) between the bolt and the cover as shown

28.21 Grease the shaft and seat the tab (A) in the cut-out (B)

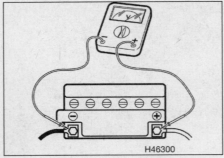

29.5 Checking the charging system output – connect the voltmeter as shown

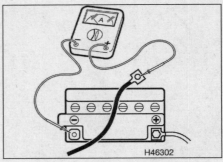

29.9 Checking the charging system leakage rate – connect the ammeter as shown

square and seat against the commutator **(see illustration)**.

22 Apply a smear of grease to the front cover oil seal lip. Slide the front cover on, aligning the marks **(see illustration 28.5b)**.

23 Check the alignment marks are correctly aligned **(see illustration 28.4)**, then fit the long bolts and tighten to 5 Nm **(see illustration 28.5a)**.

24 Install the starter motor (Section 27).

29 Charging system testing

1 If the performance of the charging system is suspect, the system as a whole should be checked first, followed by testing of the individual components. Before beginning the checks, make sure the battery is fully charged and that all system connections are clean and tight.

2 Checking the output of the charging system and the performance of the various components within the charging system requires the use of a multimeter (with voltage, current and resistance checking facilities). If a multimeter is not available, the job of checking the charging system should be left to a Yamaha dealer or automotive electrician.

3 When making the checks, follow the procedures carefully to prevent incorrect connections or short circuits, as irreparable damage to electrical system components may result if short circuits occur.

Output test

4 Start the engine and warm it up to normal operating temperature. To access the battery terminals, on MT-07 (FZ-07) models remove the rider's seat, and on MT-07TR and XSR models remove the seat (see Chapter 7).

5 To check the regulated voltage output, allow the engine to idle and connect a multimeter set to the 0 to 20 volts DC scale (voltmeter) across the terminals of the battery, positive (+) lead to battery positive (+) terminal, negative (–) lead to battery negative (–) terminal **(see illustration)**. Slowly increase the engine speed to 5000 rpm and note the reading obtained.

6 The regulated voltage should be as given in the Specifications. If the voltage is outside these limits, check the alternator, then the regulator/rectifier (Section 30and Section 31).

7 Stop the engine and disconnect the test meter.

Leakage test

Caution: Always connect an ammeter in series with the battery, never in parallel, otherwise it will be damaged. Do not turn the ignition ON or operate the starter motor when the ammeter is connected – a sudden surge in current will blow the meter's fuse.

8 Turn the ignition switch OFF. Disconnect the lead from the battery negative (–) terminal (Section 3).

9 Set the multimeter to the Amps function – set the meter to a high amps range initially and then bring it down to the mA (milli Amps) range; if there is a high current flow in the circuit it may blow the meter's fuse. Connect the meter negative (–) probe to the battery negative (–) terminal, and the positive (+) probe to the disconnected negative (–) lead **(see illustration)**.

10 No current flow should be indicated. If current leakage is indicated (generally greater than 1mA, but may be more if an alarm is fitted), there is a short circuit in the wiring. Using the wiring diagrams at the end of this Chapter, systematically disconnect individual electrical components, checking the meter each time until the source is identified.

30.2 Disconnect the alternator wiring connector from the regulator/rectifier

11 If no leakage is indicated, disconnect the meter and connect the negative (–) lead to the battery.

30 Alternator

Check

1 On MT-07 (FZ-07) models remove the left-hand fuel tank side cover (see Chapter 7). On MT-07TR models remove the left-hand fairing side panel and inner panel (see Chapter 7). On XSR models remove the left-hand air scoop (see Chapter 7).

2 Disconnect the white connector containing the three white wires from the regulator/rectifier **(see illustration)**.

3 Using a multimeter set to the ohms x 1 (ohmmeter) scale, measure the resistance between the centre wire and each of the other two on the alternator side of the connector, then between the outer two wires, taking a total of three readings, then check for continuity between each terminal and ground (earth). If the stator coil windings are in good condition the resistance readings should be within the range given in the Specifications, and there should be no continuity (infinite resistance) between the terminals and ground (earth). If not, check the fault is not due to damaged wiring between the connector and coils. If the wiring is good, the alternator stator coil assembly is at fault and should be replaced with a new one.

Alternator cover removal

4 On MT-07 (FZ-07) models remove the left-hand fuel tank cover (see Chapter 7). On MT-07TR models remove the left-hand fairing side panel and inner panel (see Chapter 7). On XSR models remove the left-hand air scoop (Chapter 7).

5 Drain the engine oil (see Chapter 1).

6 Remove the coolant reservoir (see Chapter 3).

7 Remove the front sprocket cover (see Chapter 6).

8 Disconnect the alternator wiring connector **(see illustration 30.2)**, and the CKP sensor wiring connector – for best access to the CKP sensor connector disconnect the cooling fan connector first **(see illustrations)**. Feed the wiring to the alternator cover, noting its routing.

9 Unscrew and remove the alternator cover bolts **(see illustration)**. Remove the cover, being prepared to catch any residual oil, and noting that you need to pull against the attraction of the magnets in the alternator rotor **(see illustration 30.21b)**. If necessary break the gasket seal by tapping gently around the edge with a soft-faced hammer or block of wood – do not try to lever between the cover/crankcases mating surfaces as they could be damaged. Remove the gasket – a new one must be used. Remove the dowels from either the cover or the crankcase if they are loose **(see illustration 30.21a)**.

Alternator rotor and stator removal

Special Tool: *A puller is essential for removal of the alternator rotor from the crankshaft.*

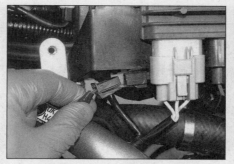

30.8a Disconnect the fan wiring connector...

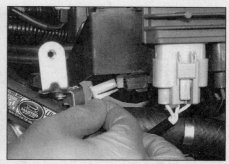

30.8b ... then disconnect the CKP sensor wiring connector

10 Remove the starter torque limiter **(see illustration)**. Withdraw the idle/reduction gear shaft and remove the gear **(see illustration)**.
11 To remove the rotor bolt it is necessary to stop the rotor from turning. This is best achieved using a rotor holding tool, either Yamaha Part No. 90890-04166 or YM-04166,

or there are several commercially available types. Keep the tool strap away from the timing triggers on the rotor. Unscrew the rotor bolt and remove the washer **(see illustration)** – a new washer must be used.
12 To remove the rotor from the shaft it is necessary to use a rotor puller. Yamaha make a

30.9 Alternator cover bolts (arrowed)

30.10a Remove the torque limiter...

30.10b ... and the idle/reduction gear

30.11 Using a rotor holder while unscrewing the bolt

30.12a Fit the puller onto the rotor...

30.12b ... then hold the rotor and tighten the puller bolt

30.13 Woodruff key (arrowed)

tool (Part Nos. 90890-01362 or YU-33270-B), or alternatively a similar tool can be obtained commercially **(see illustration)**. The rotor has three threaded holes designed to accept the bolts of the puller – there are many types of puller available, so if buying one make sure you get the correct type as shown. Fit the

puller, hold the rotor as before, and tighten the puller centre bolt until the rotor is displaced from the shaft **(see illustration)** – remove the starter driven gear along with the rotor **(see illustration 30.18)**.

13 Remove the Woodruff key from its slot in the end of the crankshaft if it is loose **(see illustration)**. If required, refer to Chapter 2, Section 14 and remove the starter driven gear and starter clutch from the back of the rotor.

14 To remove the stator from the cover, undo the bolts securing the CKP sensor and the bolts securing the stator, then remove the assembly, noting how the wiring grommet locates **(see illustration)**.

Alternator rotor and stator installation

15 Fit the stator and CKP sensor, aligning the wiring grommet with the recess in the alternator cover **(see illustration 30.14)**. Clean the sensor and stator bolt threads and apply a suitable non-permanent thread

locking compound, then fit the bolts and tighten them to 10 Nm.

16 Apply a suitable sealant to the wiring grommet, then press it into the recess in the cover.

17 If removed, refer to Chapter 2, Section 14 and fit the starter clutch and starter driven gear onto the back of the rotor.

18 Lubricate the flat section on the end of the crankshaft (where the starter driven gear runs) with engine oil. Clean the tapered end of the crankshaft and the corresponding mating surface on the inside of the rotor with a suitable solvent. Fit the Woodruff key into its slot if removed **(see illustration 30.13)**. Make sure that no metal objects have attached themselves to the magnet on the inside of the rotor, then align the slot in the hub with the key and slide the rotor onto the shaft **(see illustration)**.

19 Apply some clean engine oil to the rotor bolt threads and new washer, fit the washer onto the bolt and thread the bolt in **(see**

30.14 Alternator stator and CKP sensor bolts (arrowed)

30.18 Slide the rotor onto the shaft

30.19a Fit the bolt and washer...

30.19b ...and tighten the bolt to the specified torque

30.21a Fit a new gasket onto the dowels (arrowed)...

30.21b ... and make sure the cover locates correctly on them

30.21c Fit the two threadlocked bolts at the bottom

illustration). Hold the rotor as on removal and tighten the bolt to 70 Nm (see illustration).
20 Lubricate the idle/reduction gear shaft with clean engine oil. Position the gear with the smaller pinion facing in, and mesh the teeth with the teeth of the starter driven gear, then insert the shaft (see illustration 30.10b). Lubricate the torque limiter bearings in the crankcase and alternator cover with oil then fit the torque limiter, meshing its teeth with the idle/reduction gear and the starter motor shaft (see illustration 30.10a).

Alternator cover installation

21 If removed, fit the dowels in the crankcase, then fit a new gasket onto the dowels (see illustration). Fit the alternator cover onto the dowels and the idle gear shaft, noting that it will be forcibly drawn on by the magnets, and make sure it is seated all around (see illustration). Clean the threads of two bolts and apply some fresh threadlock. Fit all the bolts, threadlocked ones at the bottom, and tighten them evenly in a criss-cross sequence to 12 Nm (see illustration).
22 Feed the wiring back to the connectors and reconnect them (see illustrations 30.8b and a and 30.2).
23 Install the front sprocket cover (see

Chapter 6). Install and fill the coolant reservoir (see Chapter 3). Add engine oil (see Chapter 1).
24 Install the removed body parts (see Chapter 7).

31 Regulator/rectifier

Check

1 Yamaha provide no test specifications for the regulator/rectifier other than the charging system output test (Section 29). If the regulator/rectifier is suspected of being faulty, first check all other components and the wiring and connectors in the charging circuit, referring to the relevant Sections in this Chapter and to the Wiring Diagrams at the end.
2 If all other components and the wiring are good, remove the unit (see below) and take it to a Yamaha dealer for testing. Alternatively, substitute the suspect unit with a known good one and see if the fault is cured.

Removal and installation

3 The regulator/rectifier is mounted on the

left-hand side of the fuel tank. On MT-07 (FZ-07) models remove the left-hand fuel tank side cover (see Chapter 7). On MT-07TR models remove the left-hand fairing side panel and inner panel, and if required for improved access the fuel tank cover (see Chapter 7). On XSR models remove the left-hand air scoop (see Chapter 7).
4 Disconnect the wiring connectors from the regulator/rectifier, then unscrew the bolts (see illustration).
5 Installation is the reverse of removal.

31.4 Disconnect the wiring, then unscrew the bolts (arrowed)

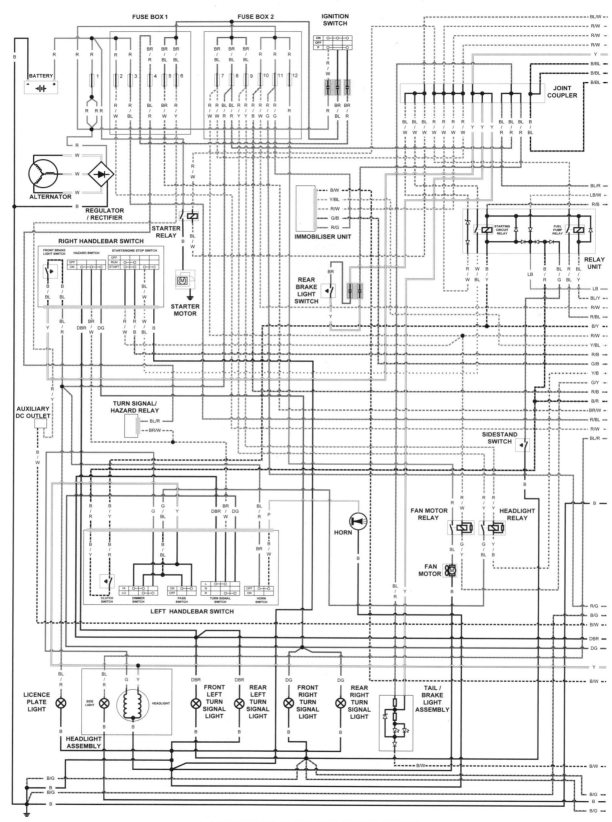

YAMAHA MT-07 EUROPE

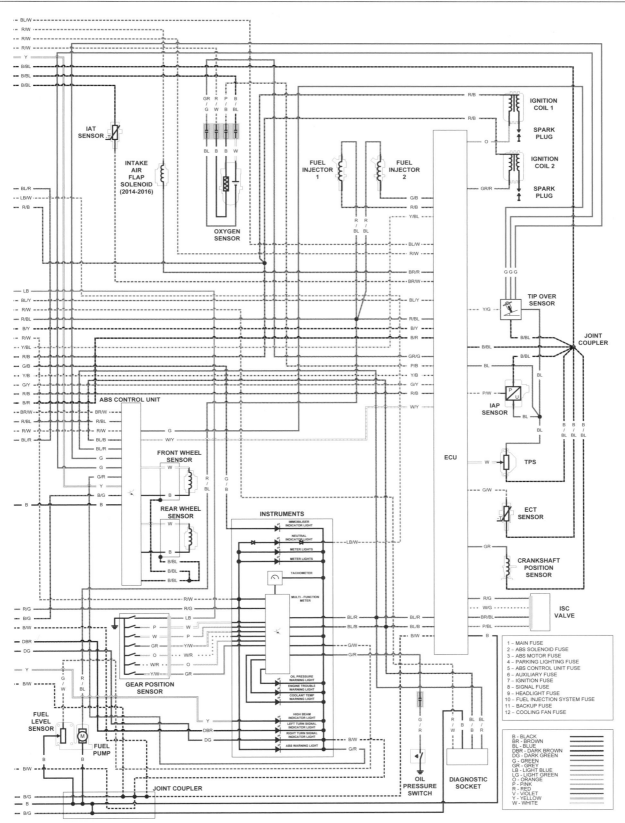

YAMAHA MT-07 EUROPE

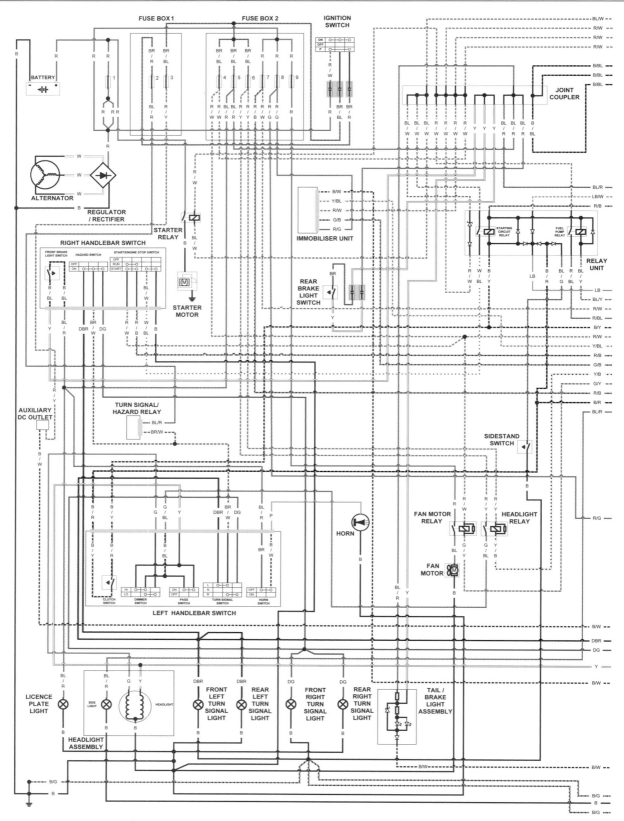

YAMAHA MT-07 WITHOUT ABS EUROPE

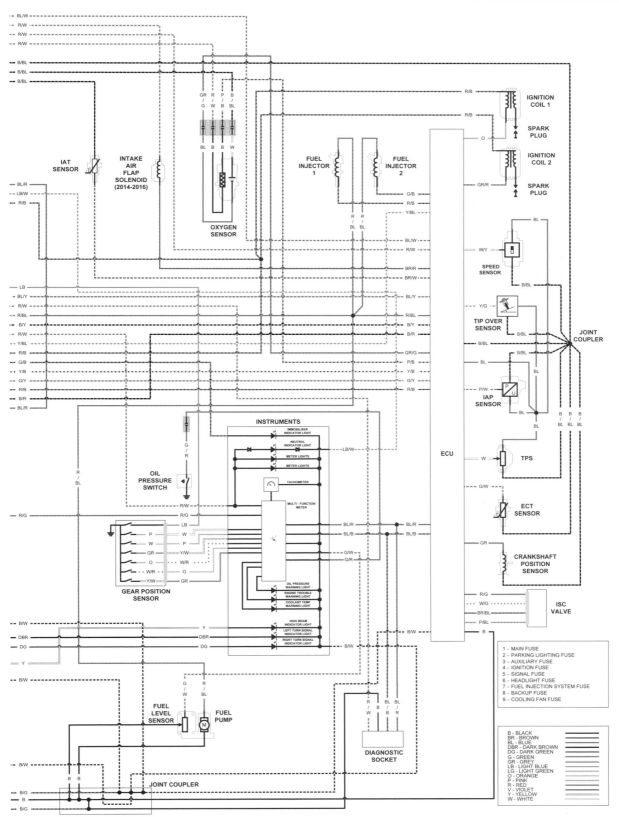

YAMAHA MT-07 WITHOUT ABS EUROPE

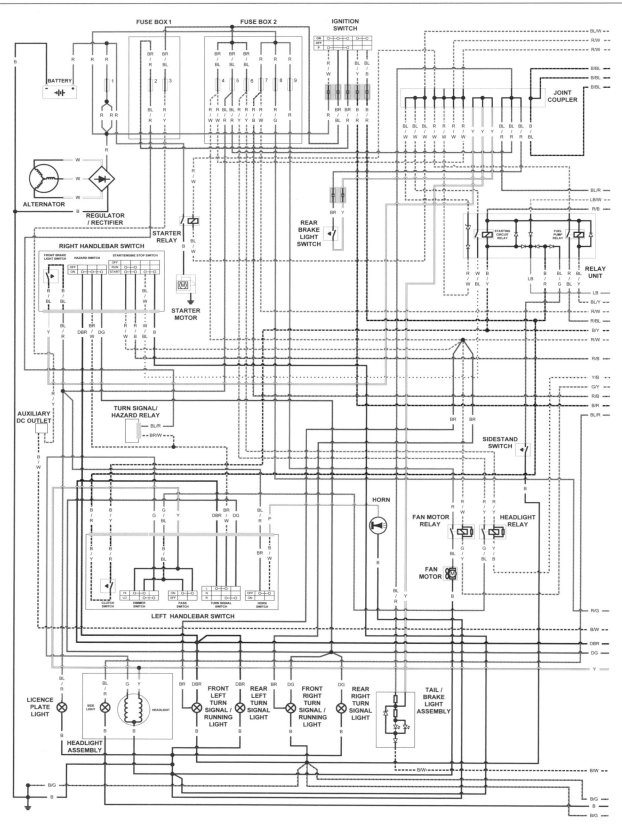

YAMAHA FZ-07 US

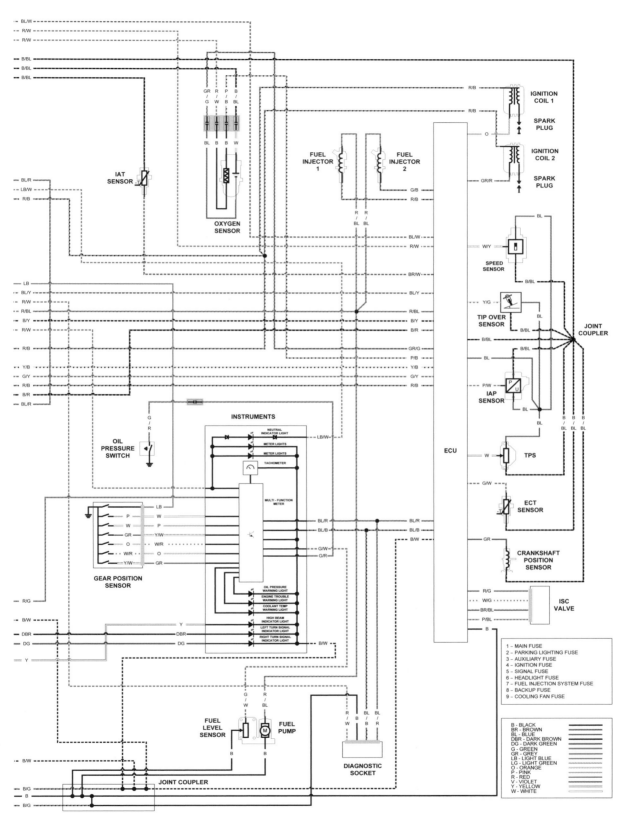

YAMAHA FZ-07 US

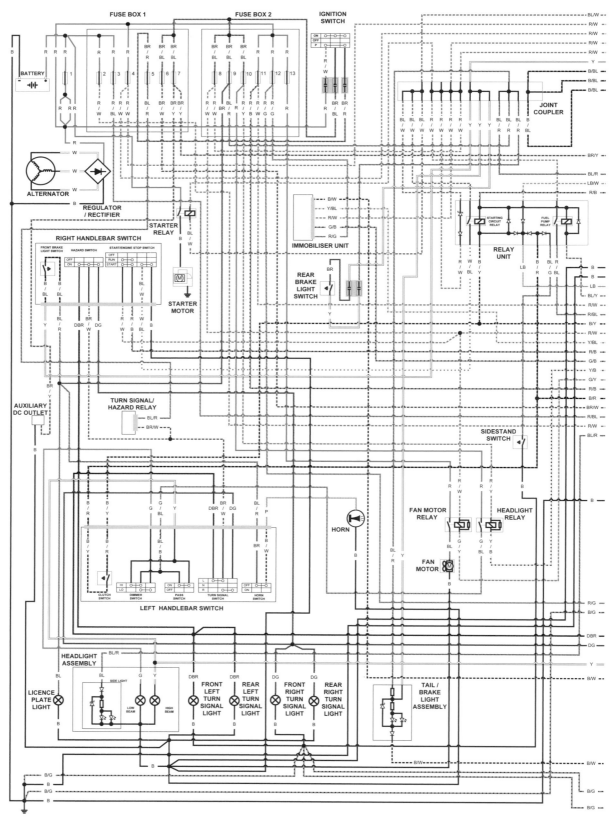

YAMAHA MT-07 TR TRACER EUROPE

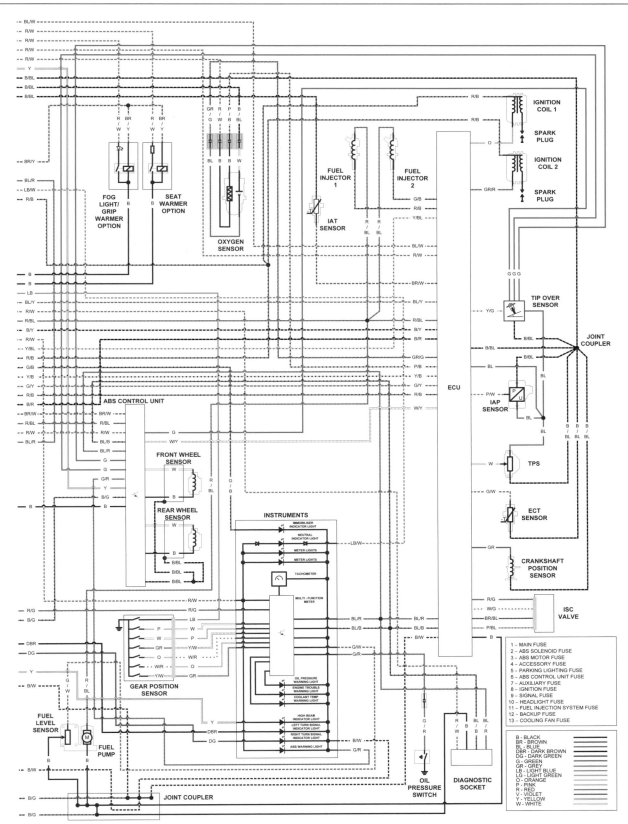

YAMAHA MT-07 TR TRACER EUROPE

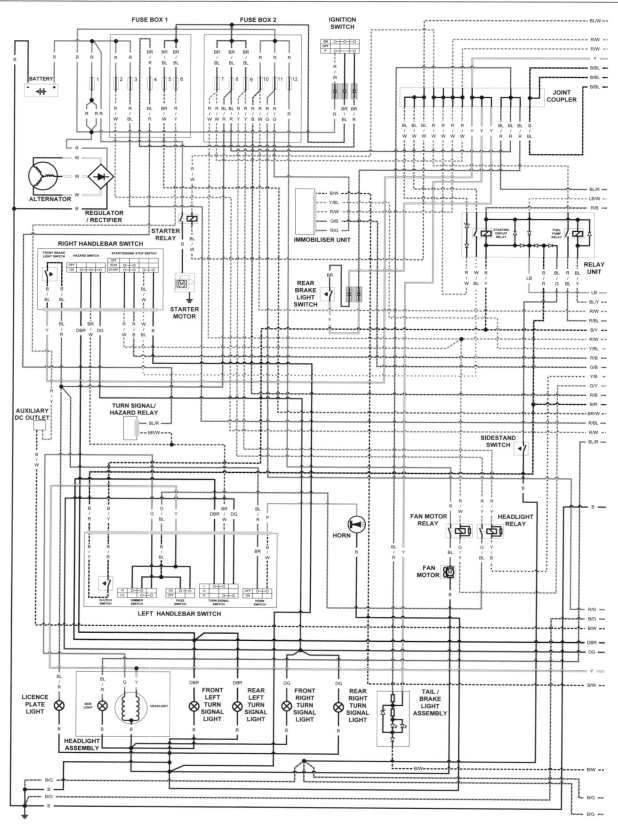

YAMAHA XSR700

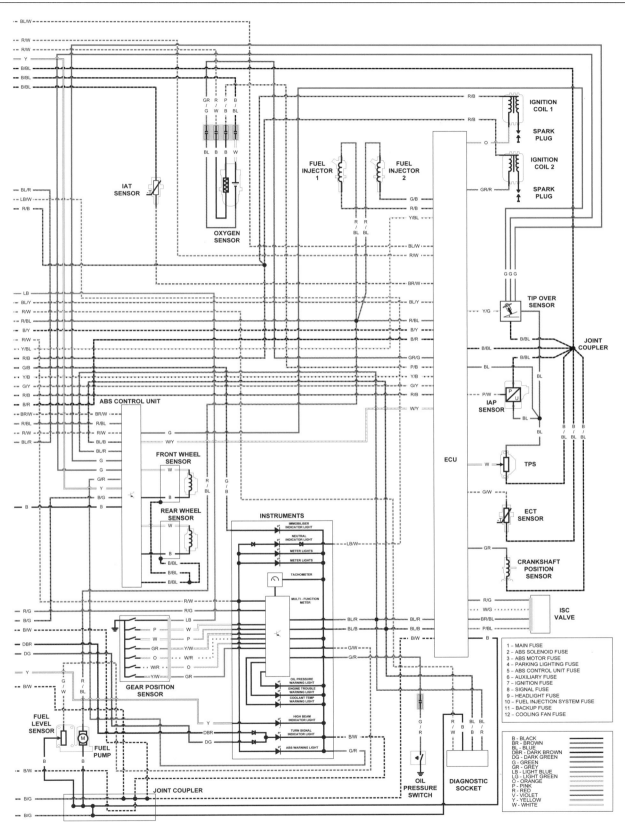

YAMAHA XSR700

Reference

Tools and Workshop Tips

● Building up a tool kit and equipping your workshop ● Using tools ● Understanding bearing, seal, fastener and chain sizes and markings ● Repair techniques

Security

● Locks and chains ● U-locks ● Disc locks ● Alarms and immobilisers ● Security marking systems ● Tips on how to prevent bike theft

Lubricants and fluids

● Engine oils ● Transmission (gear) oils ● Coolant/anti-freeze ● Fork oils and suspension fluids ● Brake/clutch fluids ● Spray lubes, degreasers and solvents

MOT Test Checks

● A guide to the UK MOT test ● Which items are tested ● How to prepare your motorcycle for the test and perform a pre-test check

Storage

● How to prepare your motorcycle for going into storage and protect essential systems ● How to get the motorcycle back on the road

Conversion Factors

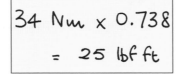

$$34 \ Nm \times 0.738 = 25 \ lbf \ ft$$

● Formulae for conversion of the metric (SI) units used throughout the manual into Imperial measures

Fault Finding

● Common faults and their likely causes ● Links to main chapters for testing and repair procedures

Technical Terms Explained

● Component names, technical terms and common abbreviations explained

Index

Buying tools

A toolkit is a fundamental requirement for servicing and repairing a motorcycle. Although there will be an initial expense in building up enough tools for servicing, this will soon be offset by the savings made by doing the job yourself. As experience and confidence grow, additional tools can be added to enable the repair and overhaul of the motorcycle. Many of the specialist tools are expensive and not often used so it may be preferable to hire them, or for a group of friends or motorcycle club to join in the purchase.

As a rule, it is better to buy more expensive, good quality tools. Cheaper tools are likely to wear out faster and need to be renewed more often, nullifying the original saving.

> **Warning: To avoid the risk of a poor quality tool breaking in use, causing injury or damage to the component being worked on, always aim to purchase tools which meet the relevant national safety standards.**

The following lists of tools do not represent the manufacturer's service tools, but serve as a guide to help the owner decide which tools are needed for this level of work. In addition, items such as an electric drill, hacksaw, files, soldering iron and a workbench equipped with a vice, may be needed. Although not classed as tools, a selection of bolts, screws, nuts, washers and pieces of tubing always come in useful.

For more information about tools, refer to the Haynes *Motorcycle Workshop Practice Techbook* (Bk. No. 3470).

Manufacturer's service tools

Inevitably certain tasks require the use of a service tool. Where possible an alternative tool or method of approach is recommended, but sometimes there is no option if personal injury or damage to the component is to be avoided. Where required, service tools are referred to in the relevant procedure.

Service tools can usually only be purchased from a motorcycle dealer and are identified by a part number. Some of the commonly-used tools, such as rotor pullers, are available in aftermarket form from mail-order motorcycle tool and accessory suppliers.

Maintenance and minor repair tools

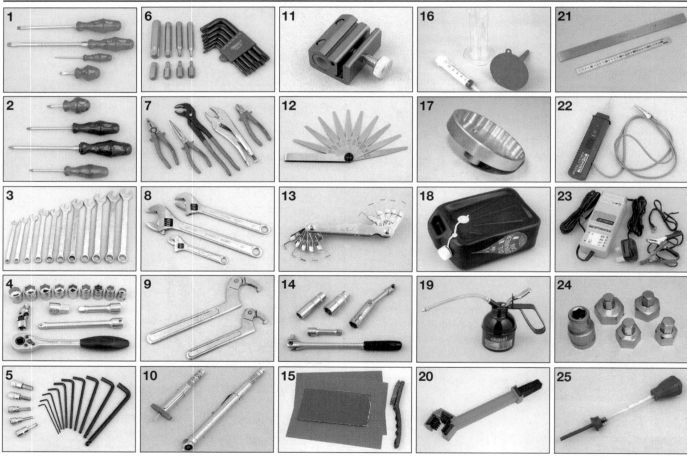

1   Set of flat-bladed screwdrivers
2   Set of Phillips head screwdrivers
3   Combination open-end and ring spanners
4   Socket set (3/8 inch or 1/2 inch drive)
5   Set of Allen keys or bits
6   Set of Torx keys or bits
7   Pliers, cutters and self-locking grips (Mole grips)
8   Adjustable spanners
9   C-spanners
10 Tread depth gauge and tyre pressure gauge
11 Cable oiler clamp
12 Feeler gauges
13 Spark plug gap measuring tool
14 Spark plug spanner or deep plug sockets
15 Wire brush and emery paper
16 Calibrated syringe, measuring vessel and funnel
17 Oil filter adapter
18 Oil drainer can or tray
19 Pump type oil can
20 Chain cleaning brush
21 Straight-edge and steel rule
22 Continuity tester
23 Battery charger
24 Wheel axle hex-bit set
25 Anti-freeze tester (for liquid-cooled engines)

Repair and overhaul tools

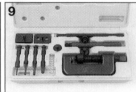

1 Torque wrench (small and mid-ranges)
2 Conventional, plastic or soft-faced hammers
3 Impact driver set
4 Vernier gauge
5 Circlip pliers (internal and external, or combination)
6 Set of cold chisels and punches
7 Selection of pullers
8 Breaker bars
9 Chain breaking/ riveting tool set
10 Wire stripper and crimper tool
11 Multimeter (measures amps, volts and ohms)
12 Angle-tightening gauge
13 Hose clamp (wingnut type shown)
14 Clutch holding tool
15 One-man brake/clutch bleeder kit

Specialist tools

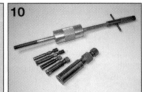

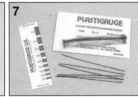

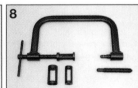

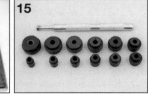

1 Micrometers (external type)
2 Telescoping gauges
3 Dial gauge
4 Cylinder compression gauge
5 Fork seal driver
6 Oil pressure gauge
7 Plastigauge kit
8 Valve spring compressor (4-stroke engines)
9 Piston pin drawbolt tool
10 Slide-hammer and knife-edged bearing extractors
11 Piston ring clamps
12 Tap and die set
13 Stud extractor
14 Screw extractor set
15 Bearing driver set

1 Workshop equipment and facilities

The workbench

● Work is made much easier by raising the bike up on a ramp - components are much more accessible if raised to waist level. The hydraulic or pneumatic types seen in the dealer's workshop are a sound investment if you undertake a lot of repairs or overhauls **(see illustration 1.1)**.

1.1 Hydraulic motorcycle ramp

● If raised off ground level, the bike must be supported on the ramp to avoid it falling. Most ramps incorporate a front wheel locating clamp which can be adjusted to suit different diameter wheels. When tightening the clamp, take care not to mark the wheel rim or damage the tyre - use wood blocks on each side to prevent this.
● Secure the bike to the ramp using tie-downs **(see illustration 1.2)**. If the bike has only a sidestand, and hence leans at a dangerous angle when raised, support the bike on an auxiliary stand.

1.2 Tie-downs are used around the passenger footrests to secure the bike

● Auxiliary (paddock) stands are widely available from mail order companies or motorcycle dealers and attach either to the wheel axle or swingarm pivot **(see illustration 1.3)**. If the motorcycle has a centrestand, you can support it under the crankcase to prevent it toppling whilst either wheel is removed **(see illustration 1.4)**.

1.3 This auxiliary stand attaches to the swingarm pivot

1.4 Always use a block of wood between the engine and jack head when supporting the engine in this way

Fumes and fire

● Refer to the Safety first! page at the beginning of the manual for full details. Make sure your workshop is equipped with a fire extinguisher suitable for fuel-related fires (Class B fire - flammable liquids) - it is not sufficient to have a water-filled extinguisher.
● Always ensure adequate ventilation is available. Unless an exhaust gas extraction system is available for use, ensure that the engine is run outside of the workshop.
● If working on the fuel system, make sure the workshop is ventilated to avoid a build-up of fumes. This applies equally to fume build-up when charging a battery. Do not smoke or allow anyone else to smoke in the workshop.

Fluids

● If you need to drain fuel from the tank, store it in an approved container marked as suitable for the storage of petrol (gasoline) **(see illustration 1.5)**. Do not store fuel in glass jars or bottles.

1.5 Use an approved can only for storing petrol (gasoline)

● Use proprietary engine degreasers or solvents which have a high flash-point, such as paraffin (kerosene), for cleaning off oil, grease and dirt - never use petrol (gasoline) for cleaning. Wear rubber gloves when handling solvent and engine degreaser. The fumes from certain solvents can be dangerous - always work in a well-ventilated area.

Dust, eye and hand protection

● Protect your lungs from inhalation of dust particles by wearing a filtering mask over the nose and mouth. Many frictional materials still contain asbestos which is dangerous to your health. Protect your eyes from spouts of liquid and sprung components by wearing a pair of protective goggles **(see illustration 1.6)**.

1.6 A fire extinguisher, goggles, mask and protective gloves should be at hand in the workshop

● Protect your hands from contact with solvents, fuel and oils by wearing rubber gloves. Alternatively apply a barrier cream to your hands before starting work. If handling hot components or fluids, wear suitable gloves to protect your hands from scalding and burns.

What to do with old fluids

● Old cleaning solvent, fuel, coolant and oils should not be poured down domestic drains or onto the ground. Package the fluid up in old oil containers, label it accordingly, and take it to a garage or disposal facility. Contact your local authority for location of such sites or ring the oil care hotline.

OIL CARE

Note: It is antisocial and illegal to dump oil down the drain. To find the location of your local oil recycling bank in the UK, call 03708 506 506 or visit www.oilbankline.org.uk

In the USA, note that any oil supplier must accept used oil for recycling.

2 Fasteners - screws, bolts and nuts

Fastener types and applications

Bolts and screws

● Fastener head types are either of hexagonal, Torx or splined design, with internal and external versions of each type **(see illustrations 2.1 and 2.2)**; splined head fasteners are not in common use on motorcycles. The conventional slotted or Phillips head design is used for certain screws. Bolt or screw length is always measured from the underside of the head to the end of the item **(see illustration 2.11)**.

2.1 Internal hexagon/Allen (A), Torx (B) and splined (C) fasteners, with corresponding bits

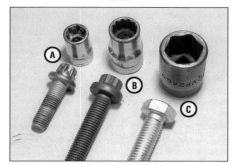

2.2 External Torx (A), splined (B) and hexagon (C) fasteners, with corresponding sockets

● Certain fasteners on the motorcycle have a tensile marking on their heads, the higher the marking the stronger the fastener. High tensile fasteners generally carry a 10 or higher marking. Never replace a high tensile fastener with one of a lower tensile strength.

Washers **(see illustration 2.3)**

● Plain washers are used between a fastener head and a component to prevent damage to the component or to spread the load when torque is applied. Plain washers can also be used as spacers or shims in certain assemblies. Copper or aluminium plain washers are often used as sealing washers on drain plugs.

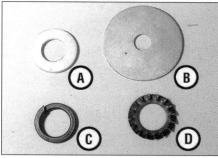

2.3 Plain washer (A), penny washer (B), spring washer (C) and serrated washer (D)

● The split-ring spring washer works by applying axial tension between the fastener head and component. If flattened, it is fatigued and must be renewed. If a plain (flat) washer is used on the fastener, position the spring washer between the fastener and the plain washer.
● Serrated star type washers dig into the fastener and component faces, preventing loosening. They are often used on electrical earth (ground) connections to the frame.
● Cone type washers (sometimes called Belleville) are conical and when tightened apply axial tension between the fastener head and component. They must be installed with the dished side against the component and often carry an OUTSIDE marking on their outer face. If flattened, they are fatigued and must be renewed.
● Tab washers are used to lock plain nuts or bolts on a shaft. A portion of the tab washer is bent up hard against one flat of the nut or bolt to prevent it loosening. Due to the tab washer being deformed in use, a new tab washer should be used every time it is disturbed.
● Wave washers are used to take up endfloat on a shaft. They provide light springing and prevent excessive side-to-side play of a component. Can be found on rocker arm shafts.

Nuts and split pins

● Conventional plain nuts are usually six-sided **(see illustration 2.4)**. They are sized by thread diameter and pitch. High tensile nuts carry a number on one end to denote their tensile strength.

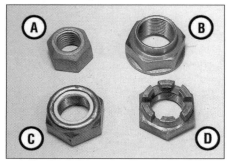

2.4 Plain nut (A), shouldered locknut (B), nylon insert nut (C) and castellated nut (D)

● Self-locking nuts either have a nylon insert, or two spring metal tabs, or a shoulder which is staked into a groove in the shaft - their advantage over conventional plain nuts is a resistance to loosening due to vibration. The nylon insert type can be used a number of times, but must be renewed when the friction of the nylon insert is reduced, ie when the nut spins freely on the shaft. The spring tab type can be reused unless the tabs are damaged. The shouldered type must be renewed every time it is disturbed.
● Split pins (cotter pins) are used to lock a castellated nut to a shaft or to prevent slackening of a plain nut. Common applications are wheel axles and brake torque arms. Because the split pin arms are deformed to lock around the nut a new split pin must always be used on installation - always fit the correct size split pin which will fit snugly in the shaft hole. Make sure the split pin arms are correctly located around the nut **(see illustrations 2.5 and 2.6)**.

2.5 Bend split pin (cotter pin) arms as shown (arrows) to secure a castellated nut

2.6 Bend split pin (cotter pin) arms as shown to secure a plain nut

Caution: If the castellated nut slots do not align with the shaft hole after tightening to the torque setting, tighten the nut until the next slot aligns with the hole - never slacken the nut to align its slot.

● R-pins (shaped like the letter R), or slip pins as they are sometimes called, are sprung and can be reused if they are otherwise in good condition. Always install R-pins with their closed end facing forwards **(see illustration 2.7)**.

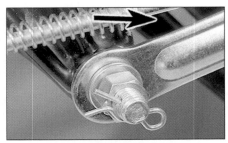

2.7 Correct fitting of R-pin. Arrow indicates forward direction

Circlips (see illustration 2.8)

● Circlips (sometimes called snap-rings) are used to retain components on a shaft or in a housing and have corresponding external or internal ears to permit removal. Parallel-sided (machined) circlips can be installed either way round in their groove, whereas stamped circlips (which have a chamfered edge on one face) must be installed with the chamfer facing away from the direction of thrust load (see illustration 2.9).

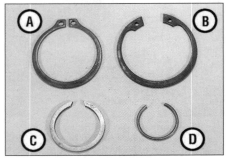

2.8 External stamped circlip (A), internal stamped circlip (B), machined circlip (C) and wire circlip (D)

● Always use circlip pliers to remove and install circlips; expand or compress them just enough to remove them. After installation, rotate the circlip in its groove to ensure it is securely seated. If installing a circlip on a splined shaft, always align its opening with a shaft channel to ensure the circlip ends are well supported and unlikely to catch (see illustration 2.10).

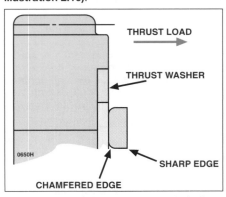

THRUST LOAD

THRUST WASHER

SHARP EDGE

CHAMFERED EDGE

0650H

2.9 Correct fitting of a stamped circlip

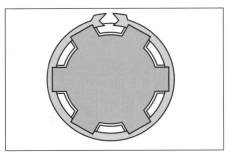

2.10 Align circlip opening with shaft channel

● Circlips can wear due to the thrust of components and become loose in their grooves, with the subsequent danger of becoming dislodged in operation. For this reason, renewal is advised every time a circlip is disturbed.

● Wire circlips are commonly used as piston pin retaining clips. If a removal tang is provided, long-nosed pliers can be used to dislodge them, otherwise careful use of a small flat-bladed screwdriver is necessary. Wire circlips should be renewed every time they are disturbed.

Thread diameter and pitch

● Diameter of a male thread (screw, bolt or stud) is the outside diameter of the threaded portion (see illustration 2.11). Most motorcycle manufacturers use the ISO (International Standards Organisation) metric system expressed in millimetres, eg M6 refers to a 6 mm diameter thread. Sizing is the same for nuts, except that the thread diameter is measured across the valleys of the nut.

● Pitch is the distance between the peaks of the thread (see illustration 2.11). It is expressed in millimetres, thus a common bolt size may be expressed as 6.0 x 1.0 mm (6 mm thread diameter and 1 mm pitch). Generally pitch increases in proportion to thread diameter, although there are always exceptions.

● Thread diameter and pitch are related for conventional fastener applications and the accompanying table can be used as a guide. Additionally, the AF (Across Flats), spanner or socket size dimension of the bolt or nut (see illustration 2.11) is linked to thread and pitch specification. Thread pitch can be measured with a thread gauge (see illustration 2.12).

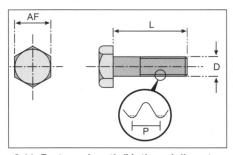

AF

L

D

P

2.11 Fastener length (L), thread diameter (D), thread pitch (P) and head size (AF)

2.12 Using a thread gauge to measure pitch

AF size	Thread diameter x pitch (mm)
8 mm	M5 x 0.8
8 mm	M6 x 1.0
10 mm	M6 x 1.0
12 mm	M8 x 1.25
14 mm	M10 x 1.25
17 mm	M12 x 1.25

● The threads of most fasteners are of the right-hand type, ie they are turned clockwise to tighten and anti-clockwise to loosen. The reverse situation applies to left-hand thread fasteners, which are turned anti-clockwise to tighten and clockwise to loosen. Left-hand threads are used where rotation of a component might loosen a conventional right-hand thread fastener.

Seized fasteners

● Corrosion of external fasteners due to water or reaction between two dissimilar metals can occur over a period of time. It will build up sooner in wet conditions or in countries where salt is used on the roads during the winter. If a fastener is severely corroded it is likely that normal methods of removal will fail and result in its head being ruined. When you attempt removal, the fastener thread should be heard to crack free and unscrew easily - if it doesn't, stop there before damaging something.

● A smart tap on the head of the fastener will often succeed in breaking free corrosion which has occurred in the threads (see illustration 2.13).

● An aerosol penetrating fluid (such as WD-40) applied the night beforehand may work its way down into the thread and ease removal. Depending on the location, you may be able to make up a Plasticine well around the fastener head and fill it with penetrating fluid.

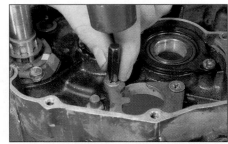

2.13 A sharp tap on the head of a fastener will often break free a corroded thread

● If you are working on an engine internal component, corrosion will most likely not be a problem due to the well lubricated environment. However, components can be very tight and an impact driver is a useful tool in freeing them **(see illustration 2.14)**.

2.14 Using an impact driver to free a fastener

● Where corrosion has occurred between dissimilar metals (eg steel and aluminium alloy), the application of heat to the fastener head will create a disproportionate expansion rate between the two metals and break the seizure caused by the corrosion. Whether heat can be applied depends on the location of the fastener - any surrounding components likely to be damaged must first be removed **(see illustration 2.15)**. Heat can be applied using a paint stripper heat gun or clothes iron, or by immersing the component in boiling water - wear protective gloves to prevent scalding or burns to the hands.

2.15 Using heat to free a seized fastener

● As a last resort, it is possible to use a hammer and cold chisel to work the fastener head unscrewed **(see illustration 2.16)**. This will damage the fastener, but more importantly extreme care must be taken not to damage the surrounding component.

Caution: Remember that the component being secured is generally of more value than the bolt, nut or screw - when the fastener is freed, do not unscrew it with force, instead work the fastener back and forth when resistance is felt to prevent thread damage.

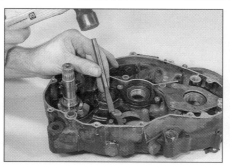

2.16 Using a hammer and chisel to free a seized fastener

Broken fasteners and damaged heads

● If the shank of a broken bolt or screw is accessible you can grip it with self-locking grips. The knurled wheel type stud extractor tool or self-gripping stud puller tool is particularly useful for removing the long studs which screw into the cylinder mouth surface of the crankcase or bolts and screws from which the head has broken off **(see illustration 2.17)**. Studs can also be removed by locking two nuts together on the threaded end of the stud and using a spanner on the lower nut **(see illustration 2.18)**.

2.17 Using a stud extractor tool to remove a broken crankcase stud

2.18 Two nuts can be locked together to unscrew a stud from a component

● A bolt or screw which has broken off below or level with the casing must be extracted using a screw extractor set. Centre punch the fastener to centralise the drill bit, then drill a hole in the fastener **(see illustration 2.19)**. Select a drill bit which is approximately half to three-quarters the diameter of the fastener

2.19 When using a screw extractor, first drill a hole in the fastener . . .

and drill to a depth which will accommodate the extractor. Use the largest size extractor possible, but avoid leaving too small a wall thickness otherwise the extractor will merely force the fastener walls outwards wedging it in the casing thread.

● If a spiral type extractor is used, thread it anti-clockwise into the fastener. As it is screwed in, it will grip the fastener and unscrew it from the casing **(see illustration 2.20)**.

2.20 . . . then thread the extractor anti-clockwise into the fastener

● If a taper type extractor is used, tap it into the fastener so that it is firmly wedged in place. Unscrew the extractor (anti-clockwise) to draw the fastener out.

> ⚠ *Warning: Stud extractors are very hard and may break off in the fastener if care is not taken - ask an engineer about spark erosion if this happens.*

● Alternatively, the broken bolt/screw can be drilled out and the hole retapped for an oversize bolt/screw or a diamond-section thread insert. It is essential that the drilling is carried out squarely and to the correct depth, otherwise the casing may be ruined - if in doubt, entrust the work to an engineer.

● Bolts and nuts with rounded corners cause the correct size spanner or socket to slip when force is applied. Of the types of spanner/socket available always use a six-point type rather than an eight or twelve-point type - better grip

2.21 Comparison of surface drive ring spanner (left) with 12-point type (right)

is obtained. Surface drive spanners grip the middle of the hex flats, rather than the corners, and are thus good in cases of damaged heads **(see illustration 2.21)**.

● Slotted-head or Phillips-head screws are often damaged by the use of the wrong size screwdriver. Allen-head and Torx-head screws are much less likely to sustain damage. If enough of the screw head is exposed you can use a hacksaw to cut a slot in its head and then use a conventional flat-bladed screwdriver to remove it. Alternatively use a hammer and cold chisel to tap the head of the fastener around to slacken it. Always replace damaged fasteners with new ones, preferably Torx or Allen-head type.

HAYNES HiNT

A dab of valve grinding compound between the screw head and screw-driver tip will often give a good grip.

Thread repair

● Threads (particularly those in aluminium alloy components) can be damaged by overtightening, being assembled with dirt in the threads, or from a component working loose and vibrating. Eventually the thread will fail completely, and it will be impossible to tighten the fastener.

● If a thread is damaged or clogged with old locking compound it can be renovated with a thread repair tool (thread chaser) **(see illustrations 2.22 and 2.23)**; special thread

2.22 A thread repair tool being used to correct an internal thread

2.23 A thread repair tool being used to correct an external thread

chasers are available for spark plug hole threads. The tool will not cut a new thread, but clean and true the original thread. Make sure that you use the correct diameter and pitch tool. Similarly, external threads can be cleaned up with a die or a thread restorer file **(see illustration 2.24)**.

2.24 Using a thread restorer file

● It is possible to drill out the old thread and retap the component to the next thread size. This will work where there is enough surrounding material and a new bolt or screw can be obtained. Sometimes, however, this is not possible - such as where the bolt/screw passes through another component which must also be suitably modified, and in cases where a spark plug or oil drain plug cannot be obtained in a larger diameter thread size.

● The diamond-section thread insert (often known by its popular trade name of Heli-Coil) is a simple and effective method of renewing the thread and retaining the original size. A kit can be purchased which contains the tap, insert and installing tool **(see illustration 2.25)**. Drill out the damaged thread with the size drill specified **(see illustration 2.26)**. Carefully retap the thread **(see illustration 2.27)**. Install the

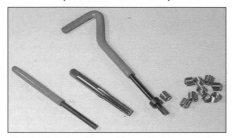

2.25 Obtain a thread insert kit to suit the thread diameter and pitch required

2.26 To install a thread insert, first drill out the original thread . . .

2.27 . . . tap a new thread . . .

2.28 . . . fit insert on the installing tool . . .

2.29 . . . and thread into the component . . .

2.30 . . . break off the tang when complete

insert on the installing tool and thread it slowly into place using a light downward pressure **(see illustrations 2.28 and 2.29)**. When positioned between a 1/4 and 1/2 turn below the surface withdraw the installing tool and use the break-off tool to press down on the tang, breaking it off **(see illustration 2.30)**.

● There are epoxy thread repair kits on the market which can rebuild stripped internal threads, although this repair should not be used on high load-bearing components.

Thread locking and sealing compounds

● Locking compounds are used in locations where the fastener is prone to loosening due to vibration or on important safety-related items which might cause loss of control of the motorcycle if they fail. It is also used where important fasteners cannot be secured by other means such as lockwashers or split pins.

● Before applying locking compound, make sure that the threads (internal and external) are clean and dry with all old compound removed. Select a compound to suit the component being secured - a non-permanent general locking and sealing type is suitable for most applications, but a high strength type is needed for permanent fixing of studs in castings. Apply a drop or two of the compound to the first few threads of the fastener, then thread it into place and tighten to the specified torque. Do not apply excessive thread locking compound otherwise the thread may be damaged on subsequent removal.

● Certain fasteners are impregnated with a dry film type coating of locking compound on their threads. Always renew this type of fastener if disturbed.

● Anti-seize compounds, such as copper-based greases, can be applied to protect threads from seizure due to extreme heat and corrosion. A common instance is spark plug threads and exhaust system fasteners.

3 Measuring tools and gauges

Feeler gauges

● Feeler gauges (or blades) are used for measuring small gaps and clearances (see illustration 3.1). They can also be used to measure endfloat (sideplay) of a component on a shaft where access is not possible with a dial gauge.

● Feeler gauge sets should be treated with care and not bent or damaged. They are etched with their size on one face. Keep them clean and very lightly oiled to prevent corrosion build-up.

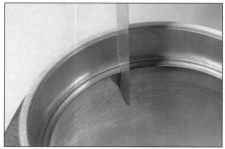

3.1 Feeler gauges are used for measuring small gaps and clearances - thickness is marked on one face of gauge

● When measuring a clearance, select a gauge which is a light sliding fit between the two components. You may need to use two gauges together to measure the clearance accurately.

Micrometers

● A micrometer is a precision tool capable of measuring to 0.01 or 0.001 of a millimetre. It should always be stored in its case and not in the general toolbox. It must be kept clean and never dropped, otherwise its frame or measuring anvils could be distorted resulting in inaccurate readings.

● External micrometers are used for measuring outside diameters of components and have many more applications than internal micrometers. Micrometers are available in different size ranges, eg 0 to 25 mm, 25 to 50 mm, and upwards in 25 mm steps; some large micrometers have interchangeable anvils to allow a range of measurements to be taken. Generally the largest precision measurement you are likely to take on a motorcycle is the piston diameter.

● Internal micrometers (or bore micrometers) are used for measuring inside diameters, such as valve guides and cylinder bores. Telescoping gauges and small hole gauges are used in conjunction with an external micrometer, whereas the more expensive internal micrometers have their own measuring device.

External micrometer

Note: *The conventional analogue type instrument is described. Although much easier to read, digital micrometers are considerably more expensive.*

● Always check the calibration of the micrometer before use. With the anvils closed (0 to 25 mm type) or set over a test gauge

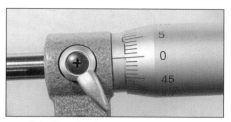

3.2 Check micrometer calibration before use

(for the larger types) the scale should read zero (see illustration 3.2); make sure that the anvils (and test piece) are clean first. Any discrepancy can be adjusted by referring to the instructions supplied with the tool. Remember that the micrometer is a precision measuring tool - don't force the anvils closed, use the ratchet (4) on the end of the micrometer to close it. In this way, a measured force is always applied.

● To use, first make sure that the item being measured is clean. Place the anvil of the micrometer (1) against the item and use the thimble (2) to bring the spindle (3) lightly into contact with the other side of the item (see illustration 3.3). Don't tighten the thimble down because this will damage the micrometer - instead use the ratchet (4) on the end of the micrometer. The ratchet mechanism applies a measured force preventing damage to the instrument.

● The micrometer is read by referring to the linear scale on the sleeve and the annular scale on the thimble. Read off the sleeve first to obtain the base measurement, then add the fine measurement from the thimble to obtain the overall reading. The linear scale on the sleeve represents the measuring range of the micrometer (eg 0 to 25 mm). The annular scale

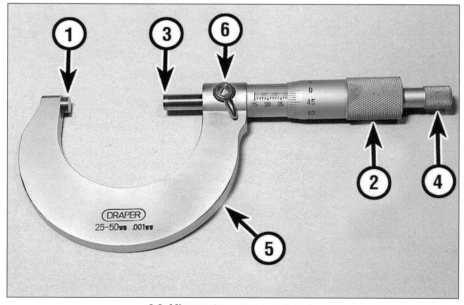

3.3 Micrometer component parts

1	Anvil	3	Spindle	5	Frame
2	Thimble	4	Ratchet	6	Locking lever

on the thimble will be in graduations of 0.01 mm (or as marked on the frame) - one full revolution of the thimble will move 0.5 mm on the linear scale. Take the reading where the datum line on the sleeve intersects the thimble's scale. Always position the eye directly above the scale otherwise an inaccurate reading will result.

In the example shown the item measures 2.95 mm **(see illustration 3.4)**:

Linear scale	2.00 mm
Linear scale	0.50 mm
Annular scale	0.45 mm
Total figure	2.95 mm

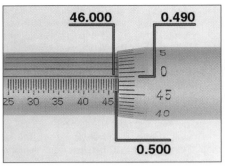

3.5 **Micrometer reading of 46.99 mm on linear and annular scales . . .**

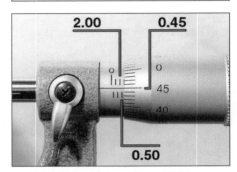

3.4 **Micrometer reading of 2.95 mm**

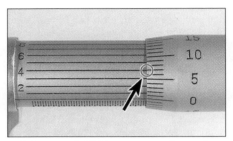

3.6 **. . . and 0.004 mm on vernier scale**

Most micrometers have a locking lever (6) on the frame to hold the setting in place, allowing the item to be removed from the micrometer.

● Some micrometers have a vernier scale on their sleeve, providing an even finer measurement to be taken, in 0.001 increments of a millimetre. Take the sleeve and thimble measurement as described above, then check which graduation on the vernier scale aligns with that of the annular scale on the thimble. **Note:** *The eye must be perpendicular to the scale when taking the vernier reading - if necessary rotate the body of the micrometer to ensure this.* Multiply the vernier scale figure by 0.001 and add it to the base and fine measurement figures.

In the example shown the item measures 46.994 mm **(see illustrations 3.5 and 3.6)**:

Linear scale (base)	46.000 mm
Linear scale (base)	00.500 mm
Annular scale (fine)	00.490 mm
Vernier scale	00.004 mm
Total figure	46.994 mm

Internal micrometer

● Internal micrometers are available for measuring bore diameters, but are expensive and unlikely to be available for home use. It is suggested that a set of telescoping gauges and small hole gauges, both of which must be used with an external micrometer, will suffice for taking internal measurements on a motorcycle.

● Telescoping gauges can be used to measure internal diameters of components. Select a gauge with the correct size range, make sure its ends are clean and insert it into the bore. Expand the gauge, then lock its position and withdraw it from the bore **(see illustration 3.7)**. Measure across the gauge ends with a micrometer **(see illustration 3.8)**.

● Very small diameter bores (such as valve guides) are measured with a small hole gauge. Once adjusted to a slip-fit inside the component, its position is locked and the gauge withdrawn for measurement with a micrometer **(see illustrations 3.9 and 3.10)**.

Vernier caliper

Note: *The conventional linear and dial gauge type instruments are described. Digital types are easier to read, but are far more expensive.*

● The vernier caliper does not provide the precision of a micrometer, but is versatile in being able to measure internal and external diameters. Some types also incorporate a depth gauge. It is ideal for measuring clutch plate friction material and spring free lengths.

● To use the conventional linear scale vernier, slacken off the vernier clamp screws (1) and set its jaws over (2), or inside (3), the item to be measured **(see illustration 3.11)**. Slide the jaw into contact, using the thumbwheel (4) for fine movement of the sliding scale (5) then tighten the clamp screws (1). Read off the main scale (6) where the zero on the sliding scale (5) intersects it, taking the whole number to the left of the zero; this provides the base measurement. View along the sliding scale and select the division which

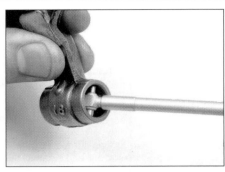

3.7 **Expand the telescoping gauge in the bore, lock its position . . .**

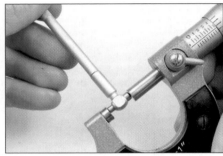

3.8 **. . . then measure the gauge with a micrometer**

3.9 **Expand the small hole gauge in the bore, lock its position . . .**

3.10 **. . . then measure the gauge with a micrometer**

lines up exactly with any of the divisions on the main scale, noting that the divisions usually represents 0.02 of a millimetre. Add this fine measurement to the base measurement to obtain the total reading.

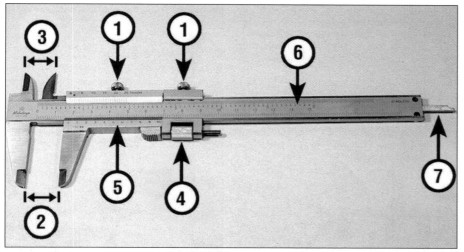

3.11 Vernier component parts (linear gauge)

1	Clamp screws	5	Sliding scale	7	Depth gauge
2	External jaws	6	Main scale		
3	Internal jaws				
4	Thumbwheel				

In the example shown the item measures 55.92 mm **(see illustration 3.12)**:

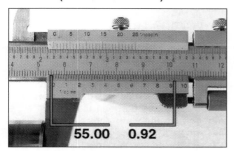

3.12 Vernier gauge reading of 55.92 mm

Base measurement	55.00 mm
Fine measurement	00.92 mm
Total figure	55.92 mm

● Some vernier calipers are equipped with a dial gauge for fine measurement. Before use, check that the jaws are clean, then close them fully and check that the dial gauge reads zero. If necessary adjust the gauge ring accordingly. Slacken the vernier clamp screw (1) and set its jaws over (2), or inside (3), the item to be measured **(see illustration 3.13)**. Slide the jaws into contact, using the thumbwheel (4) for fine movement. Read off the main scale (5) where the edge of the sliding scale (6) intersects it, taking the whole number to the left of the zero; this provides the base measurement. Read off the needle position on the dial gauge (7) scale to provide the fine measurement; each division represents 0.05 of a millimetre. Add this fine measurement to the base measurement to obtain the total reading.

In the example shown the item measures 55.95 mm **(see illustration 3.14)**:

Base measurement	55.00 mm
Fine measurement	00.95 mm
Total figure	55.95 mm

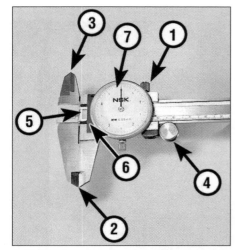

3.13 Vernier component parts (dial gauge)

1	Clamp screw	5	Main scale
2	External jaws	6	Sliding scale
3	Internal jaws	7	Dial gauge
4	Thumbwheel		

3.14 Vernier gauge reading of 55.95 mm

Plastigauge

● Plastigauge is a plastic material which can be compressed between two surfaces to measure the oil clearance between them. The width of the compressed Plastigauge is measured against a calibrated scale to determine the clearance.

● Common uses of Plastigauge are for measuring the clearance between crankshaft journal and main bearing inserts, between crankshaft journal and big-end bearing inserts, and between camshaft and bearing surfaces. The following example describes big-end oil clearance measurement.

● Handle the Plastigauge material carefully to prevent distortion. Using a sharp knife, cut a length which corresponds with the width of the bearing being measured and place it carefully across the journal so that it is parallel with the shaft **(see illustration 3.15)**. Carefully install both bearing shells and the connecting rod. Without rotating the rod on the journal tighten its bolts or nuts (as applicable) to the specified torque. The connecting rod and bearings are then disassembled and the crushed Plastigauge examined.

3.15 Plastigauge placed across shaft journal

● Using the scale provided in the Plastigauge kit, measure the width of the material to determine the oil clearance **(see illustration 3.16)**. Always remove all traces of Plastigauge after use using your fingernails.

Caution: Arriving at the correct clearance demands that the assembly is torqued correctly, according to the settings and sequence (where applicable) provided by the motorcycle manufacturer.

3.16 Measuring the width of the crushed Plastigauge

Dial gauge or DTI (Dial Test Indicator)

● A dial gauge can be used to accurately measure small amounts of movement. Typical uses are measuring shaft runout or shaft endfloat (sideplay) and setting piston position for ignition timing on two-strokes. A dial gauge set usually comes with a range of different probes and adapters and mounting equipment.

● The gauge needle must point to zero when at rest. Rotate the ring around its periphery to zero the gauge.

● Check that the gauge is capable of reading the extent of movement in the work. Most gauges have a small dial set in the face which records whole millimetres of movement as well as the fine scale around the face periphery which is calibrated in 0.01 mm divisions. Read off the small dial first to obtain the base measurement, then add the measurement from the fine scale to obtain the total reading.

In the example shown the gauge reads 1.48 mm **(see illustration 3.17)**:

Base measurement	1.00 mm
Fine measurement	0.48 mm
Total figure	1.48 mm

3.17 Dial gauge reading of 1.48 mm

● If measuring shaft runout, the shaft must be supported in vee-blocks and the gauge mounted on a stand perpendicular to the shaft. Rest the tip of the gauge against the centre of the shaft and rotate the shaft slowly whilst watching the gauge reading **(see illustration 3.18)**. Take several measurements along the length of the shaft and record the

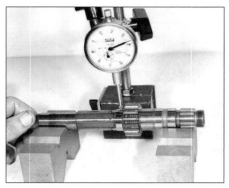

3.18 Using a dial gauge to measure shaft runout

maximum gauge reading as the amount of runout in the shaft. **Note:** *The reading obtained will be total runout at that point - some manufacturers specify that the runout figure is halved to compare with their specified runout limit.*

● Endfloat (sideplay) measurement requires that the gauge is mounted securely to the surrounding component with its probe touching the end of the shaft. Using hand pressure, push and pull on the shaft noting the maximum endfloat recorded on the gauge **(see illustration 3.19)**.

3.19 Using a dial gauge to measure shaft endfloat

● A dial gauge with suitable adapters can be used to determine piston position BTDC on two-stroke engines for the purposes of ignition timing. The gauge, adapter and suitable length probe are installed in the place of the spark plug and the gauge zeroed at TDC. If the piston position is specified as 1.14 mm BTDC, rotate the engine back to 2.00 mm BTDC, then slowly forwards to 1.14 mm BTDC.

Cylinder compression gauges

● A compression gauge is used for measuring cylinder compression. Either the rubber-cone type or the threaded adapter type can be used. The latter is preferred to ensure a perfect seal against the cylinder head. A 0 to 300 psi (0 to 20 Bar) type gauge (for petrol/gasoline engines) will be suitable for motorcycles.

● The spark plug is removed and the gauge either held hard against the cylinder head (cone type) or the gauge adapter screwed into the cylinder head (threaded type) **(see illustration 3.20)**. Cylinder compression is measured with the engine turning over, but not running. The

3.20 Using a rubber-cone type cylinder compression gauge

gauge will hold the reading until manually released.

Oil pressure gauge

● An oil pressure gauge is used for measuring engine oil pressure. Most gauges come with a set of adapters to fit the thread of the take-off point **(see illustration 3.21)**. If the take-off point specified by the motorcycle manufacturer is an external oil pipe union, make sure that the specified replacement union is used to prevent oil starvation.

3.21 Oil pressure gauge and take-off point adapter (arrow)

● Oil pressure is measured with the engine running (at a specific rpm) and often the manufacturer will specify pressure limits for a cold and hot engine.

Straight-edge and surface plate

● If checking the gasket face of a component for warpage, place a steel rule or precision straight-edge across the gasket face and measure any gap between the straight-edge and component with feeler gauges **(see illustration 3.22)**. Check diagonally across the component and between mounting holes **(see illustration 3.23)**.

3.22 Use a straight-edge and feeler gauges to check for warpage

3.23 Check for warpage in these directions

● Checking individual components for warpage, such as clutch plain (metal) plates, requires a perfectly flat plate or piece or plate glass and feeler gauges.

4 Torque and leverage

What is torque?

● Torque describes the twisting force about a shaft. The amount of torque applied is determined by the distance from the centre of the shaft to the end of the lever and the amount of force being applied to the end of the lever; distance multiplied by force equals torque.

● The manufacturer applies a measured torque to a bolt or nut to ensure that it will not slacken in use and to hold two components securely together without movement in the joint. The actual torque setting depends on the thread size, bolt or nut material and the composition of the components being held.

● Too little torque may cause the fastener to loosen due to vibration, whereas too much torque will distort the joint faces of the component or cause the fastener to shear off. Always stick to the specified torque setting.

Using a torque wrench

● Check the calibration of the torque wrench and make sure it has a suitable range for the job. Torque wrenches are available in Nm (Newton-metres), kgf m (kilograms-force metre), lbf ft (pounds-feet), lbf in (inch-pounds). Do not confuse lbf ft with lbf in.

● Adjust the tool to the desired torque on the scale (see illustration 4.1). If your torque wrench is not calibrated in the units specified, carefully convert the figure (see Conversion Factors). A manufacturer sometimes gives a torque setting as a range (8 to 10 Nm) rather than a single figure - in this case set the tool midway between the two settings. The same torque may be expressed as 9 Nm ± 1 Nm. Some torque wrenches have a method of locking the setting so that it isn't inadvertently altered during use.

4.1 Set the torque wrench index mark to the setting required, in this case 12 Nm

● Install the bolts/nuts in their correct location and secure them lightly. Their threads must be clean and free of any old locking compound. Unless specified the threads and flange should be dry - oiled threads are necessary in certain circumstances and the manufacturer will take this into account in the specified torque figure. Similarly, the manufacturer may also specify the application of thread-locking compound.

● Tighten the fasteners in the specified sequence until the torque wrench clicks, indicating that the torque setting has been reached. Apply the torque again to double-check the setting. Where different thread diameter fasteners secure the component, as a rule tighten the larger diameter ones first.

● When the torque wrench has been finished with, release the lock (where applicable) and fully back off its setting to zero - do not leave the torque wrench tensioned. Also, do not use a torque wrench for slackening a fastener.

Angle-tightening

● Manufacturers often specify a figure in degrees for final tightening of a fastener. This usually follows tightening to a specific torque setting.

● A degree disc can be set and attached to the socket (see illustration 4.2) or a protractor can be used to mark the angle of movement on the bolt/nut head and the surrounding casting (see illustration 4.3).

4.2 Angle tightening can be accomplished with a torque-angle gauge . . .

4.3 . . . or by marking the angle on the surrounding component

Loosening sequences

● Where more than one bolt/nut secures a component, loosen each fastener evenly a little at a time. In this way, not all the stress of the joint is held by one fastener and the components are not likely to distort.

● If a tightening sequence is provided, work in the REVERSE of this, but if not, work from the outside in, in a criss-cross sequence (see illustration 4.4).

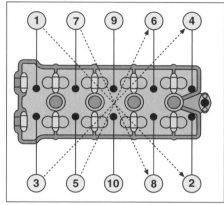

4.4 When slackening, work from the outside inwards

Tightening sequences

● If a component is held by more than one fastener it is important that the retaining bolts/nuts are tightened evenly to prevent uneven stress build-up and distortion of sealing faces. This is especially important on high-compression joints such as the cylinder head.

● A sequence is usually provided by the manufacturer, either in a diagram or actually marked in the casting. If not, always start in the centre and work outwards in a criss-cross pattern (see illustration 4.5). Start off by securing all bolts/nuts finger-tight, then set the torque wrench and tighten each fastener by a small amount in sequence until the final torque is reached. By following this practice,

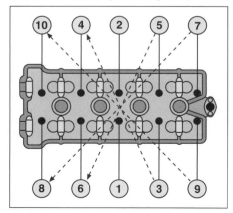

4.5 When tightening, work from the inside outwards

the joint will be held evenly and will not be distorted. Important joints, such as the cylinder head and big-end fasteners often have two- or three-stage torque settings.

Applying leverage

● Use tools at the correct angle. Position a socket wrench or spanner on the bolt/nut so that you pull it towards you when loosening. If this can't be done, push the spanner without curling your fingers around it **(see illustration 4.6)** - the spanner may slip or the fastener loosen suddenly, resulting in your fingers being crushed against a component.

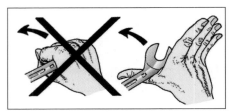

4.6 If you can't pull on the spanner to loosen a fastener, push with your hand open

● Additional leverage is gained by extending the length of the lever. The best way to do this is to use a breaker bar instead of the regular length tool, or to slip a length of tubing over the end of the spanner or socket wrench.
● If additional leverage will not work, the fastener head is either damaged or firmly corroded in place (see Fasteners).

5 Bearings

Bearing removal and installation

Drivers and sockets

● Before removing a bearing, always inspect the casing to see which way it must be driven out - some casings will have retaining plates or a cast step. Also check for any identifying markings on the bearing and if installed to a certain depth, measure this at this stage. Some roller bearings are sealed on one side - take note of the original fitted position.
● Bearings can be driven out of a casing using a bearing driver tool (with the correct size head) or a socket of the correct diameter. Select the driver head or socket so that it contacts the outer race of the bearing, not the balls/rollers or inner race. Always support the casing around the bearing housing with wood blocks, otherwise there is a risk of fracture. The bearing is driven out with a few blows on the driver or socket from a heavy mallet. Unless access is severely restricted (as with wheel bearings), a pin-punch is not recommended unless it is moved around the bearing to keep it square in its housing.

● The same equipment can be used to install bearings. Make sure the bearing housing is supported on wood blocks and line up the bearing in its housing. Fit the bearing as noted on removal - generally they are installed with their marked side facing outwards. Tap the bearing squarely into its housing using a driver or socket which bears only on the bearing's outer race - contact with the bearing balls/rollers or inner race will destroy it **(see illustrations 5.1 and 5.2)**.
● Check that the bearing inner race and balls/rollers rotate freely.

5.1 Using a bearing driver against the bearing's outer race

5.2 Using a large socket against the bearing's outer race

Pullers and slide-hammers

● Where a bearing is pressed on a shaft a puller will be required to extract it **(see illustration 5.3)**. Make sure that the puller clamp or legs fit securely behind the bearing and are unlikely to slip out. If pulling a bearing

5.3 This bearing puller clamps behind the bearing and pressure is applied to the shaft end to draw the bearing off

off a gear shaft for example, you may have to locate the puller behind a gear pinion if there is no access to the race and draw the gear pinion off the shaft as well **(see illustration 5.4)**.

> *Caution: Ensure that the puller's centre bolt locates securely against the end of the shaft and will not slip when pressure is applied. Also ensure that puller does not damage the shaft end.*

5.4 Where no access is available to the rear of the bearing, it is sometimes possible to draw off the adjacent component

● Operate the puller so that its centre bolt exerts pressure on the shaft end and draws the bearing off the shaft.
● When installing the bearing on the shaft, tap only on the bearing's inner race - contact with the balls/rollers or outer race with destroy the bearing. Use a socket or length of tubing as a drift which fits over the shaft end **(see illustration 5.5)**.

5.5 When installing a bearing on a shaft use a piece of tubing which bears only on the bearing's inner race

● Where a bearing locates in a blind hole in a casing, it cannot be driven or pulled out as described above. A slide-hammer with knife-edged bearing puller attachment will be required. The puller attachment passes through the bearing and when tightened expands to fit firmly behind the bearing **(see illustration 5.6)**. By operating the slide-hammer part of the tool the bearing is jarred out of its housing **(see illustration 5.7)**.
● It is possible, if the bearing is of reasonable weight, for it to drop out of its housing if the casing is heated as described opposite.

5.6 Expand the bearing puller so that it locks behind the bearing . . .

5.7 . . . attach the slide hammer to the bearing puller

If this method is attempted, first prepare a work surface which will enable the casing to be tapped face down to help dislodge the bearing - a wood surface is ideal since it will not damage the casing's gasket surface. Wearing protective gloves, tap the heated casing several times against the work surface to dislodge the bearing under its own weight **(see illustration 5.8)**.

5.8 Tapping a casing face down on wood blocks can often dislodge a bearing

● Bearings can be installed in blind holes using the driver or socket method described above.

Drawbolts

● Where a bearing or bush is set in the eye of a component, such as a suspension linkage arm or connecting rod small-end, removal by drift may damage the component. Furthermore, a rubber bushing in a shock absorber eye cannot successfully be driven out of position. If access is available to a engineering press, the task is straightforward. If not, a drawbolt can be fabricated to extract the bearing or bush.

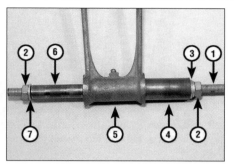

5.9 Drawbolt component parts assembled on a suspension arm

1 Bolt or length of threaded bar
2 Nuts
3 Washer (external diameter greater than tubing internal diameter)
4 Tubing (internal diameter sufficient to accommodate bearing)
5 Suspension arm with bearing
6 Tubing (external diameter slightly smaller than bearing)
7 Washer (external diameter slightly smaller than bearing)

5.10 Drawing the bearing out of the suspension arm

● To extract the bearing/bush you will need a long bolt with nut (or piece of threaded bar with two nuts), a piece of tubing which has an internal diameter larger than the bearing/bush, another piece of tubing which has an external diameter slightly smaller than the bearing/bush, and a selection of washers **(see illustrations 5.9 and 5.10)**. Note that the pieces of tubing must be of the same length, or longer, than the bearing/bush.
● The same kit (without the pieces of tubing) can be used to draw the new bearing/bush back into place **(see illustration 5.11)**.

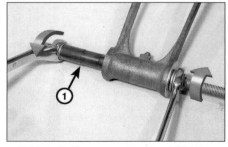

5.11 Installing a new bearing (1) in the suspension arm

Temperature change

● If the bearing's outer race is a tight fit in the casing, the aluminium casing can be heated to release its grip on the bearing. Aluminium will expand at a greater rate than the steel bearing outer race. There are several ways to do this, but avoid any localised extreme heat (such as a blow torch) - aluminium alloy has a low melting point.
● Approved methods of heating a casing are using a domestic oven (heated to 100°C) or immersing the casing in boiling water **(see illustration 5.12)**. Low temperature range localised heat sources such as a paint stripper heat gun or clothes iron can also be used **(see illustration 5.13)**. Alternatively, soak a rag in boiling water, wring it out and wrap it around the bearing housing.

> ⚠️ **Warning: All of these methods require care in use to prevent scalding and burns to the hands. Wear protective gloves when handling hot components.**

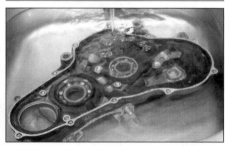

5.12 A casing can be immersed in a sink of boiling water to aid bearing removal

5.13 Using a localised heat source to aid bearing removal

● If heating the whole casing note that plastic components, such as the neutral switch, may suffer - remove them beforehand.
● After heating, remove the bearing as described above. You may find that the expansion is sufficient for the bearing to fall out of the casing under its own weight or with a light tap on the driver or socket.
● If necessary, the casing can be heated to aid bearing installation, and this is sometimes the recommended procedure if the motorcycle manufacturer has designed the housing and bearing fit with this intention.

● Installation of bearings can be eased by placing them in a freezer the night before installation. The steel bearing will contract slightly, allowing easy insertion in its housing. This is often useful when installing steering head outer races in the frame.

Bearing types and markings

● Plain shell bearings, ball bearings, needle roller bearings and tapered roller bearings will all be found on motorcycles **(see illustrations 5.14 and 5.15)**. The ball and roller types are usually caged between an inner and outer race, but uncaged variations may be found.

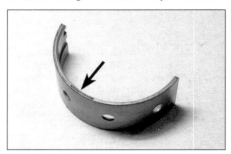

5.14 Shell bearings are either plain or grooved. They are usually identified by colour code (arrow)

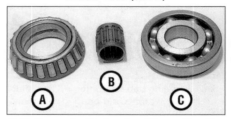

5.15 Tapered roller bearing (A), needle roller bearing (B) and ball journal bearing (C)

● Shell bearings (often called inserts) are usually found at the crankshaft main and connecting rod big-end where they are good at coping with high loads. They are made of a phosphor-bronze material and are impregnated with self-lubricating properties.

● Ball bearings and needle roller bearings consist of a steel inner and outer race with the balls or rollers between the races. They require constant lubrication by oil or grease and are good at coping with axial loads. Taper roller bearings consist of rollers set in a tapered cage set on the inner race; the outer race is separate. They are good at coping with axial loads and prevent movement along the shaft - a typical application is in the steering head.

● Bearing manufacturers produce bearings to ISO size standards and stamp one face of the bearing to indicate its internal and external diameter, load capacity and type **(see illustration 5.16)**.

● Metal bushes are usually of phosphor-bronze material. Rubber bushes are used in suspension mounting eyes. Fibre bushes have also been used in suspension pivots.

5.16 Typical bearing marking

Bearing fault finding

● If a bearing outer race has spun in its housing, the housing material will be damaged. You can use a bearing locking compound to bond the outer race in place if damage is not too severe.

● Shell bearings will fail due to damage of their working surface, as a result of lack of lubrication, corrosion or abrasive particles in the oil **(see illustration 5.17)**. Small particles of dirt in the oil may embed in the bearing material whereas larger particles will score the bearing and shaft journal. If a number of short journeys are made, insufficient heat will be generated to drive off condensation which has built up on the bearings.

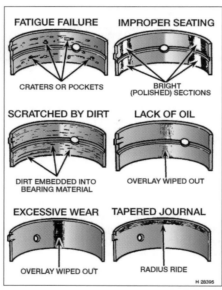

5.17 Typical bearing failures

● Ball and roller bearings will fail due to lack of lubrication or damage to the balls or rollers. Tapered-roller bearings can be damaged by overloading them. Unless the bearing is sealed on both sides, wash it in paraffin (kerosene) to remove all old grease then allow it to dry. Make a visual inspection looking to dented balls or rollers, damaged cages and worn or pitted races **(see illustration 5.18)**.

● A ball bearing can be checked for wear by listening to it when spun. Apply a film of light oil to the bearing and hold it close to the ear - hold the outer race with one hand and spin the

5.18 Example of ball journal bearing with damaged balls and cages

5.19 Hold outer race and listen to inner race when spun

inner race with the other hand **(see illustration 5.19)**. The bearing should be almost silent when spun; if it grates or rattles it is worn.

6 Oil seals

Oil seal removal and installation

● Oil seals should be renewed every time a component is dismantled. This is because the seal lips will become set to the sealing surface and will not necessarily reseal.

● Oil seals can be prised out of position using a large flat-bladed screwdriver **(see illustration 6.1)**. In the case of crankcase seals, check first that the seal is not lipped on the inside, preventing its removal with the crankcases joined.

6.1 Prise out oil seals with a large flat-bladed screwdriver

● New seals are usually installed with their marked face (containing the seal reference code) outwards and the spring side towards the fluid being retained. In certain cases, such as a two-stroke engine crankshaft seal, a double lipped seal may be used due to there being fluid or gas on each side of the joint.

● Use a bearing driver or socket which bears only on the outer hard edge of the seal to install it in the casing - tapping on the inner edge will damage the sealing lip.

Oil seal types and markings

● Oil seals are usually of the single-lipped type. Double-lipped seals are found where a liquid or gas is on both sides of the joint.

● Oil seals can harden and lose their sealing ability if the motorcycle has been in storage for a long period - renewal is the only solution.

● Oil seal manufacturers also conform to the ISO markings for seal size - these are moulded into the outer face of the seal **(see illustration 6.2)**.

6.2 These oil seal markings indicate inside diameter, outside diameter and seal thickness

7 Gaskets and sealants

Types of gasket and sealant

● Gaskets are used to seal the mating surfaces between components and keep lubricants, fluids, vacuum or pressure contained within the assembly. Aluminium gaskets are sometimes found at the cylinder joints, but most gaskets are paper-based. If the mating surfaces of the components being joined are undamaged the gasket can be installed dry, although a dab of sealant or grease will be useful to hold it in place during assembly.

● RTV (Room Temperature Vulcanising) silicone rubber sealants cure when exposed to moisture in the atmosphere. These sealants are good at filling pits or irregular gasket faces, but will tend to be forced out of the joint under very high torque. They can be used to replace a paper gasket, but first make sure that the width of the paper gasket is not essential to the shimming of internal components. RTV sealants should not be used on components containing petrol (gasoline).

● Non-hardening, semi-hardening and hard setting liquid gasket compounds can be used with a gasket or between a metal-to-metal joint. Select the sealant to suit the application: universal non-hardening sealant can be used on virtually all joints; semi-hardening on joint faces which are rough or damaged; hard setting sealant on joints which require a permanent bond and are subjected to high temperature and pressure. **Note:** *Check first if the paper gasket has a bead of sealant*

impregnated in its surface before applying additional sealant.

● When choosing a sealant, make sure it is suitable for the application, particularly if being applied in a high-temperature area or in the vicinity of fuel. Certain manufacturers produce sealants in either clear, silver or black colours to match the finish of the engine. This has a particular application on motorcycles where much of the engine is exposed.

● Do not over-apply sealant. That which is squeezed out on the outside of the joint can be wiped off, whereas an excess of sealant on the inside can break off and clog oilways.

Breaking a sealed joint

● Age, heat, pressure and the use of hard setting sealant can cause two components to stick together so tightly that they are difficult to separate using finger pressure alone. Do not resort to using levers unless there is a pry point provided for this purpose **(see illustration 7.1)** or else the gasket surfaces will be damaged.

● Use a soft-faced hammer **(see illustration 7.2)** or a wood block and conventional hammer to strike the component near the mating surface. Avoid hammering against cast extremities since they may break off. If this method fails, try using a wood wedge between the two components.

> **Caution: If the joint will not separate, double-check that you have removed all the fasteners.**

7.1 If a pry point is provided, apply gently pressure with a flat-bladed screwdriver

7.2 Tap around the joint with a soft-faced mallet if necessary - don't strike cooling fins

Removal of old gasket and sealant

● Paper gaskets will most likely come away complete, leaving only a few traces stuck

Most components have one or two hollow locating dowels between the two gasket faces. If a dowel cannot be removed, do not resort to gripping it with pliers - it will almost certainly be distorted. Install a close-fitting socket or Phillips screwdriver into the dowel and then grip the outer edge of the dowel to free it.

on the sealing faces of the components. It is imperative that all traces are removed to ensure correct sealing of the new gasket.

● Very carefully scrape all traces of gasket away making sure that the sealing surfaces are not gouged or scored by the scraper **(see illustrations 7.3, 7.4 and 7.5)**. Stubborn deposits can be removed by spraying with an aerosol gasket remover. Final preparation of

7.3 Paper gaskets can be scraped off with a gasket scraper tool . . .

7.4 . . . a knife blade . . .

7.5 . . . or a household scraper

7.6 Fine abrasive paper is wrapped around a flat file to clean up the gasket face

7.7 A kitchen scourer can be used on stubborn deposits

the gasket surface can be made with very fine abrasive paper or a plastic kitchen scourer **(see illustrations 7.6 and 7.7)**.

● Old sealant can be scraped or peeled off components, depending on the type originally used. Note that gasket removal compounds are available to avoid scraping the components clean; make sure the gasket remover suits the type of sealant used.

8 Chains

Breaking and joining final drive chains

● Drive chains for all but small bikes are continuous and do not have a clip-type connecting link. The chain must be broken using a chain breaker tool and the new chain securely riveted together using a new soft rivet-type link. Never use a clip-type connecting link instead of a rivet-type link, except in an emergency. Various chain breaking and riveting tools are available, either as separate tools or combined as illustrated in the accompanying photographs - read the instructions supplied with the tool carefully.

> ⚠ **Warning: The need to rivet the new link pins correctly cannot be overstressed - loss of control of the motorcycle is very likely to result if the chain breaks in use.**

● Rotate the chain and look for the soft link. The soft link pins look like they have been

8.1 Tighten the chain breaker to push the pin out of the link . . .

8.2 . . . withdraw the pin, remove the tool . . .

8.3 . . . and separate the chain link

deeply centre-punched instead of peened over like all the other pins **(see illustration 8.9)** and its sideplate may be a different colour. Position the soft link midway between the sprockets and assemble the chain breaker tool over one of the soft link pins **(see illustration 8.1)**. Operate the tool to push the pin out through the chain **(see illustration 8.2)**. On an O-ring chain, remove the O-rings **(see illustration 8.3)**. Carry out the same procedure on the other soft link pin.

> **Caution: Certain soft link pins (particularly on the larger chains) may require their ends to be filed or ground off before they can be pressed out using the tool.**

● Check that you have the correct size and strength (standard or heavy duty) new soft link - do not reuse the old link. Look for the size marking on the chain sideplates **(see illustration 8.10)**.

● Position the chain ends so that they are engaged over the rear sprocket. On an O-ring

8.4 Insert the new soft link, with O-rings, through the chain ends . . .

8.5 . . . install the O-rings over the pin ends . . .

8.6 . . . followed by the sideplate

chain, install a new O-ring over each pin of the link and insert the link through the two chain ends **(see illustration 8.4)**. Install a new O-ring over the end of each pin, followed by the sideplate (with the chain manufacturer's marking facing outwards) **(see illustrations 8.5 and 8.6)**. On an unsealed chain, insert the link through the two chain ends, then install the sideplate with the chain manufacturer's marking facing outwards.

● Note that it may not be possible to install the sideplate using finger pressure alone. If using a joining tool, assemble it so that the plates of the tool clamp the link and press the sideplate over the pins **(see illustration 8.7)**. Otherwise, use two small sockets placed over

8.7 Push the sideplate into position using a clamp

8.8 Assemble the chain riveting tool over one pin at a time and tighten it fully

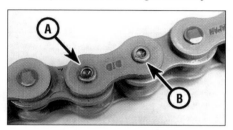

8.9 Pin end correctly riveted (A), pin end unriveted (B)

the rivet ends and two pieces of the wood between a G-clamp. Operate the clamp to press the sideplate over the pins.

● Assemble the joining tool over one pin (following the maker's instructions) and tighten the tool down to spread the pin end securely **(see illustrations 8.8 and 8.9)**. Do the same on the other pin.

> ⚠ **Warning: Check that the pin ends are secure and that there is no danger of the sideplate coming loose. If the pin ends are cracked the soft link must be renewed.**

Final drive chain sizing

● Chains are sized using a three digit number, followed by a suffix to denote the chain type **(see illustration 8.10)**. Chain type is either standard or heavy duty (thicker sideplates), and also unsealed or O-ring/X-ring type.

● The first digit of the number relates to the pitch of the chain, ie the distance from the centre of one pin to the centre of the next pin **(see illustration 8.11)**. Pitch is expressed in eighths of an inch, as follows:

8.10 Typical chain size and type marking

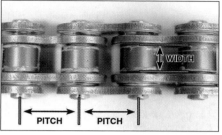

8.11 Chain dimensions

| Sizes commencing with a 4 (eg 428) have a pitch of 1/2 inch (12.7 mm) |
| Sizes commencing with a 5 (eg 520) have a pitch of 5/8 inch (15.9 mm) |
| Sizes commencing with a 6 (eg 630) have a pitch of 3/4 inch (19.1 mm) |

● The second and third digits of the chain size relate to the width of the rollers, again in imperial units, eg the 525 shown has 5/16 inch (7.94 mm) rollers **(see illustration 8.11)**.

9 Hoses

Clamping to prevent flow

● Small-bore flexible hoses can be clamped to prevent fluid flow whilst a component is worked on. Whichever method is used, ensure that the hose material is not permanently distorted or damaged by the clamp.

a) A brake hose clamp available from auto accessory shops **(see illustration 9.1)**.
b) A wingnut type hose clamp **(see illustration 9.2)**.

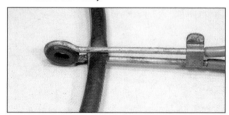

9.1 Hoses can be clamped with an automotive brake hose clamp . . .

9.2 . . . a wingnut type hose clamp . . .

c) Two sockets placed each side of the hose and held with straight-jawed self-locking grips **(see illustration 9.3)**.
d) Thick card each side of the hose held between straight-jawed self-locking grips **(see illustration 9.4)**.

9.3 . . . two sockets and a pair of self-locking grips . . .

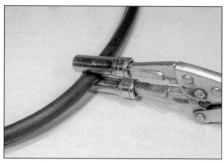

9.4 . . . or thick card and self-locking grips

Freeing and fitting hoses

● Always make sure the hose clamp is moved well clear of the hose end. Grip the hose with your hand and rotate it whilst pulling it off the union. If the hose has hardened due to age and will not move, slit it with a sharp knife and peel its ends off the union **(see illustration 9.5)**.

● Resist the temptation to use grease or soap on the unions to aid installation; although it helps the hose slip over the union it will equally aid the escape of fluid from the joint. It is preferable to soften the hose ends in hot water and wet the inside surface of the hose with water or a fluid which will evaporate.

9.5 Cutting a coolant hose free with a sharp knife

Introduction

In less time than it takes to read this introduction, a thief could steal your motorcycle. Returning only to find your bike has gone is one of the worst feelings in the world. Even if the motorcycle is insured against theft, once you've got over the initial shock, you will have the inconvenience of dealing with the police and your insurance company.

The motorcycle is an easy target for the professional thief and the joyrider alike and the official figures on motorcycle theft make for depressing reading; on average a motor-cycle is stolen every 16 minutes in the UK!

Motorcycle thefts fall into two categories, those stolen 'to order' and those taken by opportunists. The thief stealing to order will be on the look out for a specific make and model and will go to extraordinary lengths to obtain that motorcycle. The opportunist thief on the other hand will look for easy targets which can be stolen with the minimum of effort and risk.

Whilst it is never going to be possible to make your machine 100% secure, it is estimated that around half of all stolen motorcycles are taken by opportunist thieves. Remember that the opportunist thief is always on the look out for the easy option: if there are two similar motorcycles parked side-by-side, they will target the one with the lowest level of security. By taking a few precautions, you can reduce the chances of your motorcycle being stolen.

Security equipment

There are many specialised motorcycle security devices available and the following text summarises their applications and their good and bad points.

Once you have decided on the type of security equipment which best suits your needs, we recommended that you read one of the many equipment tests regularly carried out by the motorcycle press. These tests compare the products from all the major manufacturers and give impartial ratings on their effectiveness, value-for-money and ease of use.

No one item of security equipment can provide complete protection. It is highly recommended that two or more of the items described below are combined to increase the security of your motorcycle (a lock and chain plus an alarm system is just about ideal). The more security measures fitted to the bike, the less likely it is to be stolen.

Ensure the lock and chain you buy is of good quality and long enough to shackle your bike to a solid object

Lock and chain

Pros: *Very flexible to use; can be used to secure the motorcycle to almost any immovable object. On some locks and chains, the lock can be used on its own as a disc lock (see below).*

Cons: *Can be very heavy and awkward to carry on the motorcycle, although some types* will be supplied with a carry bag which can be strapped to the pillion seat.

● Heavy-duty chains and locks are an excellent security measure **(see illustration 1).** Whenever the motorcycle is parked, use the lock and chain to secure the machine to a solid, immovable object such as a post or railings. This will prevent the machine from being ridden away or being lifted into the back of a van.

● When fitting the chain, always ensure the chain is routed around the motorcycle frame or swingarm **(see illustrations 2 and 3).** Never merely pass the chain around one of the wheel rims; a thief may unbolt the wheel and lift the rest of the machine into a van, leaving you with just the wheel! Try to avoid having excess chain free, thus making it difficult to use cutting tools, and keep the chain and lock off the ground to prevent thieves attacking it with a cold chisel. Position the lock so that its lock barrel is facing downwards; this will make it harder for the thief to attack the lock mechanism.

Pass the chain through the bike's frame, rather than just through a wheel . . .

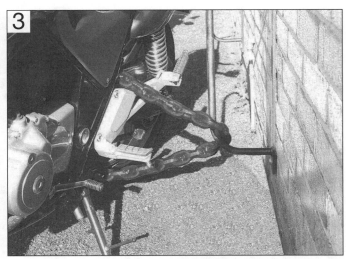

. . . and loop it around a solid object

U-locks

Pros: *Highly effective deterrent which can be used to secure the bike to a post or railings. Most U-locks come with a carrier which allows the lock to be easily carried on the bike.*

Cons: *Not as flexible to use as a lock and chain.*

● These are solid locks which are similar in use to a lock and chain. U-locks are lighter than a lock and chain but not so flexible to use. The length and shape of the lock shackle limit the objects to which the bike can be secured **(see illustration 4)**.

Disc locks

Pros: *Small, light and very easy to carry; most can be stored underneath the seat.*

Cons: *Does not prevent the motorcycle being lifted into a van. Can be very embarrassing if*

U-locks can be used to secure the bike to a solid object – ensure you purchase one which is long enough

you forget to remove the lock before attempting to ride off!

● Disc locks are designed to be attached to the front brake disc. The lock passes through one of the holes in the disc and prevents the wheel rotating by jamming against the fork/brake caliper **(see illustration 5)**. Some are equipped with an alarm siren which sounds if the disc lock is moved; this not only acts as a theft deterrent but also as a handy reminder if you try to move the bike with the lock still fitted.

● Combining the disc lock with a length of cable which can be looped around a post or railings provides an additional measure of security **(see illustration 6)**.

Alarms and immobilisers

Pros: *Once installed it is completely hassle-free to use. If the system is 'Thatcham' or 'Sold Secure-approved', insurance companies may give you a discount.*

Cons: *Can be expensive to buy and complex to install. No system will prevent the motorcycle from being lifted into a van and taken away.*

● Electronic alarms and immobilisers are available to suit a variety of budgets. There are three different types of system available: pure alarms, pure immobilisers, and the more expensive systems which are combined alarm/immobilisers **(see illustration 7)**.

● An alarm system is designed to emit an audible warning if the motorcycle is being tampered with.

● An immobiliser prevents the motorcycle being started and ridden away by disabling its electrical systems.

● When purchasing an alarm/immobiliser system, check the cost of installing the system unless you are able to do it yourself. If the motorcycle is not used regularly, another consideration is the current drain of the system. All alarm/immobiliser systems are powered by the motorcycle's battery; purchasing a system with a very low current drain could prevent the battery losing its charge whilst the motorcycle is not being used.

A typical disc lock attached through one of the holes in the disc

A disc lock combined with a security cable provides additional protection

A typical alarm/immobiliser system

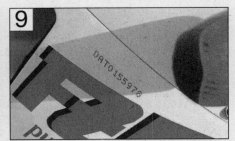

Indelible markings can be applied to most areas of the bike – always apply the manufacturer's sticker to warn off thieves

Chemically-etched code numbers can be applied to main body panels . . .

. . . again, always ensure that the kit manufacturer's sticker is applied in a prominent position

Security marking kits

Pros: *Very cheap and effective deterrent. Many insurance companies will give you a discount on your insurance premium if a recognised security marking kit is used on your motorcycle.*

Cons: *Does not prevent the motorcycle being stolen by joyriders.*

● There are many different types of security marking kits available. The idea is to mark as many parts of the motorcycle as possible with a unique security number **(see illustrations 8, 9 and 10)**. A form will be included with the kit to register your personal details and those of the motorcycle with the kit manufacturer. This register is made available to the police to help them trace the rightful owner of any motorcycle or components which they recover should all other forms of identification have been removed. Always apply the warning stickers provided with the kit to deter thieves.

Ground anchors, wheel clamps and security posts

Pros: *An excellent form of security which will deter all but the most determined of thieves.*

Cons: *Awkward to install and can be expensive.*

● Whilst the motorcycle is at home, it is a good idea to attach it securely to the floor or a solid wall, even if it is kept in a securely locked garage. Various types of ground anchors, security posts and wheel clamps are available for this purpose **(see illustration 11)**. These security devices are either bolted to a solid concrete or brick structure or can be cemented into the ground.

Permanent ground anchors provide an excellent level of security when the bike is at home

Security at home

A high percentage of motorcycle thefts are from the owner's home. Here are some things to consider whenever your motorcycle is at home:

● Where possible, always keep the motorcycle in a securely locked garage. Never rely solely on the standard lock on the garage door, these are usual hopelessly inadequate. Fit an additional locking mechanism to the door and consider having the garage alarmed. A security light, activated by a movement sensor, is also a good investment.

● Always secure the motorcycle to the ground or a wall, even if it is inside a securely locked garage.
● Do not regularly leave the motorcycle outside your home, try to keep it out of sight wherever possible. If a garage is not available, fit a motorcycle cover over the bike to disguise its true identity.
● It is not uncommon for thieves to follow a motorcyclist home to find out where the bike is kept. They will then return at a later date. Be aware of this whenever you are returning home on your motorcycle. If you suspect you are being followed, do not return home, instead ride to a garage or shop and stop as a precaution.
● When selling a motorcycle, do not provide your home address or the location where the bike is normally kept. Arrange to meet the buyer at a location away from your home. Thieves have been known to pose as potential buyers to find out where motorcycles are kept and then return later to steal them.

Security away from the home

As well as fitting security equipment to your motorcycle here are a few general rules to follow whenever you park your motorcycle.
● Park in a busy, public place.
● Use car parks which incorporate security features, such as CCTV.

● At night, park in a well-lit area, preferably directly underneath a street light.
● Engage the steering lock.
● Secure the motorcycle to a solid, immovable object such as a post or railings with an additional lock. If this is not possible, secure the bike to a friend's motorcycle. Some public parking places provide security loops for motorcycles.
● Never leave your helmet or luggage attached to the motorcycle. Take them with you at all times.

Lubricants and fluids

A wide range of lubricants, fluids and cleaning agents is available for motor-cycles. This is a guide as to what is available, its applications and properties.

Four-stroke engine oil

● Engine oil is without doubt the most important component of any four-stroke engine. Modern motorcycle engines place a lot of demands on their oil and choosing the right type is essential. Using an unsuitable oil will lead to an increased rate of engine wear and could result in serious engine damage. Before purchasing oil, always check the recommended oil specification given by the manufacturer. The manufacturer will state a recommended 'type or classification' and also a specific 'viscosity' range for engine oil.

● The oil 'type or classification' is identified by its API (American Petroleum Institute) rating. The API rating will be in the form of two letters, e.g. SG. The S identifies the oil as being suitable for use in a petrol (gasoline) engine (S stands for spark ignition) and the second letter, ranging from A to J, identifies the oil's performance rating. The later this letter, the higher the specification of the oil; for example API SG oil exceeds the requirements of API SF oil. **Note:** *On some oils there may also be a second rating consisting of another two letters, the first letter being C, e.g. API SF/CD. This rating indicates the oil is also suitable for use in a diesel engines (the C stands for compression ignition) and is thus of no relevance for motorcycle use.*

● The 'viscosity' of the oil is identified by its SAE (Society of Automotive Engineers) rating. All modern engines require multigrade oils and the SAE rating will consist of two numbers, the first followed by a W, e.g. 10W/40. The first number indicates the viscosity rating of the oil at low temperatures (W stands for winter – tested at –20ºC) and the second number represents the viscosity of the oil at high temperatures (tested at 100ºC). The lower the number, the thinner the oil. For example an oil with an SAE 10W/40 rating will give better cold starting and running than an SAE 15W/40 oil.

● As well as ensuring the 'type' and 'viscosity' of the oil match the recommendations, another consideration to make when buying engine oil is whether to purchase a standard mineral-based oil, a semi-synthetic oil (also known as a synthetic blend or synthetic-based oil) or a fully-synthetic oil. Although all oils will have a similar rating and viscosity, their cost will vary considerably; mineral-based oils are the cheapest, the fully-synthetic oils the most expensive with the semi-synthetic oils falling somewhere in-between. This decision is very much up to the owner, but it should be noted that modern synthetic oils have far better lubricating and cleaning qualities than traditional mineral-based oils and tend to retain these properties for far longer. Bearing in mind the operating conditions inside a modern, high-revving motorcycle engine it is highly recommended that a fully synthetic oil is used. The extra expense at each service could save you money in the long term by preventing premature engine wear.

● As a final note always ensure that the oil is specifically designed for use in motorcycle engines. Engine oils designed primarily for use in car engines sometimes contain additives or friction modifiers which could cause clutch slip on a motorcycle fitted with a wet-clutch.

Two-stroke engine oil

● Modern two-stroke engines, with their high power outputs, place high demands on their oil. If engine seizure is to be avoided it is essential that a high-quality oil is used. Two-stroke oils differ hugely from four-stroke oils. The oil lubricates only the crankshaft and piston(s) (the transmission has its own lubricating oil) and is used on a total-loss basis where it is burnt completely during the combustion process.

● The Japanese have recently introduced a classification system for two-stroke oils, the JASO rating. This rating is in the form of two letters, either FA, FB or FC – FA is the lowest classification and FC the highest. Ensure the oil being used meets or exceeds the recommended rating specified by the manufacturer.

● As well as ensuring the oil rating matches the recommendation, another consideration to make when buying engine oil is whether to purchase a standard mineral-based oil, a semi-synthetic oil (also known as a synthetic blend or synthetic-based oil) or a fully-synthetic oil. The cost of each type of oil varies considerably; mineral-based oils are the cheapest, the fully-synthetic oils the most expensive with the semi-synthetic oils falling somewhere in-between. This decision is very much up to the owner, but it should be noted that modern synthetic oils have far better lubricating properties and burn cleaner than traditional mineral-based oils. It is therefore recommended that a fully synthetic oil is used. The extra expense could save you money in the long term by preventing premature engine wear, engine performance will be improved, carbon deposits and exhaust smoke will be reduced.

● Always ensure that the oil is specifically designed for use in an injector system. Many high quality two-stroke oils are designed for competition use and need to be pre-mixed with fuel. These oils are of a much higher viscosity and are not designed to flow through the injector pumps used on road-going two-stroke motorcycles.

Transmission (gear) oil

● On a two-stroke engine, the transmission and clutch are lubricated by their own separate oil bath which must be changed in accordance with the Maintenance Schedule.
● Although the engine and transmission units of most four-strokes use a common lubrication supply, there are some exceptions where the engine and gearbox have separate oil reservoirs and a dry clutch is used.
● Motorcycle manufacturers will either recommend a monograde transmission oil or a four-stroke multigrade engine oil to lubricate the transmission.
● Transmission oils, or gear oils as they are often called, are designed specifically for use in transmission systems. The viscosity of these oils is represented by an SAE number, but the scale of measurement applied is different to that used to grade engine oils. As a rough guide a SAE90 gear oil will be of the same viscosity as an SAE50 engine oil.

Shaft drive oil

● On models equipped with shaft final drive, the shaft drive gears are will have their own oil supply. The manufacturer will state a recommended 'type or classification' and also a specific 'viscosity' range in the same manner as for four-stroke engine oil.
● Gear oil classification is given by the number which follows the API GL (GL standing for gear lubricant) rating, the higher the number, the higher the specification of the oil, e.g. API GL5 oil is a higher specification than API GL4 oil. Ensure the oil meets or

exceeds the classification specified and is of the correct viscosity. The viscosity of gear oils is also represented by an SAE number but the scale of measurement used is different to that used to grade engine oils. As a rough guide an SAE90 gear oil will be of the same viscosity as an SAE50 engine oil.
● If the use of an EP (Extreme Pressure) gear oil is specified, ensure the oil purchased is suitable.

Fork oil and suspension fluid

● Conventional telescopic front forks are hydraulic and require fork oil to work. To ensure the forks function correctly, the fork oil must be changed in accordance with the Maintenance Schedule.
● Fork oil is available in a variety of viscosities, identified by their SAE rating; fork oil ratings vary from light (SAE 5) to heavy (SAE 30). When purchasing fork oil, ensure the viscosity rating matches that specified by the manufacturer.
● Some lubricant manufacturers also produce a range of high-quality suspension fluids which are very similar to fork oil but are designed mainly for competition use. These fluids may have a different viscosity rating system which is not to be confused with the SAE rating of normal fork oil. Refer to the manufacturer's instructions if in any doubt.

Brake and clutch fluid

● All disc brake systems and some clutch systems are hydraulically operated. To ensure correct operation, the hydraulic fluid must be changed in accordance with the Maintenance Schedule.
● Brake and clutch fluid is classified by its DOT rating with most motorcycle manufacturers specifying DOT 3 or 4 fluid. Both fluid types are glycol-based and can be mixed together without adverse effect; DOT 4 fluid exceeds the requirements

of DOT 3 fluid. Although it is safe to use DOT 4 fluid in a system designed for use with DOT 3 fluid, never use DOT 3 fluid in a system which specifies the use of DOT 4 as this will adversely affect the system's performance. The type required for the system will be marked on the fluid reservoir cap.
● Some manufacturers also produce a DOT 5 hydraulic fluid. DOT 5 hydraulic fluid is silicone-based and is not compatible with the glycol-based DOT 3 and 4 fluids. Never mix DOT 5 fluid with DOT 3 or 4 fluid as this will seriously affect the performance of the hydraulic system.

Coolant/antifreeze

● When purchasing coolant/antifreeze, always ensure it is suitable for use in an aluminium engine and contains corrosion inhibitors to prevent possible blockages of the internal coolant passages of the system. As a general rule, most coolants are designed to be used neat and should not be diluted whereas antifreeze can be mixed with distilled water to provide a coolant solution of the required strength. Refer to the manufacturer's instructions on the bottle.
● Ensure the coolant is changed in accordance with the Maintenance Schedule.

Chain lube

● Chain lube is an aerosol-type spray lubricant specifically designed for use on motorcycle final drive chains. Chain lube has two functions, to minimise friction between the final drive chain and sprockets and to prevent corrosion of the chain. Regular use of a good-quality chain lube will extend the life of the drive chain and sprockets and thus maximise the power being transmitted from the transmission to the rear wheel.
● When using chain lube, always allow some time for the solvents in the lube to evaporate before riding the motorcycle. This will minimise the amount of lube which will

'fling' off from the chain when the motorcycle is used. If the motorcycle is equipped with an 'O-ring' chain, ensure the chain lube is labelled as being suitable for use on 'O-ring' chains.

Degreasers and solvents

● There are many different types of solvents and degreasers available to remove the grime and grease which accumulate around the motorcycle during normal use. Degreasers and solvents are usually available as an aerosol-type spray or as a liquid which you apply with a brush. Always closely follow the manufacturer's instructions and wear eye protection during use. Be aware that many solvents are flammable and may give off noxious fumes; take adequate precautions when using them (see Safety First!).

● For general cleaning, use one of the many solvents or degreasers available from most motorcycle accessory shops. These solvents are usually applied then left for a certain time before being washed off with water.

Brake cleaner is a solvent specifically designed to remove all traces of oil, grease and dust from braking system components. Brake cleaner is designed to evaporate quickly and leaves behind no residue.

Carburettor cleaner is an aerosol-type solvent specifically designed to clear carburettor blockages and break down the hard deposits and gum often found inside carburettors during overhaul.

Contact cleaner is an aerosol-type solvent designed for cleaning electrical components. The cleaner will remove all traces of oil and dirt from components such as switch contacts or fouled spark plugs and then dry, leaving behind no residue.

Gasket remover is an aerosol-type solvent designed for removing stubborn gaskets from engine components during overhaul. Gasket remover will minimise the amount of scraping required to remove the gasket and therefore reduce the risk of damage to the mating surface.

Spray lubricants

● Aerosol-based spray lubricants are widely available and are excellent for lubricating lever pivots and exposed cables and switches. Try to use a lubricant which is of the dry-film type as the fluid evaporates, leaving behind a dry-film of lubricant. Lubricants which leave behind an oily residue will attract dust and dirt which will increase the rate of wear of the cable/lever.

● Most lubricants also act as a moisture dispersant and a penetrating fluid. This means they can also be used to 'dry out' electrical components such as wiring connectors or switches as well as helping to free seized fasteners.

Greases

● Grease is used to lubricate many of the pivot-points. A good-quality multi-purpose grease is suitable for most applications but some manufacturers will specify the use of specialist greases for use on components such as swingarm and suspension linkage bushes. These specialist greases can be purchased from most motorcycle (or car) accessory shops; commonly specified types include molybdenum disulphide grease, lithium-based grease, graphite-based grease, silicone-based grease and high-temperature copper-based grease.

Gasket sealing compounds

● Gasket sealing compounds can be used in conjunction with gaskets, to improve their sealing capabilities, or on their own to seal metal-to-metal joints. Depending on their type, sealing compounds either set hard or stay relatively soft and pliable.

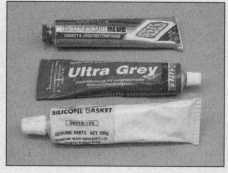

● When purchasing a gasket sealing compound, ensure that it is designed specifically for use on an internal combustion engine. General multi-purpose sealants available from DIY stores may appear visibly similar but they are not designed to withstand the extreme heat or contact with fuel and oil encountered when used on an engine (see 'Tools and Workshop Tips' for further information).

Thread locking compound

● Thread locking compounds are used to secure certain threaded fasteners in position to prevent them from loosening due to vibration. Thread locking compounds can be purchased from most motorcycle (and car) accessory shops. Ensure the threads of the both components are completely clean and dry before sparingly applying the locking compound (see 'Tools and Workshop Tips' for further information).

Fuel additives

● Fuel additives which protect and clean the fuel system components are widely available. These additives are designed to remove all traces of deposits that build up on the carburettors/injectors and prevent wear, helping the fuel system to operate more efficiently. If a fuel additive is being used, check that it is suitable for use with your motorcycle, especially if your motorcycle is equipped with a catalytic converter.

● Octane boosters are also available. These additives are designed to improve the performance of highly-tuned engines being run on normal pump-fuel and are of no real use on standard motorcycles.

About the MOT Test

In the UK, all vehicles more than three years old are subject to an annual test to ensure that they meet minimum safety requirements. A current test certificate must be issued before a machine can be used on public roads, and is required before a road fund licence can be issued. Riding without a current test certificate will also invalidate your insurance.

For most owners, the MOT test is an annual cause for anxiety, and this is largely due to owners not being sure what needs to be checked prior to submitting the motorcycle for testing. The simple answer is that a fully roadworthy motorcycle will have no difficulty in passing the test.

This is a guide to getting your motorcycle through the MOT test. Obviously it will not be possible to examine the motorcycle to the same standard as the professional MOT tester, particularly in view of the equipment required for some of the checks. However, working through the following procedures will enable you to identify any problem areas before submitting the motorcycle for the test.

It has only been possible to summarise the test requirements here, based on the regulations in force at the time of printing. Test standards are becoming increasingly stringent, although there are some exemptions for older vehicles. More information about the test can be obtained from the MOT Inspection Manual for Motor Bicycle and Side Car Testing at www.gov.uk

Many of the checks require that one of the wheels is raised off the ground. If the motorcycle doesn't have a centre stand, note that an auxiliary stand will be required. Additionally, the help of an assistant may prove useful.

Certain exceptions apply to machines under 50 cc, machines without a lighting system, and Classic bikes - if in doubt about any of the requirements listed below seek confirmation from an MOT tester prior to submitting the motorcycle for the test.

Check that the frame number is clearly visible.

Electrical System

Lights, turn signals, horn and reflector

● With the ignition on, check the operation of the following electrical components. **Note:** *The electrical components on certain small-capacity machines are powered by the generator, requiring that the engine is run for this check.*

a) *Headlight and tail light. Check that both illuminate in the low and high beam switch positions.*

b) *Position lights. Check that the front position (or sidelight) and tail light illuminate in this switch position.*

c) *Turn signals. Check that all flash at the correct rate, and that the warning light(s) function correctly. Check that the turn signal switch works correctly.*

d) *Hazard warning system (where fitted). Check that all four turn signals flash in this switch position.*

e) *Brake stop light. Check that the light comes on when the front and rear brakes are independently applied. Models first used on or after 1st April 1986 must have a brake light switch on each brake.*

f) *Horn. Check that the sound is continuous and of reasonable volume.*

● Check that there is a red reflector on the rear of the machine, either mounted separately or as part of the tail light lens.

● Check the condition of the headlight, tail light and turn signal lenses.

Headlight beam height

● The MOT tester will perform a headlight beam height check using specialised beam setting equipment **(see illustration 1)**. This equipment will not be available to the home mechanic, but if you suspect that the headlight is incorrectly set or may have been maladjusted in the past, you can perform a rough test as follows.

● Position the bike in a straight line facing a brick wall. The bike must be off its stand, upright and with a rider seated. Measure the height from the ground to the centre of the headlight and mark a horizontal line on the wall at this height. Position the motorcycle 3.8 metres from the wall and draw a vertical

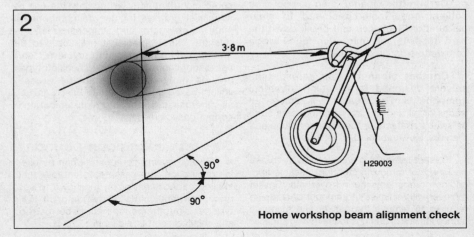

Headlight beam height checking equipment

line up the wall central to the centreline of the motorcycle. Switch to dipped beam and check that the beam pattern falls slightly lower than the horizontal line and to the left of the vertical line **(see illustration 2)**.

Home workshop beam alignment check

Exhaust System and Final Drive

Exhaust

● Check that the exhaust mountings are secure and that the system does not foul any of the rear suspension components.
● Start the motorcycle. When the revs are increased, check that the exhaust is neither holed nor leaking from any of its joints. On a linked system, check that the collector box is not leaking due to corrosion.

● Note that the exhaust decibel level ("loudness" of the exhaust) is assessed at the discretion of the tester. If the motorcycle was first used on or after 1st January 1985 the silencer must carry the BSAU 193 stamp, or a marking relating to its make and model, or be of OE (original equipment) manufacture. If the silencer is marked NOT FOR ROAD USE, RACING USE ONLY or similar, it will fail the MOT.

Final drive

● On chain or belt drive machines, check that the chain/belt is in good condition and does not have excessive slack. Also check that the sprocket is securely mounted on the rear wheel hub. Check that the chain/belt guard is in place.
● On shaft drive bikes, check for oil leaking from the drive unit and fouling the rear tyre.

Steering and Suspension

Steering

● With the front wheel raised off the ground, rotate the steering from lock to lock. The handlebar or switches must not contact the fuel tank or be close enough to trap the rider's hand. Problems can be caused by damaged lock stops on the lower yoke and frame, or by the fitting of non-standard handlebars.
● When performing the lock to lock check, also ensure that the steering moves freely without drag or notchiness. Steering movement can be impaired by poorly routed cables, or by overtight head bearings or worn bvearings. The tester will perform a check of the steering head bearing lower race by mounting the front wheel on a surface plate, then performing a lock to

lock check with the weight of the machine on the lower bearing (see illustration 3).
● Grasp the fork sliders (lower legs) and attempt to push and pull on the forks

Front wheel mounted on a surface plate for steering head bearing lower race check

(see illustration 4). Any play in the steering head bearings will be felt. Note that in extreme cases, wear of the front fork bushes can be misinterpreted for head bearing play.
● Check that the handlebars are securely mounted.
● Check that the handlebar grip rubbers are secure. They should by bonded to the bar left end and to the throttle cable pulley on the right end.

Front suspension

● With the motorcycle off the stand, hold the front brake on and pump the front forks up and down (see illustration 5). Check that they are adequately damped.

Checking the steering head bearings for freeplay

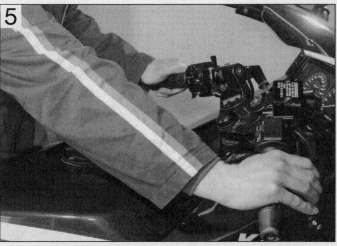

Hold the front brake on and pump the front forks up and down to check operation

6

Inspect the area around the fork dust seal for oil leakage (arrow)

7

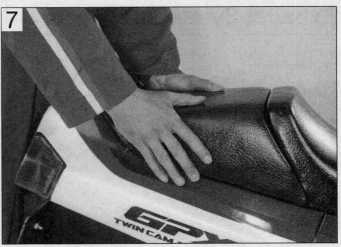

Bounce the rear of the motorcycle to check rear suspension operation

8

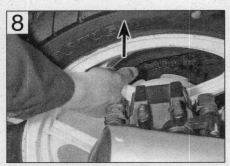

Checking for rear suspension linkage play

● Inspect the area above and around the front fork oil seals **(see illustration 6)**. There should be no sign of oil on the fork tube (stanchion) nor leaking down the slider (lower

leg). On models so equipped, check that there is no oil leaking from the anti-dive units.
● On models with swingarm front suspension, check that there is no freeplay in the linkage when moved from side to side.

Rear suspension

● With the motorcycle off the stand and an assistant supporting the motorcycle by its handlebars, bounce the rear suspension **(see illustration 7)**. Check that the suspension components do not foul on any of the cycle parts and check that the shock absorber(s) provide adequate damping.
● Visually inspect the shock absorber(s)

and check that there is no sign of oil leakage from its damper. This is somewhat restricted on certain single shock models due to the location of the shock absorber.
● With the rear wheel raised off the ground, grasp the wheel at the highest point and attempt to pull it up **(see illustration 8)**. Any play in the swingarm pivot or suspension linkage bearings will be felt as movement. **Note:** *Do not confuse play with actual suspension movement. Failure to lubricate suspension linkage bearings can lead to bearing failure* **(see illustration 9)**.
● With the rear wheel raised off the ground, grasp the swingarm ends and attempt to move the swingarm from side to side and forwards and backwards - any play indicates wear of the swingarm pivot bearings **(see illustration 10)**.

9

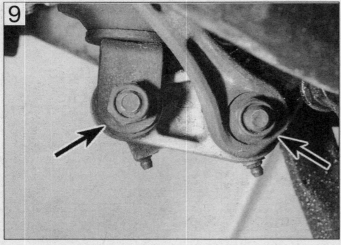

Worn suspension linkage pivots (arrows) are usually the cause of play in the rear suspension

10

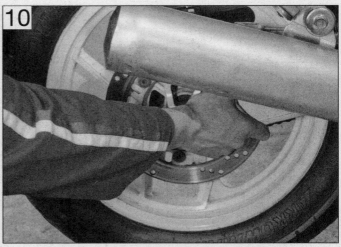

Grasp the swingarm at the ends to check for play in its pivot bearings

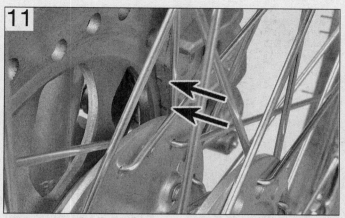

Brake pad wear can usually be viewed without removing the caliper. Most pads have wear indicator grooves (arrowed) and some also have indicator tangs or cut-outs.

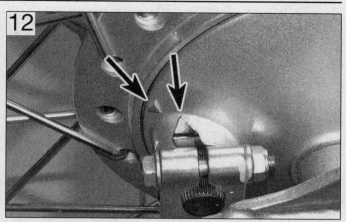

On drum brakes, check the angle of the operating lever with the brake fully applied. Most drum brakes have a wear indicator pointer or scale.

Brakes, Wheels and Tyres

Brakes

● With the wheel raised off the ground, apply the brake then free it off, and check that the wheel is about to revolve freely without brake drag.

● On disc brakes, examine the disc itself. Check that it is securely mounted and not cracked.

● On disc brakes, view the pad material through the caliper mouth and check that the pads are not worn down beyond the limit (see illustration 11).

● On drum brakes, check that when the brake is applied the angle between the operating lever and cable or rod is not too great (see illustration 12). Check also that the operating lever doesn't foul any other components.

● On disc brakes, examine the flexible hoses from top to bottom. Have an assistant hold the brake on so that the fluid in the hose is under pressure, and check that there is no sign of fluid leakage, bulges or cracking. If there are any metal brake pipes or unions, check that these are free from corrosion and damage. Where a brake-linked anti-dive system is fitted, check the hoses to the anti-dive in a similar manner.

● Check that the rear brake torque arm is secure and that its fasteners are secured by self-locking nuts or castellated nuts with split-pins or R-pins (see illustration 13).

● On models with ABS, check that the self-check warning light in the instrument panel works.

● The MOT tester will perform a test of the motorcycle's braking efficiency based on a calculation of rider and motorcycle weight. Although this cannot be carried out at home, you can at least ensure that the braking systems are properly maintained. For hydraulic disc brakes, check the fluid level, lever/pedal feel (bleed of air if its spongy) and pad material. For drum brakes, check adjustment, cable or rod operation and shoe lining thickness.

Wheels and tyres

● Check the wheel condition. Cast wheels should be free from cracks and if of the built-up design, all fasteners should be secure. Spoked wheels should be checked for broken, corroded, loose or bent spokes.

● With the wheel raised off the ground, spin the wheel and visually check that the tyre and wheel run true. Check that the tyre does not foul the suspension or mudguards.

● With the wheel raised off the ground, grasp the wheel and attempt to move it about the axle (spindle) (see illustration 14). Any play felt here indicates wheel bearing failure.

Brake torque arm must be properly secured at both ends

Check for wheel bearing play by trying to move the wheel about the axle (spindle)

Checking the tyre tread depth

Tyre direction of rotation arrow can be found on tyre sidewall

Castellated type wheel axle (spindle) nut must be secured by a split pin or R-pin

Two straightedges are used to check wheel alignment

● Check the tyre tread depth, tread condition and sidewall condition (see illustration 15).
● Check the tyre type. Front and rear tyre

types must be compatible and be suitable for road use. Tyres marked NOT FOR ROAD USE, COMPETITION USE ONLY or similar, will fail the MOT.

● If the tyre sidewall carries a direction of rotation arrow, this must be pointing in the direction of normal wheel rotation (see illustration 16).
● Check that the wheel axle (spindle) nuts (where applicable) are properly secured. A self-locking nut or castellated nut with a split-pin or R-pin can be used (see illustration 17).
● Wheel alignment is checked with the motorcycle off the stand and a rider seated. With the front wheel pointing straight ahead, two perfectly straight lengths of metal or wood and placed against the sidewalls of both tyres (see illustration 18). The gap each side of the front tyre must be equidistant on both sides. Incorrect wheel alignment may be due to a cocked rear wheel (often as the result of poor chain adjustment) or in extreme cases, a bent frame.

General checks and condition

● Check the security of all major fasteners, bodypanels, seat, fairings (where fitted) and mudguards.

● Check that the rider and pillion footrests, handlebar levers and brake pedal are securely mounted.

● Check for corrosion on the frame or any load-bearing components. If severe, this may affect the structure, particularly under stress.

Sidecars

A motorcycle fitted with a sidecar requires additional checks relating to the stability of the machine and security of attachment and

swivel joints, plus specific wheel alignment (toe-in) requirements. Additionally, tyre and lighting requirements differ from conventional

motorcycle use. Owners are advised to check MOT test requirements with an official test centre.

Preparing for storage

Before you start

If repairs or an overhaul is needed, see that this is carried out now rather than left until you want to ride the bike again.

Give the bike a good wash and scrub all dirt from its underside. Make sure the bike dries completely before preparing for storage.

Engine

● Remove the spark plug(s) and lubricate the cylinder bores with approximately a teaspoon of motor oil using a spout-type oil can (see illustration 1). Reinstall the spark plug(s). Crank the engine over a couple of times to coat the piston rings and bores with oil. If the bike has a kickstart, use this to turn the engine over. If not, flick the kill switch to the OFF position and crank the engine over on the starter (see illustration 2). If the nature on the ignition system prevents the starter operating with the kill switch in the OFF position, remove the spark plugs and fit them back in their caps; ensure that the plugs are earthed (grounded) against the cylinder head when the starter is operated (see illustration 3).

 Warning: It is important that the plugs are earthed (grounded) away from the spark plug holes otherwise there is a risk of atomised fuel from the cylinders igniting.

 On a single cylinder four-stroke engine, you can seal the combustion chamber completely by positioning the piston at TDC on the compression stroke.

● Drain the carburettor(s) otherwise there is a risk of jets becoming blocked by gum deposits from the fuel (see illustration 4).

● If the bike is going into long-term storage, consider adding a fuel stabiliser to the fuel in the tank. If the tank is drained completely, corrosion of its internal surfaces may occur if left unprotected for a long period. The tank can be treated with a rust preventative especially for this purpose. Alternatively, remove the tank and pour half a litre of motor oil into it, install the filler cap and shake the tank to coat its internals with oil before draining off the excess. The same effect can also be achieved by spraying WD40 or a similar water-dispersant around the inside of the tank via its flexible nozzle.

● Make sure the cooling system contains the correct mix of antifreeze. Antifreeze also contains important corrosion inhibitors.

● The air intakes and exhaust can be sealed off by covering or plugging the openings. Ensure that you do not seal in any condensation; run the engine until it is hot,

Squirt a drop of motor oil into each cylinder

Flick the kill switch to OFF . . .

. . . and ensure that the metal bodies of the plugs (arrows) are earthed against the cylinder head

Connect a hose to the carburettor float chamber drain stub (arrow) and unscrew the drain screw

Exhausts can be sealed off with a plastic bag

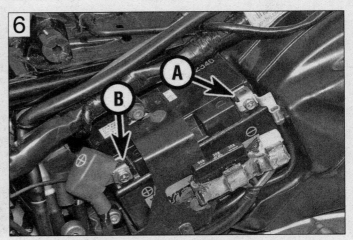

Disconnect the negative lead (A) first, followed by the positive lead (B)

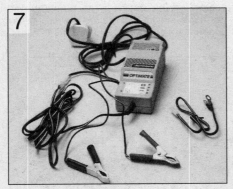

Use a suitable battery charger - this kit also assess battery condition

then switch off and allow to cool. Tape a piece of thick plastic over the silencer end(s) (see illustration 5). Note that some advocate pouring a tablespoon of motor oil into the silencer(s) before sealing them off.

Battery

● Remove it from the bike - in extreme cases of cold the battery may freeze and crack its case (see illustration 6).

● Check the electrolyte level and top up if necessary (conventional refillable batteries). Clean the terminals.
● Store the battery off the motorcycle and away from any sources of fire. Position a wooden block under the battery if it is to sit on the ground.
● Give the battery a trickle charge for a few hours every month (see illustration 7).

Tyres

● Place the bike on its centrestand or an auxiliary stand which will support the motorcycle in an upright position. Position wood blocks under the tyres to keep them off the ground and to provide insulation from damp. If the bike is being put into long-term storage, ideally both tyres should be off the ground; not only will this protect the tyres, but will also ensure that no load is placed on the steering head or wheel bearings.
● Deflate each tyre by 5 to 10 psi, no more or the beads may unseat from the rim, making subsequent inflation difficult on tubeless tyres.

Pivots and controls

● Lubricate all lever, pedal, stand and footrest

pivot points. If grease nipples are fitted to the rear suspension components, apply lubricant to the pivots.
● Lubricate all control cables.

Cycle components

● Apply a wax protectant to all painted and plastic components. Wipe off any excess, but don't polish to a shine. Where fitted, clean the screen with soap and water.
● Coat metal parts with Vaseline (petroleum jelly). When applying this to the fork tubes, do not compress the forks otherwise the seals will rot from contact with the Vaseline.
● Apply a vinyl cleaner to the seat.

Storage conditions

● Aim to store the bike in a shed or garage which does not leak and is free from damp.
● Drape an old blanket or bedspread over the bike to protect it from dust and direct contact with sunlight (which will fade paint). This also hides the bike from prying eyes. Beware of tight-fitting plastic covers which may allow condensation to form and settle on the bike.

Getting back on the road

Engine and transmission

● Change the oil and replace the oil filter. If this was done prior to storage, check that the oil hasn't emulsified - a thick whitish substance which occurs through condensation.
● Remove the spark plugs. Using a spout-type oil can, squirt a few drops of oil into the cylinder(s). This will provide initial lubrication as the piston rings and bores comes back into contact. Service the spark plugs, or fit new ones, and install them in the engine.

● Check that the clutch isn't stuck on. The plates can stick together if left standing for some time, preventing clutch operation. Engage a gear and try rocking the bike back and forth with the clutch lever held against the handlebar. If this doesn't work on cable-operated clutches, hold the clutch lever back against the handlebar with a strong elastic band or cable tie for a couple of hours (see illustration 8).
● If the air intakes or silencer end(s) were blocked off, remove the bung or cover used.
● If the fuel tank was coated with a rust

Hold clutch lever back against the handlebar with elastic bands or a cable tie

preventative, oil or a stabiliser added to the fuel, drain and flush the tank and dispose of the fuel sensibly. If no action was taken with the fuel tank prior to storage, it is advised that the old fuel is disposed of since it will go off over a period of time. Refill the fuel tank with fresh fuel.

Frame and running gear

● Oil all pivot points and cables.
● Check the tyre pressures. They will definitely need inflating if pressures were reduced for storage.
● Lubricate the final drive chain (where applicable).
● Remove any protective coating applied to the fork tubes (stanchions) since this may well destroy the fork seals. If the fork tubes weren't protected and have picked up rust spots, remove them with very fine abrasive paper and refinish with metal polish.
● Check that both brakes operate correctly. Apply each brake hard and check that it's not possible to move the motorcycle forwards, then check that the brake frees off again once released. Brake caliper pistons can stick due to corrosion around the piston head, or on the sliding caliper types, due to corrosion of the slider pins. If the brake doesn't free after repeated operation, take the caliper off for examination. Similarly drum brakes can stick

due to a seized operating cam, cable or rod linkage.
● If the motorcycle has been in long-term storage, renew the brake fluid and clutch fluid (where applicable).
● Depending on where the bike has been stored, the wiring, cables and hoses may have been nibbled by rodents. Make a visual check and investigate disturbed wiring loom tape.

Battery

● If the battery has been previously removal and given top up charges it can simply be reconnected. Remember to connect the positive cable first and the negative cable last.
● On conventional refillable batteries, if the battery has not received any attention, remove it from the motorcycle and check its electrolyte level. Top up if necessary then charge the battery. If the battery fails to hold a charge and a visual checks show heavy white sulphation of the plates, the battery is probably defective and must be renewed. This is particularly likely if the battery is old. Confirm battery condition with a specific gravity check.
● On sealed (MF) batteries, if the battery has not received any attention, remove it from the motorcycle and charge it according to the information on the battery case - if the battery fails to hold a charge it must be renewed.

Starting procedure

● If a kickstart is fitted, turn the engine over a couple of times with the ignition OFF to distribute oil around the engine. If no kickstart is fitted, flick the engine kill switch OFF and the ignition ON and crank the engine over a couple of times to work oil around the upper cylinder components. If the nature of the ignition system is such that the starter won't work with the kill switch OFF, remove the spark plugs, fit them back into their caps and earth (ground) their bodies on the cylinder head. Reinstall the spark plugs afterwards.
● Switch the kill switch to RUN, operate the choke and start the engine. If the engine won't start don't continue cranking the engine - not only will this flatten the battery, but the starter motor will overheat. Switch the ignition off and try again later. If the engine refuses to start, go through the fault finding procedures in this manual. **Note:** *If the bike has been in storage for a long time, old fuel or a carburettor blockage may be the problem. Gum deposits in carburettors can block jets - if a carburettor cleaner doesn't prove successful the carburettors must be dismantled for cleaning.*
● Once the engine has started, check that the lights, turn signals and horn work properly.
● Treat the bike gently for the first ride and check all fluid levels on completion. Settle the bike back into the maintenance schedule.

Conversion factors

Length (distance)

Inches (in)	x 25.4	=	Millimetres (mm)	x 0.0394	= Inches (in)
Feet (ft)	x 0.305	=	Metres (m)	x 3.281	= Feet (ft)
Miles	x 1.609	=	Kilometres (km)	x 0.621	= Miles

Volume (capacity)

Cubic inches (cu in; in³)	x 16.387	=	Cubic centimetres (cc; cm³)	x 0.061	= Cubic inches (cu in; in³)
Imperial pints (Imp pt)	x 0.568	=	Litres (l)	x 1.76	= Imperial pints (Imp pt)
Imperial quarts (Imp qt)	x 1.137	=	Litres (l)	x 0.88	= Imperial quarts (Imp qt)
Imperial quarts (Imp qt)	x 1.201	=	US quarts (US qt)	x 0.833	= Imperial quarts (Imp qt)
US quarts (US qt)	x 0.946	=	Litres (l)	x 1.057	= US quarts (US qt)
Imperial gallons (Imp gal)	x 4.546	=	Litres (l)	x 0.22	= Imperial gallons (Imp gal)
Imperial gallons (Imp gal)	x 1.201	=	US gallons (US gal)	x 0.833	= Imperial gallons (Imp gal)
US gallons (US gal)	x 3.785	=	Litres (l)	x 0.264	= US gallons (US gal)

Mass (weight)

Ounces (oz)	x 28.35	=	Grams (g)	x 0.035	= Ounces (oz)
Pounds (lb)	x 0.454	=	Kilograms (kg)	x 2.205	= Pounds (lb)

Force

Ounces-force (ozf; oz)	x 0.278	=	Newtons (N)	x 3.6	= Ounces-force (ozf; oz)
Pounds-force (lbf; lb)	x 4.448	=	Newtons (N)	x 0.225	= Pounds-force (lbf; lb)
Newtons (N)	x 0.1	=	Kilograms-force (kgf; kg)	x 9.81	= Newtons (N)

Pressure

Pounds-force per square inch (psi; lbf/in²; lb/in²)	x 0.070	=	Kilograms-force per square centimetre (kgf/cm²; kg/cm²)	x 14.223	= Pounds-force per square inch (psi; lbf/in²; lb/in²)
Pounds-force per square inch (psi; lbf/in²; lb/in²)	x 0.068	=	Atmospheres (atm)	x 14.696	= Pounds-force per square inch (psi; lbf/in²; lb/in²)
Pounds-force per square inch (psi; lbf/in²; lb/in²)	x 0.069	=	Bars	x 14.5	= Pounds-force per square inch (psi; lbf/in²; lb/in²)
Pounds-force per square inch (psi; lbf/in²; lb/in²)	x 6.895	=	Kilopascals (kPa)	x 0.145	= Pounds-force per square inch (psi; lbf/in²; lb/in²)
Kilopascals (kPa)	x 0.01	=	Kilograms-force per square centimetre (kgf/cm²; kg/cm²)	x 98.1	= Kilopascals (kPa)
Millibar (mbar)	x 100	=	Pascals (Pa)	x 0.01	= Millibar (mbar)
Millibar (mbar)	x 0.0145	=	Pounds-force per square inch (psi; lbf/in²; lb/in²)	x 68.947	= Millibar (mbar)
Millibar (mbar)	x 0.75	=	Millimetres of mercury (mmHg)	x 1.333	= Millibar (mbar)
Millibar (mbar)	x 0.401	=	Inches of water (inH₂O)	x 2.491	= Millibar (mbar)
Millimetres of mercury (mmHg)	x 0.535	=	Inches of water (inH₂O)	x 1.868	= Millimetres of mercury (mmHg)
Inches of water (inH₂O)	x 0.036	=	Pounds-force per square inch (psi; lbf/in²; lb/in²)	x 27.68	= Inches of water (inH₂O)

Torque (moment of force)

Pounds-force inches (lbf in; lb in)	x 1.152	=	Kilograms-force centimetre (kgf cm; kg cm)	x 0.868	= Pounds-force inches (lbf in; lb in)
Pounds-force inches (lbf in; lb in)	x 0.113	=	Newton metres (Nm)	x 8.85	= Pounds-force inches (lbf in; lb in)
Pounds-force inches (lbf in; lb in)	x 0.083	=	Pounds-force feet (lbf ft; lb ft)	x 12	= Pounds-force inches (lbf in; lb in)
Pounds-force feet (lbf ft; lb ft)	x 0.138	=	Kilograms-force metres (kgf m; kg m)	x 7.233	= Pounds-force feet (lbf ft; lb ft)
Pounds-force feet (lbf ft; lb ft)	x 1.356	=	Newton metres (Nm)	x 0.738	= Pounds-force feet (lbf ft; lb ft)
Newton metres (Nm)	x 0.102	=	Kilograms-force metres (kgf m; kg m)	x 9.804	= Newton metres (Nm)

Power

Horsepower (hp)	x 745.7	=	Watts (W)	x 0.0013	= Horsepower (hp)

Velocity (speed)

Miles per hour (miles/hr; mph)	x 1.609	=	Kilometres per hour (km/hr; kph)	x 0.621	= Miles per hour (miles/hr; mph)

Fuel consumption*

Miles per gallon, Imperial (mpg)	x 0.354	=	Kilometres per litre (km/l)	x 2.825	= Miles per gallon, Imperial (mpg)
Miles per gallon, US (mpg)	x 0.425	=	Kilometres per litre (km/l)	x 2.352	= Miles per gallon, US (mpg)

Temperature

Degrees Fahrenheit = ($°C$ x 1.8) + 32   Degrees Celsius (Degrees Centigrade; $°C$) = ($°F$ - 32) x 0.56

It is common practice to convert from miles per gallon (mpg) to litres/100 kilometres (l/100km), where mpg x l/100 km = 282

This Section provides an easy reference-guide to the more common faults that are likely to afflict your machine. Obviously, the opportunities are almost limitless for faults to occur as a result of obscure failures, and to try and cover all eventualities would require a book. Indeed, a number have been written on the subject.

Successful troubleshooting is not a mysterious 'black art' but the application of a bit of knowledge combined with a systematic and logical approach to the problem. Approach any troubleshooting by first accurately identifying the symptom and then checking through the list of possible causes, starting with the simplest or most obvious and progressing in stages to the most complex.

Take nothing for granted, but above all apply liberal quantities of common sense.

The main symptom of a fault is given in the text as a major heading below which are listed the various systems or areas which may contain the fault. Details of each possible cause for a fault and the remedial action to be taken are given, in brief, in the paragraphs below each heading. Further information should be sought in the relevant Chapter.

Engine doesn't start or is difficult to start
- [ ] Starter motor doesn't rotate
- [ ] Starter motor rotates but engine does not turn over
- [ ] Starter works but engine won't turn over (seized)
- [ ] No fuel flow
- [ ] Engine flooded
- [ ] No spark or weak spark
- [ ] Compression low
- [ ] Stalls after starting
- [ ] Rough idle

Poor running at low speeds
- [ ] Spark weak
- [ ] Fuel/air mixture incorrect
- [ ] Compression low
- [ ] Poor acceleration

Poor running or no power at high speed
- [ ] Firing incorrect
- [ ] Fuel/air mixture incorrect
- [ ] Compression low
- [ ] Knocking or pinking
- [ ] Miscellaneous causes

Overheating
- [ ] Engine overheats
- [ ] Firing incorrect
- [ ] Fuel/air mixture incorrect
- [ ] Compression too high
- [ ] Engine load excessive
- [ ] Lubrication inadequate
- [ ] Miscellaneous causes

Clutch problems
- [ ] Clutch slipping
- [ ] Clutch not disengaging completely

Gearchanging problems
- [ ] Doesn't go into gear or lever doesn't return
- [ ] Jumps out of gear
- [ ] Overselects

Abnormal engine noise
- [ ] Knocking or pinking
- [ ] Piston slap or rattling
- [ ] Valve noise
- [ ] Other noise

Abnormal driveline noise
- [ ] Clutch noise
- [ ] Transmission noise
- [ ] Final drive noise

Abnormal frame and suspension noise
- [ ] Front end noise
- [ ] Rear end noise
- [ ] Brake noise

Engine lubrication system
- [ ] Oil pressure warning light comes on

Excessive exhaust smoke
- [ ] White smoke
- [ ] Black smoke
- [ ] Brown smoke

Poor handling or stability
- [ ] Handlebars hard to turn
- [ ] Handlebar shakes or vibrates excessively
- [ ] Machine pulls to one side
- [ ] Poor shock absorbing qualities

Braking problems
- [ ] Brakes are spongy, don't hold
- [ ] Brake lever or pedal pulsates
- [ ] Brakes drag
- [ ] ABS system (where fitted)

Electrical problems
- [ ] Battery dead or weak
- [ ] Battery overcharged

Engine doesn't start or is difficult to start

Starter motor doesn't rotate

- [ ] Engine kill switch OFF.
- [ ] Fuse blown. Check main fuse, ignition fuse and fuel injection fuse (Chapter 8).
- [ ] Battery voltage low. Check battery condition and recharge or replace battery (Chapter 8).
- [ ] Loose or corroded battery connections/terminals. Tighten or clean connections (Chapter 8).
- [ ] Starter motor defective. Make sure the wiring to the starter is secure and free of corrosion. Replace or repair the motor if defective (Chapter 8).
- [ ] Starter relay defective. Make sure the wiring to relay is secure and free of corrosion. Test the operation of the relay, internal corrosion or arcing can cause the relay to not pass sufficient current to the starter motor even if it clicks when the start button is operated (Chapter 8).
- [ ] Starter switch not contacting. The contacts could be wet, corroded or dirty. Disassemble and clean the switch (Chapter 8).
- [ ] Wiring open or shorted. Check all wiring connections and harnesses to make sure that they are dry, tight and not corroded. Also check for broken or frayed wires that can cause a short to ground (earth) (see Wiring diagrams, Chapter 8).
- [ ] Ignition or kill switch defective..This is usually caused by water, corrosion, damage or excessive wear. The switches can be disassembled and cleaned with electrical contact cleaner. If cleaning does not help, replace the switches (Chapter 8).
- [ ] Faulty gear position switch, sidestand switch or clutch switch. Check the wiring to each switch and the switch itself (see Chapter 8).
- [ ] Faulty starter circuit cut-off relay or diode (Chapter 8).
- [ ] Fuel injection system shutdown due to system fault (Chapter 4).

Starter motor rotates but engine does not turn over

- [ ] Starter clutch defective. Inspect and repair or replace with a new one (see Chapter 2).
- [ ] Damaged idler or starter gears. Inspect and replace the damaged parts (see Chapter 2).

Starter works but engine won't turn over (seized)

- [ ] Seized engine caused by one or more internally damaged components. Failure due to wear, abuse or lack of lubrication. Damage can include seized valves, followers, camshafts, pistons, crankshaft, connecting rod bearings, or transmission gears or bearings. Refer to Chapter 2 for engine disassembly.

No fuel flow

- [ ] No fuel in tank.
- [ ] Fuel tank breather hose obstructed (Chapter 4).
- [ ] Faulty fuel injection system relay. Check the relay (see Chapter 4).
- [ ] Fuel pump or pressure regulator faulty, or the pump's internal filter is blocked (see Chapter 4).
- [ ] Engine control unit (ECU) defective (Chapter 4).
- [ ] Ignition key not recognised by immobiliser system (where fitted) (Chapter 4).
- [ ] Fuel hose kinked. Fit a new hose (Chapter 4).
- [ ] Fuel rail or injector clogged. For both injectors to be clogged, either a very bad batch of fuel with an unusual additive has been used, or some other foreign material has entered the tank. Check the fuel pump. In some cases, if a machine has been unused for several months, the fuel turns to a varnish-like liquid which can cause an injector needle to stick to its seat. Drain the tank and fuel system, ultrasonically clean or replace fuel injectors (Chapter 4).

Engine flooded

- [ ] Injector needle valve worn or stuck open. A piece of dirt, rust or other debris can cause the needle to seat improperly, causing excess fuel to be admitted to the throttle body. In this case, the injector should be cleaned and the needle and seat inspected (see Chapter 4). If the needle and seat are worn, then the leaking will persist and the parts should be renewed.
- [ ] Starting technique incorrect. Under normal circumstances (i.e. if all the components of the fuel injection system are good) the machine should start with the throttle closed.

No spark or weak spark

- [ ] Ignition switch OFF.
- [ ] Engine kill switch turned to the OFF position.
- [ ] Ignition or kill switch shorted. This is usually caused by water, corrosion, damage or excessive wear. The switches can be disassembled and cleaned with electrical contact cleaner. If cleaning does not help, replace the switches (see Chapter 8).
- [ ] Battery voltage low. Check battery condition and recharge or replace battery (Chapter 8).
- [ ] Spark plug cap not making good contact. Make sure that the coils are pushed fully onto the spark plugs (Chapter 1).
- [ ] Spark plugs dirty, defective or worn out. Locate reason for fouled plugs using the firing end condition photos and follow the plug maintenance procedures (see Chapter 1).
- [ ] Incorrect spark plugs. Wrong type or heat range. Check and install correct plugs (see Chapter 1).
- [ ] Ignition coil defective. Check the coils (Chapter 4).
- [ ] Fuel injection system shutdown due to system fault (Chapter 4).
- [ ] Crankshaft position (CKP) sensor defective (see Chapter 4).
- [ ] Faulty fuel injection relay or tip-over sensor (Chapter 4).
- [ ] Engine control unit (ECU) defective (see Chapter 4).
- [ ] Wiring shorted or broken between: ignition switch and engine kill switch (or blown fuse); ECU and kill switch; ECU and ignition coils; ECU and CKP sensor. Make sure that all wiring connections are clean, dry and tight. Look for chafed and broken wires (see Chapter 8)

Compression low

- [ ] Spark plugs loose. Remove the plugs and inspect their threads. Reinstall and tighten securely (see Chapter 1).
- [ ] Cylinder head not sufficiently tightened down. If the cylinder head is suspected of being loose, then there's a chance that the gasket or head is damaged if the problem has persisted for any length of time. The head bolts should be tightened to the proper torque and in the correct sequence (Chapter 2).
- [ ] Improper valve clearance. This means that the valve is not closing completely and compression pressure is leaking past the valve. Check and adjust the valve clearances (Chapter 1).
- [ ] Cylinder and/or piston worn. Excessive wear will cause compression pressure to leak past the rings. This is usually accompanied by worn rings as well. A top-end overhaul is necessary (Chapter 2).
- [ ] Piston rings worn, weak, broken, or sticking. Broken or sticking piston rings usually indicate a lubrication or fuelling problem that causes excess carbon deposits to form on the pistons and rings. Top-end overhaul is necessary (Chapter 2).
- [ ] Piston ring-to-groove clearance excessive. This is caused by excessive wear of the piston ring lands. Piston renewal is necessary (Chapter 2).
- [ ] Cylinder head gasket damaged. If a head is allowed to become loose, or if excessive carbon build-up on the piston crown and combustion chamber causes extremely high compression, the head gasket may leak. Retorquing the head is not always sufficient to restore the seal, so a new gasket is necessary (Chapter 2).
- [ ] Cylinder head warped. This is caused by overheating or improperly tightened head bolts. Machine shop resurfacing or a new head is necessary (Chapter 2).
- [ ] Valve spring broken or weak. Caused by component failure or wear; the springs must be replaced with new ones (Chapter 2).
- [ ] Valve not seating properly. This is caused by a bent valve (from over-revving or improper valve adjustment), burned valve or seat (incorrect air/fuel mixture) or an accumulation of carbon deposits on the seat. The valves must be cleaned and/or renewed and the seats very lightly lapped (Chapter 2).

Engine doesn't start or is difficult to start (continued)

Stalls after starting

☐ Engine idle speed incorrect (Chapter 1).

☐ Ignition malfunction (see Chapter 4).

☐ Fuel injection system malfunction (see Chapter 4).

☐ Fuel contaminated. The fuel can be contaminated with either dirt or water, or can change chemically if the machine has been unused for several months. Drain the tank and fuel system (Chapter 4).

☐ Intake air leak. Check for loose throttle body-to-intake manifold connections, loose or damaged throttle body synchronising hose plug (Chapter 4).

Rough idle

☐ Idle speed incorrect (see Chapter 1).

☐ Ignition fault (see Chapter 4).

☐ Throttle bodies out of balance. Synchronise them as described in Chapter 1.

☐ Throttle body vacuum take off plug missing or vacuum hose disconnected or damaged (Chapter 4).

☐ Fuel injection system malfunction (see Chapter 4).

☐ Fuel contaminated. The fuel can be contaminated with either dirt or water, or can change chemically if the machine has been unused for several months. Drain the tank and the fuel system (Chapter 4).

☐ Intake air leak. Check for loose throttle body-to-intake duct connections, loose or damaged throttle body vacuum hoses (Chapter 4).

☐ Air filter clogged. Fit a new filter and clean its housing (Chapter 1).

Poor running at low speeds

Spark weak

☐ Battery voltage low. Check battery condition and recharge or replace battery (Chapter 8).

☐ Spark plug caps not making good contact. Make sure that the coils are pushed fully onto the spark plugs (Chapter 1).

☐ Spark plugs dirty, defective or worn out. Locate reason for fouled plugs using spark plug condition chart on the inside back cover and follow the plug maintenance procedures (see Chapter 1).

☐ Incorrect spark plugs. Wrong type or heat range. Check and install correct plugs (see Chapter 1).

☐ Ignition coil or spark plug cap defective (Chapter 4).

☐ Loose or corroded coil wiring connectors. Check security and clean connections (Chapter 4).

Fuel/air mixture incorrect

☐ Fuel tank breather hose obstructed (Chapter 4).

☐ Fuel pump or pressure regulator faulty, or the pump's internal filter is blocked (see Chapter 4).

☐ Fuel hose kinked. Replace the fuel hose (Chapter 4).

☐ Fuel rail or injector clogged. For both injectors to be clogged, either a very bad batch of fuel with an unusual additive has been used, or some other foreign material has entered the tank. Check the fuel pump. In some cases, if a machine has been unused for several months, the fuel turns to a varnish-like liquid which can cause an injector needle to stick to its seat. Drain the tank and fuel system, ultrasonically clean or replace fuel injectors (Chapter 4).

☐ Intake air leak. Check for loose throttle body-to-intake duct connections, loose or damaged vacuum hose or blanking plug (Chapter 4).

☐ Air filter clogged. Fit a new filter and clean its housing (Chapter 1).

Compression low

Note: *Check by performing a compression test (see Chapter 2).*

☐ Spark plugs loose. Remove the plugs and inspect their threads. Reinstall and tighten securely (see Chapter 1).

☐ Cylinder head not sufficiently tightened down. If a cylinder head is suspected of being loose, then there's a chance that the gasket or head is damaged if the problem has persisted for any length of time. The head bolts should be tightened to the proper torque and in the correct sequence (Chapter 2).

☐ Improper valve clearance. This means that the valve is not closing completely and compression pressure is leaking past the valve. Check and adjust the valve clearances (Chapter 1).

☐ Cylinder and/or piston worn. Excessive wear will cause compression pressure to leak past the rings. This is usually accompanied by worn rings as well. A top-end overhaul is necessary (Chapter 2).

☐ Piston rings worn, weak, broken, or sticking. Broken or sticking piston rings usually indicate a lubrication or fuelling problem that causes excess carbon deposits to form on the pistons and rings. Top-end overhaul is necessary (Chapter 2).

☐ Piston ring-to-groove clearance excessive. This is caused by excessive wear of the piston ring lands. Piston renewal is necessary (Chapter 2).

☐ Cylinder head gasket damaged. If the head is allowed to become loose, or if excessive carbon build-up on the piston crown and combustion chamber causes extremely high compression, the head gasket may leak. Retorquing the head is not always sufficient to restore the seal, so a new gasket is necessary (Chapter 2).

☐ Cylinder head warped. This is caused by overheating or improperly tightened head bolts. Machine shop resurfacing or head renewal is necessary (Chapter 2).

☐ Valve spring broken or weak. Caused by component failure or wear; the springs must be renewed (Chapter 2).

☐ Valve not seating properly. This is caused by a bent valve (from over-revving or improper valve adjustment), burned valve or seat (improper fuelling) or an accumulation of carbon deposits on the seat (from fuelling or lubrication problems). The valves must be cleaned and/or renewed and the seats very lightly lapped (Chapter 2).

Poor acceleration

☐ Timing not advancing. The crankshaft position sensor (CKP) or the engine control unit (ECU) may be defective (see Chapter 4).

☐ Engine oil viscosity too high. Using a heavier oil than that recommended in Chapter 1 can damage the oil pump or lubrication system and cause drag on the engine.

☐ Brakes dragging. Usually caused by corrosion behind dust seals, ingestion of dirt past a deteriorated seal or from a warped disc or bent axle (Chapter 6).

Poor running or no power at high speed

Firing incorrect

- [ ] Spark plug caps not making good contact. Make sure that the coils are pushed fully onto the spark plugs (Chapter 1).
- [ ] Spark plugs dirty, defective or worn out. Locate reason for fouled plugs using spark plug condition chart on the inside back cover and follow the plug maintenance procedures (see Chapter 1).
- [ ] Incorrect spark plugs. Wrong type or heat range. Check and install correct plugs (see Chapter 1).
- [ ] Ignition coil defective. Test and renew if necessary (see Chapter 4).
- [ ] Faulty ECU (engine control unit) (see Chapter 4).

Fuel/air mixture incorrect

- [ ] Fuel tank breather hose obstructed (Chapter 4).
- [ ] Fuel pump faulty or blocked pump internal filter. Inspect and replace if necessary (Chapter 4).
- [ ] Fuel hose kinked. Replace the fuel hose (Chapter 4).
- [ ] Fuel rail or injector clogged. For both injectors to be clogged, either a very bad batch of fuel with an unusual additive has been used, or some other foreign material has entered the tank. Check the fuel pump. In some cases, if a machine has been unused for several months, the fuel turns to a varnish-like liquid which can cause an injector needle to stick to its seat. Drain the tank and fuel system, ultrasonically clean or replace fuel injectors (Chapter 4).
- [ ] Intake air leak. Check for loose throttle body-to-intake duct connections, loose or damaged vacuum hose or blanking plug (Chapter 4).
- [ ] Air filter clogged. Fit a new filter and clean its housing (Chapter 1).

Compression low

Note: *Check by performing a compression test (see Chapter 2).*

- [ ] Spark plugs loose. Remove the plugs and inspect their threads. Reinstall and tighten securely (see Chapter 1).
- [ ] Cylinder head not sufficiently tightened down. If a cylinder head is suspected of being loose, then there's a chance that the gasket or head is damaged if the problem has persisted for any length of time. The head bolts should be tightened to the proper torque and in the correct sequence (Chapter 2).
- [ ] Improper valve clearance. This means that the valve is not closing completely and compression pressure is leaking past the valve. Check and adjust the valve clearances (Chapter 1).
- [ ] Cylinder and/or piston worn. Excessive wear will cause compression pressure to leak past the rings. This is usually accompanied by worn rings as well. A top-end overhaul is necessary (Chapter 2).
- [ ] Piston rings worn, weak, broken, or sticking. Broken or sticking piston rings usually indicate a lubrication or fuelling problem that causes excess carbon deposits to form on the pistons and rings. Top-end overhaul is necessary (Chapter 2).
- [ ] Piston ring-to-groove clearance excessive. This is caused by excessive wear of the piston ring lands. Piston renewal is necessary (Chapter 2).
- [ ] Cylinder head gasket damaged. If a head is allowed to become loose, or if excessive carbon build-up on the piston crown and combustion chamber causes extremely high compression, the head gasket may leak. Retorquing the head is not always sufficient to restore the seal, so a new gasket is necessary (Chapter 2).
- [ ] Cylinder head warped. This is caused by overheating or improperly tightened head bolts. Machine shop resurfacing or head renewal is necessary (Chapter 2).
- [ ] Valve spring broken or weak. Caused by component failure or wear; the springs must be replaced with new ones (Chapter 2).
- [ ] Valve not seating properly. This is caused by a bent valve (from over-revving or improper valve adjustment), burned valve or seat (improper fuelling) or an accumulation of carbon deposits on the seat (from fuelling or lubrication problems). The valves must be cleaned and/or renewed and the seats serviced (Chapter 2).

Knocking or pinking

- [ ] Carbon build-up in combustion chamber. Use of a fuel additive that will dissolve the adhesive bonding the carbon particles to the piston crown and chamber is the easiest way to remove the build-up. Otherwise, the cylinder head will have to be removed and decarbonised (Chapter 2).
- [ ] Incorrect or poor quality fuel. Old or improper grades of fuel can cause detonation. This causes the pistons to rattle, thus the knocking or pinking sound. Drain old fuel and always use the recommended fuel grade.
- [ ] Spark plug heat range incorrect. Uncontrolled detonation indicates the plug heat range is too hot. The plug in effect becomes a glow plug, raising cylinder temperatures. Install the proper heat range plug (Chapter 1).
- [ ] Improper air/fuel mixture. This will cause the cylinders to run hot, which leads to detonation. A blockage in the fuel system or an air leak can cause this imbalance (see Chapter 4).

Miscellaneous causes

- [ ] Throttle valve doesn't open fully. Check the throttle cables and adjust cable freeplay (see Chapter 1).
- [ ] Clutch slipping due loose or worn clutch components (see Chapter 2).
- [ ] Timing not advancing. The crankshaft position sensor (CKP) or the engine control unit (ECU) may be defective (see Chapter 4). If so, they must be replaced with new ones.
- [ ] Engine oil viscosity too high. Using a heavier oil than the one recommended in Chapter 1 can damage the oil pump or lubrication system and cause drag on the engine.
- [ ] Brakes dragging. Usually caused by corrosion behind dust seals, ingestion of dirt past a deteriorated seal or from a warped disc or bent axle (Chapter 6).

Overheating

Engine overheats

☐ Coolant level low. Check and add coolant (see *Pre-ride checks*).
☐ Leak in cooling system. Check cooling system hoses and radiator for leaks and other damage. Repair or renew parts as necessary (see Chapter 3).
☐ Faulty thermostat. Check and renew as described in Chapter 3.
☐ Faulty radiator cap. Remove the cap and have it pressure tested (Chapter 3).
☐ Coolant passages clogged. Drain, flush and refill with fresh coolant (Chapter 1).
☐ Water pump defective. Remove the pump and check the components (see Chapter 3).
☐ Clogged or damaged radiator fins (see Chapter 1).
☐ Faulty cooling fan, relay or coolant temperature sensor (see Chapter 3).

Firing incorrect

☐ Spark plugs dirty, defective or worn out. Locate reason for fouled plugs using spark plug condition chart on the inside back cover and follow the plug maintenance procedures (see Chapter 1).
☐ Incorrect spark plugs. Wrong type or heat range. Check and install correct plugs (see Chapter 1).
☐ Ignition coil defective. Test and replace with a new one if necessary (see Chapter 4).
☐ Faulty engine control unit (ECU) (see Chapter 4).

Fuel/air mixture incorrect

☐ Fuel tank breather hose obstructed (Chapter 4).
☐ Fuel pump faulty or blocked internal filter. Inspect the pump and renew if necessary (Chapter 4).
☐ Fuel hose kinked. Replace the fuel hose (Chapter 4).
☐ Fuel rail or injector clogged. For both injectors to be clogged, either a very bad batch of fuel with an unusual additive has been used, or some other foreign material has entered the tank. Check the fuel pump. In some cases, if a machine has been unused for several months, the fuel turns to a varnish-like liquid which can cause an injector needle to stick to its seat. Drain the tank and fuel system, ultrasonically clean or replace fuel injectors (Chapter 4).
☐ Intake air leak. Check for loose throttle body-to-intake duct connections, loose or damaged vacuum hose or blanking plug (Chapter 4).
☐ Air filter clogged. Fit a new filter and clean its housing (Chapter 1).

Compression too high

Note: *Check by performing a compression test (see Chapter 2).*
☐ Carbon build-up in combustion chamber. Use of a fuel additive that will dissolve the adhesive bonding the carbon particles to the piston crown and chamber is the easiest way to remove the build-up. Otherwise, the cylinder head will have to be removed and decarbonised (Chapter 2).

Engine load excessive

☐ Clutch slipping due loose or worn clutch components (see Chapter 2).
☐ Engine oil level too high. Too much oil will cause pressurisation of the crankcase and inefficient engine operation. Check Specifications and drain to proper level (Chapter 1 and *Pre-ride checks*).
☐ Engine oil viscosity too high. Using a heavier oil than the one recommended in Chapter 1 can damage the oil pump or lubrication system as well as cause drag on the engine.
☐ Brakes dragging. Usually caused by corrosion behind dust seals, ingestion of dirt past deteriorated seal or from a warped disc or bent axle (Chapter 6).

Lubrication inadequate

☐ Engine oil level too low. Friction caused by intermittent lack of lubrication or from oil that is overworked can cause overheating. The oil provides a definite cooling function in the engine. Check the oil level (see *Pre-ride checks*).
☐ Low engine oil pressure. Check the pressure (see Chapter 2).
☐ Blocked oil filter or oil cooler (see Chapter 2).

Miscellaneous causes

☐ Modification to exhaust system. Most aftermarket exhaust systems cause the engine to run leaner, which make them run hotter. When installing an aftermarket exhaust system, always check with the manufacturer/supplier as to whether the fuel system requires adjustment.

Clutch problems

Clutch slipping

☐ Insufficient clutch cable freeplay. Check and adjust (see Chapter 1).
☐ Clutch plates worn or warped. Overhaul the clutch assembly (see Chapter 2).
☐ Clutch springs broken or weak. Old or heat-damaged (from slipping clutch) springs should be renewed (Chapter 2).
☐ Clutch release mechanism faulty (see Chapter 2).
☐ Clutch centre or housing unevenly worn. This causes improper engagement of the plates. Replace the damaged or worn parts (see Chapter 2).
☐ Incorrect oil used in engine. Oils designed for car engines often contain friction modifiers, which if used in an engine with a wet clutch can promote clutch slip. Always use the correct oil designed for motorcycle engines (see *Pre-ride checks*).

Clutch not disengaging completely

☐ Excessive clutch cable freeplay. Check and adjust (see Chapter 1).
☐ Clutch release mechanism faulty or wrongly adjusted (see Chapter 2).
☐ Clutch plates warped or damaged. This will cause clutch drag, which in turn will cause the machine to creep. Overhaul the clutch assembly (see Chapter 2).
☐ Clutch springs fatigued or broken. Check and renew the springs (see Chapter 2).
☐ Engine oil deteriorated. Old, thin oil will not provide proper lubrication for the plates, causing the clutch to drag. Renew the oil and filter (see Chapter 1).
☐ Engine oil viscosity too high. Using a heavier oil than recommended in Chapter 1 can cause the plates to stick together. Change to the correct weight oil.
☐ Clutch housing bearing seized on the transmission input shaft. Lack of lubrication, severe wear or damage can cause the bearing to seize. Overhaul of the clutch, and perhaps transmission, may be necessary to repair the damage (see Chapter 2).
☐ Loose clutch centre nut. Causes housing and centre misalignment putting a drag on the engine. Engagement adjustment continually varies. Overhaul the clutch assembly (see Chapter 2).

Gearchanging problems

Doesn't go into gear or lever doesn't return

- [ ] Clutch not disengaging (see above).
- [ ] Gearchange mechanism stopper arm spring weak or broken, or arm roller broken or worn. Replace the spring or arm with a new one (see Chapter 2).
- [ ] Selector fork(s) bent, worn or seized. Overhaul the transmission (see Chapter 2).
- [ ] Gear(s) stuck on shaft. Most often caused by a lack of lubrication or excessive wear in transmission bearings and bushes. Overhaul the transmission (see Chapter 2).
- [ ] Selector drum binding. Caused by lubrication failure or excessive wear. Replace the drum and/or its bearing with a new one (see Chapter 2).
- [ ] Gearchange mechanism return spring weak or broken (see Chapter 2).

- [ ] Gearchange linkage arm broken. Splines stripped out of arm or shaft, caused by a loose linkage arm pinch bolt or from dropping the bike (see Chapter 2).

Jumps out of gear

- [ ] Selector fork(s) worn (see Chapter 2).
- [ ] Selector fork groove(s) in selector drum worn (see Chapter 2).
- [ ] Gear pinion dogs or dog slots worn or damaged. The gear pinions should be inspected and renewed (Chapter 2). No attempt should be made to repair the worn parts.

Overselects

- [ ] Gearchange mechanism stopper arm spring weak or broken, or arm roller broken or worn. Renew the spring or arm (see Chapter 2).
- [ ] Gearchange mechanism return spring weak or broken (see Chapter 2).

Abnormal engine noise

Knocking or pinking

- [ ] Carbon build-up in combustion chamber. Use of a fuel additive that will dissolve the adhesive bonding the carbon particles to the piston crown and chamber is the easiest way to remove the build-up. Otherwise, the cylinder head will have to be removed and decarbonised (Chapter 2).
- [ ] Incorrect or poor quality fuel. Old or improper grades of fuel can cause detonation. This causes the pistons to rattle, thus the knocking or pinking sound. Drain old fuel and always use the recommended fuel grade (Chapter 4).
- [ ] Spark plug heat range incorrect. Uncontrolled detonation indicates the plug heat range is too hot. The plug in effect becomes a glow plug, raising cylinder temperatures. Install the proper heat range plug (Chapter 1).
- [ ] Improper air/fuel mixture. This will cause the cylinders to run hot, which leads to detonation. A blockage in the fuel system or an air leak can cause this imbalance (see Chapter 4).

Piston slap or rattling

- [ ] Cylinder-to-piston clearance excessive. Cylinder and/or piston worn, usually accompanied by worn rings as well. A top-end overhaul is necessary (see Chapter 2).
- [ ] Piston ring(s) worn, broken or sticking. Overhaul the top-end (see Chapter 2).
- [ ] Piston pin, piston pin bore or connecting rod small-end worn from high mileage or seized due to lack of lubrication (see Chapter 2).
- [ ] Piston seizure damage. Usually from lack of lubrication or overheating. Replace the pistons and upper crankcase, as necessary (see Chapter 2).
- [ ] Connecting rod big-end clearance excessive. Caused by excessive wear or lack of lubrication. Replace worn parts (Chapter 2).

- [ ] Connecting rod bent. Caused by over-revving, trying to start a badly flooded engine or from ingesting a foreign object into the combustion chamber. Replace the damaged parts (Chapter 2).

Valve noise

- [ ] Incorrect valve clearances – check and adjust (see Chapter 1).
- [ ] Valve spring broken or weak. Check and replace weak valve springs with new ones (see Chapter 2).
- [ ] Camshaft or camshaft journals in the cylinder head worn or damaged. Lubrication failure at high rpm is usually the cause of damage due to insufficient oil or failure to change the oil at the recommended intervals. Since there are no replaceable bearings in the head, the head and camshaft holders will have to be renewed (see Chapter 2).

Other noise

- [ ] Cylinder head gasket leaking. Check around the joint for blowing with the engine running.
- [ ] Exhaust pipe leaking at cylinder head connection. Caused by incorrect fit of pipe(s), loose exhaust flange or damaged gasket. All exhaust system fasteners should be tightened evenly and carefully to avoid leaks (see Chapter 4).
- [ ] Crankshaft runout excessive (Chapter 2). Caused by a bent crankshaft (from over-revving) or damage from an upper cylinder component failure. Can also be attributed to dropping the machine on either of the crankshaft ends.
- [ ] Engine mounting bolts loose – ensure all the bolts are tightened to the specified torque settings (see Chapter 2).
- [ ] Crankshaft bearings worn (see Chapter 2).
- [ ] Cam chain rattle, due to worn chain or defective tensioner. Also worn chain tensioner/guide blades (see Chapter 2).

Abnormal driveline noise

Clutch noise

- ☐ Clutch housing/friction plate clearance excessive (Chapter 2).
- ☐ Wear between the clutch housing splines and input shaft splines (Chapter 2).
- ☐ Worn release bearing (Chapter 2).

Transmission noise

- ☐ Bearings worn. Also includes the possibility that the shafts are worn. Overhaul the transmission (Chapter 2).
- ☐ Gears worn or chipped (Chapter 2).
- ☐ Metal chips jammed in gear teeth. Probably pieces from a broken clutch, gear or selector mechanism that were picked up by the gears. This will cause early bearing failure (Chapter 2).

- ☐ Engine oil level too low, causes a howl from transmission (*Pre-ride checks*).

Final drive noise

- ☐ Drive chain excessively loose/worn or drive sprockets excessively worn. Adjust chain or replace chain and sprockets as a set (Chapter 1 and Chapter 6).
- ☐ Front or rear sprocket loose. Tighten fasteners (Chapter 6).
- ☐ Sprockets and/or chain worn. Fit new sprockets and chain (Chapter 6).
- ☐ Rear sprocket warped. Fit a new sprocket (Chapter 6).
- ☐ Rubber dampers in rear wheel worn (Chapter 6).

Abnormal frame and suspension noise

Front end noise

- ☐ Low fluid level or improper viscosity oil in forks. This can sound like spurting and is usually accompanied by irregular fork action (Chapter 5).
- ☐ Spring weak or broken. Makes a clicking or scraping sound. Fork oil, when drained, will have a lot of metal particles in it (Chapter 5).
- ☐ Steering head bearings loose or damaged. Clicks when braking. Check and adjust or replace with new ones as necessary (Chapter 1 and Chapter 5).
- ☐ Fork yoke clamp bolts loose – ensure all the bolts are tightened to the specified torque (Chapter 6).
- ☐ Forks bent. Good possibility if machine has been dropped. Replace the inner tubes with new ones as required (Chapter 5).
- ☐ Front axle or axle pinch bolt loose. Tighten them to the specified torque (Chapter 6).
- ☐ Loose or worn wheel bearings. Check and replace with new ones as needed (Chapter 1 and Chapter 6).

Rear end noise

- ☐ Shock absorber fluid level incorrect. Indicates a leak caused by defective seal. Shock will be covered with oil. Replace shock with a new one or seek advice on repair from a suspension specialist (Chapter 5).
- ☐ Defective shock absorber with internal damage. This is in the body of the shock and can't be remedied. The shock must be replaced with a new one or rebuilt (Chapter 5).
- ☐ Bent or damaged shock body. Replace the shock with a new one (Chapter 5).
- ☐ Loose or worn swingarm and/or suspension linkage bearings.

- ☐ Check and replace with new ones as necessary (Chapter 5).
- ☐ Loose or worn wheel bearings/sprocket bearing. Check and replace with new ones as needed (Chapter 1 and Chapter 6).

Brake noise

- ☐ Squeal caused by pad shim not installed or positioned correctly (where fitted) (Chapter 6).
- ☐ Squeal caused by dust on brake pads. Usually found in combination with glazed pads. Clean using brake cleaning solvent (Chapter 6).
- ☐ Pads glazed. Caused by excessive heat from prolonged hard use or from contamination. DO NOT use sandpaper, emery cloth, carborundum cloth or any other abrasive to roughen the pad surfaces as abrasives will stay in the pad material and damage the disc. A very fine flat file can be used, but new pads is the best remedy (Chapter 6).
- ☐ Contamination of brake pads. Oil or brake fluid can cause the brake pads to chatter or squeal. Fit new pads. Identify the cause of the contamination, especially check the caliper piston seals for leaking fluid. Clean disc thoroughly with brake system cleaner (Chapter 6).
- ☐ Disc warped. Can cause a chattering, clicking or intermittent squeal. Usually accompanied by a pulsating lever and uneven braking. Replace the disc and pads (Chapter 6).
- ☐ Loose or worn wheel bearings. Check and replace with new ones as needed (Chapter 1 and Chapter 6).
- ☐ Forks incorrectly aligned on front wheel axle causing caliper or mounting to contact disc. Loosen front axle pinch bolt and re-align (Chapter 6).

Engine lubrication system

Oil pressure warning light comes on

- ☐ Oil level low. Inspect for leak or other problem causing low oil level and add recommended oil (see Pre-ride checks).
- ☐ Oil pump defective, blocked oil strainer gauze or failed pressure relief valve. Carry out an oil pressure check (Chapter 2).
- ☐ Oil viscosity too low. Very old, thin oil or an improper weight of oil

used in the engine. Change to correct oil (Chapter 1).
- ☐ Camshaft or crankshaft journals worn. Excessive wear causing drop in oil pressure. Abnormal wear could be caused by oil starvation at high rpm from low oil level or improper weight or type of oil (Chapter 1).
- ☐ Oil pressure switch defective. Check the switch according to the procedure in Chapter 8. Replace it with a new one if it is defective.

Excessive exhaust smoke

White smoke

☐ Piston rings worn or broken, causing oil from the crankcase to be pulled past the piston into the combustion chamber. Replace the rings with new ones (Chapter 2).

☐ Cylinders worn or scored. Caused by overheating or oil starvation. Install a new upper crankcase and new pistons (Chapter 2).

☐ Valve stem oil seal damaged or worn. Replace the oil seals with new ones (Chapter 2).

☐ Valve guide worn. Perform a complete valve job (Chapter 2).

☐ Engine oil level too high, which causes the oil to be forced past the rings. Drain oil to the proper level (see Chapter 1 and *Pre-ride checks*).

☐ Head gasket broken between oil return and cylinder. Causes oil to be pulled into the combustion chamber. Replace the head gasket with a new one and check the head for warpage (Chapter 2).

☐ Abnormal crankcase pressurisation which forces oil past the rings, usually caused by a clogged breather.

Black smoke

☐ Air filter clogged. Replace it with a new one (Chapter 1).

☐ Fuel injection system malfunction (Chapter 4).

Brown smoke

☐ Air filter poorly sealed or not installed (Chapter 1).

☐ Fuel injection system malfunction (Chapter 4).

Poor handling or stability

Handlebars hard to turn

☐ Steering head bearing adjuster nut too tight. Check adjustment as described in Chapter 1.

☐ Bearings damaged. Roughness can be felt as the bars are turned from side-to-side. Replace the bearings with new ones (Chapter 5).

☐ Races dented or worn. Denting results from wear in only one position (e.g., straight ahead), from a collision or hitting a pothole or from dropping the machine. Replace the bearings with new ones (Chapter 5).

☐ Steering stem lubrication inadequate. Causes are grease getting hard from age or being washed out by high pressure car washes. Disassemble steering head and repack bearings (Chapter 5).

☐ Steering stem bent. Caused by a collision, hitting a pothole or by dropping the machine. Replace damaged part. Don't try to straighten the steering stem (Chapter 5).

☐ Front tyre air pressure too low (*Pre-ride checks*).

Handlebar shakes or vibrates excessively

☐ Tyres worn or out of balance.

☐ Swingarm bearings worn. Replace the bearings with new ones (Chapter 5).

☐ Wheel rim(s) warped or damaged. Inspect wheels for runout (Chapter 6).

☐ Wheel bearings worn. Worn front or rear wheel bearings can cause poor tracking. Worn front bearings will cause wobble (Chapter 1 and Chapter 6).

☐ Fork yoke clamp bolts or handlebar clamp bolts loose. Tighten them to the specified torque (Chapter 5).

☐ Engine mounting bolts loose. Will cause excessive vibration with increased engine rpm – ensure all the bolts are tightened to the specified torque settings (see Chapter 2).

Machine pulls to one side

☐ Frame bent. Definitely suspect this if the machine has been dropped. May or may not be accompanied by cracking near the steering head, swingarm mountings or engine mountings. Replace the frame with a new one (Chapter 5).

☐ Wheels out of alignment. Caused by improper location of axle spacers or from bent steering stem or frame (Chapter 5).

☐ Forks bent. Disassemble the forks and replace the damaged parts (Chapter 5).

☐ Swingarm bent or twisted. Replace the swingarm with a new one (Chapter 5).

☐ Fork oil level uneven. Check and add or drain as necessary (Chapter 5).

Poor shock absorbing qualities

☐ Too hard – Front fork oil level excessive (Chapter 5).

☐ Too hard – Front fork oil viscosity too high. Use the correct oil (see the Specifications in Chapter 5).

☐ Too hard – Front fork tube bent. Causes a harsh, sticking feeling (Chapter 5).

☐ Too hard – Fork internal damage (Chapter 5).

☐ Too hard – Rear shock pre-load too high (Chapter 5).

☐ Too hard – Rear shock shaft or body bent or damaged, or shock internal failure (Chapter 5).

☐ Too hard – Tyre pressure too high (*Pre-ride checks*).

☐ Too soft – Front fork oil level too low (Chapter 5).

☐ Too soft – Front fork oil viscosity too light (Chapter 5).

☐ Too soft – Front fork springs weak or broken (Chapter 5).

☐ Too soft – Front fork oil leaking. Strip fork and renew seals (Chapter 5).

☐ Too soft – Rear shock pre-load too low for weight load (Chapter 5).

☐ Too soft – Rear shock oil leaking or internal damage (Chapter 5).

Braking problems

Brakes are spongy, don't hold

☐ Low brake fluid level (see *Pre-ride checks*).
☐ Air in hydraulic system. Caused by inattention to master cylinder fluid level or by leakage. Locate problem and bleed brakes (Chapter 6).
☐ Pads worn. Fit new pads (Chapter 1 and Chapter 6).
☐ Disc worn. Measure disc thickness and replace with a new one if necessary (Chapter 6).
☐ Contaminated pads. Caused by contamination with oil, grease, brake fluid, etc. Fit new pads. Identify the cause of the contamination, especially check the caliper piston seals for leaking fluid. Clean disc thoroughly with brake system cleaner (Chapter 6).
☐ Brake fluid deteriorated. Fluid is old or contaminated. Drain system, replenish with new fluid and bleed the system (Chapter 6).
☐ Master cylinder internal seals worn or damaged causing fluid to bypass (Chapter 6).
☐ Master cylinder bore scratched by foreign material or broken spring. Fit a new master cylinder (Chapter 6).
☐ Disc warped. Replace disc with new one (Chapter 6)

Brake lever or pedal pulsates

☐ Disc warped. Replace disc with new one (Chapter 6).
☐ Axle bent. Replace axle with new one (Chapter 6).

☐ Brake caliper bolts loose – tighten the bolts to the specified torque (Chapter 6).
☐ Wheel warped or otherwise damaged (Chapter 6).
☐ Wheel bearings damaged or worn (Chapters 1 and 6).

Brakes drag

☐ Brake caliper piston seized in bore. Caused by corrosion behind dust seals or ingestion of dirt past deteriorated seal (Chapter 6).
☐ Brake caliper slider pins sticking or corroded, preventing full movement of rear caliper (Chapter 6).
☐ Brake pad damaged. Pad material separated from backing plate. Usually caused by faulty manufacturing process or from contact with chemicals. Fit new pads (Chapter 6).
☐ Pads improperly installed (Chapter 6).
☐ Brake caliper incorrectly installed (Chapter 6).
☐ Master cylinder piston seized. Caused by wear or damage to piston or cylinder bore (Chapter 6).
☐ Lever balky or stuck. Check pivot and lubricate (Chapter 6).
☐ Forks incorrectly aligned on front wheel axle. Loosen front axle pinch bolt and re-align (Chapter 6).

ABS system (where fitted)

☐ System fault indicated by indicator light coming on while the machine is being ridden. Download the fault code to identify the problem (Chapter 6).

Electrical problems

Battery dead or weak

☐ Battery faulty. Caused by sulphated plates which are shorted through sedimentation. Confirm by terminal voltage check (Chapter 8).
☐ Broken battery terminal making only occasional contact (Chapter 8).
☐ Battery leads making poor contact (Chapter 8).
☐ Load excessive. Caused by addition of high wattage lights or other electrical accessories.
☐ Ignition switch defective. Switch either grounds (earths) internally or fails to shut off system. Renew the switch (Chapter 8).
☐ Regulator/rectifier defective (Chapter 8).
☐ Alternator stator coil open or shorted (Chapter 8).

☐ Electrical system fault. Check for excessive current leakage (Chapter 8).
☐ Wiring faulty. Wiring grounded (earthed) or connections loose in ignition, charging or lighting circuits (Chapter 8).

Battery overcharged

☐ Regulator/rectifier defective. Overcharging is noticed when battery gets excessively warm (Chapter 8).
☐ Battery faulty. Confirm with battery terminal voltage check (Chapter 8).
☐ Battery amperage too low, wrong type or size of battery. Install manufacturer's specified amp-hour battery to handle charging load (Chapter 8).

A

ABS (Anti-lock braking system) A system, usually electronically controlled, that senses incipient wheel lockup during braking and relieves hydraulic pressure at wheel which is about to skid.

Aftermarket Components suitable for the motorcycle, but not produced by the motorcycle manufacturer.

Allen key A hexagonal wrench which fits into a recessed hexagonal hole.

Alternating current (ac) Current produced by an alternator. Requires converting to direct current by a rectifier for charging purposes.

Alternator Converts mechanical energy from the engine into electrical energy to charge the battery and power the electrical system.

Ampere (amp) A unit of measurement for the flow of electrical current. Current = Volts ÷ Ohms.

Ampere-hour (Ah) Measure of battery capacity.

Angle-tightening A torque expressed in degrees. Often follows a conventional tightening torque for cylinder head or main bearing fasteners **(see illustration)**.

Angle-tightening con-rod bolts

Antifreeze A substance (usually ethylene glycol) mixed with water, and added to the cooling system, to prevent freezing of the coolant in winter. Antifreeze also contains chemicals to inhibit corrosion and the formation of rust and other deposits that would tend to clog the radiator and coolant passages and reduce cooling efficiency.

Anti-dive System attached to the fork lower leg (slider) to prevent fork dive when braking hard.

Anti-seize compound A coating that reduces the risk of seizing on fasteners that are subjected to high temperatures, such as exhaust clamp bolts and nuts.

API American Petroleum Institute. A quality standard for 4-stroke motor oils.

Asbestos A natural fibrous mineral with great heat resistance, commonly used in the composition of brake friction materials. Asbestos is a health hazard and the dust created by brake systems should never be inhaled or ingested.

ATF Automatic Transmission Fluid. Often used in front forks.

ATU Automatic Timing Unit. Mechanical device for advancing the ignition timing on early engines.

ATV All Terrain Vehicle. Often called a Quad.

Axial play Side-to-side movement.

Axle A shaft on which a wheel revolves. Also known as a spindle.

B

Backlash The amount of movement between meshed components when one component is held still. Usually applies to gear teeth.

Ball bearing A bearing consisting of a hardened inner and outer race with hardened steel balls between the two races.

Bearings Used between two working surfaces to prevent wear of the components and a build-up of heat. Four types of bearing are commonly used on motorcycles: plain shell bearings, ball bearings, tapered roller bearings and needle roller bearings.

Bevel gears Used to turn the drive through 90°. Typical applications are shaft final drive and camshaft drive **(see illustration)**.

Bevel gears are used to turn the drive through 90°

BHP Brake Horsepower. The British measurement for engine power output. Power output is now usually expressed in kilowatts (kW).

Bias-belted tyre Similar construction to radial tyre, but with outer belt running at an angle to the wheel rim.

Big-end bearing The bearing in the end of the connecting rod that's attached to the crankshaft.

Bleeding The process of removing air from an hydraulic system via a bleed nipple or bleed screw.

Bottom-end A description of an engine's crankcase components and all components contained there-in.

BTDC Before Top Dead Centre in terms of piston position. Ignition timing is often expressed in terms of degrees or millimetres BTDC.

Bush A cylindrical metal or rubber component used between two moving parts.

Burr Rough edge left on a component after machining or as a result of excessive wear.

C

Cam chain The chain which takes drive from the crankshaft to the camshaft(s).

Canister The main component in an evaporative emission control system (California market only); contains activated charcoal granules to trap vapours from the fuel system rather than allowing them to vent to the atmosphere.

Castellated Resembling the parapets along the top of a castle wall. For example, a castellated wheel axle or spindle nut.

Catalytic converter A device in the exhaust system of some machines which converts certain pollutants in the exhaust gases into less harmful substances.

Charging system Description of the components which charge the battery, ie the alternator, rectifier and regulator.

Circlip A ring-shaped clip used to prevent endwise movement of cylindrical parts and shafts. An internal circlip is installed in a groove in a housing; an external circlip fits into a groove on the outside of a cylindrical piece such as a shaft. Also known as a snap-ring.

Clearance The amount of space between two parts. For example, between a piston and a cylinder, between a bearing and a journal, etc.

Coil spring A spiral of elastic steel found in various sizes throughout a vehicle, for example as a springing medium in the suspension and in the valve train.

Compression Reduction in volume, and increase in pressure and temperature, of a gas, caused by squeezing it into a smaller space.

Compression damping Controls the speed the suspension compresses when hitting a bump.

Compression ratio The relationship between cylinder volume when the piston is at top dead centre and cylinder volume when the piston is at bottom dead centre.

Continuity The uninterrupted path in the flow of electricity. Little or no measurable resistance.

Continuity tester Self-powered bleeper or test light which indicates continuity.

Cp Candlepower. Bulb rating commonly found on US motorcycles.

Crossply tyre Tyre plies arranged in a criss-cross pattern. Usually four or six plies used, hence 4PR or 6PR in tyre size codes.

Cush drive Rubber damper segments fitted between the rear wheel and final drive sprocket to absorb transmission shocks **(see illustration)**.

Cush drive rubbers dampen out transmission shocks

D

Decarbonisation The process of removing carbon deposits - typically from the combustion chamber, valves and exhaust port/system.

Degree disc Calibrated disc for measuring piston position. Expressed in degrees.

Detonation Destructive and damaging explosion of fuel/air mixture in combustion chamber instead of controlled burning.

Dial gauge Clock-type gauge with adapters for measuring runout and piston position. Expressed in mm or inches.

Diaphragm The rubber membrane in a master cylinder or carburettor which seals the upper chamber.

Diaphragm spring A single sprung plate often used in clutches.

Direct current (dc) Current produced by a dc generator.

Diode An electrical valve which only allows current to flow in one direction. Commonly used in rectifiers and starter interlock systems.

Disc valve (or rotary valve) A induction system used on some two-stroke engines.

Double-overhead camshaft (DOHC) An engine that uses two overhead camshafts, one for the intake valves and one for the exhaust valves.

Drivebelt A toothed belt used to transmit drive to the rear wheel on some motorcycles. A drivebelt has also been used to drive the camshafts. Drivebelts are usually made of Kevlar.

Driveshaft Any shaft used to transmit motion. Commonly used when referring to the final driveshaft on shaft drive motorcycles.

E

Earth return The return path of an electrical circuit, utilising the motorcycle's frame.

ECU (Electronic Control Unit) A computer which controls (for instance) an ignition system, or an anti-lock braking system.

EGO Exhaust Gas Oxygen sensor. Sometimes called a Lambda sensor.

Electrolyte The fluid in a lead-acid battery.

EMS (Engine Management System) A computer controlled system which manages the fuel injection and the ignition systems in an integrated fashion.

Endfloat The amount of lengthways movement between two parts. As applied to a crankshaft, the distance that the crankshaft can move side-to-side in the crankcase.

Endless chain A chain having no joining link. Common use for cam chains and final drive chains.

EP (Extreme Pressure) Oil type used in locations where high loads are applied, such as between gear teeth.

Evaporative emission control system Describes a charcoal filled canister which stores fuel vapours from the tank rather than allowing them to vent to the atmosphere. Usually only fitted to California models and referred to as an EVAP system.

Expansion chamber Section of two-stroke engine exhaust system so designed to improve engine efficiency and boost power.

F

Feeler blade or gauge A thin strip or blade of hardened steel, ground to an exact thickness, used to check or measure clearances between parts.

Final drive Description of the drive from the transmission to the rear wheel. Usually by chain or shaft, but sometimes by belt.

Firing order The order in which the engine cylinders fire, or deliver their power strokes, beginning with the number one cylinder.

Flooding Term used to describe a high fuel level in the carburettor float chambers, leading to fuel overflow. Also refers to excess fuel in the combustion chamber due to incorrect starting technique.

Free length The no-load state of a component when measured. Clutch, valve and fork spring lengths are measured at rest, without any preload.

Freeplay The amount of travel before any action takes place. The looseness in a linkage, or an assembly of parts, between the initial application of force and actual movement. For example, the distance the rear brake pedal moves before the rear brake is actuated.

Fuel injection The fuel/air mixture is metered electronically and directed into the engine intake ports (indirect injection) or into the cylinders (direct injection). Sensors supply information on engine speed and conditions.

Fuel/air mixture The charge of fuel and air going into the engine. See Stoichiometric ratio.

Fuse An electrical device which protects a circuit against accidental overload. The typical fuse contains a soft piece of metal which is calibrated to melt at a predetermined current flow (expressed as amps) and break the circuit.

G

Gap The distance the spark must travel in jumping from the centre electrode to the side electrode in a spark plug. Also refers to the distance between the ignition rotor and the pickup coil in an electronic ignition system.

Gasket Any thin, soft material - usually cork, cardboard, asbestos or soft metal - installed between two metal surfaces to ensure a good seal. For instance, the cylinder head gasket seals the joint between the block and the cylinder head.

Gauge An instrument panel display used to monitor engine conditions. A gauge with a movable pointer on a dial or a fixed scale is an analogue gauge. A gauge with a numerical readout is called a digital gauge.

Gear ratios The drive ratio of a pair of gears in a gearbox, calculated on their number of teeth.

Glaze-busting see Honing

Grinding Process for renovating the valve face and valve seat contact area in the cylinder head.

Gudgeon pin The shaft which connects the connecting rod small-end with the piston. Often called a piston pin or wrist pin.

H

Helical gears Gear teeth are slightly curved and produce less gear noise that straight-cut gears. Often used for primary drives.

Helicoil A thread insert repair system. Commonly used as a repair for stripped spark plug threads **(see illustration)**.

Installing a Helicoil thread insert

Honing A process used to break down the glaze on a cylinder bore (also called glaze-busting). Can also be carried out to roughen a rebored cylinder to aid ring bedding-in.

HT (High Tension) Description of the electrical circuit from the secondary winding of the ignition coil to the spark plug.

Hydraulic A liquid filled system used to transmit pressure from one component to another. Common uses on motorcycles are brakes and clutches.

Hydrometer An instrument for measuring the specific gravity of a lead-acid battery.

Hygroscopic Water absorbing. In motorcycle applications, braking efficiency will be reduced if DOT 3 or 4 hydraulic fluid absorbs water from the air - care must be taken to keep new brake fluid in tightly sealed containers.

I

Ibf ft Pounds-force feet. An imperial unit of torque. Sometimes written as ft-lbs.

Ibf in Pound-force inch. An imperial unit of torque, applied to components where a very low torque is required. Sometimes written as in-lbs.

IC Abbreviation for Integrated Circuit.

Ignition advance Means of increasing the timing of the spark at higher engine speeds. Done by mechanical means (ATU) on early engines or electronically by the ignition control unit on later engines.

Ignition timing The moment at which the spark plug fires, expressed in the number of crankshaft degrees before the piston reaches the top of its stroke, or in the number of millimetres before the piston reaches the top of its stroke.

Infinity (∞) Description of an open-circuit electrical state, where no continuity exists.

Inverted forks (upside down forks) The sliders or lower legs are held in the yokes and the fork tubes or stanchions are connected to the wheel axle (spindle). Less unsprung weight and stiffer construction than conventional forks.

J

JASO Quality standard for 2-stroke oils.

Joule The unit of electrical energy.

Journal The bearing surface of a shaft.

K

Kickstart Mechanical means of turning the engine over for starting purposes. Only usually fitted to mopeds, small capacity motorcycles and off-road motorcycles.

Kill switch Handebar-mounted switch for emergency ignition cut-out. Cuts the ignition circuit on all models, and additionally prevent starter motor operation on others.

km Symbol for kilometre.

kmh Abbreviation for kilometres per hour.

L

Lambda (λ) sensor A sensor fitted in the exhaust system to measure the exhaust gas oxygen content (excess air factor).

Lapping see Grinding.

LCD Abbreviation for Liquid Crystal Display.

LED Abbreviation for Light Emitting Diode.

Liner A steel cylinder liner inserted in a aluminium alloy cylinder block.

Locknut A nut used to lock an adjustment nut, or other threaded component, in place.

Lockstops The lugs on the lower triple clamp (yoke) which abut those on the frame, preventing handlebar-to-fuel tank contact.

Lockwasher A form of washer designed to prevent an attaching nut from working loose.

LT Low Tension Description of the electrical circuit from the power supply to the primary winding of the ignition coil.

M

Main bearings The bearings between the crankshaft and crankcase.

Maintenance-free (MF) battery A sealed battery which cannot be topped up.

Manometer Mercury-filled calibrated tubes used to measure intake tract vacuum. Used to synchronise carburettors on multi-cylinder engines.

Micrometer A precision measuring instrument that measures component outside diameters **(see illustration)**.

Tappet shims are measured with a micrometer

MON (Motor Octane Number) A measure of a fuel's resistance to knock.

Monograde oil An oil with a single viscosity, eg SAE80W.

Monoshock A single suspension unit linking the swingarm or suspension linkage to the frame.

mph Abbreviation for miles per hour.

Multigrade oil Having a wide viscosity range (eg 10W40). The W stands for Winter, thus the viscosity ranges from SAE10 when cold to SAE40 when hot.

Multimeter An electrical test instrument with the capability to measure voltage, current and resistance. Some meters also incorporate a continuity tester and buzzer.

N

Needle roller bearing Inner race of caged needle rollers and hardened outer race. Examples of uncaged needle rollers can be found on some engines. Commonly used in rear suspension applications and in two-stroke engines.

Nm Newton metres.

NOx Oxides of Nitrogen. A common toxic pollutant emitted by petrol engines at higher temperatures.

O

Octane The measure of a fuel's resistance to knock.

OE (Original Equipment) Relates to components fitted to a motorcycle as standard or replacement parts supplied by the motorcycle manufacturer.

Ohm The unit of electrical resistance. Ohms = Volts ÷ Current.

Ohmmeter An instrument for measuring electrical resistance.

Oil cooler System for diverting engine oil outside of the engine to a radiator for cooling purposes.

Oil injection A system of two-stroke engine lubrication where oil is pump-fed to the engine in accordance with throttle position.

Open-circuit An electrical condition where there is a break in the flow of electricity - no continuity (high resistance).

O-ring A type of sealing ring made of a special rubber-like material; in use, the O-ring is compressed into a groove to provide the sealing action.

Oversize (OS) Term used for piston and ring size options fitted to a rebored cylinder.

Overhead cam (sohc) engine An engine with single camshaft located on top of the cylinder head.

Overhead valve (ohv) engine An engine with the valves located in the cylinder head, but with the camshaft located in the engine block or crankcase.

Oxygen sensor A device installed in the exhaust system which senses the oxygen content in the exhaust and converts this information into an electric current. Also called a Lambda sensor.

P

Plastigauge A thin strip of plastic thread, available in different sizes, used for measuring clearances. For example, a strip of Plastigauge is laid across a bearing journal. The parts are assembled and dismantled; the width of the crushed strip indicates the clearance between journal and bearing.

Polarity Either negative or positive earth (ground), determined by which battery lead is connected to the frame (earth return). Modern motorcycles are usually negative earth.

Pre-ignition A situation where the fuel/air mixture ignites before the spark plug fires. Often due to a hot spot in the combustion chamber caused by carbon build-up. Engine has a tendency to 'run-on'.

Pre-load (suspension) The amount a spring is compressed when in the unloaded state. Preload can be applied by gas, spacer or mechanical adjuster.

Premix The method of engine lubrication on older two-stroke engines. Engine oil is mixed with the petrol in the fuel tank in a specific ratio. The fuel/oil mix is sometimes referred to as "petroil".

Primary drive Description of the drive from the crankshaft to the clutch. Usually by gear or chain.

PS Pfedestärke - a German interpretation of BHP.

PSI Pounds-force per square inch. Imperial measurement of tyre pressure and cylinder pressure measurement.

PTFE Polytetrafluroethylene. A low friction substance.

Pulse secondary air injection system A process of promoting the burning of excess fuel present in the exhaust gases by routing fresh air into the exhaust ports.

Q

Quartz halogen bulb Tungsten filament surrounded by a halogen gas. Typically used for the headlight **(see illustration)**.

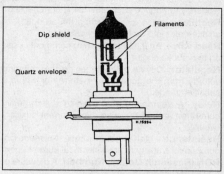

Quartz halogen headlight bulb construction

R

Rack-and-pinion A pinion gear on the end of a shaft that mates with a rack (think of a geared wheel opened up and laid flat). Sometimes used in clutch operating systems.

Radial play Up and down movement about a shaft.

Radial ply tyres Tyre plies run across the tyre (from bead to bead) and around the circumference of the tyre. Less resistant to tread distortion than other tyre types.

Radiator A liquid-to-air heat transfer device designed to reduce the temperature of the coolant in a liquid cooled engine.

Rake A feature of steering geometry - the angle of the steering head in relation to the vertical **(see illustration)**.

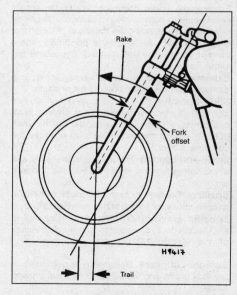

Steering geometry

Rebore Providing a new working surface to the cylinder bore by boring out the old surface. Necessitates the use of oversize piston and rings.

Rebound damping A means of controlling the oscillation of a suspension unit spring after it has been compressed. Resists the spring's natural tendency to bounce back after being compressed.

Rectifier Device for converting the ac output of an alternator into dc for battery charging.

Reed valve An induction system commonly used on two-stroke engines.

Regulator Device for maintaining the charging voltage from the generator or alternator within a specified range.

Relay A electrical device used to switch heavy current on and off by using a low current auxiliary circuit.

Resistance Measured in ohms. An electrical component's ability to pass electrical current.

RON (Research Octane Number) A measure of a fuel's resistance to knock.

rpm revolutions per minute.

Runout The amount of wobble (in-and-out movement) of a wheel or shaft as it's rotated. The amount a shaft rotates `out-of-true'. The out-of-round condition of a rotating part.

S

SAE (Society of Automotive Engineers) A standard for the viscosity of a fluid.

Sealant A liquid or paste used to prevent leakage at a joint. Sometimes used in conjunction with a gasket.

Service limit Term for the point where a component is no longer useable and must be renewed.

Shaft drive A method of transmitting drive from the transmission to the rear wheel.

Shell bearings Plain bearings consisting of two shell halves. Most often used as big-end and main bearings in a four-stroke engine. Often called bearing inserts.

Shim Thin spacer, commonly used to adjust the clearance or relative positions between two parts. For example, shims inserted into or under tappets or followers to control valve clearances. Clearance is adjusted by changing the thickness of the shim.

Short-circuit An electrical condition where current shorts to earth (ground) bypassing the circuit components.

Skimming Process to correct warpage or repair a damaged surface, eg on brake discs or drums.

Slide-hammer A special puller that screws into or hooks onto a component such as a shaft or bearing; a heavy sliding handle on the shaft bottoms against the end of the shaft to knock the component free.

Small-end bearing The bearing in the upper end of the connecting rod at its joint with the gudgeon pin.

Spalling Damage to camshaft lobes or bearing journals shown as pitting of the working surface.

Specific gravity (SG) The state of charge of the electrolyte in a lead-acid battery. A measure of the electrolyte's density compared with water.

Straight-cut gears Common type gear used on gearbox shafts and for oil pump and water pump drives.

Stanchion The inner sliding part of the front forks, held by the yokes. Often called a fork tube.

Stoichiometric ratio The optimum chemical air/fuel ratio for a petrol engine, said to be 14.7 parts of air to 1 part of fuel.

Sulphuric acid The liquid (electrolyte) used in a lead-acid battery. Poisonous and extremely corrosive.

Surface grinding (lapping) Process to correct a warped gasket face, commonly used on cylinder heads.

T

Tapered-roller bearing Tapered inner race of caged needle rollers and separate tapered outer race. Examples of taper roller bearings can be found on steering heads.

Tappet A cylindrical component which transmits motion from the cam to the valve stem, either directly or via a pushrod and rocker arm. Also called a cam follower.

TCS Traction Control System. An electronically-controlled system which senses wheel spin and reduces engine speed accordingly.

TDC Top Dead Centre denotes that the piston is at its highest point in the cylinder.

Thread-locking compound Solution applied to fastener threads to prevent slackening. Select type to suit application.

Thrust washer A washer positioned between two moving components on a shaft. For example, between gear pinions on gearshaft.

Timing chain See **Cam Chain**.

Timing light Stroboscopic lamp for carrying out ignition timing checks with the engine running.

Top-end A description of an engine's cylinder block, head and valve gear components.

Torque Turning or twisting force about a shaft.

Torque setting A prescribed tightness specified by the motorcycle manufacturer to ensure that the bolt or nut is secured correctly. Undertightening can result in the bolt or nut coming loose or a surface not being sealed. Overtightening can result in stripped threads, distortion or damage to the component being retained.

Torx key A six-point wrench.

Tracer A stripe of a second colour applied to a wire insulator to distinguish that wire from another one with the same colour insulator. For example, Br/W is often used to denote a brown insulator with a white tracer.

Trail A feature of steering geometry. Distance from the steering head axis to the tyre's central contact point.

Triple clamps The cast components which extend from the steering head and support the fork stanchions or tubes. Often called fork yokes.

Turbocharger A centrifugal device, driven by exhaust gases, that pressurises the intake air. Normally used to increase the power output from a given engine displacement.

TWI Abbreviation for Tyre Wear Indicator. Indicates the location of the tread depth indicator bars on tyres.

U

Universal joint or U-joint (UJ) A double-pivoted connection for transmitting power from a driving to a driven shaft through an angle. Typically found in shaft drive assemblies.

Unsprung weight Anything not supported by the bike's suspension (ie the wheel, tyres, brakes, final drive and bottom (moving) part of the suspension).

V

Vacuum gauges Clock-type gauges for measuring intake tract vacuum. Used for carburettor synchronisation on multi-cylinder engines.

Valve A device through which the flow of liquid, gas or vacuum may be stopped, started or regulated by a moveable part that opens, shuts or partially obstructs one or more ports or passageways. The intake and exhaust valves in the cylinder head are of the poppet type.

Valve clearance The clearance between the valve tip (the end of the valve stem) and the rocker arm or tappet/follower. The valve clearance is measured when the valve is closed. The correct clearance is important - if too small the valve won't close fully and will burn out, whereas if too large noisy operation will result.

Valve lift The amount a valve is lifted off its seat by the camshaft lobe.

Valve timing The exact setting for the opening and closing of the valves in relation to piston position.

Vernier caliper A precision measuring instrument that measures inside and outside dimensions. Not quite as accurate as a micrometer, but more convenient.

Wet liner arrangement

VIN Vehicle Identification Number. Term for the bike's engine and frame numbers.

Viscosity The thickness of a liquid or its resistance to flow.

Volt A unit for expressing electrical "pressure" in a circuit. Volts = current x ohms.

W

Water pump A mechanically-driven device for moving coolant around the engine.

Watt A unit for expressing electrical power. Watts = volts x current.

Wear limit see **Service limit**

Wet liner A liquid-cooled engine design where the pistons run in liners which are directly surrounded by coolant (**see illustration**).

Wheelbase Distance from the centre of the front wheel to the centre of the rear wheel.

Wiring harness or loom Describes the electrical wires running the length of the motorcycle and enclosed in tape or plastic sheathing. Wiring coming off the main harness is usually referred to as a sub harness.

Woodruff key A key of semi-circular or square section used to locate a gear to a shaft. Often used to locate the alternator rotor on the crankshaft.

Wrist pin Another name for gudgeon or piston pin.

Note: *References throughout this index are in the form - "Chapter number" • "Page number"*

Note: *References throughout this index are in the form - "Chapter number" • "Page number"*

Preserving Our Motoring Heritage

< The Model J Duesenberg Derham Tourster. Only eight of these magnificent cars were ever built – this is the only example to be found outside the United States of America

Almost every car you've ever loved, loathed or desired is gathered under one roof at the Haynes Motor Museum. Over 300 immaculately presented cars and motorbikes represent every aspect of our motoring heritage, from elegant reminders of bygone days, such as the superb Model J Duesenberg to curiosities like the bug-eyed BMW Isetta. There are also many old friends and flames. Perhaps you remember the 1959 Ford Popular that you did your courting in? The magnificent 'Red Collection' is a spectacle of classic sports cars including AC, Alfa Romeo, Austin Healey, Ferrari, Lamborghini, Maserati, MG, Riley, Porsche and Triumph.

A Perfect Day Out

Each and every vehicle at the Haynes Motor Museum has played its part in the history and culture of Motoring. Today, they make a wonderful spectacle and a great day out for all the family. Bring the kids, bring Mum and Dad, but above all bring your camera to capture those golden memories for ever. You will also find an impressive array of motoring memorabilia, a comfortable 70 seat video cinema and one of the most extensive transport book shops in Britain. The Pit Stop Cafe serves everything from a cup of tea to wholesome, home-made meals or, if you prefer, you can enjoy the large picnic area nestled in the beautiful rural surroundings of Somerset.

John Haynes O.B.E., Founder and Chairman of the museum at the wheel of a Haynes Light 12.

< The 1936 490cc sohc-engined International Norton – well known for its racing success

The Museum is situated on the A359 Yeovil to Frome road at Sparkford, just off the A303 in Somerset. It is about 40 miles south of Bristol, and 25 minutes drive from the M5 intersection at Taunton.

Open 9.30am - 5.30pm (10.00am - 4.00pm Winter) 7 days a week, *except Christmas Day, Boxing Day and New Years Day*

Special rates available for schools, coach parties and outings Charitable Trust No. 292048